TECHNOLOGY AND ENGINEERING APPLICATIONS OF SIMULINK

Edited by **S.C. Chakravarty**

Technology and Engineering Applications of Simulink
Edited by S.C. Chakravarty

Published by InTech
Janeza Trdine 9, 51000 Rijeka, Croatia

Publishing Process Manager Romina Skomersic

Technical Editor Teodora Smiljanic

Cover Designer InTech Design Team

Additional hard copies can be obtained from orders@intechopen.com

Technology and Engineering Applications of Simulink, Edited by S.C. Chakravarty
p. cm.
ISBN 978-953-51-0635-7

For EU product safety concerns:
IN TECH d.o.o., Prolaz Marije Krucifikse Kozulić 3, 51000 Rijeka, Croatia,
info@intechopen.com or visit our website at intechopen.com.

Meet the editor

Dr S. C. Chakravarty did his Ph.D degree in space physics from the Physical Research Laboratory (PRL) , Ahmedabad, India and joined the Indian Space Research Organisation (ISRO) at Bangalore during 1973. He assumed various responsibilities to plan, organise and implement the coordinated atmospheric and space science research programmes sponsored by ISRO. As the Programme Director of Space Science research activities, Dr Chakravarty was involved in the planning and coordination of work related to India's first moon mission, Chandrayaan-1. He also coordinated large number of scientific research programmes involving scientific balloon and sounding rocket experiments, space science satellite missions including Astrosat, SROSS-C, and Megha-Tropiques. Dr Chakravarty also helped to enable Indian participation in internationally coordinated programmes like MAP, INDOEX, CAWSES etc. Presently his research activities include development of physics based and real time models on monsoon dynamics, the total electron content (TEC) of the ionosphere and aspects of mesospheric phenomena.

Contents

Preface

Building on MATLAB (the language of technical computing), Simulink provides a platform for engineers to plan, model, design, simulate, test and implement complex electromechanical, dynamic control, signal processing and communication systems. Simulink-Matlab combination is very useful for developing algorithms, GUI assisted creation of block diagrams and realisation of interactive simulation based designs. The eleven chapters of the book demonstrate the power and capabilities of Simulink to solve engineering problems with varied degree of complexity in the virtual environment. The first four chapters provide details of design, analysis, simulation and implementation of flexible AC transmission system devices to control the power variables, multi-component electric circuits, signal transmission through power distribution lines of different kinds and PID/fuzzy logic control of a boom suspension. Details of enhanced capabilities in simulation effects constitute the subject matter of the next three chapters on S-functions for custom made subroutines and bond graph models, development of model and HDL code on FPGA system and harmonic linearization method of non-linear characteristics of modulation techniques. The last four chapters deal with examples of electromagnetic and dynamic systems of thermo-electrical micro hot plate with temperature control circuit, braked railed vehicle wheel slide protection, replacement in a car battery by a hybrid supply of battery and super capacitors and a novel speed control logic for electric vehicle. I hope that both newcomers and professionals in the field would benefit by going through the details given in the above chapters of the book.

S.C. Chakravarty
Scientist (retired), Indian Space Research Organisation (ISRO), Bangalore or Hon Senior Professor, Indian Centre for Space Physics (ICSP), Kolkata, India

1

Analysis of Power Electronic Controllers in Electric Power Systems Using Simulink

Juan Segundo-Ramirez[1] and A. Medina[2]
[1]*Universidad Autónoma de San Luis Potosí*
[2]*Universidad Michoacana de San Nicolás de Hidalgo*
México

1. Introduction

Flexible ac Transmission Systems (FACTS) devices have emerged in power system because of the development of power electronics components for high voltage and power. The FACTS devices provide higher controllability in power systems by means of power electronic devices. Several FACTS equipments have been already introduced for various applications worldwide, and new types of FACTS are in the stage of being introduced in practice. FACTS technology provides a better ability to varying operational conditions and improves the usage of existing installations.

2. Power electronic application in transmission systems

It can be seen that with growing line length and with higher power demand the opportunity for FACTS devices gets more important. The devices work electrically as fast current, voltage or impedance controllers. The power electronic allows very short reaction times down to far below one second (~ms). Detailed introductions in FACTS devices can also be found in the literature (Hingorani & Gyudyi, 2000) (Acha, et al. 2004) (Mathur & Varma, 2002)(Padiyar, 2007) (Zhang, Rehtanz, & Pal, 2006) with the main focus on new topologies, modeling and control.

Basically, there are two groups of FACTS, one is based on thyristor valve operation (Hingorani & Gyudyi, 2000), and the other is based on Voltage Source Converters (VSCs) (Segundo-Ramírez & Medina, 2008) (Segundo-Ramírez & Medina, 2009). A list of some FACTS devices are shown in Table 1. The FACTS devices based on VSCs provide a controllable voltage magnitude and phase angle due to a Pulse Width Modulation (PWM) technique (Mohan, Underland, & Robins, 1995). The Static Compensator (STATCOM) (Hingorani & Gyudyi, 2000) is a shunt connected device that is able to provide reactive power support at a network location far away from the generators. Through this reactive power injection, the STATCOM can regulate the voltage at the connection node. The Static Synchronous Series compensator (SSSC) (Hingorani & Gyudyi, 2000) is a series device which injects a voltage in series with the transmission line. The Unified Power Flow Controller (UPFC) (Hingorani & Gyudyi, 2000) is the most versatile device of the family of FACTS devices, since it is able to control the active and the reactive power, respectively, as well as the voltage at the connection node. In Figure 1 a schematic representation of the STATCOM, the SSSC, and the UPFC are presented. The compensating FACTS devices under analysis in this chapter are briefly described below.

Connection Type	FACTS Devices	
	Thyristor-Based FACTS	VSC-Based FACTS
Shunt Connected	Static Var Compensator (SVC)	Static Compensator (STATCOM)
Series Connected	Thyristor Controlled Series Compensator (TCSC)	Static Series Synchronous Compensator (SSSC)
Back-to-Back Connected	HVDC	Unified Power Flow Controller (UPFC)
		HVDC VSC

Table 1. Overview of the principal FACTS-Devices.

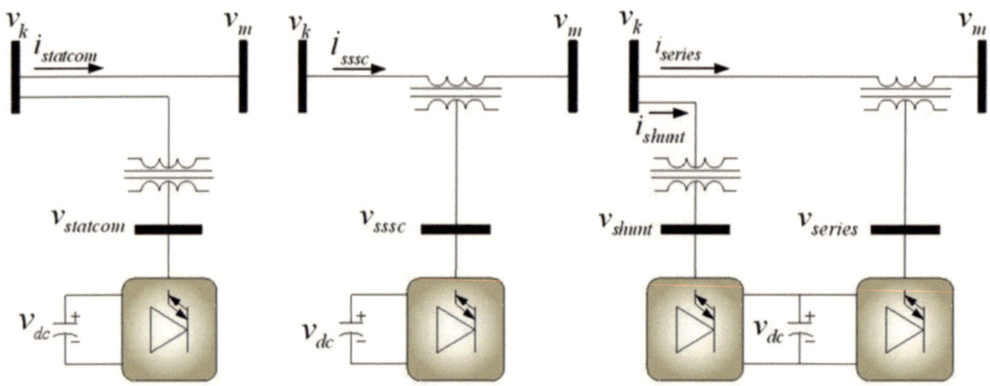

(a) STATCOM (b) SSSC (c) UPFC

Fig. 1. FACTS devices based on VSCs. (a) STATCOM, (b) SSSC, and (c) UPFC.

2.1 Static compensator (STATCOM)

It is a shunt device that does not require passive elements for reactive compensation. The STATCOM operation is based on a VSC, which is supplied by a dc storage capacitor. The VSC terminals are connected to the dc system through a coupling transformer. The VSC produces a quasi-sine wave voltage at the fundamental frequency (50 or 60 Hz). The STATCOM can generate or absorb reactive power. A schematic representation of the STATCOM is shown in Figure 1(a).

Assuming that the losses in the VSC and the coupling transformer are negligible, $v_{statcom}$ is in phase with the voltage at the terminal bus v_k. In this situation, the current $i_{statcom}$ is completely reactive. If the magnitude of the voltage v_k is higher than the magnitude of $v_{statcom}$, the reactive current flows from the bus to the VSC, which means that the STATCOM absorbs reactive power. On the other hand, if the magnitude of $v_{statcom}$ is higher than the magnitude of v_k, the reactive current flows from the VSC to the ac system. Then, the STATCOM injects reactive power to the system. In practice, the power losses of the STATCOM are not negligible and must be drawn from the ac system to maintain constant the dc capacitor voltage.

2.2 Static synchronous series compensator (SSSC)

The SSSC is a series device in which a synchronous voltage source injects a fundamental frequency voltage in series with the transmission line through a coupling transformer. The synchronous voltage source is supplied by a VSC. A schematic representation of the SSSC is shown in Figure 1(b).

Ideally, the injected voltage is in quadrature with the line current. In this mode the VSC does not absorb or inject any real power. However, in practice, the VSC losses must be replenished by the ac system, in consequence a small phase lag is introduced for this purpose. The operating characteristics make this device very attractive for power transmission application. The main limitation of application is due to the losses and cost of the converter. The SSSC is a device which has so far not been built at transmission level because Series Compensator (fixed capacitor) and thyristor controlled series capacitor (TCSC) (Hingorani & Gyudyi, 2000) are fulfilling all the today's operational requirements at a low cost.

2.3 Unified power flow controller (UPFC)

This device contains two VSCs connected together through a dc link storage capacitor. One of the VSCs is connected in series with the transmission line, while the other VSC is connected in shunt with the transmission line. The UPFC can control the active and reactive power flow in the transmission line, and at the same time can regulate the voltage magnitude at the connection node. To control the real and reactive power flow in the series side, the UPFC allows interchange of real power between the shunt and the series converters. The main disadvantage of this device is the high cost level due to the complex systems setup (Zhang, Rehtanz, & Pal, 2006). A schematic representation of the UPFC is shown in Figure 1(c).

3. PSB/SIMULINK

Power System Blockset (PSB) for use with Matlab/Simulink employs state-variable analysis. In PSB complex control algorithms can be implemented into the models in an easy and fast way. Besides, PSB can use several Matlab toolboxes. In particular, it has the PWM generator and the VSC blocks. The main advantage of the PSB is that it is developed in Matlab/Simulink environment, this fact makes possible to use it together with several other control design tools. It is possible to use the Simulink Accelerator and the Real-Time Workshop to improve the PSB performance; a C code is generated. Additionally, the PSB can use several integration methods, which make it a powerful simulation tool.

3.1 Modeling and analysis of FACTS by PSB/SIMULINK

This section is divided into three parts. Simulations relating to the STATCOM are presented first. This is followed by simulations carried out for the SSSC and then for the UPFC. The study case related to the STATCOM is described in detail using PSB/Simulink. For the cases of the SSSC and the UPFC, only the general implementation is described.

3.2 Static compensator (STATCOM)

The test case is shown in Figure 2, where the STATCOM includes the control system described in (Mahyavanshi & Radman, 2006). The initial conditions are zero, the reference line to line voltage is 179.6292 volts at node 1, the reference voltage for the dc capacitor is 500 volts, and the modulation index is m_f=15 (900 Hz). The shunt transformer, the line 1 and the line 2 are represented by RL branches, whose impedances are $0.05 + j\omega \times 0.005\ \Omega$, $0.2 + j\omega \times 0.015\ \Omega$, and $0.15 + j\omega \times 0.01\ \Omega$, respectively. The Figure 3 shows the PI control used in this analysis. On the other hand, Figure 4 shows some important blocks parameters of the system. Figure 4 shows some important block of parameters for some components shown in Figure 2 and Figure 3. Please notice that a passive filter has been connected at bus 1, in order to drain the harmonic currents.

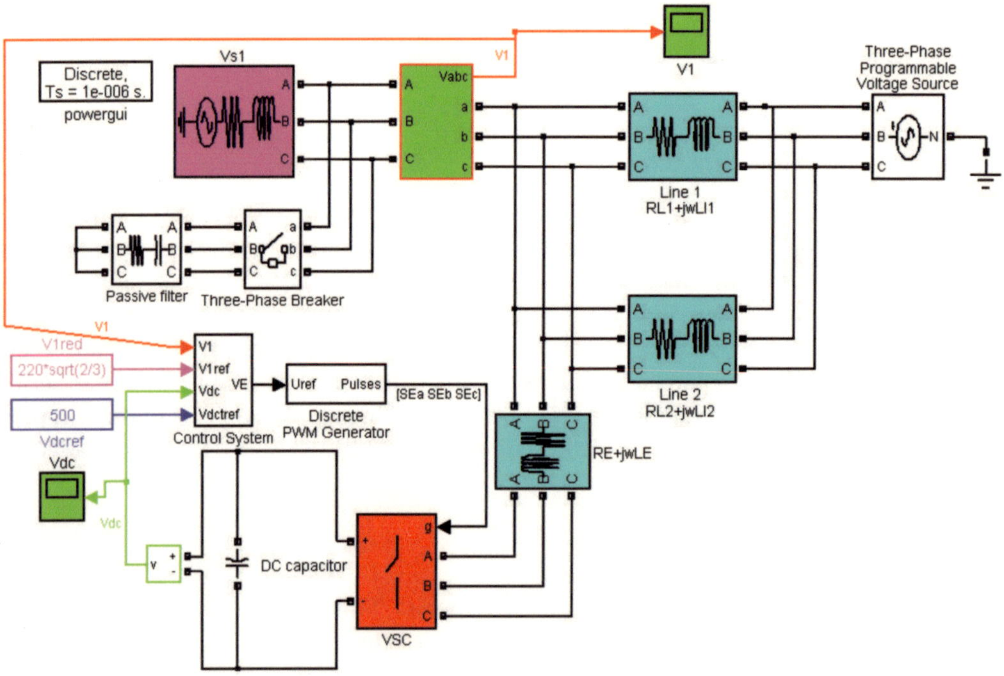

Fig. 2. Test system including the STATCOM.

The test case is initially in periodic steady state, at $t = 0.05\ s$, the voltage magnitude of the three-phase programmable voltage source is increased 15%, and finally at $t = 0.35\ s$, the initial operating point is reestablished. The study for the STATCOM is divided in two parts, firstly the three-phase breaker is open, and consequently the passive filter is disconnected. In the second part, the three-phase breaker is closed allowing the filtering function. The passive filter is represented as a RC branch with $C = 80\ \mu F$ and $R = 0.5\ \Omega$.

In the Figure 5, some selected transient waveforms of the STATCOM without the passive filter are shown: Figure 5(a) presents the output of the phase controller, alfaE, which is actually the phase angle of the voltage at the ac terminals of the VSC; Figure 5(b) presents the output of the magnitude control, which is the half part of the voltage magnitude at the ac terminal of the VSC; Figure 5(c) shows the voltage across the dc capacitor, and finally, the peak line-to-neutral voltage at the bus 1 is shown in Figure 5(d). Figure 6 shows the steady state waveform of the voltage at the bus 1 at the top of the figure, and its harmonic spectrum at the bottom of the figure. The Figure 6 was obtained using the FFT Analysis button in the powergui block.

In the Figure 7, some selected transient waveforms of the STATCOM with the passive filter are shown: Figure 7(a) presents the output of the phase controller; Figure 7(b) presents the output of the magnitude control; Figure 7(c) shows the voltage across the dc capacitor, and finally, the peak line-to-neutral voltage at the bus 1 is shown in Figure 7(d). Figure 8 shows the steady state waveform of the voltage at the bus 1 at the top of the figure, and its harmonic spectrum at the bottom of the figure.

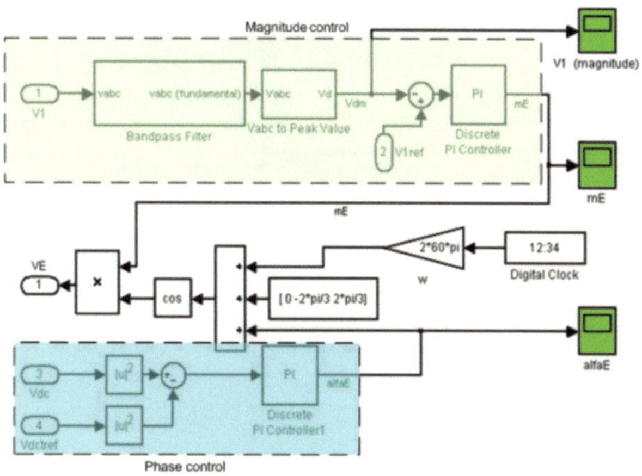

(a) Control System

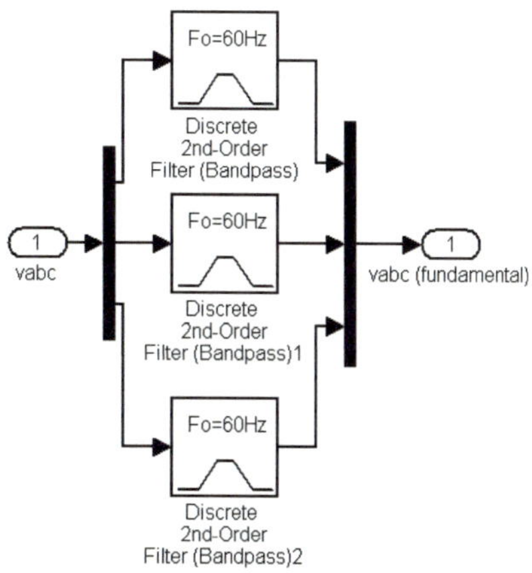

(b) Bandpass Filter

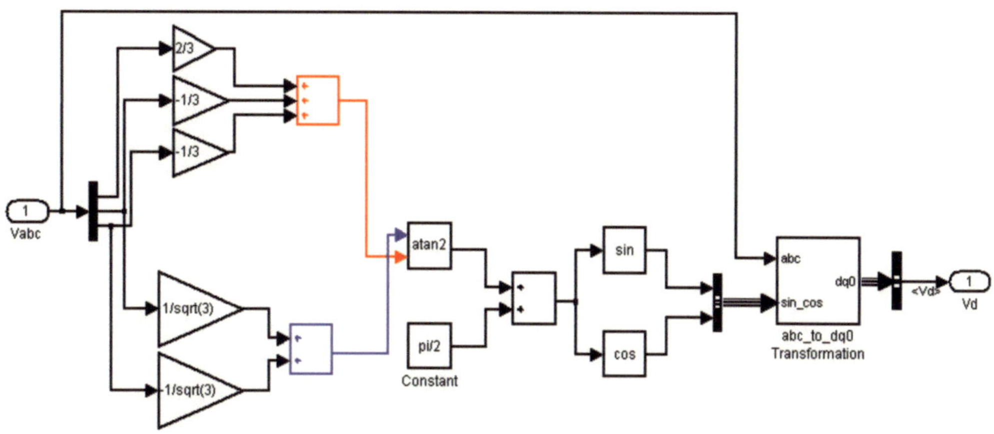

(c) Vabc to Peak Value

Fig. 3. STATCOM PI control system. (a) Main control system. (b) Bandpass filter. (c) Extraction of the peak value of a three-phase voltage in abc-reference.

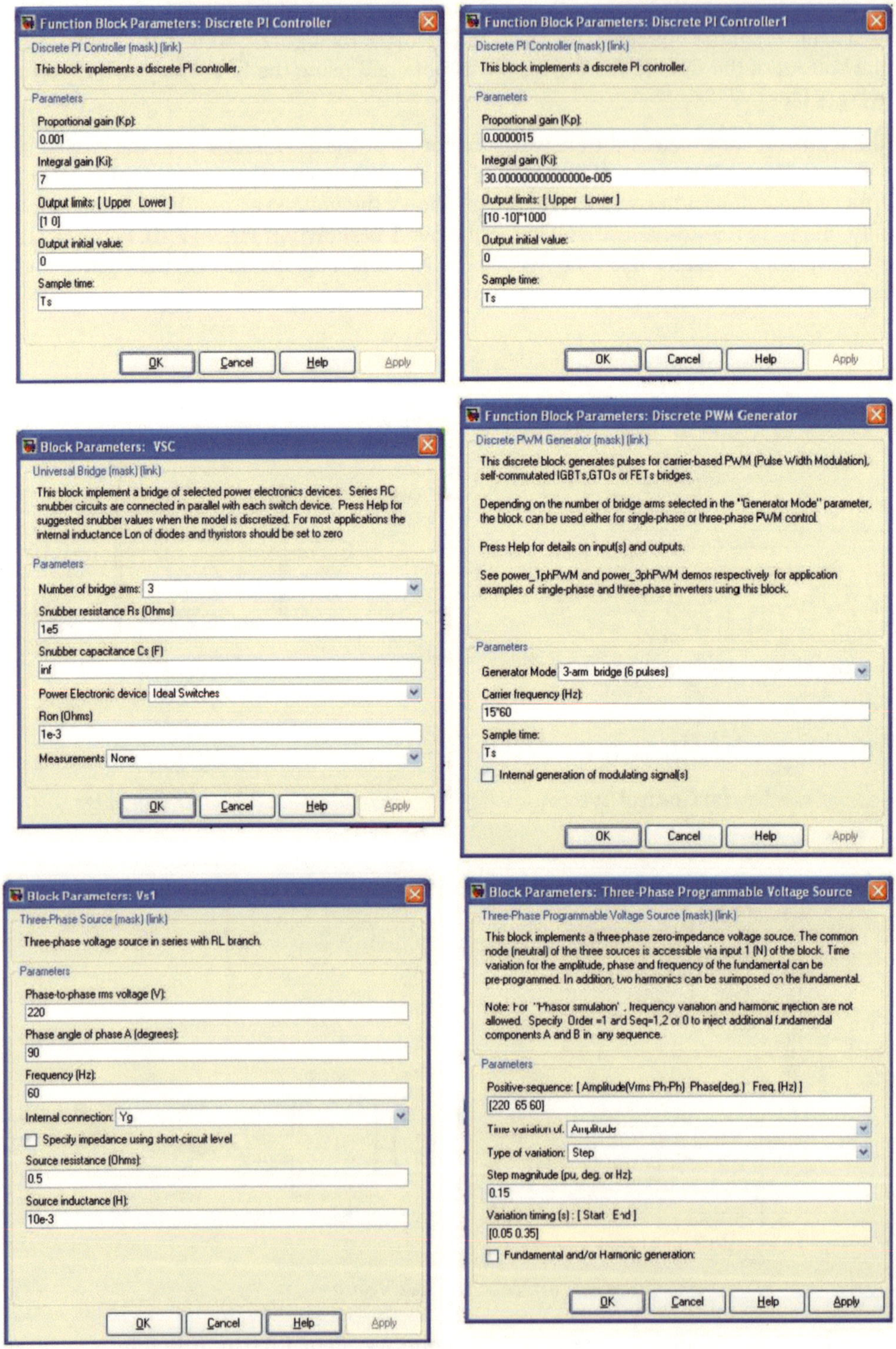

Fig. 4. Blocks parameters of important components.

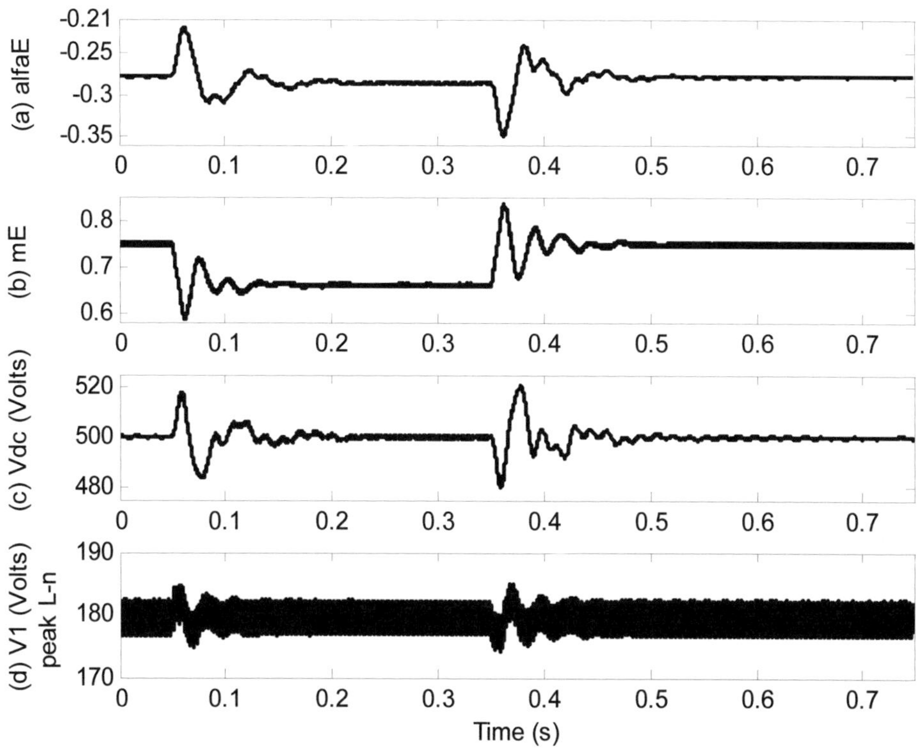

Fig. 5. Selected transient waveforms of the STATCOM without passive filter. (a) Phase angle of the voltage at the ac terminals of the VSC. (b) Amplitude modulation ratio. (c) Voltage across the dc capacitor. (d) Peak line-to-neutral voltage at the bus 1.

From Figure 5 and Figure 7 it is easy to notice that the passive filter has a positive impact on the reduction of the harmonic distortion in the power network without affecting the performance of the controller. In Figure 6, the waveform of the voltage at bus 1 is severely distorted with a total harmonic distortion (THD) of 39.88%. In this case, some harmonic components have a magnitude of almost 20% of the fundamental component, which is an undesirable operating condition in practical applications. On the other hand, the obtained voltage at bus 1 when the passive filter is on has a THD of 4.23% and the highest magnitude of the harmonic components is around 3.5% of the fundamental component, as shown in Figure 8.

In this simulation analysis, a discrete representation of the system given in Figure 2 was used in order to carry-out the simulations, an integration step of 1 μs was selected.

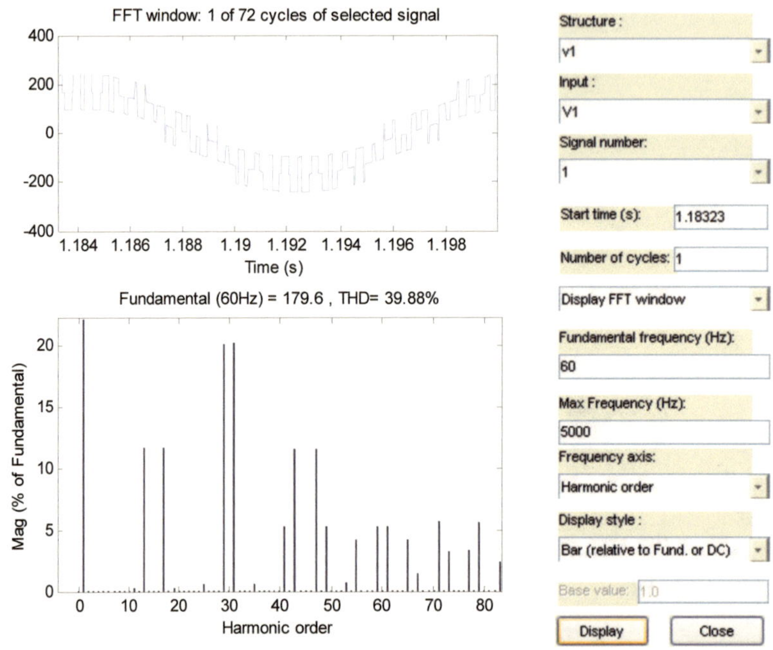

Fig. 6. Steady state waveform of the voltage at the bus 1 without passive filter (top), and its harmonic spectrum (bottom).

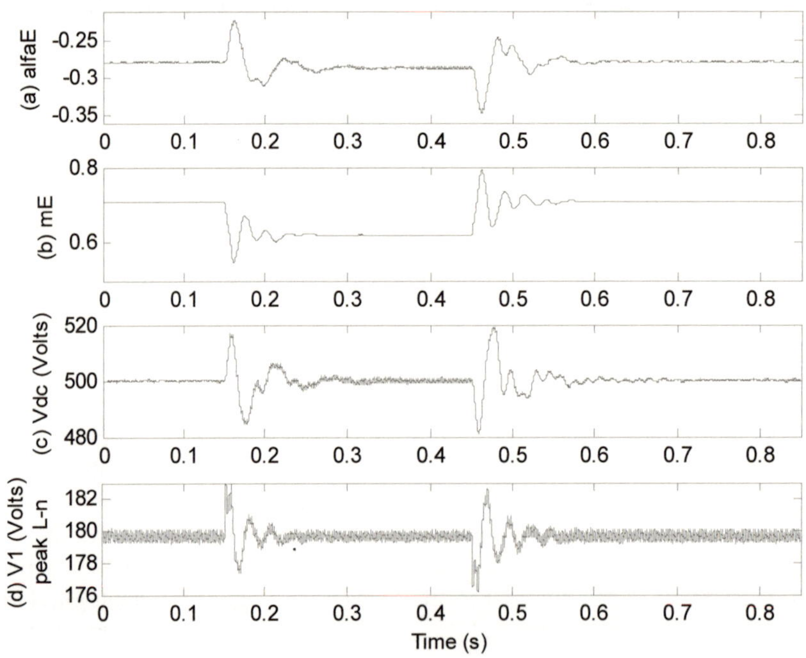

Fig. 7. Selected transient waveforms of the STATCOM with passive filter. (a) Phase angle of the voltage at the ac terminals of the VSC. (b) Amplitude modulation ratio. (c) Voltage across the dc capacitor. (d) Peak line-to-neutral voltage at the bus 1.

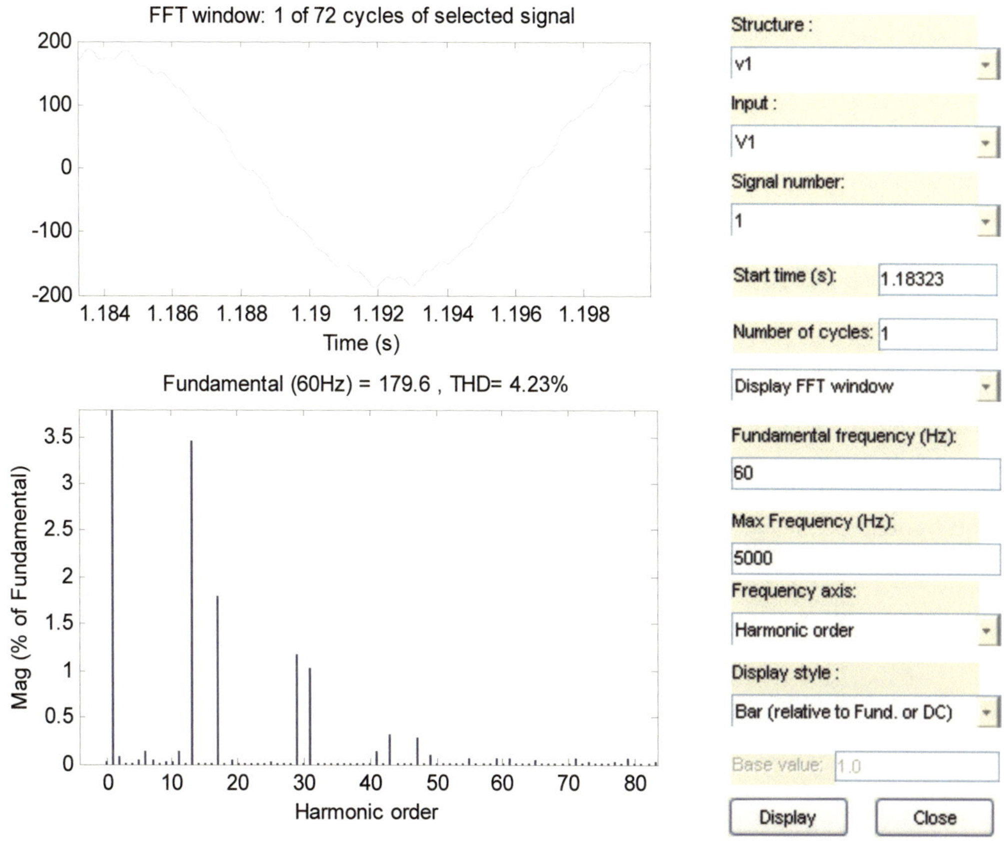

Fig. 8. Steady state waveform of the voltage at the bus 1 with passive filter (top), and its harmonic spectrum (bottom).

3.2.1 Static synchronous series compensator (SSSC)

The test system for the analysis of the SSSC is shown in Figure 9. The network parameters are the same of those of Figure 2. The series transformers are represented b an ideal model. The series active power reference Pref in the line 2 is equal to 5500 W; the dc voltage capacitor reference is equal to 500 V; the gains of the power control are Kp=0.000015 and Ki=0.004, and its limits are 0 and 1; the gains of the dc voltage control are Kp=0.03 and Ki=1, and its limits are $-\pi$ and π

The SSSC includes the control system shown in Figure 10. This control has two control objectives: to control the active power (P) that flows in the transmission line connected in series with the SSSC, and to maintain the dc voltage capacitor at its reference value. Remember that the SSSC does not interchange active power in steady-state, only the power loss; otherwise the dc capacitor is discharged. In transient state the SSSC has transient interchanges of active power with the network, which is reflected in variation of the dc voltage. Under this situation, the control regulates the interchange of active power in order to maintain the dc voltage capacitor at its steady-state. The initial conditions are zero; the active power reference Pref is 5500 W, and the index modulation is 41 (2.46 kHz). Pref is the active power reference in the transmission line in series with the SSSC.

The test case has zero initial conditions for all the state variables, except for the voltage across the dc capacitor; its initial condition is 500 V. At $t = 0.4\ s$ the voltage magnitude of the three-phase programmable voltage source is increased 15%, and finally at $t = 0.7\ s$, the initial operating point is reestablished. In this simulation analysis, a discrete representation of the system given in Figure 2 was used in order to carry-out the simulations, and an integration step of 2 μs was selected. This analysis is also carried-out with and without the passive filter.

Figure 11 shows some selected transient waveforms of the SSSC without passive filter. In this figure it is possible to notice that the series active power decreases about 25% when the voltage magnitude of the three-phase programmable voltage source increases 15%, and the series active power increases about 25% when the same voltage goes back to the original value. The control objectives of the SSSC controller are achieved in six full cycles, as shown in this figure.

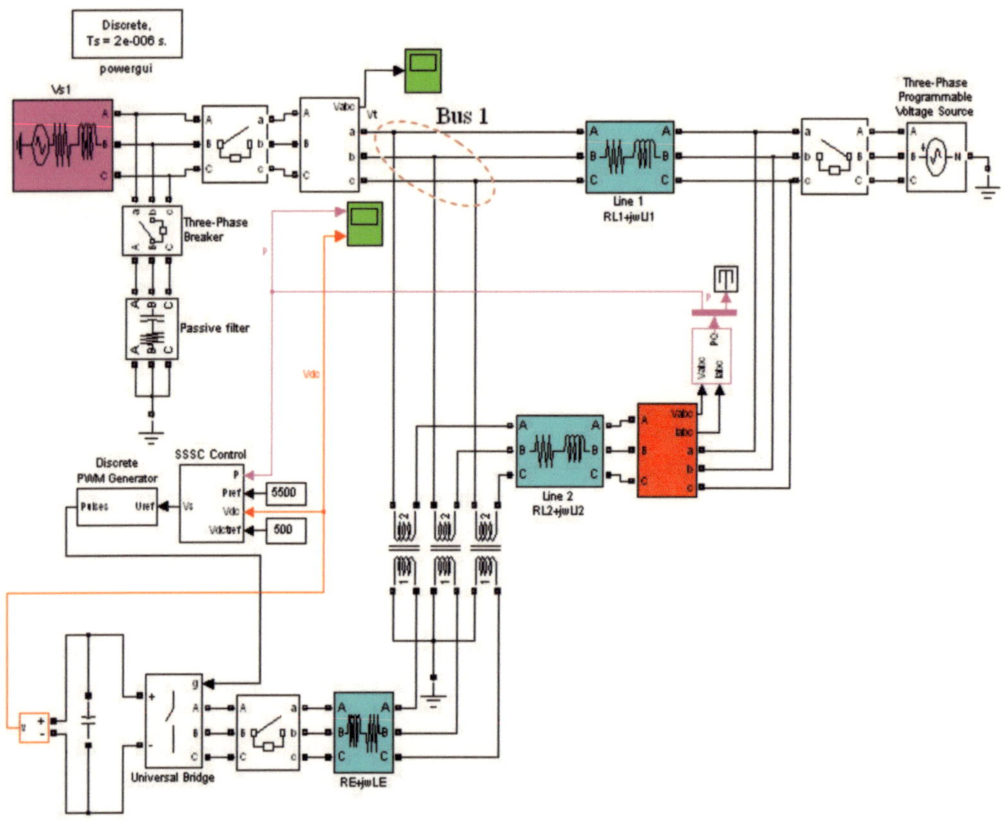

Fig. 9. Test system including the SSSC.

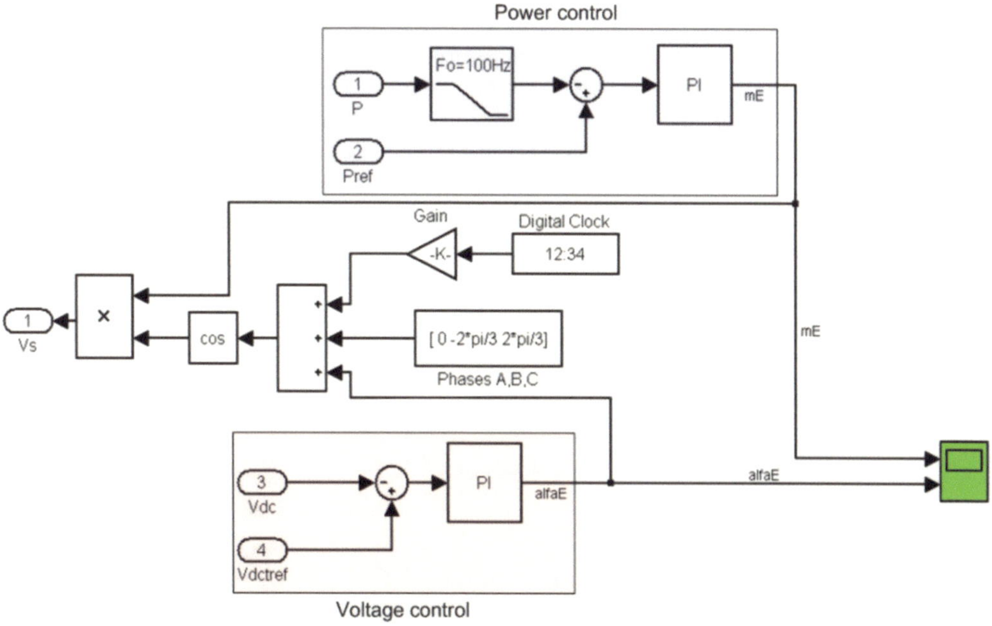

Fig. 10. SSSC control.

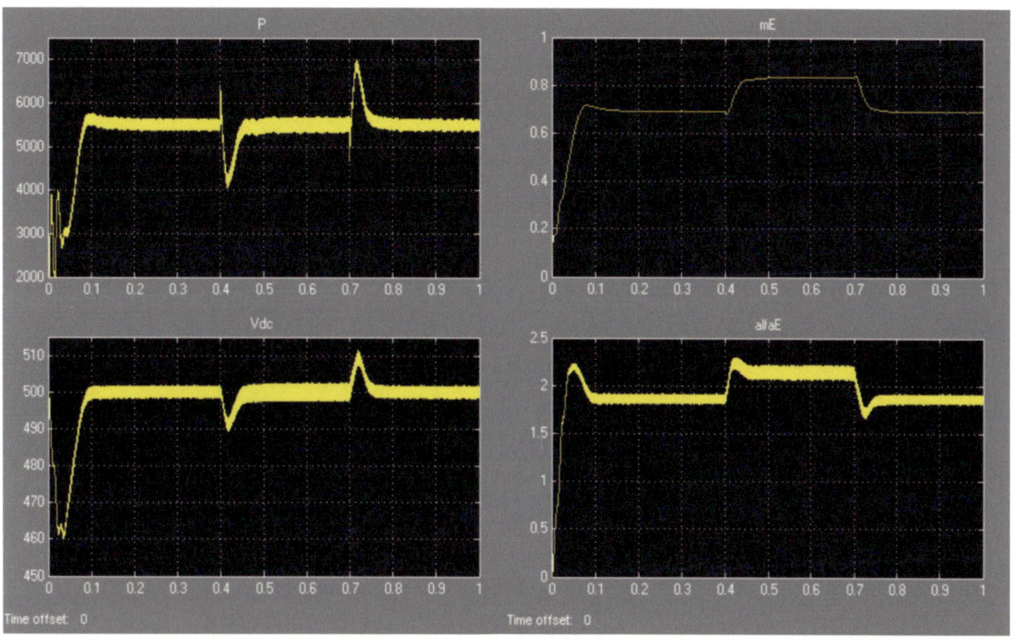

Fig. 11. Selected transient waveforms of the SSSC without passive filter. (Top left) Series active power. (Top right) Amplitude modulation ratio. (Bottom left) Voltage across the dc capacitor. (Bottom right) Phase angle of the voltage at the ac terminals.

Figure 12 shows the steady state waveform of the voltage at bus 1 without passive filter. In this operating scenario, the voltage is highly distorted; the THD is around 22.85% and the harmonics 39 and 43 have a magnitude of around 12% of the fundamental component. Notice that THD is high even when the switching frequency is 2.46 kHz. On the other hand, of some selected variables, the transient and steady state solutions of the SSSC test system including the passive filter are shown in Figure 13 and Figure 14. Comparing Figure 11 and Figure 13, it is easy to notice that difference between these figures is negligible. The most remarkable difference is the reduction of the harmonic distortion in all the system, especially in the voltage at bus 1.

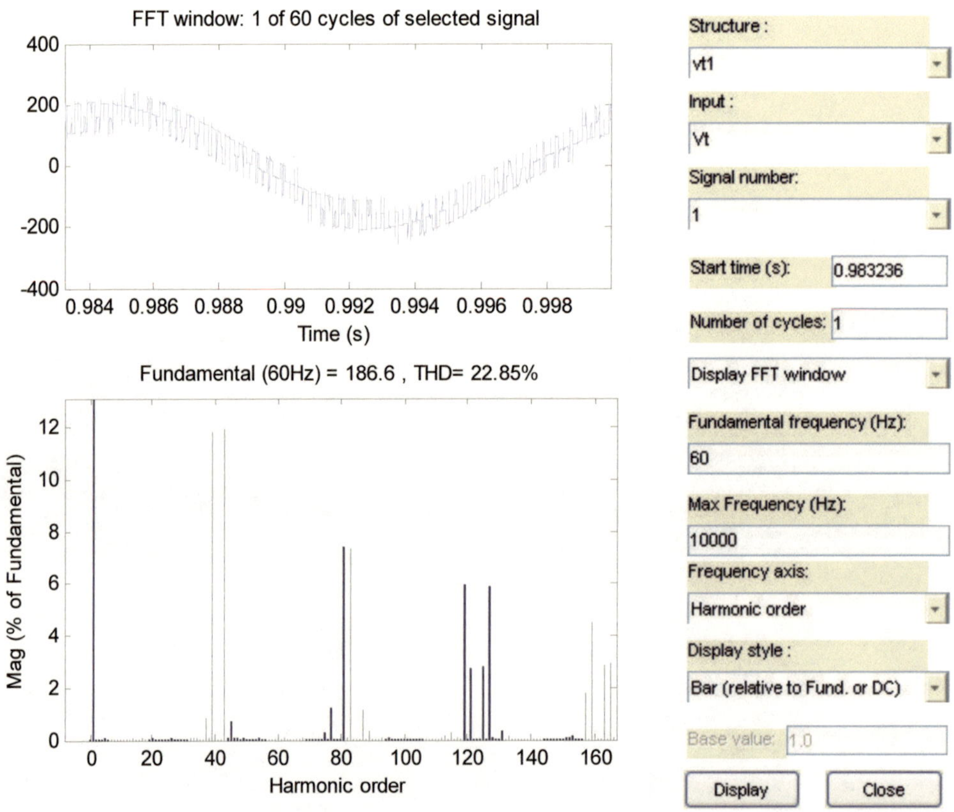

Fig. 12. Steady state waveform of the voltage at the bus 1 without passive filter (top), and its harmonic spectrum (bottom).

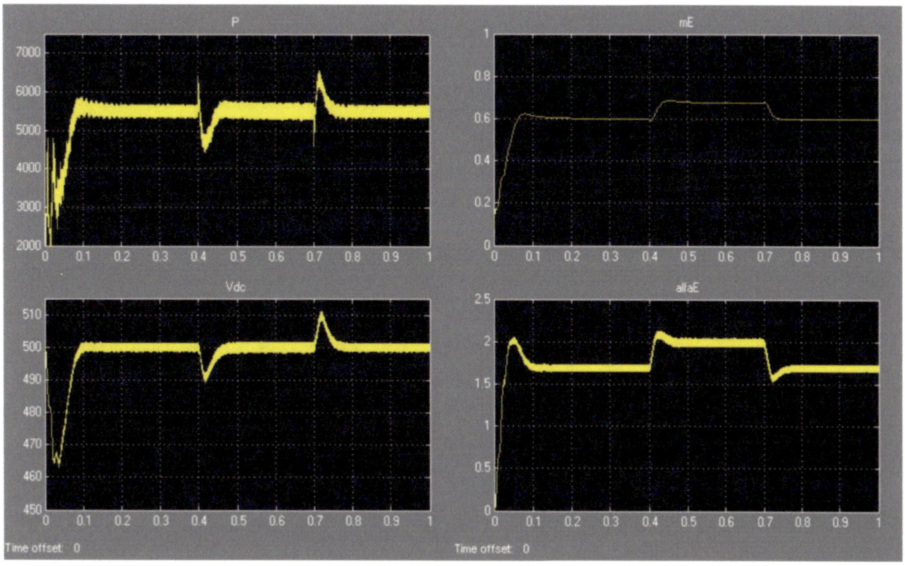

Fig. 13. Selected transient waveforms of the SSSC with passive filter. (Top left) Series active power. (Top right) Amplitude modulation ratio. (Bottom left) Voltage across the dc capacitor. (Bottom right) Phase angle of the voltage at the ac terminals.

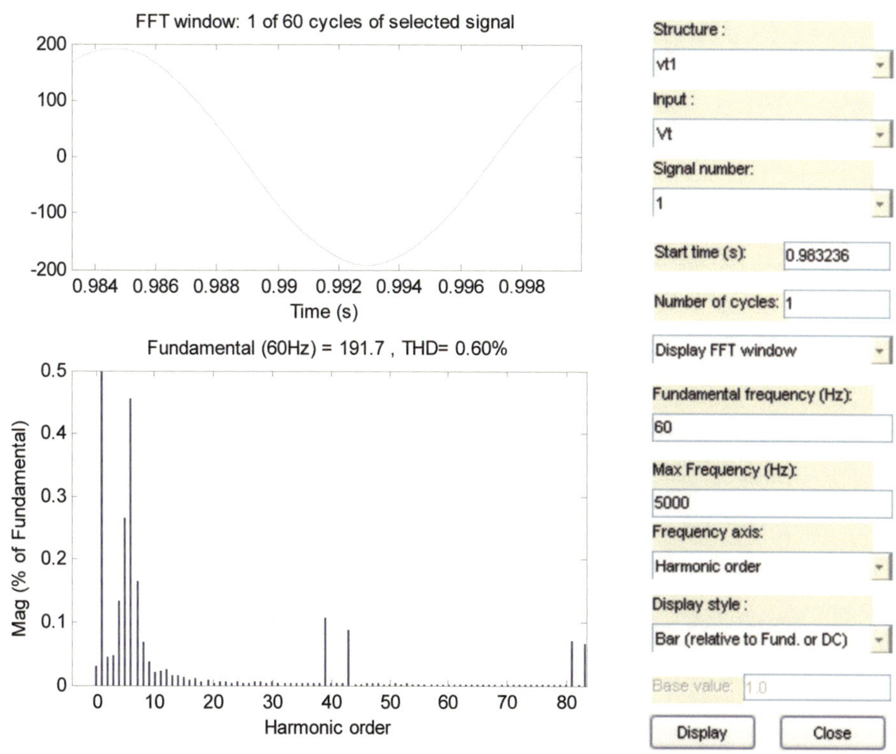

Fig. 14. Steady state waveform of the voltage at the bus 1 with passive filter (top), and its harmonic spectrum (bottom).

3.2.2 Unified power flow controller (UPFC)

The UPFC test system of Figure 15 and Figure 16 shows the Simulink implementation of the UPFC. The network parameters are the same of those of Figure 2. The UPFC including the shunt control described in (Mahyavanshi & Radman, 2006) is schematically shown in Figure 18, and the series control proposed in (Fujita, Watanabe, & Akagi, 2001) is shown in Figure 17. The initial condition is zero, except for the dc capacitor voltage, which is 500 volts.

The series controller regulates the real (*Pref*=8500 watts) and reactive (*Qref*=0 vars) power flows by adjusting the injected series voltage. The shunt converter regulates the voltage across the dc capacitor and the sending end voltage V1 at bus 1. The modulation index is m_f=27, which represents a commutation frequency of 1.61 kHz. The RC passive filter has a capacitance of 80 μF and a resistance of 0.2 Ω. The gains for the series controller are the following: Kp=1 and Ki=500 for the Discrete PI Controller 1, with no limits; Kp=2 and Ki=1000 for the Discrete PI Controller 2, with no limits. On the other hand, the gains for the shunt controller are: Kp=0.002 and Ki=1 for the Discrete PI Controller 1, with no limits; finally, Kp=0.0012 and Ki=0.09 for the Discrete PI Controller 2, with no limits. The UPFC analysis presented in this section only includes the case when the passive filter is connected, as shown in Figure 15.

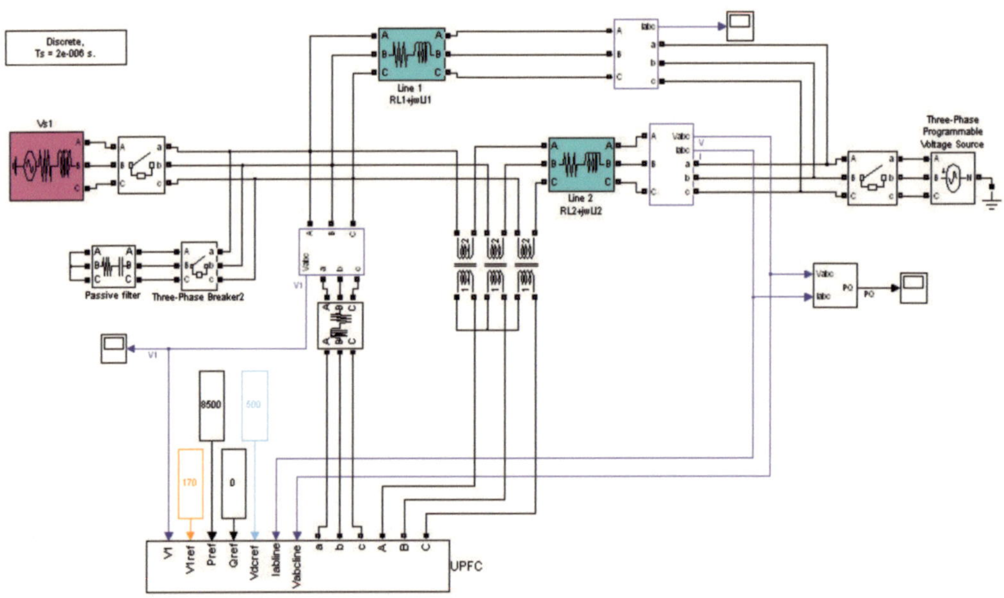

Fig. 15. Test system including the UPFC.

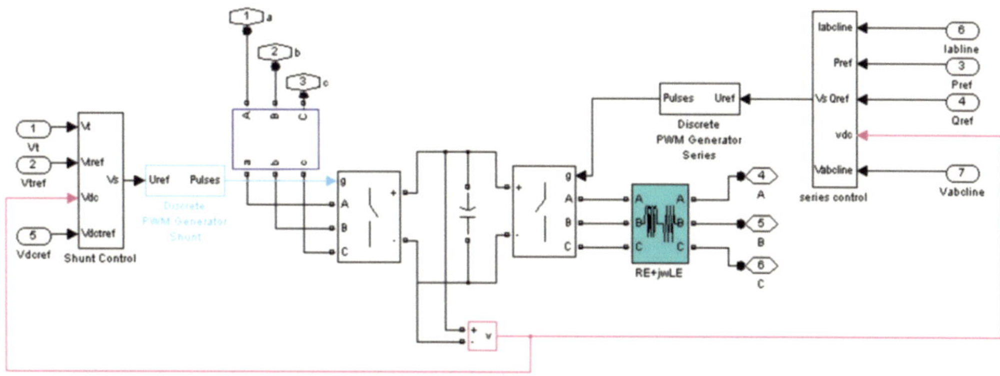

Fig. 16. UPFC and its controllers.

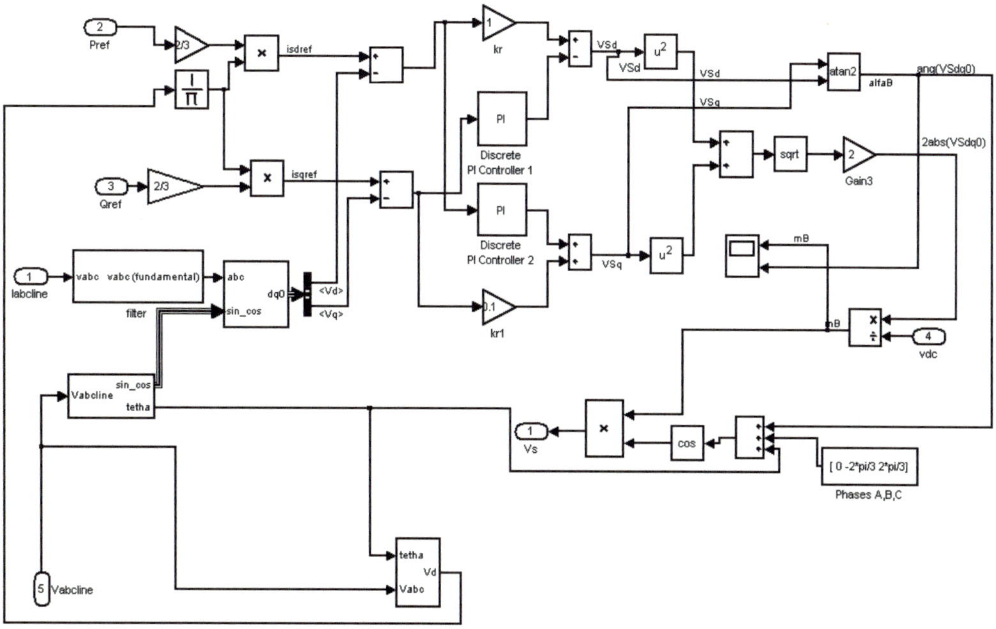

Fig. 17. Series controller.

The dynamic response of UPFC controllers are presented in Figure 19. From this figure, it is possible to observe that the variation of the three-phase programmable voltage source significantly affects the response of the series controller. This is because the magnitude of the voltages at the ends of the line controlled by the UPFC affects the power flow across the line. On the other hand, Figure 20 shows the transient waveform of the voltage across the dc capacitor and the active and reactive power flow in the controlled line. Notice that the reactive and active power remains close to the reference during the step changes in the three-phase programmable voltage source. Finally, Figure 21 presents the periodic steady-state solution of the sending end voltage V1 and its harmonic spectrum, which has a low THD of 1.74%.

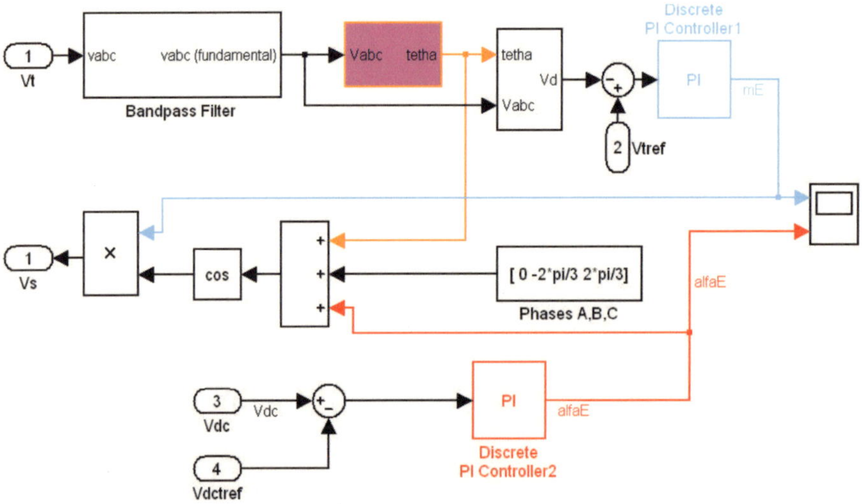

Fig. 18. Shunt controller.

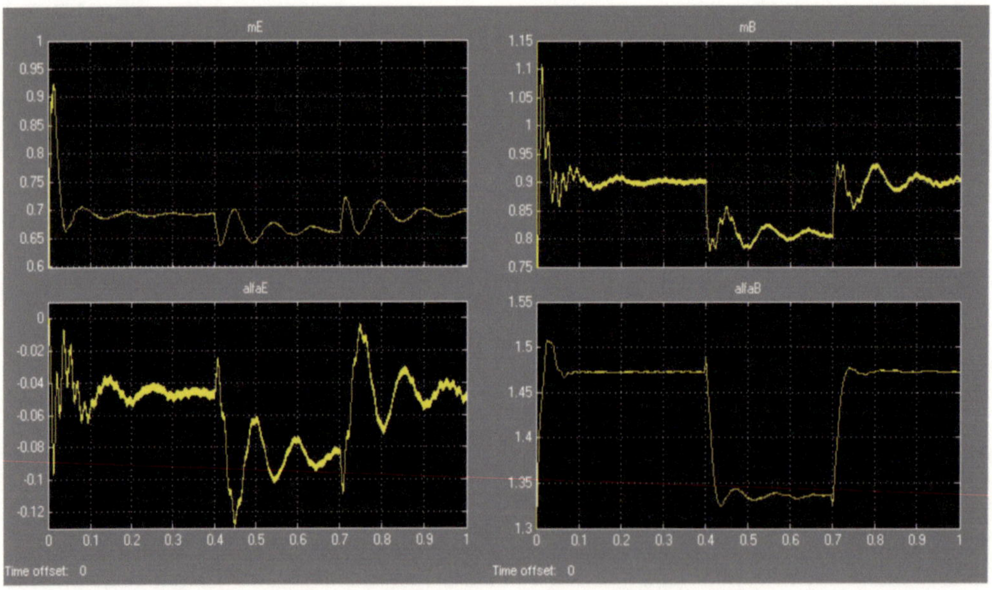

Fig. 19. Transient response of the series and shunt controllers of UPFC.

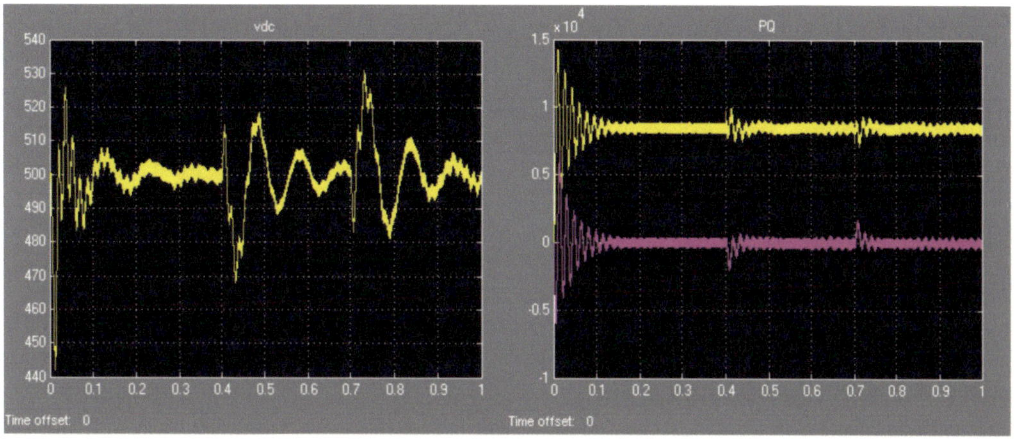

Fig. 20. Transient waveforms of selected variables: (Left) Voltage across the dc capacitor. (Right) Reactive (purple) and active (yellow) power.

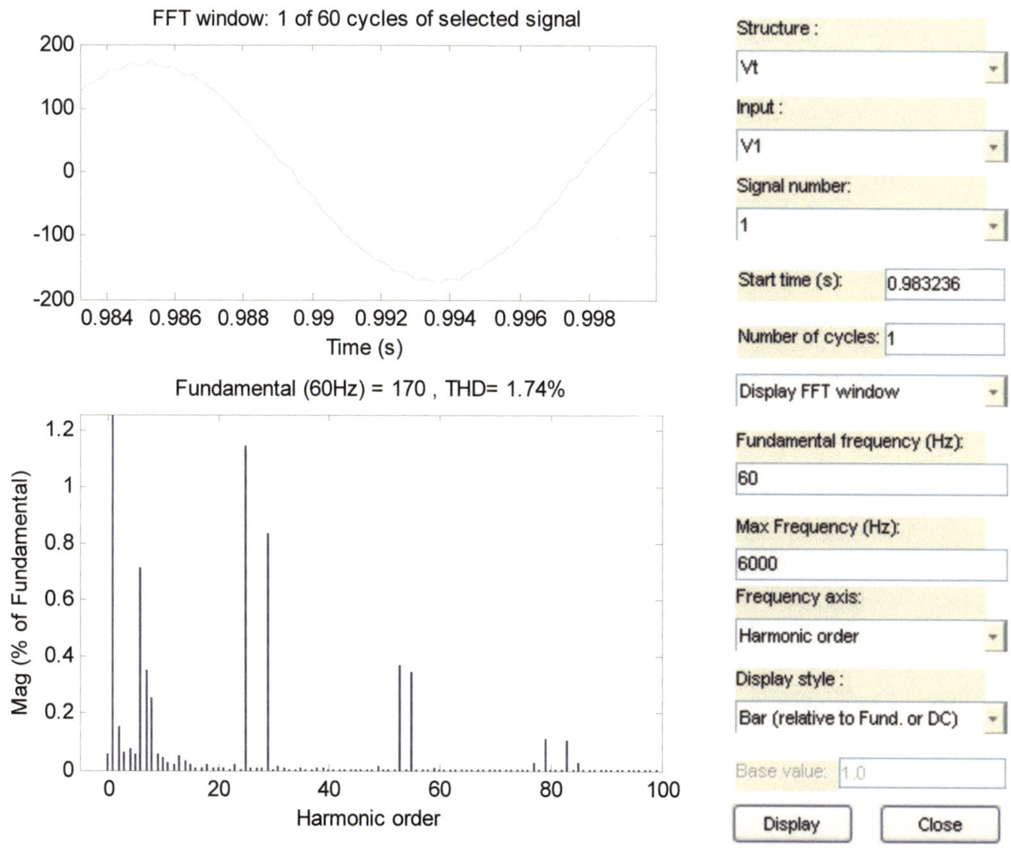

Fig. 21. Steady state waveform of the voltage at the bus 1 (top) and its harmonic spectrum (bottom).

4. Conclusions

In this chapter, implementation in Simulink of three FACTS devices based on VSC has been presented. These implementations include the STATCOM, SSSC, and the UPFC. All the implementations have been carried-out taking into account the control systems. The presented models can be used in order to analyze the dynamic and the periodic steady-state behavior of these FACTS components.

5. Acknowledgements

The authors thank the Univesidad Autónoma de San Luis Potosí (UASLP) and the Universidad Michoacana de San Nicolás de Hidalgo (UMSNH) for the facilities that were granted to carry out this chapter.

6. References

Acha, E., Fuerte-Esquivel, C., Ambriz-Pérez, H., & Angeles-Camacho, C. (2004). *FACTS Modelling and Simulation in Power Networks,* John Wiley & Sons, 9780470852712, England

Fujita, H., Watanabe, Y., & Akagi, H. (2001). Transient Analisis of a Unified Power Flow Controller and its Application to Design of the DC-Link Capacitor. *IEEE Transaction on Power Electronics*, Vol. 16, No. 5, (september 2001), pp. 735-740, 0885-8993

Hingorani, N. G., & Gyudyi, L. (2000). *Undestanding FACTS,* IEEE Press, 078033455, New York

Mahyavanshi, B., & Radman, G. (2006). A Study of Interaction Between Dynamic Load and STATCOM. *Proceedings of the 38th southeastern symposium on system theory*, 0-7803-9457-7, Cookeville, TN, march 2006

Mathur, R., & Varma, R. (2002). *Thyristor Based FACTS Controllers for Electrical Transmission Systems*, IEEE Computer Society Press, ISSN, Piscataway, New Jersey

Mohan, N., Underland, T. M., & Robins, W. P. (1995). *Power Electronics: Converters, Applications, and Design,* Wiley, 0471226939, New York

Padiyar, K. R. (2007). *FACTS Controller in Power Transmission and Distribution,* New Age, 978-81-224-2142-2, New Delhi

Segundo-Ramírez, J., & Medina, A. (2009). Modeling of FACTS Devices Based on SPWM VSCs. *IEEE Transaction on Power Delivery*, Vol. 24, No. 4, (November 2009), pp. 1815-1823, 0885-8977

Segundo-Ramírez, J., & Medina, A. (2008). Periodic Steady-State Solution of Electric Systems Including UPFCs by Extrapolation to the Limit Cycle. *IEEE Transaction on Power Delivery*, Vol. 23, No. 3, pp. 1506-1512

Zhang, X.-P., Rehtanz, C., & Pal, B. (2006). *Flexible AC Transmission Systems: Modelling and Control,* Springer-Verlag. 978-3-540-30606-1, Germany

2

Study of Inductive-Capacitive Series Circuits Using the Simulink Software Package

Titu Niculescu
University of Petrosani
Romania

1. Introduction

This chapter presents a modern method for approaching the electrical circuits using the MATLAB-SIMULINK package programs. The simple series circuits which are switched on a DC voltage at the initial moment are presented below. For the young researchers these are very useful. We can determine the current variation forms and the reactive elements voltage, by using this virtual medium. Each presented case contains an analytical presentation of the problem, but it also contains electrical diagrams of electrical parameters. The diagrams were obtained by different methods which use this programs package.

2. Study of the inductive series circuits

We will consider the RL series circuit with concentrated parameters from Fig.1. At the initial moment, the k circuit switcher is closed and we intend to study the behavior and variation of circuit electrical parameters after connection.

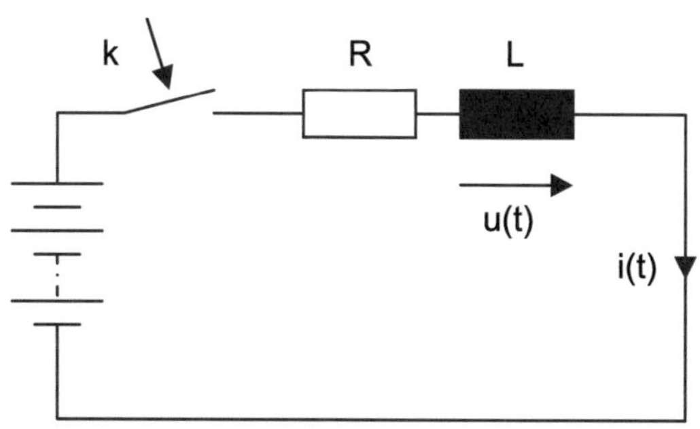

Fig. 1. RL series circuits at closing

2.1 Theoretical study of the circuit

The differential equation which corresponds to the transitory regime immediately after closing is the following:

$$Ri + L\frac{di}{dt} = E \qquad (1)$$

The current expression through the circuit after closing is the solution of the differential equation of the circuit (1).

$$i(t) = \frac{E}{R}(1 - e^{-\frac{t}{T}}) \tag{2}$$

where:

$$T = \frac{L}{R} \tag{3}$$

and it represents the time constant of the circuit.

The voltage expression on the coil after connection is:

$$u(t) = L\frac{di}{dt} = E \cdot e^{-\frac{t}{T}} \tag{4}$$

2.2 SIMULINK model of the circuit

The SIMULINK model of the circuit after closing was done on grounds of equation (1) where the derivative of the current was separated.

$$\frac{di}{dt} = \frac{1}{L}(E - Ri) \tag{5}$$

The SIMULINK model obtained in this way is shown in Fig.2 and was created in order to allow the drawing of the current diagrams through the circuit and the voltage on the coil, for different values of the R resistance and the E D.C. voltage.

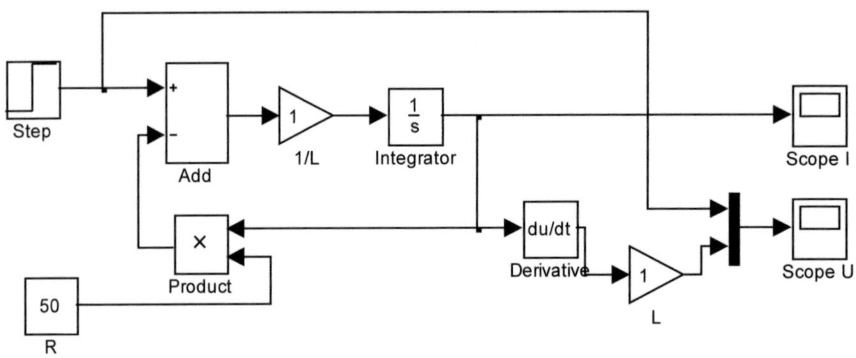

Fig. 2. SIMULINK model of the RL circuit at closing

The k switcher is realized using a voltage step signal which is applied at the terminal of the circuit, to simulate the closing of the k switcher.

If we consider the following values of the electric parameters

- D.C. voltage applied: E = 24[V];

- The resistance value: R = 50[Ω];
- The circuit inductivity: L = 1[H],

we will obtain the diagrams from Fig.3 and Fig.4.

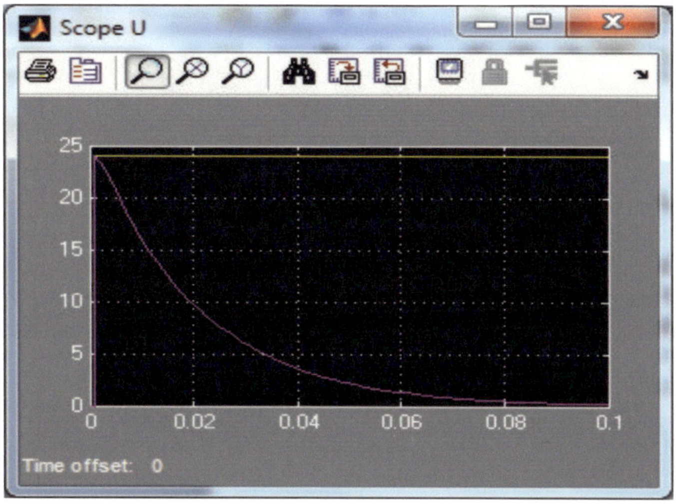

Fig. 3. Variation of the coil voltage after closing

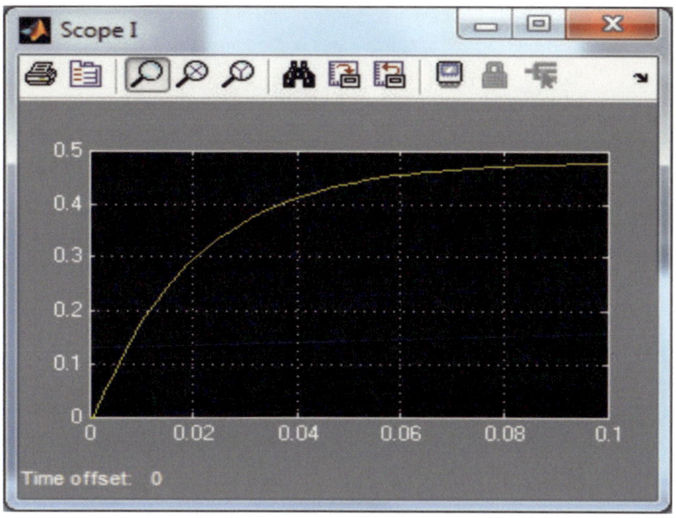

Fig. 4. Variation of the circuit current

2.3 Analysis of RL series circuits using the SimPowerSistems software package

The SimPowerSystems software package is a component of the MATLAB program which allows analyzing an electrical circuit by drawing it in an editing window. The SimPowerSystems model is presented in Fig.5 and allows the visualization of the circuit current and the coil voltage if we apply a step voltage signal and a unitary impulse. The electrical parameters of the circuit have the values:

R = 50[Ω]; L = 1[H].

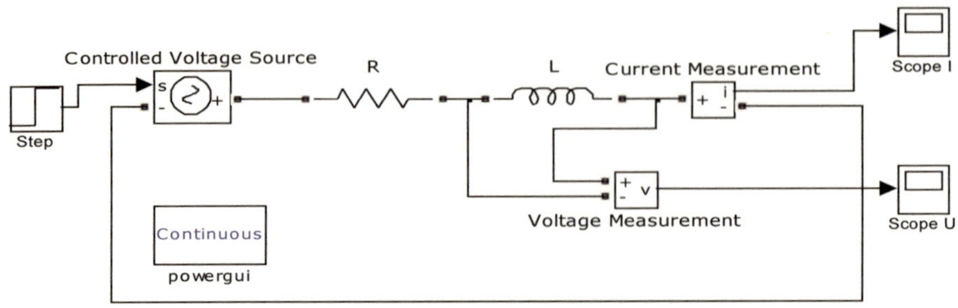

Fig. 5. SimPowerSystems model of an inductive circuit

The *Continous powergui* analyze block is required to be present in the drawing window for launching the simulation model. We will open an analysis window by double-clicking on this block, Fig. 6.

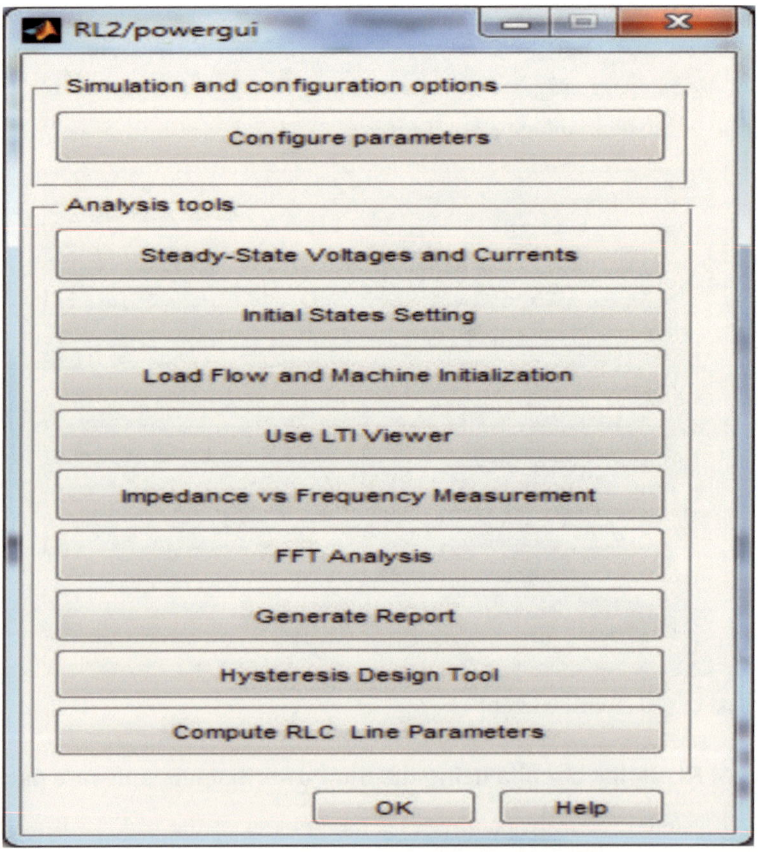

Fig. 6. The analysis window of the circuit

The selection of the *Use LTI Viewer* button will lead to the opening of the window in Fig.7, from which we can select the current diagram or the coil voltage diagram.

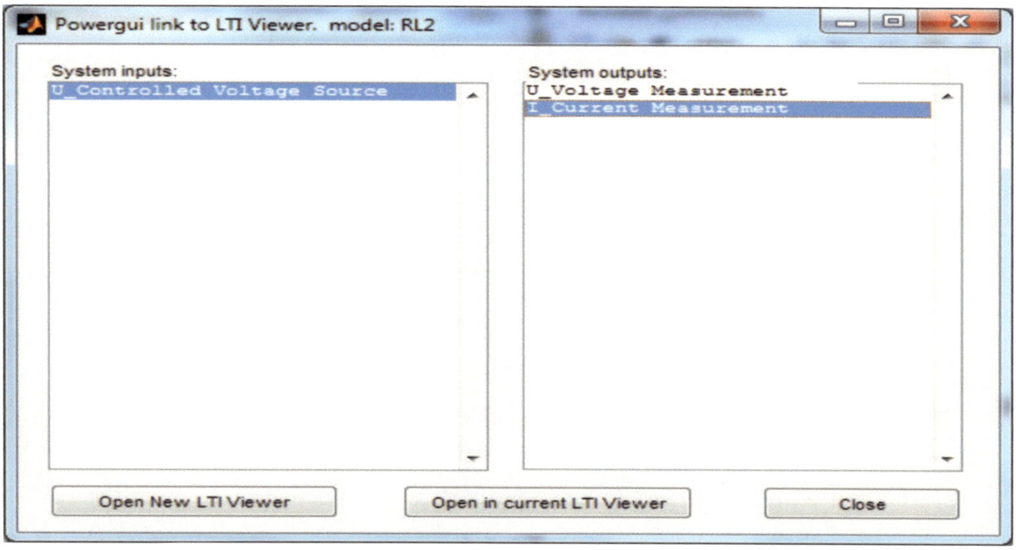

Fig. 7. The *LTI Viewer* window

The selection *of U_Voltage Measurement or I_Current Measurement* is followed by the obtaining of the coil voltage diagram and of the circuit current upon applying the step signal and a unitary impulse. These are presented in Fig.8 and Fig.9.

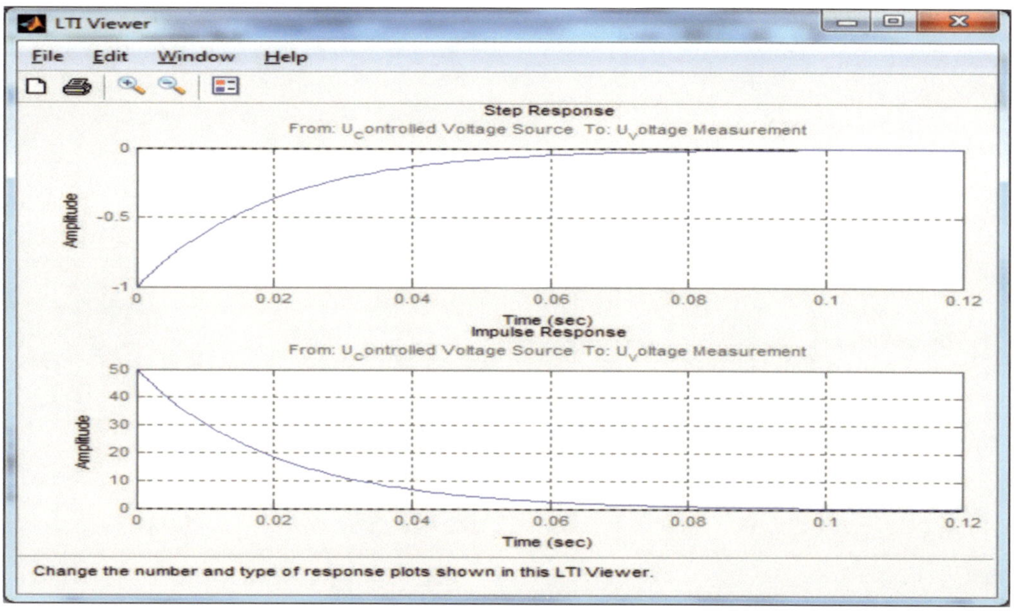

Fig. 8. The coil voltage variation upon applying a step signal and a unitary impulse.

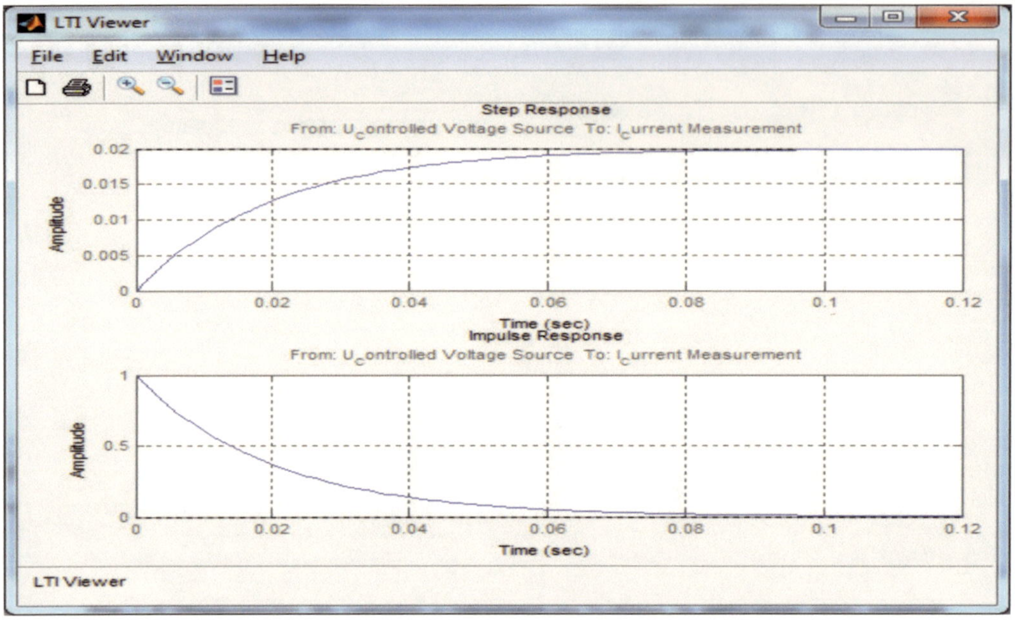

Fig. 9. The current variation upon applying a step signal and a unitary impulse.

We can use the *Edit/Plot Configurations* and *Edit/ Viewer Preferences* options, in order to create these diagrams. We can also select the *Bode* option from these menus, which allows the obtaining of the current frequency diagrams of the RL series circuit.

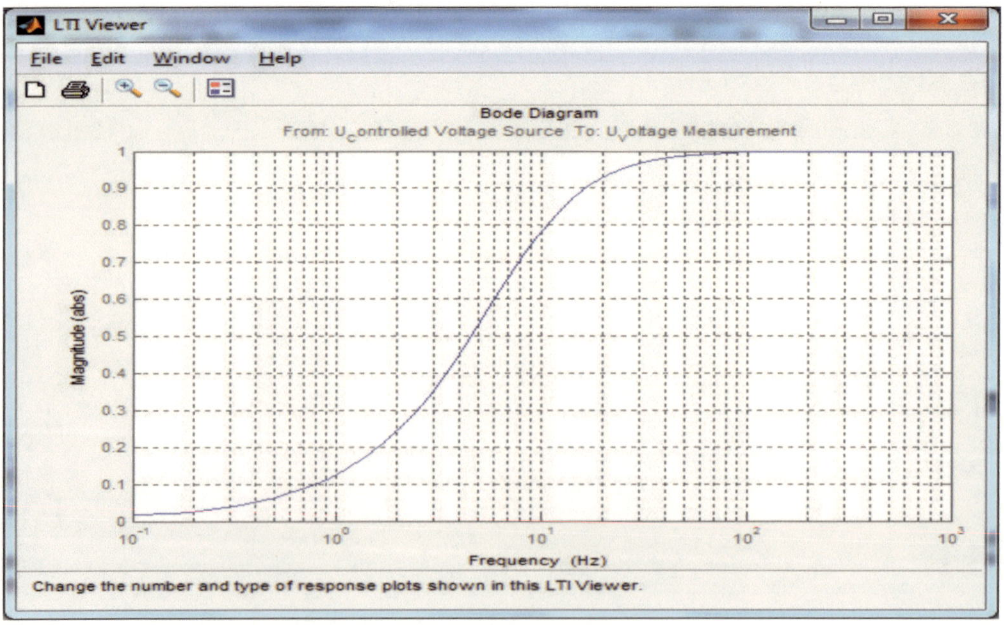

Fig. 10. The amplitude frequency diagram of the voltage coil.

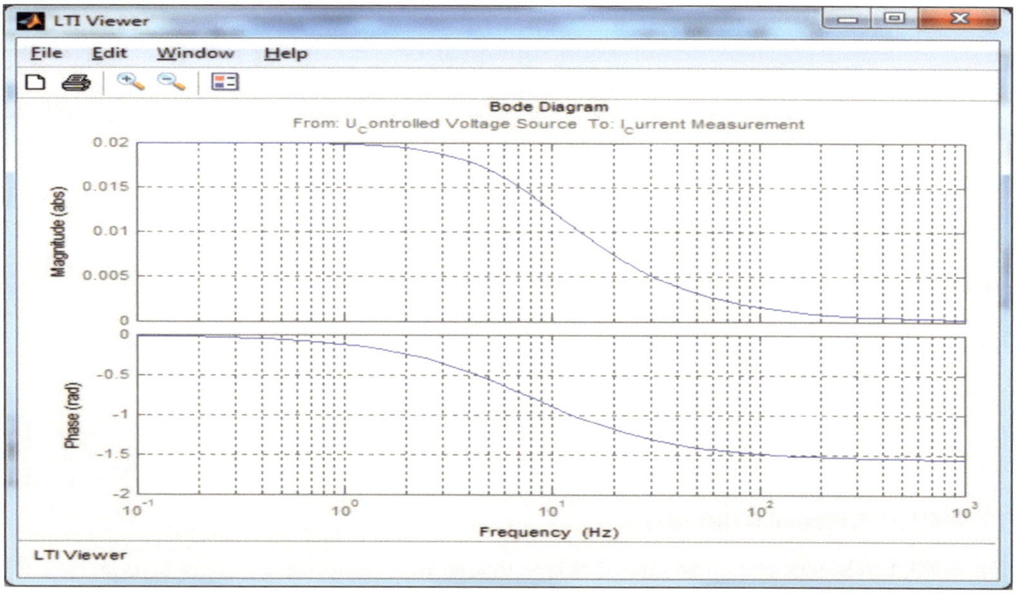

Fig. 11. The frequency current diagrams.

3. Study of the capacitive series circuits

We will consider the RC series circuit with concentrated parameters from Fig.12. At the initial moment, the k circuit switcher is closed and we want to study the current variation through the circuit and the capacitor voltage variation, after connection.

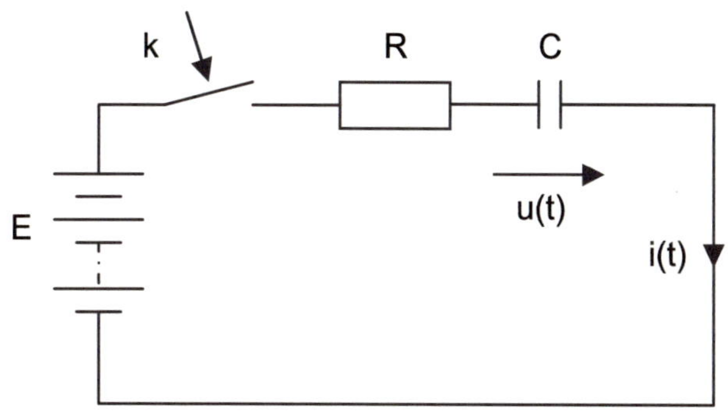

Fig. 12. RC series circuit at closing

3.1 Theoretical study of the circuit

The integral equation which corresponds to the transitory regime immediately after closing is given by:

$$Ri + \frac{1}{C}\int idt = E \tag{6}$$

Equation (6) is equivalent with differential equation:

$$RC\frac{du}{dt} + u = E \tag{7}$$

The expression of the capacitor voltage after closing is the solution of differential equation (7):

$$u(t) = E(1 - e^{-\frac{t}{T}}) \tag{8}$$

where $T = RC$, represents the time constant of the circuit.

The circuit current after closing is given by:

$$i = C\frac{du}{dt} = \frac{E}{R}e^{-\frac{t}{T}} \tag{9}$$

3.2 SIMULINK model of the circuit

The SIMULINK model of the circuit after closing was done on grounds of equation (7) where the voltage derivative was separated.

$$\frac{du}{dt} = \frac{1}{RC}(E - u) \tag{10}$$

The SIMULINK model obtained is shown in Fig.13 and was created in order to allow the drawing of the current diagrams through the circuit and the voltage capacitor, for different values of the R resistance, of the E D.C. voltage and of the C capacitor.

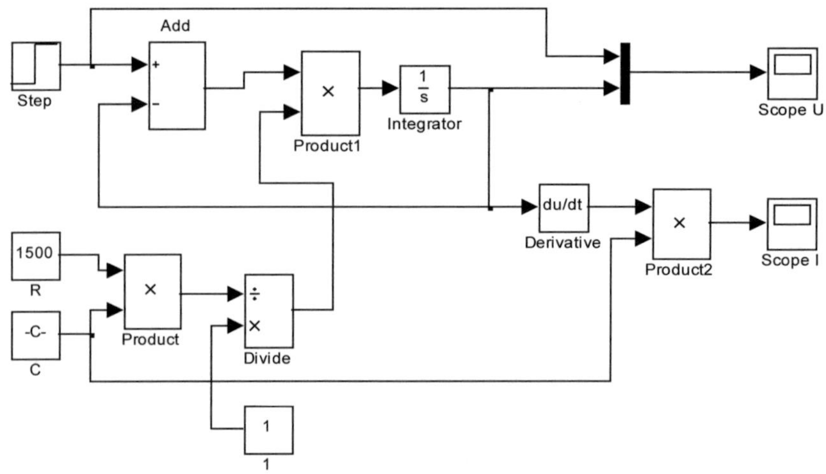

Fig. 13. SIMULINK model of the RC circuit at closing

The k switcher is realized using the same voltage step signal which is applied at the terminal of the circuit, to simulate the closing of the k switcher.

If we consider the following values of the electric parameters:

- D.C. voltage applied: E = 24[V];
- The circuit resistance: R = 50[Ω];
- The circuit capacity: C = 100[μF],

we will obtain the diagrams from Fig.14 and Fig.15.

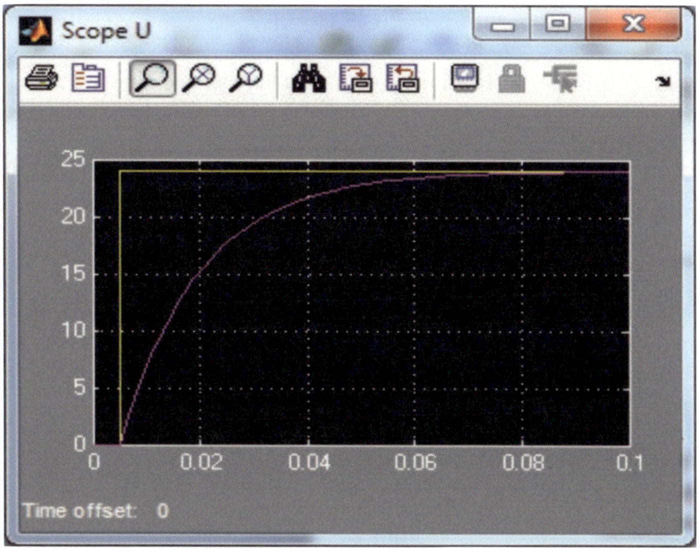

Fig. 14. The capacitor voltage variation

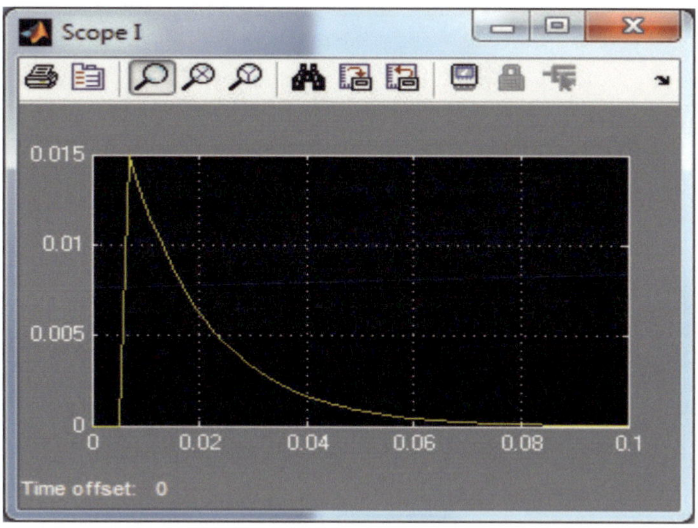

Fig. 15. The current variation after closing

3.3 Analysis of RC series circuits using the SimPowerSistems software package

The SimPowerSystems model is presented in Fig.16 and allows the visualization of the circuit current and the capacitor voltage if we apply a step voltage signal and a unitary impulse.

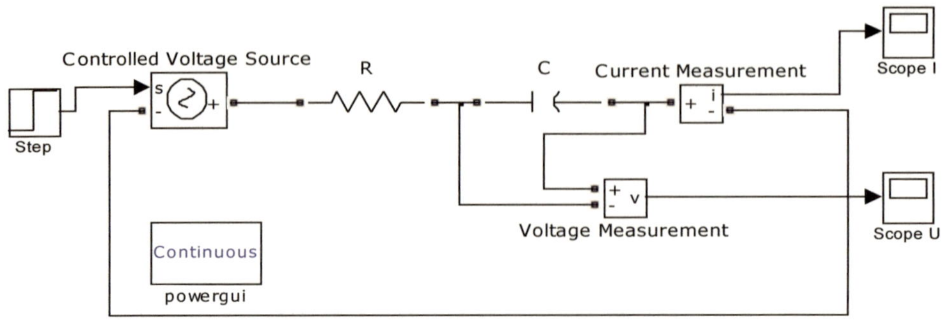

Fig. 16. SimPowerSystems model of the capacitive circuit

The electrical parameters of the circuit have the values:

- R = 50[Ω]; C = 10[μF].

To study the voltage variation on the capacitor, we follow the steps:

- Select by double clicking the *Continous powerguy* block from the simulation model.
- Select *Use LTI Wiewer* in the new window;
- We will select U Voltage *Measurement*.

This method allows us to obtain the voltage capacitor diagram upon applying the step signal and the unitary impulse (Fig.17).

The current variation through the circuit upon applying a step signal and a unitary impulse was obtained by selecting *I_Current Measurement* option (Fig.18).

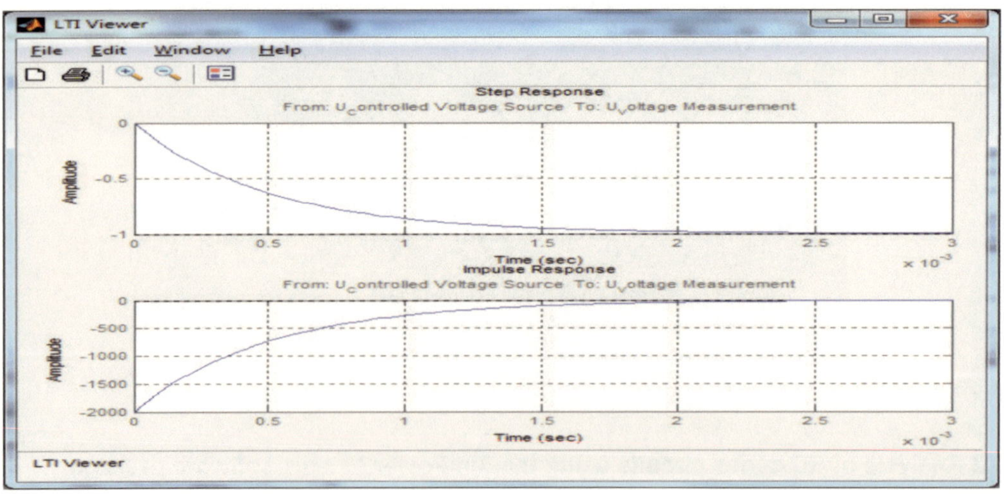

Fig. 17. The capacitor voltage variation upon applying a step signal and a unitary impulse.

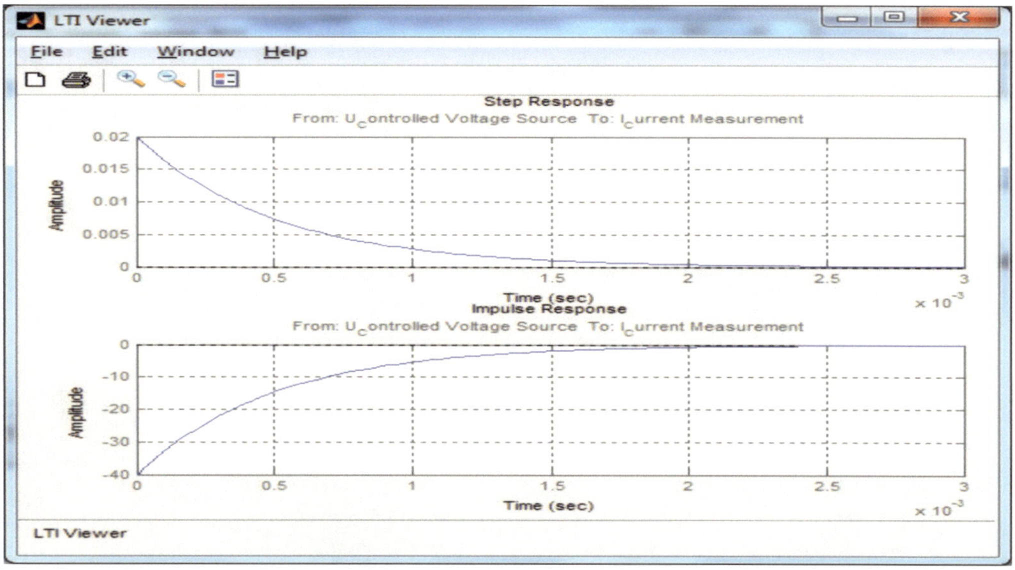

Fig. 18. The current variation upon applying a step signal and a unitary impulse.

The Bode diagrams which allow the visualization of the frequency behavior of the circuit are presented bellow:

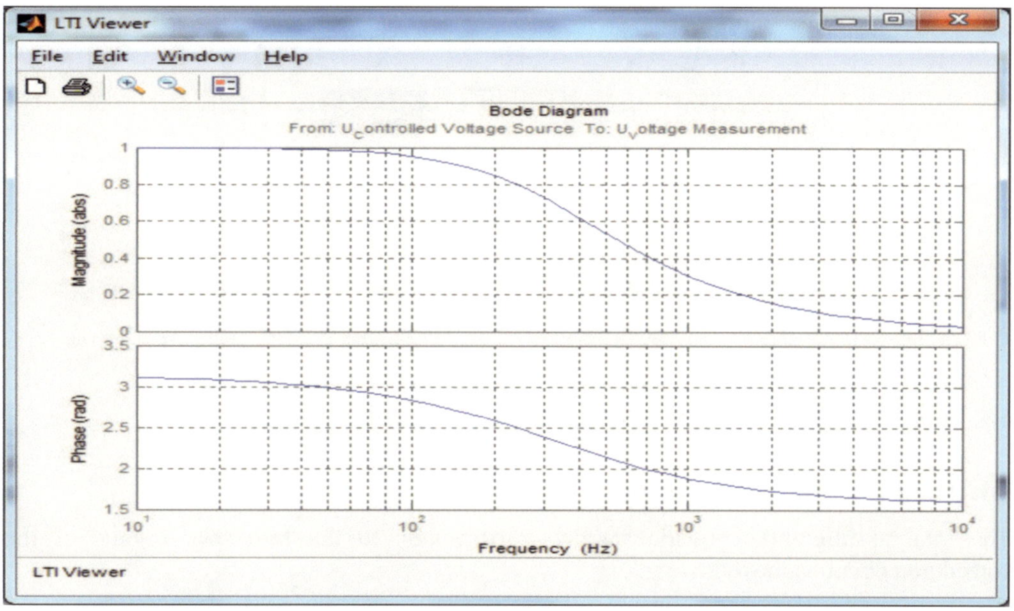

Fig. 19. The capacitor voltage frequency diagrams

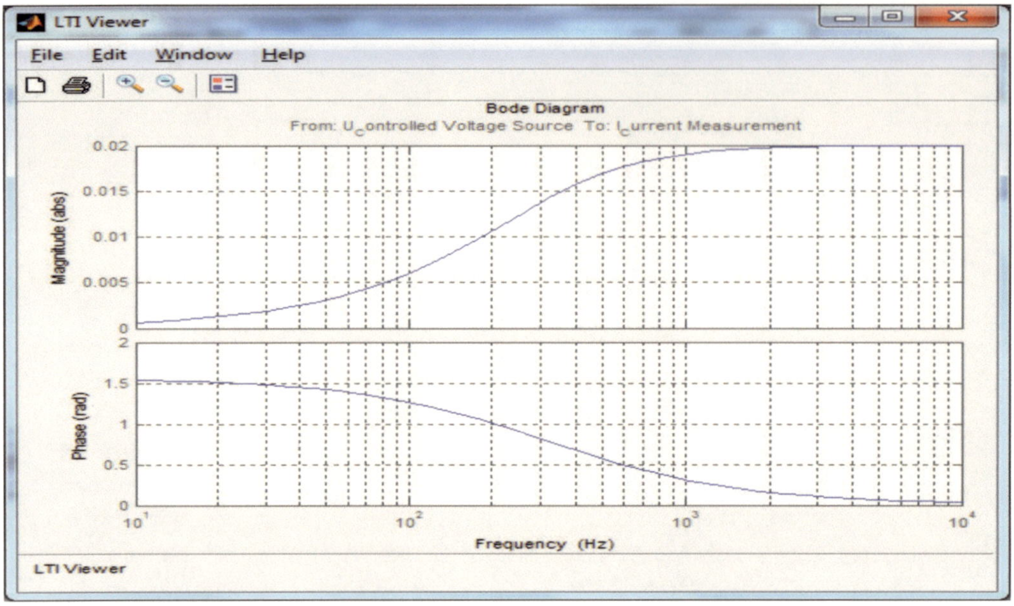

Fig. 20. The current frequency diagrams.

4. Study of the inductive-capacitive series circuits

We will consider the RLC series circuit with concentrated parameters from Fig.21. At the initial moment, the k circuit switcher is closed and we intend to study the behavior and variation of circuit electrical parameters after connection.

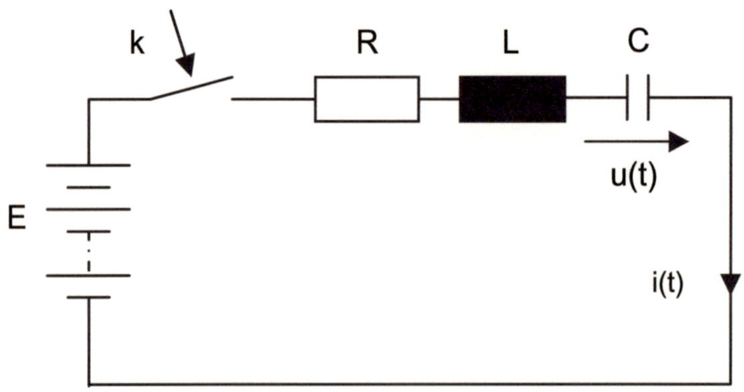

Fig. 21. RLC series circuit at connecting

4.1 Theoretical study of the circuit

The integral-differential equation which corresponds to the transitory regime of the considered circuit is the following:

$$Ri + L\frac{di}{dt} + \frac{1}{C}\int i dt = E \tag{11}$$

or:

$$LC\frac{d^2u}{dt^2}+RC\frac{du}{dt}+u\ =E \tag{12}$$

The following notations are made:

$$\delta=\frac{R}{2L} \tag{13}$$

The circuit amortization:

$$\omega_0=\frac{1}{\sqrt{LC}} \tag{14}$$

the circuit personal pulsation:

$$\omega=\sqrt{\delta^2-\omega_0^2} \tag{15}$$

We will consider the situation when $\delta>\omega_0$ or $R<2\sqrt{L/C}$, which will be checked by the resistor in the circuit.

Consequently, the solving of the differential equation gives the following solutions:

$$u(t)=E\left[[1-\frac{1}{2\sqrt{\delta^2-\omega_0^2}}(r_1e^{r_2t}-r_2e^{r_1t})]\right] \tag{16}$$

$$i(t)=\frac{E}{2L\sqrt{\delta^2-\omega_0^2}}\left(e^{r_1t}-e^{r_2t}\right) \tag{17}$$

where r1 and r2 are the roots of the characteristic equation:

$$\begin{aligned} r_1 &= -\delta+\omega \\ r_2 &= -\delta-\omega \end{aligned} \tag{18}$$

We will consider the situation when $\delta<\omega_0$ or $R<2\sqrt{L/C}$. The following notation was made:

$$\omega_0^2-\delta^2=\omega'^2 \tag{19}$$

Consequently, the solving of the differential equation gives the following solutions:

$$u(t)=E\left[[1-\frac{\omega_0}{\omega'}\bullet e^{-\delta t}\bullet\sin(\omega' t+\beta')]\right] \tag{20}$$

$$i(t)=\frac{E}{\omega' L}e^{-\delta t}\sin\omega' t \tag{21}$$

where

$$\beta' = \arccos\frac{\delta}{\omega_0} \tag{22}$$

4.2 SIMULINK model of the circuit

The SIMULINK model of the circuit after closing was done on grounds of the second order differential equation (12), which is put in the form (23) where the higher order derivative is separated:

$$\frac{d^2u}{dt} = \frac{1}{LC}\left[[E - RC\frac{du}{dt} - u]\right] \tag{23}$$

The SIMULINK model from Fig.22 generates the voltage capacitor and the current through the circuit during the transitory regime. To this purpose, two values of the R resistor are considered, which correspond to two important regimes:

- Aperiodic regime;
- Oscillatory regime.

For each regime the capacitor voltage and the circuit current variation diagrams are plotted.

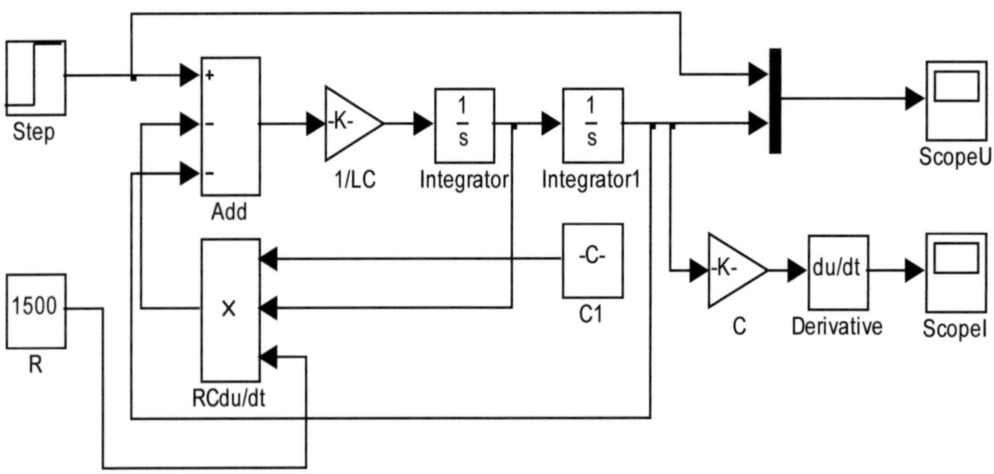

Fig. 22. SIMULINK model of the circuit

If we consider:

- The value of the D.C. voltage: E = 24 [V]
- The circuit resistance: R = 1.5 [kΩ],
- The coil inductance: L = 10^{-4} [H]
- The capacitor capacity: C = 10 [nF],

we get the following MATLAB diagrams (Fig.23 and Fig.24) according to the equations (16) and (17) for a-periodic mode, and according to the equations (20) and (21) for oscillating mode (Fig.25 and Fig.26).

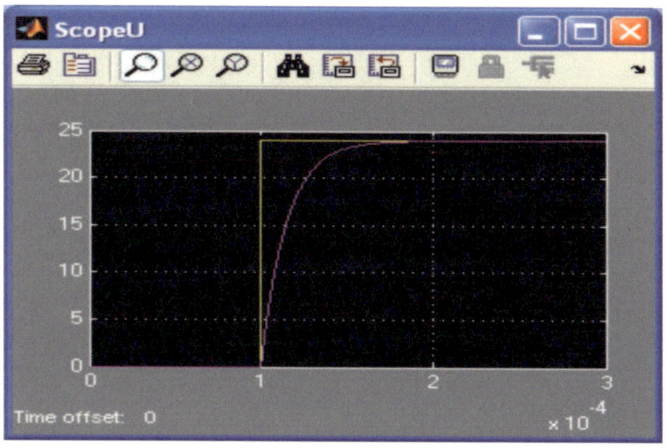

Fig. 23. The voltage capacitor variation in the a-periodic mode

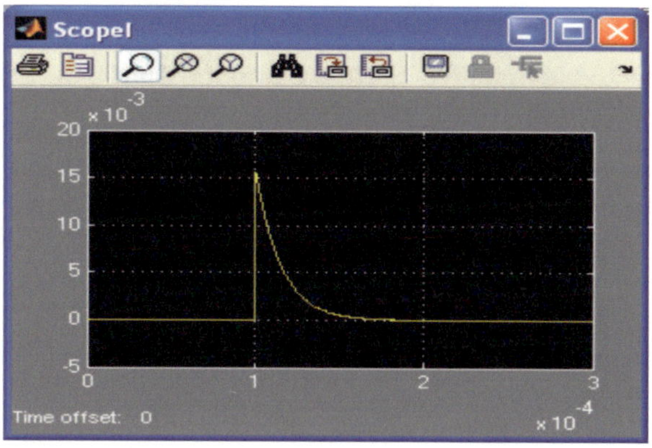

Fig. 24. The current variation in the a-periodic mode

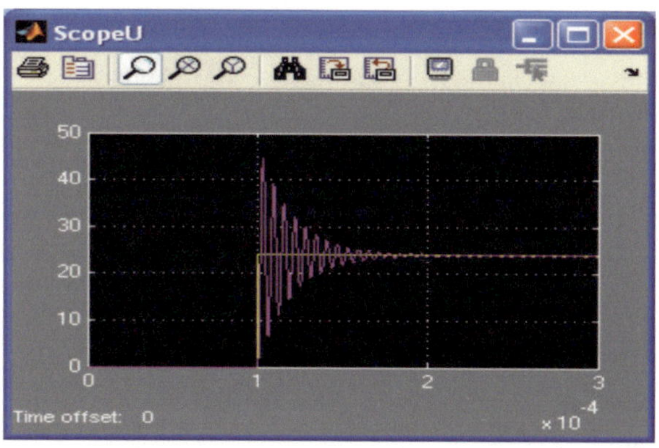

Fig. 25. The capacitor voltage variation in the oscillating regime

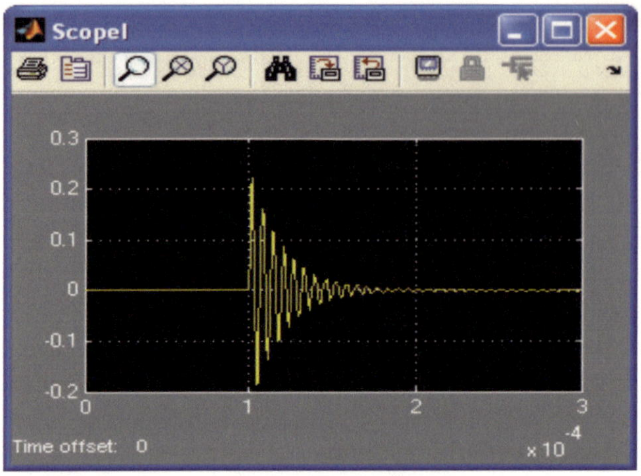

Fig. 26. The current variation in the oscillating regime

The k switcher is realized by using a voltage step signal which is applied at the terminal of the circuit, to simulate the closing of the k switcher. Changing the value of resistance, automatically leads to the updating of the voltage and current charts.

4.3. Analysis of inductive-capacitive circuits using the SimPowerSystems software package

The SimPowerSystems software package allows the study of the circuit behavior, when it is connected to a voltage step or a unitary impulse, using *Continous powerguy* block. The current variation in the circuit, the voltage variation of the capacitive element, or the frequency behavior of the circuit for different values of circuit elements can be studied.

4.3.1 SimPowerSystems model of the circuit

The MATLAB software package contains SimPowerSystems of Simulink, which can simulate the electrical circuits and analyze different operating regimes. Because the signal step response or pulse generates a transitory regime, the circuit behavior in these conditions can be studied. The simulation is shown in Fig.27:

The advantage of this simulation method is that the circuit can be tested at both signals, unit step and unitary impulse, and leads to several types of typical circuit diagrams. Two sets of values were chosen in this case for circuit parameters, which correspond to two special regimes.

In the simulation model from Fig.27 we used a *Controlled Voltage Source* controlled by a step voltage signal. In this way, the switcher closing can be simulated.

The SimPowerSystems software package allows the obtaining of a lot of diagrams for a circuit. So, we will study the capacitor voltage diagrams and current diagrams for the two occurring regimes:

- A-periodic regime:
- Oscillating regime.

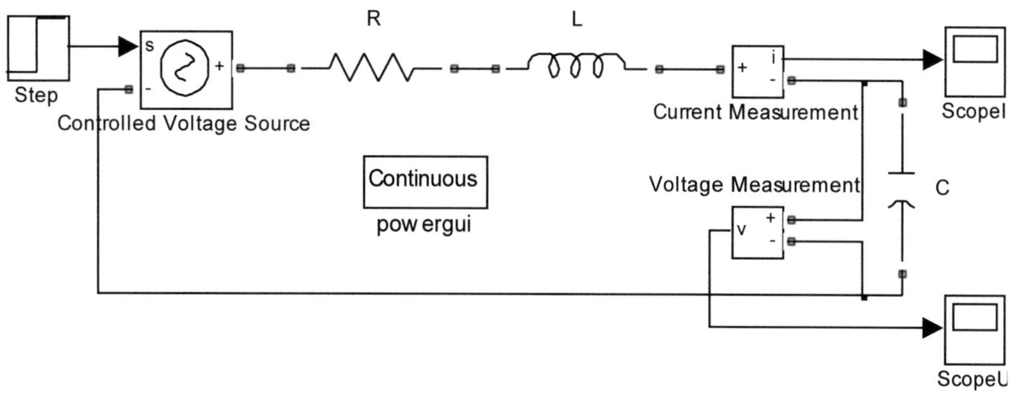

Fig. 27. SimPowerSystems model of the circuit

1. *Voltage capacitor*

The a-periodic loading of the capacitor leads to the obtaining of the capacitor voltage variation diagrams when the unit step and the unitary impulse are applied to the input. These charts are presented below.

The following values of electrical parameters were considered:

- For a-periodic regime:
- E = 24 [V], the step voltage applied;
- R = 1,5 [kΩ], the electrical circuit resistance;
- $L = 10^{-4}[H]$, the circuit inductance;
- C = 10 [nF], the circuit capacity.
- For oscillating regime:
- E = 24 [V], the step voltage applied;
- R = 10 [Ω], the electrical circuit resistance;
- $L = 10^{-4}[H]$, the circuit inductance;
- C = 10 [nF], the circuit capacity.

To study the capacitor voltage variation, we follow the steps:

- Select by double clicking the *Continous powerguy* block from the simulation model;
- Select *Use LTI Wiewer* will appear in the new window;
- We will select U Voltage *Measurement*.

The POWERGUY analysis block, with the above values, allows the obtaining of the following Matlab diagrams (Fig.28 and Fig.29):

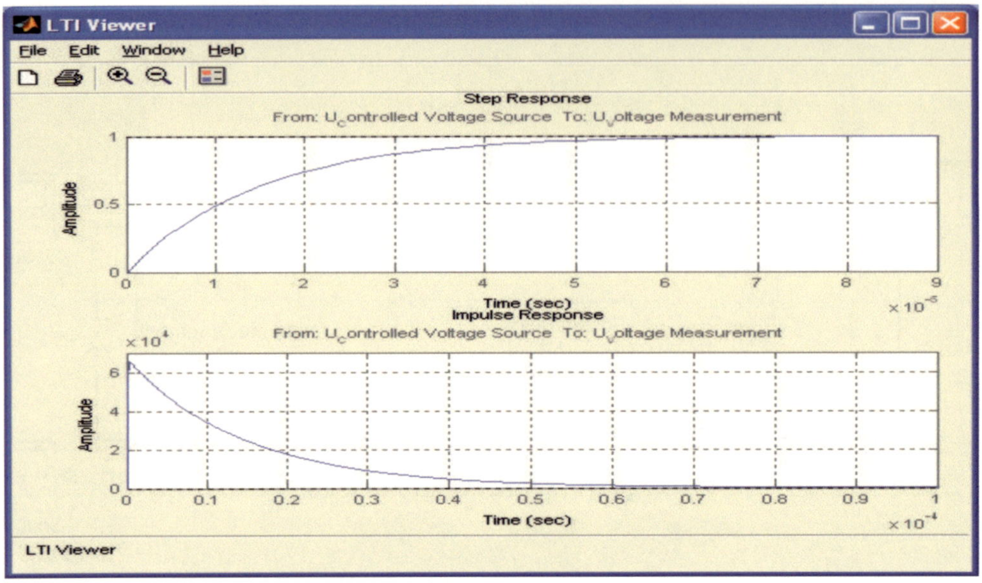

Fig. 28. The capacitor voltage variation in the a-periodic mode

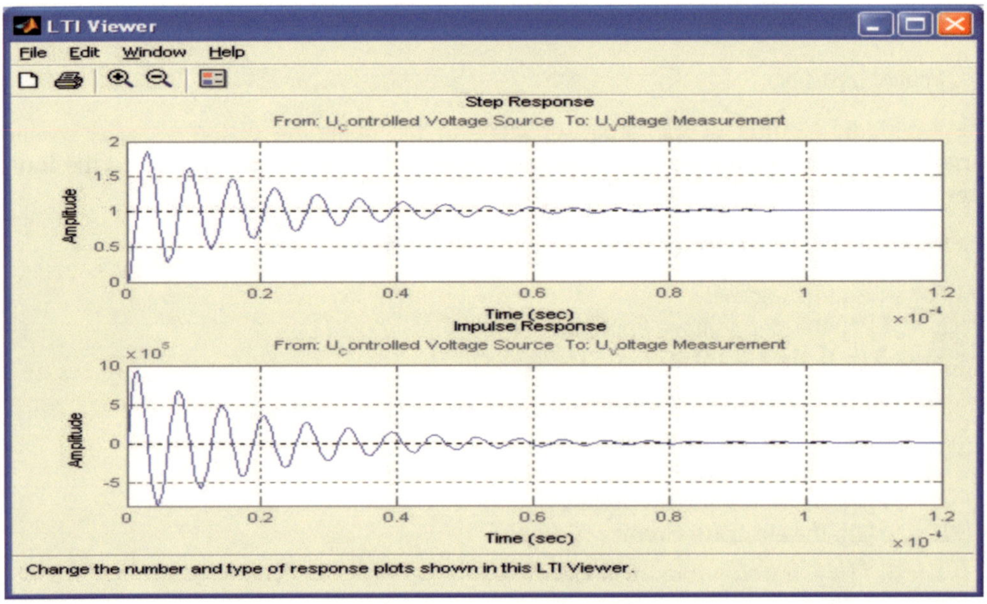

Fig. 29. The capacitor voltage variation in the oscillating regime

The POWERGUY block permits the analysis and plotting of the frequency characteristics of the capacitor voltage, where the frequency in logarithmic coordinates was considered on the horizontal axis (BODE diagram).

For this, we follow these steps:

- Select by double clicking *Continous powerguy* block ;

- *Use LTI Wiewer* will appear in the window and we will select it;
- In the occurring window we will select *U voltage Measurement;*
- Now, we will select *Edit / Plot Configuration / Bode*

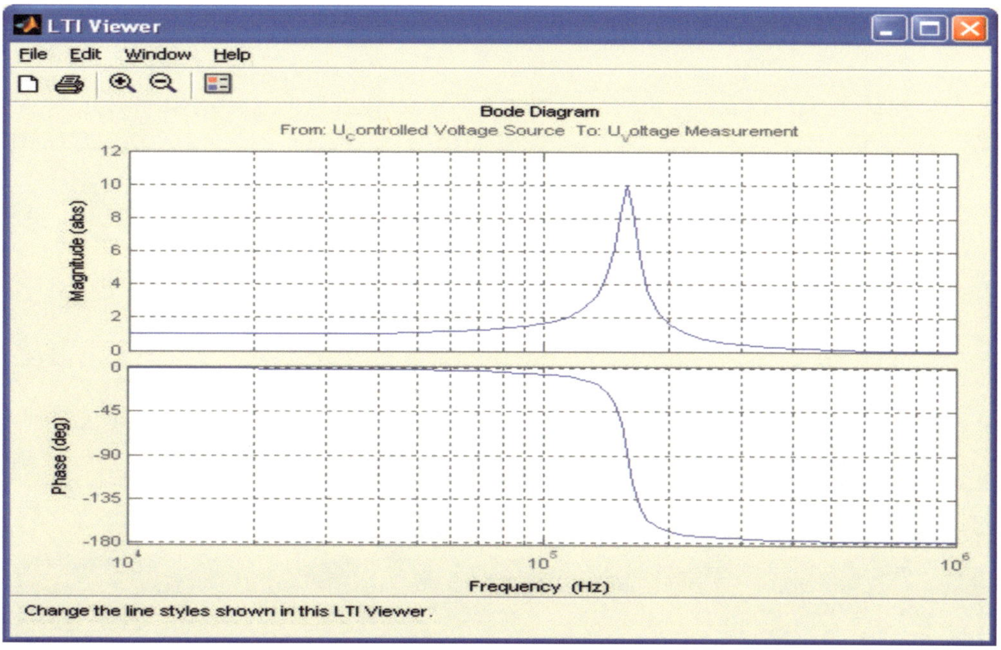

Fig. 30. Frequency diagrams of the voltage swing on the capacitive element

2. Study of circuit current

To study the circuit current variation the same procedure is used, mentioning that instead of selecting the *U voltage Measurement, I Current Measuremen*t must be selected.

A-periodic loading of the capacitor leads to obtaining the current variation diagrams when the unit step and the unitary impulse are applied to the input.

For this, we will follow these steps:

- Select *Continous powerguy* block diagram simulation by double click;
- Select *Use LTI Wiewer* in the appeared window;
- Select *I Current Measurement* in the window appeared;
- Select *Edit / Plot Configuration / Bode*

The SimPowerSystems software package allows the obtaining of two diagrams for a circuit. So, we will study the current variation diagrams for the two occurring regimes:

- A-periodical regime:
- Oscillating regime.

The a-periodical and oscillating regime according to these values are obtained in the following charts (Fig.31 and Fig.32):

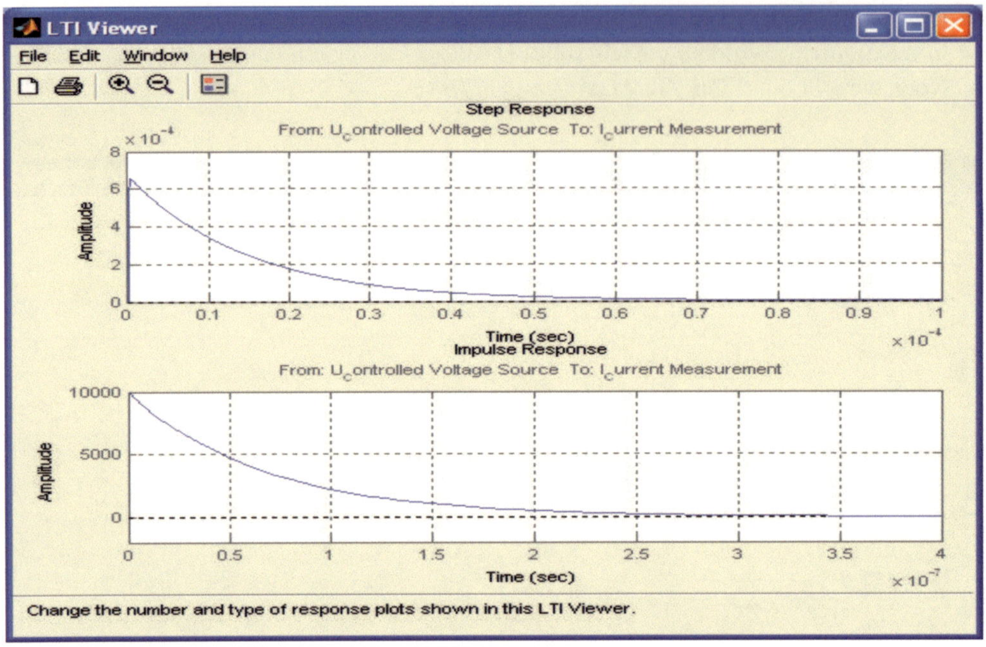

Fig. 31. The current variation for signal step and impulse in a-periodic mode

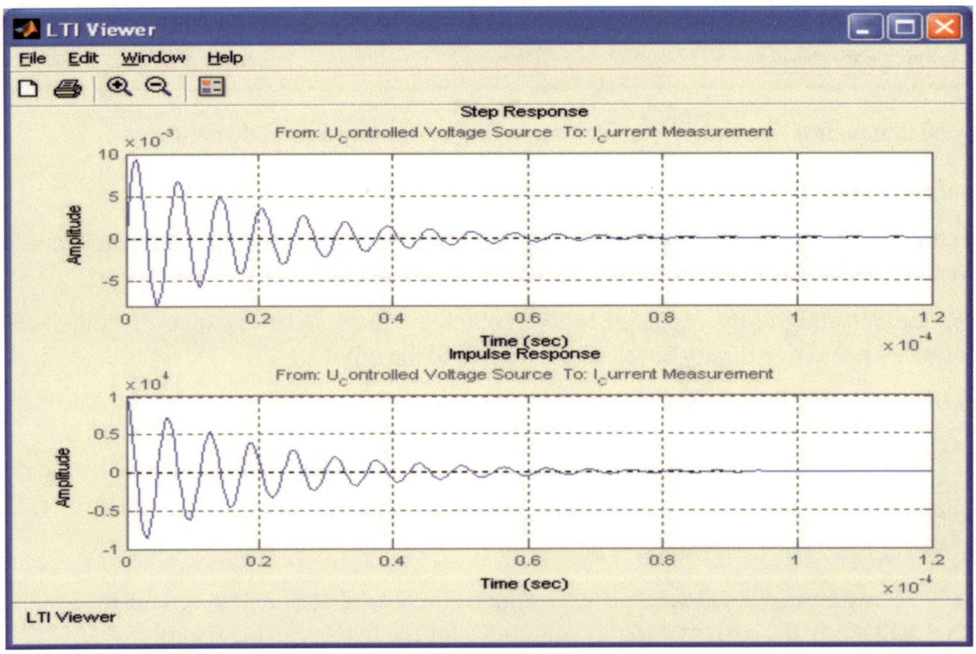

Fig. 32. The current variation for signal step and impulse in the oscillating regime

The POWERGUY block allows the analysis and plotting of frequency current characteristics, where the frequency in logarithmic coordinates was considered on the horizontal axis (BODE diagram). For this, we will follow these steps:

- Select *Continous powerguy* by double clicking the block diagram simulation;
- Select *Use LTI Wiewer* in the appeared window;
- Select *I Current Measurement* in the window appeared;
- Select *Edit / Plot Configuration / Bode*

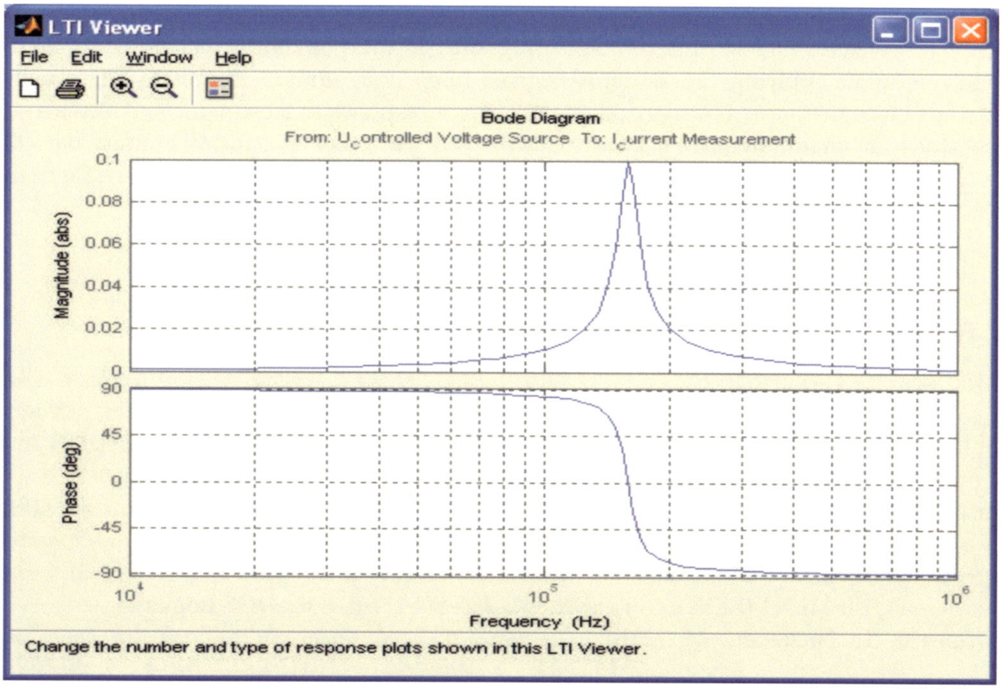

Fig. 33. Frequency diagrams of the current swing through the circuit

In the diagram from Fig.33 we can observe a maximum of current which correspond to a resonance regime. We can determine the resonance frequencies for an inductive-capacitive circuit using the simulation circuit model and the SimPowerSystems software package. With POWERGUY block, other electrical circuit parameters can be determined.

5. Conclusions

An important conclusion of this chapter is that the electrical circuits, regardless of configuration, can be studied with this modern method which involves the use of virtual medium.

Three elementary circuits are presented here, but the study modality can be extended to other circuits configuration as well.

If we consider an electric circuit, a first problem is that of writing the characteristic integral differential equations, which can be integrated with a simulation model and which uses the Simulink software package. These models can be conceived so that the electric circuit parameters must be electric input values in the simulation model. Thus, the obtained diagrams are automatically updated to any changes of circuit electrical parameters, and the influence of each parameter variation in the final diagrams can be studied.

In order to realize the simulating model which integrates the differential equations, the basic idea is to separate in the left member of equation, the higher order derivative. The analytical expressions obtained in the right member of the equation underlie the achievement of the simulating model by means of specific blocks of the virtual medium. In the case of complex circuits, the simulating model is conceived on a differential equations system.

Another given facility of this package programs, is the possibility to study the circuit behavior upon applying the standard signals (step unit, unitary impulse). The specific analysis block *Continous Powerguy* allows the circuit response to these signals. It also allows the study of circuit frequency characteristics and the other specific diagrams: the coil hysteresis diagrams, line parameters, FTF analysis, Bode Diagrams, Nyquist diagrams, Nichols diagrams and others.

This study intends to be a starting point in the approach of more complex circuits.

6. References

Niculescu, T.; Pasculescu, D.; Pana, L. (2010). *Study of the operating states of intrinsic safety Barriers of the electric equipment intended for use in atmospheres with explosion hazard,*Main Page of the Journal WSEAS TRANSACTIONS on CIRCUITS and SYSTEMS, ISSN: 1109-2734,

Pasculescu, D.; Niculescu, T.; Pana, L. (2010). *Uses of Matlab software to size intrinsic safety barriers of the electric equipment intended for use in atmospheres with explosion,* International Conference on ENERGY and ENVIRONME TECHNOLOGIES and EQUIPMENT (EEETE '10), ISBN: 978-960-474-181-6, Bucharest, Romania

Niculescu, T.; Niculescu, M. (2010). *The study of fundamental electrical circuits transitory Phenomena using MATLAB software, UNIVERSITARIA SIMPRO* ElectricalEngineering and Energetics System Control, Applied Informatics and ComputerEngineering, ISSN 1842-4449 Petrosani, Romania

Ghinea, M.; Firţeanu, V. (1999). *MATLAB calcul numeric, grafică, aplcatii,* Teora, ISBN 973-601-275-1, Bucharest, Romania

Halunga-Fratu, S.; Fratu, O. (2004) *Simularea sistemelor de transmisiune analogice şi digitale folosind mediul MATLAB/SIMULINK,* MatrixRom, ISBN 973-685-716-6, Bucharest, Romania

Tudorache, T. (2006). *Medii de calcul in ingineria electrica MATLAB,* MatrixRom, ISBN 973-775-005-6, Bucharest, Romania

Niculescu, T.;Costinaş, S. (1998) *Electrotehnică,* Printech, ISBN 973-9402-14-3, Bucharest, Romania

3

Fixed Transmission Media

Rastislav Róka
Slovak University of Technology, Bratislava
Slovakia

1. Introduction

For successful understanding of the signal transmission in access networks that utilized fixed transmission media, it is necessary exactly to recognize essential negative influences in the real environment of metallic homogeneous symmetric lines, power distribution cables and optical fibers. This chapter discusses features and frequency characteristics of negative influences on signals transmitted by means of the VDSL technology, the PLC technology and PON networks. For the expansion of communication systems on fixed transmission media, it is necessary to have a detailed knowledge of their transmission environments and negative influences in the real developing of customer installations.

A main attention of the metallic transmission media's parts is focused on the description of the proposed VDSL and PLC simulation models and on the explanation of simulation methods for substantial negative influences. Presented simulation models represent a reach enough knowledgebase for the extended digital signal processing techniques of the VDSL and PLC signal transmissions that can be extremely helpful for various tests and performance comparisons.

A main attention of the optical transmission media's part is focused on the description of the proposed optical fiber's simulation model and on the explanation of simulation methods for its substantial linear effects - transmission factors. The presented simulation model represents a reach enough knowledgebase that can be helpful for various tests and performance comparisons of various novel modulation techniques suggested and intended to be used at signal transmissions in the transmission environment of optical fibers.

2. The environment of metallic homogeneous lines

2.1 Linear negative influences on transmitted signals

Propagation loss and linear distortions (distortions of the module and the phase characteristics and the group delay characteristic) are linear negative influences dependent on physical and constructional parameters, such as a line length, a core diameter of the wire, a mismatch of impedances in cross-connecting points of sections, a frequency bandwidth and so forth (Róka, 2004).

We first discuss the propagation loss L_{dB} in a perfectly terminated line. If R, L, G and C are primary constants of the line and $\omega = 2.\pi.f$, where f is the frequency, then

$$\gamma(\omega)=\alpha(\omega)+j.\beta(\omega)=\sqrt{(R+j.\omega.L).(G+j.\omega.C)} \tag{1}$$

and

$$Z(\omega)=\sqrt{\frac{(R+j.\omega.L)}{(G+j.\omega.C)}} \tag{2}$$

where $\gamma(\omega)$ denotes the propagation constant of the line, $\alpha(\omega)$ is the specific constant of the attenuation, $\beta(\omega)$ is the specific constant of the phase shift and $Z(\omega)$ is the characteristic impedance of the line. For a perfectly terminated line with the length l, the transfer function $\mathcal{H}(l, f)$ of metallic homogeneous symmetric lines is given by

$$\mathcal{H}(l,f)=e^{-l.\gamma(f)}=e^{-l.\alpha(f)}.e^{-j.l.\beta(f)} \tag{3}$$

and the propagation loss L_{dB} is given as

$$L_{dB}(l,f)=-20.\log_{10}\left|\mathcal{H}(l,f)\right|=\frac{20}{\ln 10}.l.\alpha(f)=a_{line}(l,f)\ [dB] \tag{4}$$

We must place emphasis on the interchangeable use of terms - the line attenuation $a_{line}(l, f)$ and the propagation loss $L_{dB}(l, f)$ to designate the quantity in (4) only for the case of a perfectly terminated line. We can see that a dependency of the propagation loss L_{dB} on the line length l is linear and is also an increasing function of the frequency f as should be apparent from the expression for the propagation constant $\gamma(\omega)$ in (1). A power level of transmitted signals is also influenced by other important parameters - a diameter and constructional material of the core.

For lower frequency regions, for which $\omega.L << R$ is valid and G can be neglected, the propagation constant expressed in (1) can be simplified to

$$\gamma(\omega)\approx\sqrt{\frac{\omega.R.C}{2}}.\left[1-\frac{\omega.L}{2.R}\right]+j.\sqrt{\frac{\omega.R.C}{2}}.\left[1+\frac{\omega.L}{2.R}\right] \tag{5}$$

For frequencies less than 20 kHz, both the real and imaginary parts $\alpha(\omega)$ and $\beta(\omega)$ are approximately proportional to $\sqrt{f}$. At higher frequencies, frequency dependencies of the primary constants R and L (except for C) become noticeable and the propagation constant in (1) can be approximated by

$$\gamma(\omega)\approx\frac{R(\omega)}{2}.\sqrt{\frac{C}{L(\omega)}}+j.\omega.\sqrt{C.L(\omega)} \tag{6}$$

In this case, the imaginary part $\beta(\omega)$ is approximately a linear function of the frequency. Major variations for the real part $\alpha(\omega)$ are due to the frequency dependency of R, which becomes proportional to $\sqrt{f}$. because of the skin effect. Therefore, it is necessary to take into account increased signal attenuation in the area of higher frequencies.

The phase τ_ϕ and envelope τ_e delays of the line can be expressed as following

$$\tau_{\phi}(\omega)=\sqrt{\frac{\beta(\omega)}{\omega}} \qquad \tau_{e}(\omega)=\sqrt{\frac{d\beta(\omega)}{d\omega}} \tag{7}$$

At higher frequencies, the group envelope delay τ_e and the phase delay τ_ϕ are approximately frequency-independent and equal to the value about $\tau_e \approx \tau_\phi = 5{,}4$ μs/km.

2.2 Near-end and far-end crosstalk signals

The term "crosstalk" generally refers to the interference that enters a communication channel through some coupling paths. On Fig. 1, a kind of generating and propagating of two crosstalk types in a multipair cable is presented.

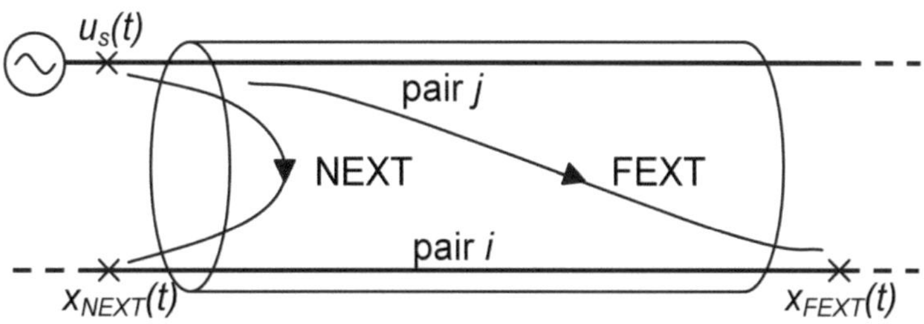

Fig. 1. Types of crosstalks in the environment of metallic homogeneous lines

At the input of pair *j*, the information signal $u_s(t)$ is generated. This signal, when propagating through the line, can generate two types of crosstalk signals arising in pair *i*. A crosstalk signal $x_{NEXT}(t)$ is called the near-end crosstalk NEXT. A crosstalk signal $x_{FEXT}(t)$ is called the far-end crosstalk FEXT. From a data communication point of view, the NEXT crosstalk is generally more damaging than the FEXT crosstalk, because the NEXT does not necessarily propagate through the line length and thus does not experience a propagation loss of the signal (Werner, 1991).

If either single or multiple interferers generate a crosstalk signal, we can define a gain of the NEXT crosstalk path according to (Werner, 1991), (Róka, 2002, 2004) using a following relation

$$\left|\mathcal{H}_{NEXT}(l,f)\right|^2=\frac{\pi^2.f^2.k_{NEXT}}{\alpha(f)}\left[1-e^{-4.\alpha(f).l}\right]\approx K_{NEXT}\cdot f^{3/2} \tag{8}$$

where variables are given as $K_{NEXT} = 0{,}882.10^{-14}.N_d^{0,6}$, N_d is the number of disturbing pairs (disturbers), *f* is the frequency in Hz. An approximation on the right in (8) is valid when the line length *l* is large and for frequency regions where the real part $\alpha(\omega)$ of the propagation constant is proportional to $\sqrt{f}$. We can also derive a gain of the FEXT crosstalk path in a similar manner using a following relation

$$\left|\mathcal{H}_{FEXT}(l,f)\right|^2=4.\pi^2.f^2.k_{FEXT}.l.e^{-2.\alpha(f).l}\approx K_{FEXT}.l.3280.f^2.\left|\mathcal{H}(l,f)\right|^2 \tag{9}$$

where variables are given as $K_{FEXT} = 3{,}083.10^{-20}$, *l* is the line length in km, *f* is the frequency in Hz and $\mathcal{H}(l,f)$ expresses the transfer function of a metallic homogeneous symmetric line.

2.3 Impulse noise signal

Due to the important effect of this negative influence, we took into account also this type of noise. The most common and the most damaging type of impulse noise seems to occur when a disturbed pair shares a common cable sheath with switched disturbing pairs – that is usual in the local access network. Sharp voltage changes can occur on analog pairs because of the opening and closing of relays. These voltage changes when are coupled into neighboring pairs through the NEXT and FEXT coupling path, create spurious, impulsive-like voltages whose amplitudes can be quite significant (Werner, 1991).

In unshielded twisted pairs, various equipments and environmental disturbances such as signaling circuits, transmission and switching gear, electrostatic discharges, lightning surges and so forth can generate an impulse noise. The impulse noise has some reasonably well-defined characteristics. Features of the typical impulse noise can be summarized as follows:

- occurs about 1-5 times per minute (on an average 4 times per minute),
- has peak values in the range 2 - 33 mV,
- has most of its energy concentrated below 40 kHz,
- has time duration in the range 30 - 150 μs.

Of course, mentioned features don't characterize all possible impulse noise signals. In the simulation model, therefore, characteristics of the impulse noise signal can be randomly varied.

2.4 Spectral characteristics of the VDSL signals

The VDSL modem uses a frequency bandwidth up to 20MHz. From this reason, the VDSL transmitter must solve situations that are not emergent in other xDSL modems. To these problems belong a spectral compatibility and cooperation with installed xDSL systems and a high level of different crosstalk signals.

In VDSL modems, various types of duplex methods and proposed modulation techniques are considered in (Cherubini et al., 2000), (Mestagh et al., 2000) and (Oksman & Werner, 2000). The ETSI recommendation binds producers to keep an established frequency plan (European Telecommunications Standards Institute [ETSI], 1999). The VDSL system can work in a frequency band bounded by frequencies f_{LOW} and f_{HIGH} (Fig. 2). In given frequency areas, the power of the VDSL signal must be adjusted to a level that can ensure the spectral compatibility with older xDSL systems. Alike, the signal level must be decreased to obviate undesirable emissions RFI, concretely caused by amateur radio stations.

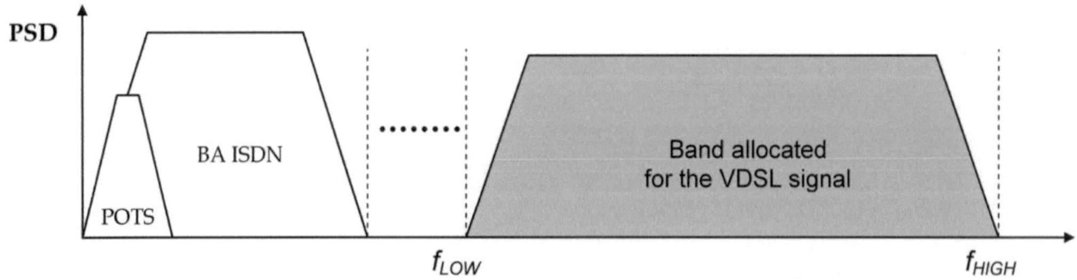

Fig. 2. The general frequency plan for the VDSL system

The lower frequency f_{LOW} is given by the spectral compatibility with narrowband services POTS and BA ISDN. The VDSL frequency plan depends on installation variations, on crosstalks from different sources and on the existence of narrowband services. Therefore, PSD masks of the VDSL signal are defined on the base of specific criteria. By (ETSI, 1999, 2001), we can discriminate between the VDSL deployment with or without the existence of narrowband services in the same cable and with or without the possibility for creating frequency apertures. The FTTEx variation seems to be the most probably variation of the VDSL deployment scenario where the line termination transceiver is placed in the central office exchange. Therefore, in our analysis, we used the FTTEx power spectral density mask. A graphical representation of the selected variation is shown on Fig. 3. If necessary, it is possible to assign any other standard spectral mask for the considered VDSL signal.

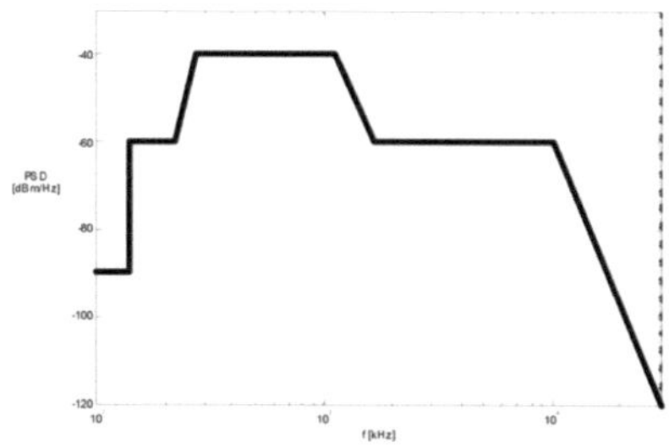

Fig. 3. The PSD mask of the VDSL signal for the FTTEx variation with narrowband services and the ADSL presence

2.5 Spectral characteristics of near-end and far-end crosstalk signals

Because crosstalk signals from the POTS service in disturbing pairs don't have significant influences on the VDSL signal in the disturbed pair, we supposed both disturbing and disturbed signals to have the same power spectral densities $PSD_1(f) = PSD_2(f)$. This situation is happened when in neighboring pairs are also VDSL signals - we can talk about the self-NEXT crosstalk and the self-FEXT crosstalk.

For local subscriber loops, we assigned the power spectral density of NEXT and FEXT crosstalks using relations (8) and (9) as follows

$$PSD_{NEXT}(f)=PSD(f).\left|\mathcal{H}_{NEXT}(l,f)\right|^2,\ \left|\mathcal{H}_{NEXT}(l,f)\right|^2\approx K_{NEXT}\cdot f^{3/2} \tag{10}$$

$$PSD_{FEXT}(f)=PSD(f).\left|\mathcal{H}_{FEXT}(l,f)\right|^2,\left|\mathcal{H}_{FEXT}(l,f)\right|^2\approx K_{FEXT}.l.3280.f^2.\left|\mathcal{H}\ (l,f)\right|^2 \tag{11}$$

where variables K_{NEXT} and K_{FEXT} are functions of disturbed pairs.

Equations (10) - (11) allow very well approximation of practically observed kind of multiple interferer crosstalks. Before starting of the simulation, we determined values of variables K_{NEXT} and K_{FEXT} in the simulation model as a function of the number of disturbing pairs N_d for typical 50-pairs cable as

$$K_{NEXT}=K_{NEXT-49}\cdot\frac{N_d^{\ 0.6}}{10} \tag{12}$$

$$K_{FEXT} = K_{FEXT-49} \frac{N_d^{\ 0.6}}{10} \tag{13}$$

The value of the $K_{NEXT\text{-}49}$ variable is given as 8,8.10^{-14}, the value of the $K_{FEXT\text{-}49}$ variable is empirically estimated as 8.10^{-20}/3280 (Aslanis & Cioffi, 1992).

3. The simulation model for the VDSL technology

For considering of the signal transmission on metallic homogeneous lines by means of the VDSL technology, it is necessary comprehensively to know characteristics of negative environmental influences and features of applied modulation techniques. It is difficult to realize of the exact analytical description of complex systems such as the VDSL system in the real environment of local access networks. In addition, due to dynamical natures of some processes, it is not suitable. For analyzing of various signal processing techniques used by the VDSL technologies, a suitable and flexible enough tool are computer simulations and modeling schemes of real environmental conditions at the signal transmission.

For modeling of the VDSL transmission path, we used the software program *Matlab* together with additional libraries like *Signal Processing Toolbox* and *Communication Toolbox*. A proposed and realized modeling scheme represents a transmission of high-speed data signals in downstream and upstream directions by means of the VDSL technology utilizing of metallic homogeneous lines. The realized model (Fig. 4) represents the signal transmission in the VDSL environment utilizing metallic homogenous lines for high-speed data signals in the downstream and upstream direction. This VDSL environment model is the enhanced version of the ADSL environment model introduced (Róka & Cisár, 2002). New features of this simulation model are VDSL transmission characteristics and applications of precoding techniques and trellis coded modulations.

Basic functional blocks realized in our simulation model are shown on Fig. 4. The VDSL simulation model (Fig. 4) can be divided into the three main parts:

1. A transmitting part - it is responsible for the encoding (using the FEC technique) and for the modulation of signals into a form suitable for the transmission channel.
2. A transmission channel (the metallic homogenous line) - this part of the model realized negative influences on the transmitted signal. Above all, it goes about a propagation loss, a signal distortion, crosstalk noises, white and impulse noises, the radio interference. Because these negative influences expressively interfere into the communication and represent its main limiting factors, they present a critical part of the model and, therefore, it is necessary exactly to recognize and express their characteristics by correct parameters.
3. A receiving part - it is conceptually inverted in a comparison with the transmitter. Its main functions are the signal amplification, the removing of the ISI, the demodulation and the correction of errored information bits.

The analysis can be based on computer simulations that cover the most important features and characteristics of the real transmission environment for the VDSL technology and result in searching for the best combination of coding and precoding techniques.

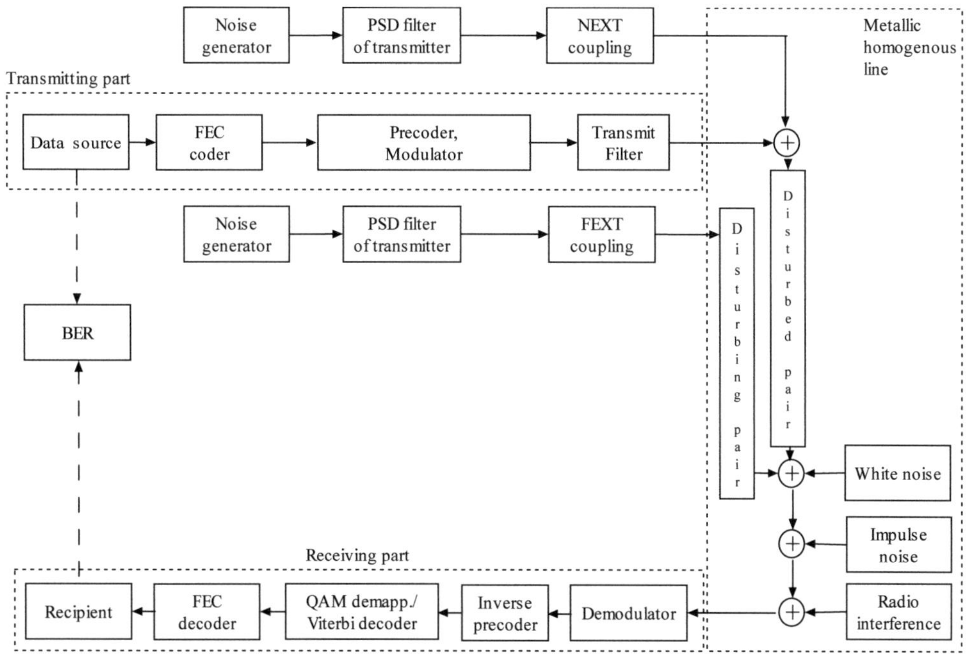

Fig. 4. The block scheme of the VDSL simulation model

3.1 The transmitting part of the model

The transmitted message carried to the receiving part is generated as a random binary chain with the given length. This message is also saved (for the BER calculation), encoded by a particular type of the FEC codes (RS, BCH) and modulated. It can be chosen from two kinds of modulations - the first one is the classical QAM modulation and the second one is a combination of the QAM and the convolutional coding, i.e. the TCM. The QAM modulation is chosen because of its compatibility with considered precoding techniques, a low distortion resistance and an easy implementation in the Matlab program environment.

3.2 The transmission line

Utilizing of local subscriber loops for the broadband access of subscribers by means of the VDSL technology assumes a replacing of the significant part of metallic lines by optical fibers. This will bring a subscriber distribution point (SDP) unit closer to subscribers, when metallic lines will distribute signals to subscriber premises. Although metallic lines will comprise only a small part of the transmission path, their influences on transmitted signals will not negligible.

Negative influences of the VDSL environment at the signal transmission depend on parameters of metallic homogeneous lines (a core material, a cable insulation, a core diameter, a number of neighboring lines in the cable binder, a cable length). If we want to achieve exact results from simulations, all these factors must be accepted. Of course, this acceptance leads to a complicated and complex simulation model. For modeling of all these influences, a theoretical description together with simulation methods is introduced (Róka & Cisár, 2002).

3.3 The receiving part of the model

At the receiver side, the distorted and attenuated signal is first amplified, next demodulated and then shifted into the inverse precoder that removes constellation changes introduced by the precoder at the transmitter side. If the TCM is used, the TCM decoder follows and the Viterbi algorithm is searching the most probably binary sequence. Otherwise, the QAM demapping block converts the constellation points sequence into the binary data sequence that is corrupted by transmission errors. They are consequently removed in the FEC decoder. Finally, the corrected sequence is compared with the original transmitted message and the bit error rate is calculated.

We should notice that individual precoding techniques suppose conceptually different manner of the signal regeneration, therefore this process is not here exactly described. For both methods, it is essential to know a transmission function of metallic lines. This information can be extracted from the signal transmission of predefined symbol sequences at the initialization process.

Before starting of the simulation, we can calculate the transmission function of the line for given parameters *(l, ξ)*. Values of this function are sampled in equal proportioned frequency intervals in the range from 0 Hz up to the half of the sampling frequency ($f_{samp}/2$). A number of samples is optional. For signal processing, it is desirable to choice the number of samples equal to *2.N*, where *N* is an integer number. Using sampled values, the impulse characteristic of the transmission line *h (t)* is calculated using the inverse Fourier transformation with the same number of samples (from practical viewpoint, the number of 512 samples is adequate). This sampled impulse characteristic is used as coefficients for the digital filter. A simulation of the signal transmission through the line itself is executed by digital filtering of the sampled modulated signal using the proposed filter. On Fig. 5, there are shown frequency characteristics of the transmission line (ϕ = 0,4 mm, Cu) for various line lengths.

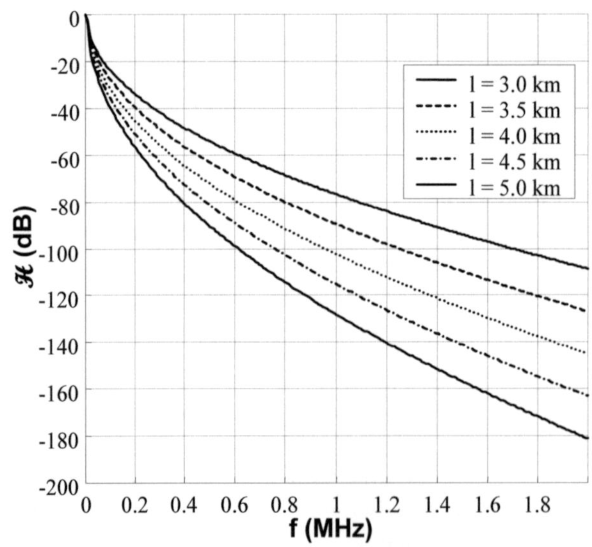

Fig. 5. Frequency characteristics of the transmission line for various line lengths

The influence of the transmission channel that we can derive from its transmission function is expressed above all at the attenuation of the transmitted signal. The signal attenuation is more accentuated for areas of higher frequency components of power spectral density characteristics. This influence is more expensive for longer line lengths. However, we can find out that the influence is decreased with increasing of the core diameter of wires. This results from a change of values for the primary constant of the line, concretely R and L.

We can create the NEXT crosstalk noise signal by forming of the white noise spectrum (with constant PSD = 0 dB/Hz) that is generated by a random number generator. First, we must calculate a frequency characteristic of the $\mathcal{H}_{NEXT}(l, f)$ crosstalk transmission function using (8). Its parameters are the number of disturbing pairs and the appropriate value of the variable K_{NEXT}. On Fig. 6, the NEXT crosstalk transmission function for various numbers of disturbers is presented. For modeling of the NEXT negative influence, the NEXT crosstalk noise signal acquired by filtering is added to the transmitted signal entering the transmission line.

The FEXT crosstalk signal is created in a similar manner as the NEXT crosstalk signal (its spectrum is presented on Fig. 6). Because this type of a crosstalk must be propagated through a disturbing line, we included into calculating the $\mathcal{H}_{FEXT}(l, f)$ crosstalk transmission function also the transmission function of the line $\mathcal{H}(l, f)$ using (9) with given parameters. The FEXT crosstalk signal is added to the transmitted information signal attenuated at a transmission through the metallic homogeneous line.

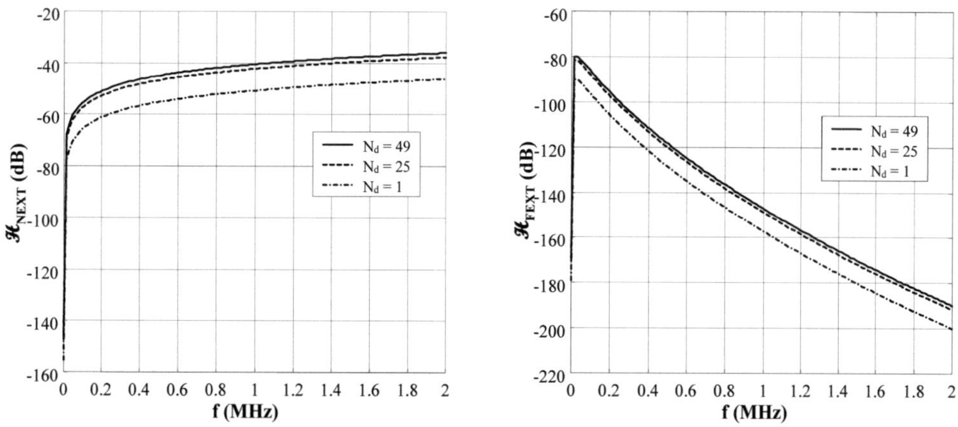

Fig. 6. The frequency characteristic of NEXT and FEXT crosstalk transmission functions for various numbers of disturbers

The influence of the FEXT crosstalk transmission function is characterized by the power spectral density of the FEXT crosstalk signal and by the FEXT crosstalk path. This FEXT crosstalk path is depend on the line length, on the frequency of signal and on the transmission function of the transmission line because of propagating of crosstalk signals through the disturbing pair. For longer line lengths, the influence of the FEXT crosstalk can be neglected. On other side, this influence is accentuated at higher frequency components of the transmitted signal. Therefore, it is necessary to take into account of the FEXT crosstalk for the new VDSL technology transmitting signals of asymmetric services and application at very high bit rates of information signals and on very short distances because of occupying higher frequency bandwidths of metallic homogeneous lines.

3.4 The analysis of environmental influences on the VDSL signals

At the analysis of the signal transmission through metallic homogeneous lines in the VDSL environment, we need to know three basic parameters - properties of the signal transmitted into the line (mainly its PSD), a transmission function of the transmission channel and features of the noise and crosstalk environmental influences.

In (Róka, 2002, 2004), particular relationships and frequency characteristics of basic noises and crosstalks occurred at the signal transmission through metallic homogeneous lines in the environment of xDSL technologies are introduced. The analysis of negative influences of noises and crosstalks on qualitative parameters of homogeneous lines can be extended to the VDSL environment. In our analysis, the NEXT crosstalk is not considered because this one can disable a communication in the VDSL frequency bandwidth. With respect to the possible VDSL deployments in conditions of the Slovak access network, we use a spectral mask defined for the FTTEx variation and for the coexistence with narrowband services in the same pair. In this spectral mask variation, the ADSL presence is supposed.

For the SCM modulation, four individual subbands are given alternatively for upstream and downstream directions of the transmission. Band transition frequencies are introduced in Tab. 1.

Band transition frequencies	f_1 [kHz]	f_2 [kHz]	f_3 [kHz]	f_4 [kHz]	f_5 [kHz]
VDSL subbands	138	3000	5100	7050	12000
Optional subbands	138	3750	5200	8500	12000
- The utilization of frequencies below f_1 and above f_5 but within the overall PSD masks is possible but is not covered (ETSI, 2001).					

Table 1. Band transition frequencies for the SCM FDD subbands according to the ETSI

Using a transmission function of the raised cosine filter and on the base of known values of carrier frequencies and symbol rates for particular subbands (Tab. 1), we can express an ideal PSD characteristic of the SCM signal. A signal transmitted into the metallic homogeneous lines must comply with the defined FTTEx spectral mask, so that a spectrum of the ideal SCM signal from the modulator must be digitally adjusted using FIR filters before transmitting. From this adjusted PSD, moreover, frequency components equivalent to subbands allocated for amateur radio stations should be eliminated (ETSI, 1999). Using appropriate FIR filters, the SCM signal can be also adjusted with respect to other FTTx spectral masks.

For the MCM modulation, a way to form the PSD of the signal transmitted from the transmitter is defined in the ETSI standard (ETSI, 2001). After simplifying, it is multiplying of every complex coefficient $Z_i = X_i + j.Y_i$ by a constant g_i and resulting complex coefficients $Z_i' = g_i . Z_i$ enter into the IFFT block. By this way, the transmitter can easy adapt any PSD characteristic of the transmitted VDSL signal for satisfying demands that are established by a chosen spectral mask. Alike, it is easy to keep frequency apertures in given subbands at occurrences of disturbing frequencies of the RFI type. Therefore, the MCM allows a high flexibility of the PSD transmitted signal and tries as effective as possible utilizations of the available bandwidth. We can therefore suppose that the transmitted VDSL signal will achieve maximum allowable levels in particular subchannels according to the FTTEx spectral mask (Fig. 3).

On Fig. 7 and 8, results of PSD characteristics of VDSL signals for the line length 0,5 km, the core diameter 0,4 mm with 24 ADSL and 9 VDSL disturbers and with the FTTEx spectral mask are introduced. On Fig. 7, the power spectral density of the SCM signal, the AWGN noise and the FEXT crosstalk are considered at the end of the line. All these characteristics are attenuated from a reason of transmitting signals through metallic homogeneous lines and, therefore, their corrections are needed. We are also using a linear equalization process to eliminate influences of the intersymbol interference (ISI). We can imitate this process by a corrector in the frequency area with a transmission function inverted to a channel transmission function. This correction in the frequency area eliminates aftereffects of the nonlinear signal attenuation by amplifying of higher frequency components. However, the correction of the received signal amplifies also the influence of noises and interferences. On Fig. 8, the PSD of the SCM signal and the total noise adjusted by the corrector are specified.

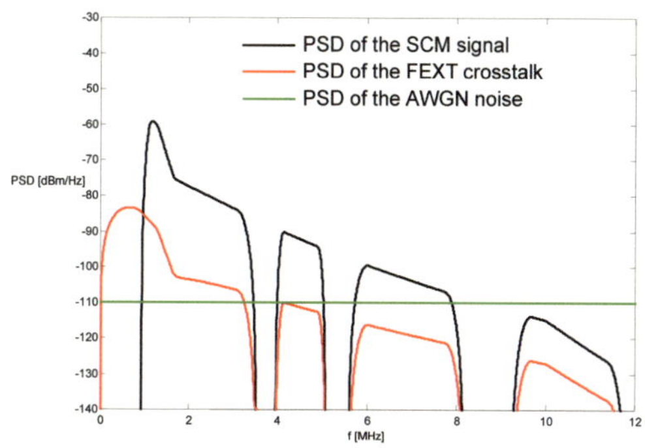

Fig. 7. The PSD characteristics of the SCM signal, the FEXT crosstalk and the AWGN noise attenuated at the end of the line

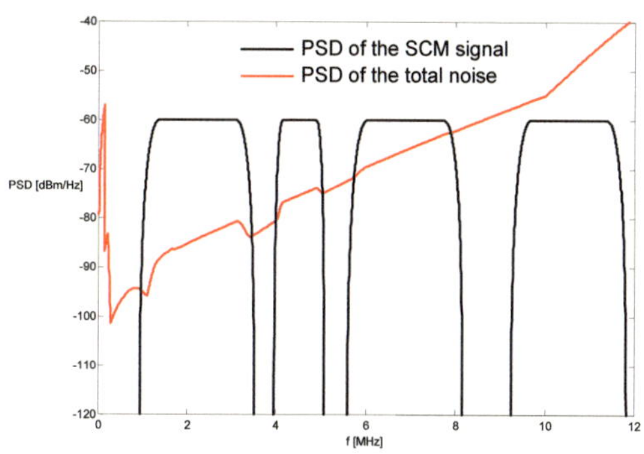

Fig. 8. The PSD characteristics of the SCM signal and the total noise adjusted by the corrector

On Fig. 9, results of PSD characteristics of the MCM signal, the AWGN noise and the FEXT crosstalk for the line length 0,5 km, the core diameter 0,4 mm with 24 ADSL and 9 VDSL disturbers and with the FTTEx spectral mask are introduced. A received signal is sampled and processed by the FFT block without a correction in the frequency area. Therefore, the SNR can be calculated in particular subchannels directly from the MCM signal power and the noise powers at the end of the line.

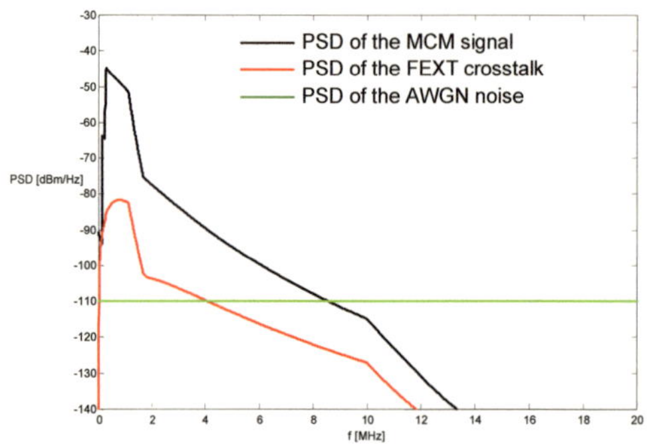

Fig. 9. The PSD characteristics of the MCM signal, the FEXT crosstalk and the AWGN noise attenuated at the end of the line

A sense of analyzing for environmental influences on the power spectral densities of VDSL signals is to identify all substantial noise resources and at the same time to determine a way for calculating of the signal-to-noise ratio for various proposed modulation techniques. For our following analysis of the VDSL system performance, the parameter *SNR* is very important. The signal-to-noise ratio for the subband given by the lowest f_{LOW} and the highest f_{HIGH} frequencies can be expressed as

$$SNR(f)=\frac{\int_{f_{LOW}}^{f_{HIGH}} PSD_S(f)df}{\int_{f_{LOW}}^{f_{HIGH}} PSD_N(f)df} \tag{14}$$

where $PSD_S(f)$ is the VDSL signal power spectral density and $PSD_N(f)$ is the noise power spectral density. The *SNR (f)* ratio must be calculated from the adjusted SCM signal power and the noise powers.

4. The environment of power distribution cables

4.1 The multipath signal propagation

The PLC transmission channel has a tree-like topology with branches formed by additional wires tapered from the main path and having various lengths and terminated loads with highly frequency-varying impedances in a range from a few ohms to some kiloohms (Zimmermann & Dostert, 2002b), (Held, 2006). That's why the PLC signal propagation does not only take place along a direct line-of-sight path between a transmitter and a receiver but also additional paths are used for a signal spreading. This multipath scenario can be easily explained by the example of a cable with one tap (Fig. 10).

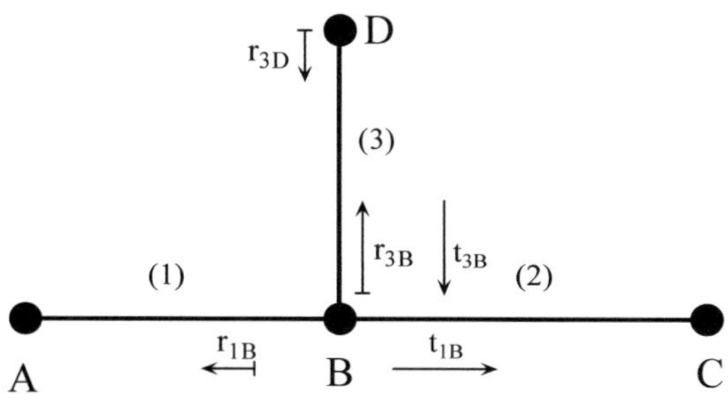

Fig. 10. The multipath signal propagation in the cable with one tap

The line consists of three segments (A-B), (B-C) and (B-D) with lengths l_1, l_2, l_3 and characteristic impedances Z_{L1}, Z_{L2} and Z_{L3}. To simplify considerations, points A and C are assumed to be matched, which means $Z_A = Z_{L1}$ and $Z_C = Z_{L2}$. Then, points B and D are reflection points with reflection factors are denoted as r_{1B}, r_{3D}, r_{3B} and transmission factors are denoted as t_{1B}, t_{3B}. Because of multiple reflections, a number of propagation paths is infinitive (i.e., A → B → C, A → B → D → B → C, and so on). An affect of all reflections and transmissions can be expressed for each propagation path i in a form of the weighting factor g_i that is mathematically equal to the product of reflection and transmission factors along the path. The value g_i is always less or equal to one because all reflection and transmission factors can be only less or equal to one. The simulation model can be simplified if we approximate infinite number of paths by only N dominant paths and make N as small as possible. When more transmissions and reflections occur along the path, then the weighting factor will be smaller. When the longer path will be considered, then the signal contribution from this part to the overall signal spreading will be small due to the higher signal attenuation (Ferreira et al., 2010).

4.2 The signal attenuation

Characteristics of the PLC transmission environment focused on the multipath signal propagation, the signal attenuation, the noise scenario and the electromagnetic compatibility are introduced in (Róka & Dlháň, 2005). First, we can present basic characteristics of the PLC channel.

A total signal attenuation on the PLC channel consists of two parts: coupling losses (depending on a transmitter design) and line losses (very high and can range from 40 to 100 dB/km). To find a mathematical formulation for the signal attenuation, we have to start with the complex propagation constant

$$\gamma(\omega) = \sqrt{(R + j.\omega.L)\cdot(G + j.\omega.C)} = \alpha(\omega) + j.\beta(\omega) \tag{15}$$

depending on the primary cable parameters R, L, G, C. Then, the frequency response of a transmission line $\mathcal{H}(f)$ (the transfer function) with the length l can be expressed as follows ($\mathcal{U}(x)$ is the voltage at the distance x):

$$\mathcal{H}(f)=\frac{\mathcal{U}(x=l)}{\mathcal{U}(x=0)}=e^{-\gamma(f)\cdot l}=e^{-\alpha(f)\cdot l}e^{-j\cdot\beta(f)\cdot l} \tag{16}$$

Considering frequencies in the megahertz range, the resistance R per length unit is dominated by the skin effect and thus is proportional to $\sqrt{f}$. The conductance G per length unit is mainly influenced by a dissipation factor of the dielectric material (usually PVC) and therefore proportional to f. With typical geometry and material properties, we can suppose $G \ll \omega.C$ and $R \ll \omega.L$ in the frequency range of interest. Then, cables can be regarded as low lossy ones with real valued characteristic impedances and a simplified expression for the complex propagation constant γ can be introduced

$$\gamma(f)=k_1\cdot\sqrt{f}+k_2\cdot f+j\cdot k_3\cdot f=\alpha(f)+j.\beta(f) \tag{17}$$

where constants k_1, k_2 and k_3 are parameters summarizing material and geometry properties. Based on these derivations and an extensive investigation of measured frequency responses, an approximating formula for the attenuation factor α *(f)* is found in a form

$$\alpha(f)=a_0+a_1\cdot f^k \tag{18}$$

that is able to characterize the attenuation of typical power distribution lines with only three parameters, being easily derived from the measured transfer function (Zimmermann & Dostert, 2002b). Now the propagation loss L_{dB} is given at the length l and the frequency f as

$$\begin{aligned} L_{dB}(l,f)=-20.\log_{10}\left|\mathcal{H}(l,f)\right|=\frac{20}{\ln 10}.l.\alpha(f)=\frac{20}{\ln 10}.l.(a_0+a_1.f^k) \quad [Np] \\ \approx 8{,}686.l.(a_0+a_1.f^k) \quad [dB] \end{aligned} \tag{19}$$

We can see a linear dependence of the propagation loss L_{dB} on the line length l. Parameters a_0, a_1 and k are characterized by measurements of the transfer function $\mathcal{H}$ *(f)* that is much easier then the measurement of primary line parameters *R, L, C, G*. If we now merge a signal spreading on all paths together (we can use a superposition), we can receive an expression for the frequency response $\mathcal{H}$ *(f)* in a form

$$\mathcal{H}(f)=\sum_{i=1}^{N} g_i\cdot a(l_i,f)\cdot e^{-j.2.\pi.f.\tau_i} \tag{20}$$

where $a\,(l_i, f)$ is the signal attenuation proportioned with the length and the frequency and N is the number of paths in the transmission channel. The delay τ_i of the transmission line can be calculated from the dielectric constant ε_r of insulating materials, the light speed c and the line length l_i as follows

$$\tau_i=\frac{l_i.\sqrt{\varepsilon_r}}{c} \tag{21}$$

4.3 The noise scenario

Unfortunately, in a case of the PLC environment, we can't stay only with the additive white Gaussian noise. The noise scenario is much more complicated, since five general classes of noise can be distinguished in power distribution line channels (Zimmermann & Dostert, 2002a), (Götz et al., 2004). These five classes are (Fig. 11):

1. *Colored background noise* - caused by a summation of numerous noise sources with low powers. Its PSD varies with the frequency in a range up to 30 MHz (significantly increases toward to lower frequencies) and also with the time in terms of minutes or even hours.
2. *Narrowband noise* - caused by ingress of broadcasting stations. It is generally varying with daytimes and consists mostly of sinusoidal signals with modulated amplitudes.
3. *Periodic impulsive noise asynchronous with the main frequency* - caused by rectifiers within DC power supplies. Its spectrum is a discrete line spectrum with a repetition rate in a range between 50 and 200 kHz.
4. *Periodic impulsive noise synchronous with the main frequency* - caused by power supplies operating synchronously with the main cycle. Its PSD is decreasing with the frequency and a repetition rate is 50 Hz or 100 Hz.
5. *Asynchronous impulsive noise* - caused by impulses generated by the switching transients' events in the network. It is considered as the worst noise in the PLC environment, because of its magnitude that can easily reach several dB over other noise types. Fortunately, the average disturbance ratio is well below 1 percent, meaning that 99 percent of the time is absolutely free of the asynchronous impulsive noise.

The noise types 1, 2 and 3 can be summarized as background noises because they are remaining stationary over periods of seconds and minutes, sometimes even of hours. On the contrary, the noise types 4 and 5 are time-variant in terms of microseconds or milliseconds and their impact on useful signals is much more stronger and may cause single-bit or burst errors in a data transmission. Time and domain analysis of impulse noises can be found in (Zimmermann & Dostert, 2002a). We will just mention a few expressions regarding a mathematical description of the impulse noise model and the impulse energy and power.

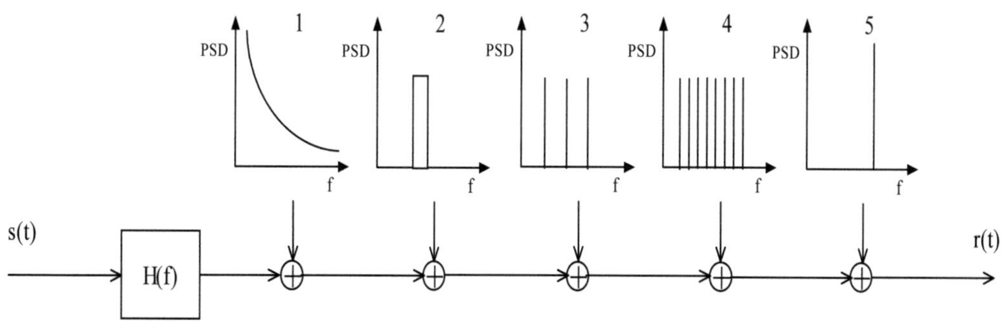

Fig. 11. The noise scenario in the PLC environment

A time behavior of the impulsive noise can be described by three basic figures, i.e. the impulse width t_w, the arrival time t_{arr} and the interarrival time t_{iat} or the impulse distance t_d. The interarrival time (the impulse distance) means a distance between two impulse events that can be described by

$$t_{iat} = t_w + t_d = t_{arr,i+1} - t_{arr,i} \tag{22}$$

Then, a train of impulses $n_{imp}(t)$ can be described as

$$n_{imp}(t) = \sum_{i=1}^{N} A_i \cdot imp\left(\frac{t - t_{arr,i}}{t_{w,i}}\right) \tag{23}$$

where A_i means the impulse amplitude and *imp (t)* is the generalized impulse function. The parameters A_i, t_w and t_{arr} are random variables, whose statistical properties may be investigated by measurements. More information can be found in (Róka & Urminský, 2008).

The best way how to characterize extent of the impact of impulses on a data transmission are values of the impulse energy and the impulse power. The impulse energy E_{imp} can be calculated from the time-domain representation $n_{imp}(t)$ as

$$E_{imp} = \int_{t_{arr}}^{t_{arr}+t_w} n_{imp}(t)^2 \, dt \tag{24}$$

As we can see from (24), the impulse energy is influenced by the impulse shape and width. Finally, the impulse power can be determined by

$$\psi_{imp} = \frac{1}{t_w} \int_{t_{arr}}^{t_{arr}+t_w} n_{imp}(t)^2 \, dt \tag{25}$$

and can be used for a comparison of impulse and background noises.

5. The simulation model for the PLC technology

The realized model (Fig. 12) represents a high-speed signal transmission in the PLC system utilizing outdoor power distribution lines in downstream and upstream directions (Róka & Dlháň, 2005). The signal transmission over outdoor power distribution lines represents the transmission between a transmitter in the transformer substation and a receiver in the customer premises.

Our realized simulation model can be divided into the three main parts:

1. A transmitting part - it is responsible for the encoding (because of using the FEC technique) and for the modulation of signals into a form suitable for the transmission channel.
2. A transmission channel (the outdoor power lines) - this part realizes negative influences of the PLC environment on the transmitted signal. Above all, it goes about the propagation loss, the signal distortion, the impulsive, colored and narrow-band noises.
3. A receiving part - it is conceptually inverted in a comparison with the transmitter. Its main functions are the signal amplification, the demodulation and the correction of error information bits.

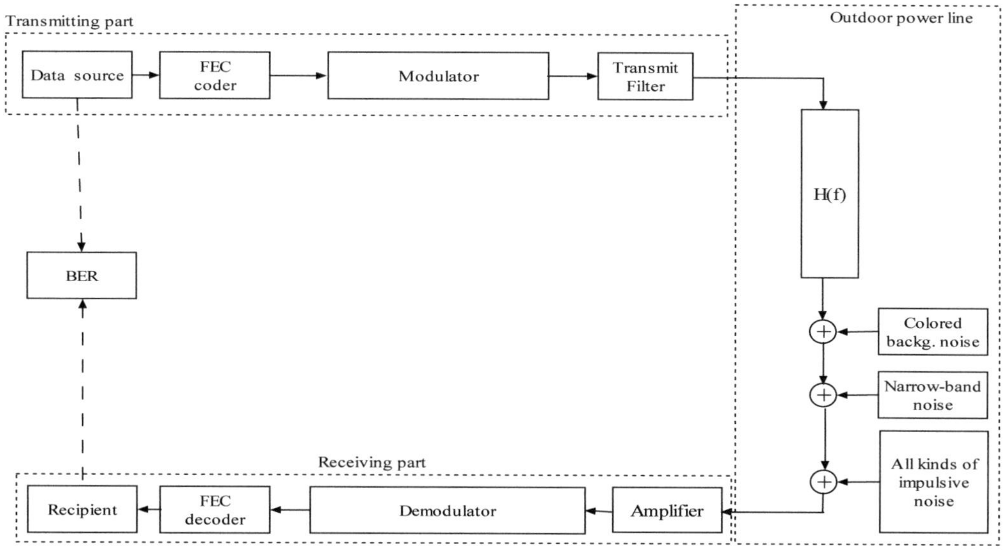

Fig. 12. The block scheme of the PLC simulation model

5.1 The transmitting part of the model

The transmitted message carried to the receiving part is generated as a random binary chain with the given length. This message is also saved (for the BER calculation), encoded by a particular type of the FEC codes and modulated. From the coding and modulation techniques, we are intending to implement several different ones to be able to compare them and find the most appropriate one.

5.2 The outdoor power distribution line

Negative influences of the PLC environment at the signal transmission depend on parameters of power distribution lines (a core material, a cable insulation, a cable length, a core diameter, a number, position and properties of additional wires tapered from the main path) as well as on number and properties of points of nonhomogenity (instrument panels, PLC signal coupling units, regenerator units, points of wires interconnections). If we want to achieve exact results from simulations, all these factors must be accepted. Of course, this acceptance leads to a complicated and complex PLC simulation model. Because of this fact we have to choose a trade-off between the model complexity and the accuracy of reality representations. For modeling of the PLC transmission channel, we chose a generalized multipath model because of its accuracy, easily implementation and understandability (Zimmermann & Dostert, 2002b). Mathematically, it can be described in a form of the expression

$$\mathcal{H}(f)=\sum_{i=1}^{N} g_i \cdot a(l_i,f)\cdot e^{-j.2.\pi.f.\tau_i}=\sum_{i=1}^{N}\left|g_i(f)\right|\cdot e^{\phi_{g_i}(f)}\cdot e^{-(a_0+a_1.f^k)\cdot l_i}\cdot e^{-j.2.\pi.f.\tau_i} \tag{26}$$

In general, the weighting factor g_i is complex and frequency-dependent because reflection points may have complex and frequency-dependent values. According to extended measurements campaigns, it is possible to consider g_i as a complex but not frequency-dependent value or as a real value even in many practical models it can be considered.

For the presented model, parameters were assumed from the paper (Zimmermann & Dostert, 2002b). In spite of its simplification, it is still accurate enough for the PLC system performance analyses. It goes about the model of the 110 m link supposing $N = 15$ main paths. The values of other parameters like k, a_0, a_1, g_i, l_i (k, a_0, a_1 are attenuation factors, g_i is weighting factor and finally l_i means length of i-th branch) can be found in Tab. 2.

N	1	2	3	4	5	6	7	8	9	10	11	12	13	14	15
g_i	0,029	0,043	0,103	-0,058	-0,045	-0,040	0,038	-0,038	0,071	-0,035	0,065	-0,055	0,042	-0,059	0,049
l_i [m]	90	102	113	143	148	200	260	322	411	490	567	740	960	1130	1250
k	1														
a_0	0														
a_1 [m/s]	$7{,}8.10^{-10}$														

Table 2. Parameters of the 15-path PLC simulation model

In the PLC transmission environment, not only a signal distortion expressed by the channel transfer function $\mathcal{H}(f)$ is presented. Also different types of noise have very negative influence on transmitted signals in a form of the time-invariant behavior of the SNR on powerline channels. The first type of noise – the colored background noise is modeled by filtering the AWGN noise through a filter with the exponentially decreasing transfer function for increasing frequencies with the average 35 dB/decade in the low frequency range up to 10 kHz and a low rate in the high frequency range (Hrasnica et al., 2004). The narrowband noise is generated in a similar way only with a difference in band-pass filters with a random selection of the lower passband edge frequency. The power of these narrow spikes is varying around the -80 dBm/Hz. The impulsive noise can be described by expression (23). From (Zimmermann & Dostert, 2002a), the parameters of periodic impulsive noises (type 3 and 4) are more and less deterministic. Concretely, the width of noise impulse is about 200 μs, the impulse amplitude is concentrated around two values; about 0.4 V and then between 0.7 and 1 V. The interarrival time values are 10 ms, 6 ms and 12 ms.

The biggest problem for modeling represents the asynchronous impulsive noise because of its random occurrence and random durations from some microseconds up to a few milliseconds. It can't be ignored since its influence with the PSD more than 50 dB is particularly devastating of the transmitted signal. As it goes about a random process, whose a future behavior only depends on the present state or on limited periods in the past, may be described by so-called the portioned Markov chain. In this model, all states are partitioned into two groups, where the first represents a case where no impulse event occurs and the second represents an occurrence of the impulse event. Transitions between states from the first group top the second and vice versa are described by two independent probability matrices U for impulse-free states and G for impulse states. The concrete values of these matrices can be found in paper (Zimmermann & Dostert, 2002a). Each impulsive noise state corresponds to an exponential distribution of the impulse width, while each impulse-free state corresponds to an exponential distribution of the impulse distance. Thus, this kind of modeling represents a superposition of several exponential distributions that approximate real scenarios very well.

5.3 The receiving part of the model

At the receiver side, the distorted and attenuated signal is first amplified and then demodulated. Part of the demodulation is also demapping block as a part of modulator, which is responsible for converting the constellation points sequence into the binary data sequence corrupted by transmission errors. They are consequently removed in the FEC decoder. Finally, the corrected sequence is compared with the original transmitted message and the bit error rate is calculated.

5.4 Characteristics of the parametric model for reference channels

The parametric model for the PLC channel is possible to adapt for any topology of the power distribution network (Róka & Urminský, 2008). Parameters of this model with various coefficients were presented in ETSI Technical Specifications (ETSI, 2000, 2001) and a following set of reference channels for a practical utilization was established:

1. *Reference channel 1* (RC1) - a channel between transformer stations with features of the HV channel. A distance between separate transformer stations is around 1000 m.
2. *Reference channel 2* (RC2) - a channel from the transformer station up to the main circuit breaker, a distance is approximately 150 m.
3. *Reference channel 3* (RC3) - a channel from the main circuit breaker up to the counting box of consumed energy in the house, a distance is maximum 250 m.
4. *Reference channel 4* (RC4) - a home scenario.

For the presented parametric model, parameters for various PLC reference channels were assumed from the paper (Zimmermann & Dostert, 2002b). In spite of their simplification, it is still accurate enough for the PLC system performance analyses. The values of other parameters like k, a_0, a_1, g_i, l_i for the multi-path signal propagation in reference channels can be found in (Róka & Urminský, 2008). Computer simulations at appropriate frequency characteristics of particular reference channels used values from a specific table. These frequency responses are graphically shown in Fig. 13.

As it can be noticed from simulation results, the signal attenuation in reference channels is straightforward proportioned with the length and the frequency. For some specific frequencies only is shown the selective attenuation caused by the multi-path effect with approximately 30 to 40 dB.

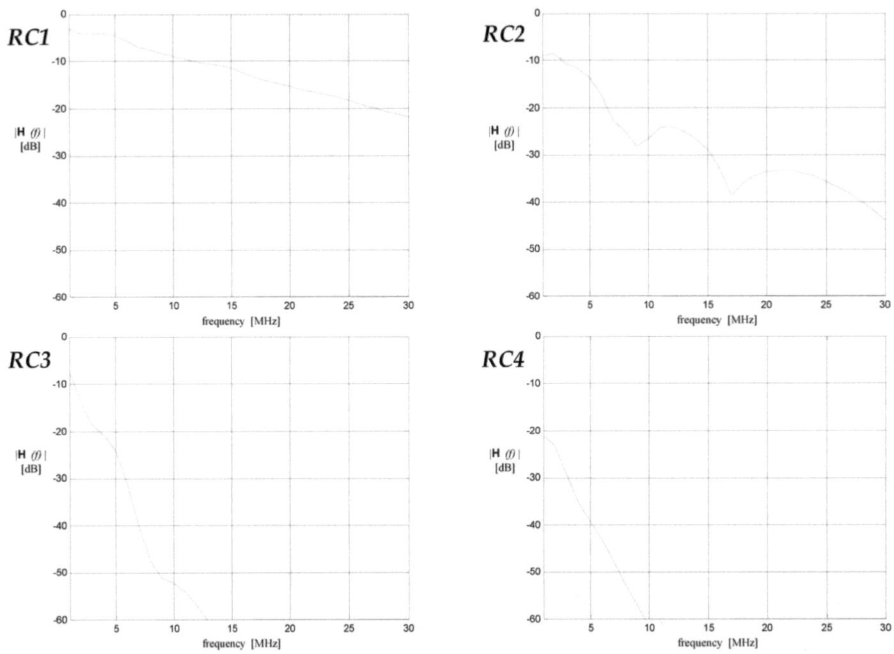

Fig. 13. Frequency responses of the RC1, RC2, RC3 and RC4 channels

6. The environment of optical fibers

6.1 Transmission parameters of the optical fiber

Basic transmission factors of the singlemode standard optical fiber are following (Čuchran & Róka, 2006):

- the attenuation,
- the dispersion
  - the chromatic dispersion CD,
  - the polarization mode dispersion PMD,
- nonlinear effects – the self phase modulation SPM,
  - the cross phase modulation XPM,
  - the cross polarization modulation XPolM,
  - the four wave mixing FWM,
  - the stimulated Raman scattering SRS,
  - the stimulated Brillouin scattering SBS.

Nonlinear effects in the optical fiber may potentially have a significant impact on the performance of WDM optical communication systems. In a WDM system, these effects place constraints on the spacing between adjacent wavelength channels and they limit the maximum power per channel, the maximum bit rate and the system reach (Mukherjee, 2006).

Knowing which fundamental linear and nonlinear interactions dominate is helpful to conceive techniques that improve a transmission of optical signals, including advanced modulation formats, a digital signal processing and a distributed optical nonlinearity management.

6.2 The attenuation

The optical fiber is an ideal medium that can be used to carry optical signals over long distances. There are several sources that contribute to the fiber attenuation, such as an absorption, a scattering and a radiation. The attenuation leads to a reduction of the signal power as the signal propagates over some distance. When determining the maximum distance that a signal propagate for a given transmitter power and receiver sensitivity, the attenuation must be considered. The attenuation coefficient α [dB/km] of the optical fiber can be obtained by measuring the input and the output optical power and then the optical power level along the fiber length L [km] can be expressed as

$$P(L)=10^{\frac{-\alpha.L}{10}}.P(0) \qquad [W] \qquad (27)$$

where $P\,(0)$ is the optical power at the transmitter, $P\,(L)$ is the optical pulse power at the distance L. For the link length L, the $P\,(L)$ must be greater than or equal to the receiver sensitivity Pr. On Fig. 14, a characteristic curve of the $\alpha\,(\lambda)$ as a function of available wavelengths is presented (Black, 2002).

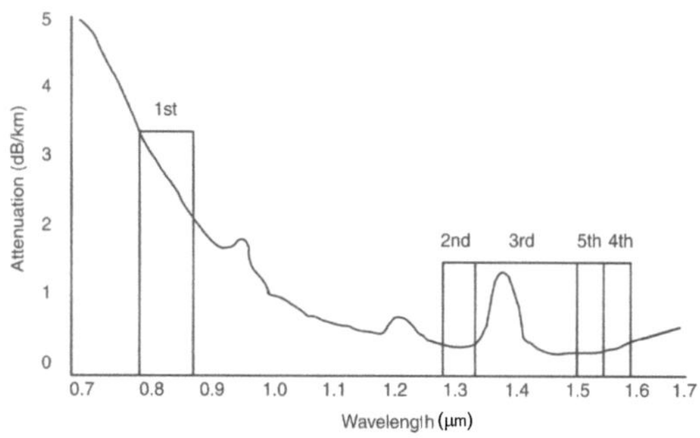

Fig. 14. The wavelength characteristic of the attenuation coefficient α

6.3 The dispersion

The dispersion is a widening of the pulse duration as it travels through the optical fiber. As a pulse widens, it can broaden enough to interfere with neighboring pulses (bits) on the fiber leading to the intersymbol interference ISI. The dispersion thus limits the maximum transmission rate on a fiber-optic channel. We distinguished two basic dispersive forms - the intermodal dispersion and the chromatic dispersion. Both cause an optical signal distortion in multimode optical fibers MMF, whereas a chromatic dispersion is the only cause of the optical signal distortion in singlemode fibers SMF.

The chromatic dispersion CD represents a fact that different wavelengths travel at different speeds, even within the same mode. In a dispersive medium, the index of refraction $n\,(\lambda)$ is a function of the wavelength. Thus, certain wavelengths of the transmitted signal will propagate faster than other wavelengths. The CD dispersion is the result of material dispersion, waveguide dispersion and profile dispersion. On Fig. 15, characteristic curves of the CD as a function of available wavelengths for various optical fiber types (USF, NZDF, DSF) are presented (Black, 2002).

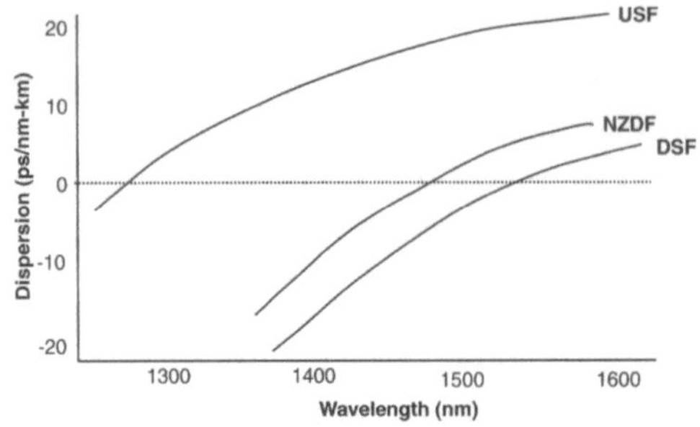

Fig. 15. Wavelength characteristics of the dispersion for USF, NZDF and DSF fibers

The polarization mode dispersion PMD is another complex optical effect that can occur in singlemode optical fibers (Black, 2002). The SMF support two perpendicular polarizations of the original transmitted signal. If a fiber is not perfect, these polarization modes may travel at different speeds and, consequently, arrive at the end of the fiber at different times. The difference in arrival times between the fast and slow mode axes is the PMD (Fig. 16). Like the CD, the PMD causes digitally-transmitted pulses to spread out as the polarization modes arrive at their destination at different times.

$$\Delta\tau = D_{PMD} \cdot \sqrt{L} \tag{28}$$

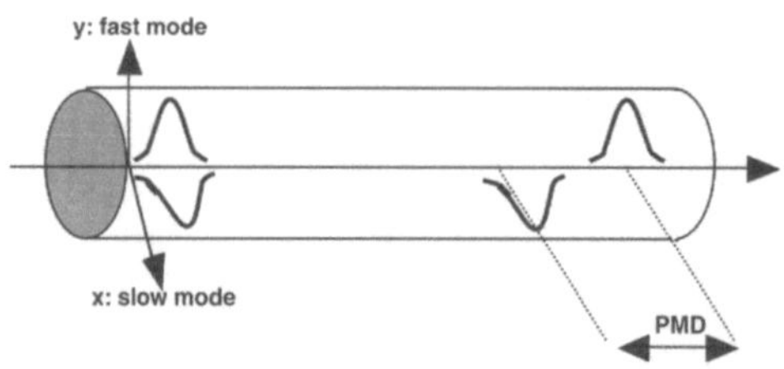

Fig. 16. The PMD generation in the environment of optical fibers

The main problem with the PMD in optical fiber systems is its stochastic nature, letting the principal state of polarization PSP and the differential group delay DGD vary on timescales between milliseconds and months (Kaminow et al., 2008).

6.4 The insertion loss

The fiber loss is not only source of the optical signal attenuation along transmission lines. Fiber splices and fiber connectors also cause the signal attenuation. The number of optical splices and connectors depends on the transmission length and must be taken into account unless the total attenuation due to fiber joints is distributed and added to the optical fiber attenuation.

7. The simulation model for the optical communications

For modeling of the optical transmission path, we used the software program *Matlab 2010 Simulink* together with additional libraries like *Communication Blockset* and *Communication Toolbox* (Schiff, 2006), (Binh, 2010). The realized model (Fig. 17) represents the signal transmission in the environment utilizing optical fibers for very high-speed data signals in both directions. Optical communication technologies will always be facing the limits of high-speed signal processing and modulation, which is an important factor to take into account when discussing advanced optical modulation formats. The main task of the simulation model is an analysis of various modulation techniques (Xiong, 2000), (Kaminow et al., 2008), (Shieh & Djordjevic, 2010).

Basic functional blocks realized in the optocommunication simulation model can be divided into the three main parts:

1. A transmitting part - it is responsible for the generating (using the Bernoulli generator) and for the modulation of generated signals according to required information inputs into a form suitable for the transmission channel. The modulation block contains a basic set OOK modulation and its variations with DBPSK and DQPSK modulations.
2. A transmission channel (the optical fiber) - this part of the model realized negative influences on the transmitted signal. Above all, it goes about an attenuation, a dispersion and a noise. Because these negative influences expressively interfere into the communication and represent its main limiting factors, they present a critical part of the model and, therefore, it is necessary exactly to recognize and express their characteristics by correct parameters.
3. A receiving part - it is conceptually inverted in a comparison with the transmitter. At the receiver side, a signal is demodulated by appropriate demodulator and the BER ratio is calculated. Also, blocks for graphical presenting of transmitted optical signals can be utilized (Fig. 18).

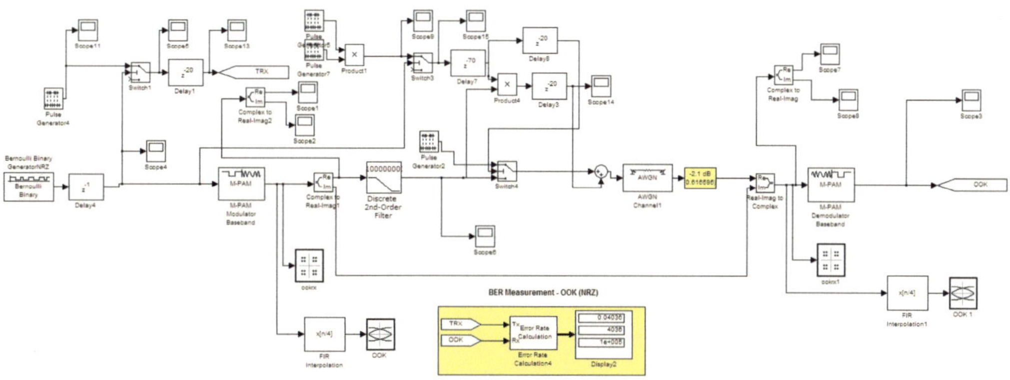

Fig. 17. The block scheme of the optocommunication simulation model

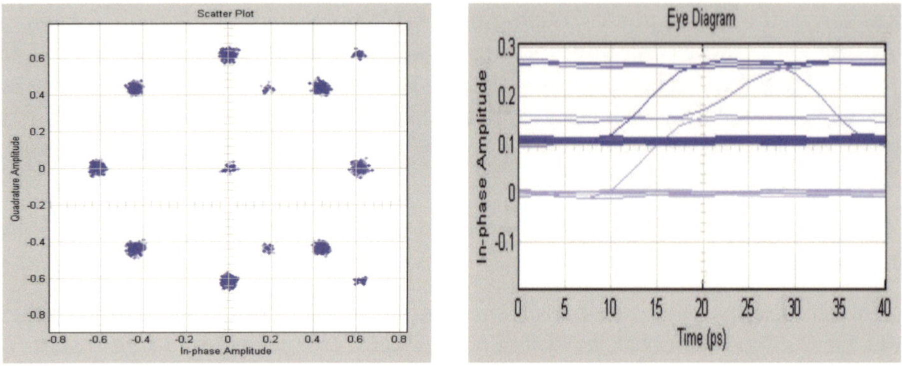

Fig. 18. Symbol constellation and eye diagrams of the DQPSK modulations

8. Conclusion

The first part of the paper analyzes basic features of the real transmission environment of metallic homogeneous lines and presents possibilities for modeling and simulating of the information signal transport in this environment by means of the VDSL technology. We focused on the determination and the analysis of concrete characteristic features for substantial negative influences of internal and external environments and on the representation of frequency dependencies of transmitted VDSL signals. The attenuation determined by the channel's transmission function is more damaged for areas of higher frequency components of power spectral density characteristics for transmitted signals. The influence of the NEXT crosstalk signal is accentuated at higher frequency components of the transmitted signal. The influence of the FEXT crosstalk signal is depending on the line length, on the frequency of signal and on the transmission function of the transmission line because of propagating of crosstalk signals through the disturbing pair. For long enough line lengths, the influence of the FEXT crosstalk can be neglected. Therefore, for the VDSL technology that transmits information signals of asymmetric and symmetric services at very high bit rates on very short distances, it is necessary to take into account both NEXT and FEXT crosstalks at signals occupying higher frequency bandwidths of metallic homogeneous lines. Due to damaging effects of the impulse noise, we must take into account also this type of negative environmental influence.

Basic features and characteristics of negative environmental influences at the signal transmission in the VDSL environment can be used for modeling spectral characteristics of signals on the transmission path. The VDSL simulation model allows determining main problems that can arise at the VDSL signal transmission. For realizing of individual model blocks, we concentrated on the choice of appropriate parameters so that these blocks could be adjusted and modified for future demands. The knowledge of the PSD characteristics of the VDSL signal can be very effectively utilized for characterizing the VDSL signal transmission on metallic homogeneous symmetric lines, especially for a determination of the SNR ratio. In addition, they can be used for analyzing singlecarrier and multicarrier modulation techniques in the overall VDSL system performance including theoretical and practical limits of transmission channels used by the VDSL technology.

The second part of the paper analyzes basic features of the real transmission environment of the outdoor power distribution lines and presents possibilities for modeling and simulation of the information signal transmission in this environment by means of the PLC technology. We focused on transmission characteristics of the PLC channel, namely the multipath signal propagation, the signal attenuation and the interference scenario revealing different classes of the impulsive noise. We created a model of the complex frequency response in a range from 500 kHz up to 30 MHz. Moreover, we realized experimental measurements for verification of the parametric model for reference channels. According the transfer functions, it has been observed the decreasing linear performance in the measured frequencies range where the number of imperfect matching points is minimum. It can be concluded that if the line length path grows it is more probable that the number of reflections produced by imperfect matching points grows too. Moreover, the transfer function slope increasing in lower frequencies is proportional to the line length.

Basic features of negative environmental influences at the signal transmission in the power distribution environment can be used for modeling spectral characteristics of PLC signals of the transmission path. The PLC simulation model is verified by measurements in the real PLC transmission environment that confirmed its satisfactory conformity with real transmission conditions. Using the PLC simulation model, it is possible to verify a correctness of the proposed model, to compare with other ones and to demonstrate its suitability for searching the most appropriate coding and modulation techniques that belong among critical requirements of the development of the next generation PLC communication systems with higher data rates. In spite of problems with a high-frequency signal transmission, power distribution lines remain a very interesting transmission medium. Therefore, it is necessary to evolve a technology that is able to overcome various noises and interferences incident in the PLC environment.

The third part of the paper analyzes transmission parameters for the transmission medium of optical fibers and presents possibilities for modeling and simulation of the information signal transmission in the environment of optical channels. We focused on linear transmission factors - the attenuation and the dispersion - and on nonlinear effects. Nonlinear effects in the optical fiber may potentially have a significant impact on the performance of WDM optical communication systems.

The simulation model for the optical communications represents the signal transmission in optical fibers for very high-speed data signals in both directions. Knowing which fundamental linear and nonlinear interactions dominate in the optical transmission medium is helpful to conceive techniques that improve a transmission of optical signals, including advanced modulation formats, a digital signal processing and a distributed optical nonlinearity management.

9. Acknowledgment

This work is a part of research activities conducted at Slovak University of Technology Bratislava, Faculty of Electrical Engineering and Information Technology, Institute of Telecommunications, within the scope of the project VEGA No. 1/0106/11 "Analysis and proposal for advanced optical access networks in the NGN converged infrastructure utilizing fixed transmission media for supporting multimedia services".

10. Abbreviations

ADSL	Asymmetric DSL
AWGN	Additive White Gaussian Noise
BA ISDN	Basic Access ISDN
BER	Bit Error Rate
BCH	Bose-Chaudury-Hocquenghem
CD	Chromatic Dispersion
DBPSK	Differential Binary Phase Shift Keying
DGD	Differential Group Delay
DQPSK	Differential Quadrature Phase Shift Keying
DSF	Dispersion Shifted Fiber
ETSI	European Telecommunications Standards Institute
FEC	Forward Error Correction
FEXT	Far-End Crosstalk
FDD	Frequency Division Duplex
FTTEx	Fiber To The Exchange
FWM	Four Wave Mixing
ISI	Inter-Symbol Interference
MCM	Multi-Carrier Modulation
MMF	Multi-Mode Fiber
NEXT	Near-End Crosstalk
NZDF	Non-Zero Dispersion shifted Fiber
OOK	On-Off Keying
PLC	Power Line Communication
PMD	Polarization Mode Dispersion
POTS	Plain Old Telephone Service
PSD	Power Spectral Density
PSP	Principal State of Polarization
QAM	Quadrature Amplitude Modulation
RC	Reference Channel
RFI	Radio Frequency Interference
RS	Reed-Solomon
SBS	Stimulated Brillouin Scattering
SCM	Single-Carrier Modulation
SDP	Subscriber Distribution Point
SMF	Single-Mode Fiber
SNR	Signal-to-Noise Ratio
SPM	Self Phase Modulation
SRS	Stimulated Raman Scattering
TCM	Trellis-Coded Modulation
USF	Dispersion Unshifted Fiber
VDSL	Very high bit rate DSL
WDM	Wavelength Division Multiplexing
xDSL	"x" Digital Subscriber Line
XPM	Cross Phase Modulation
XPolM	Cross Polarization Modulation

11. References

Aslanis, J. T.; Cioffi, J. M. (1992). Achievable information rates on digital subscriber loops: Limiting information rates with crosstalk noise. *IEEE Transactions on Communications*, Vol.40, No.2, (February 1992), pp. 361-372, ISSN 0090-6778

Binh, L.N. (2010). *Optical Fiber Communications Systems*, CRC Press, ISBN 978-1-4398-0620-3, Boca Raton, United States of America

Black, U. (2002). *Optical Networks – 3rd Generation Transport Systems*, Prentice Hall PTR Inc., ISBN 0-13-060726-6, New Jersey, United States of America

Čuchran, J.; Róka, R. (2006). *Optocommunication Systems and Networks*, STU Publishing house, ISBN 80-227-2437-8, Bratislava, Slovakia

ETSI TS 101 270-1 (1999). VDSL, Part 1 - Functional requirements, (October 1999)

ETSI TS 101 270-2 (2001). VDSL, Part 2 - Transceiver specification, (February 2001)

ETSI TS 101 475 (2000). Broadband Radio Access Networks (BRAN), HIPERLAN Type 2, Physical (PHY) Layer, Technical Specification, (April 2000)

ETSI TS 101 761-1 (2001). Broadband Radio Access Networks (BRAN), HIPERLAN Type 2, Data Link Control (DLC) Layer, Part 1: Basic Data Transport Functions, (December 2001)

Ferreira, H.C.; Lampe, L.; Newbury, J.; Swart, T.G. (2010). *Power Line Communications*, John Wiley & Sons, ISBN 978-0-470-74030-9, Chichester, United Kingdom

Götz, M.; Rapp, M.; Dostert, K. (2004). Power Line Channel Characteristics and Their Effect on Communication System Design. *IEEE Communications Magazine*, Vol.42, No.4, (April 2004), pp. 78-86, ISSN 0163-6804

Held, G. (2006). *Understanding Broadband over Power Line*, Auerbach Publications, ISBN 0-8493-9846-0, Boca Raton, United States of America

Hrasnica, H.; Haidine, A.; Lehnert, R. (2004). *Broadband Powerline Communications Networks*, John Wiley & Sons, ISBN 0-470-85741-2, Chichester, United Kingdom

Cherubini, G. et al. (2000). Filter Bank Modulation Techniques for Very High-Speed Digital Subscriber Lines. *IEEE Communication Magazine*, Vol.38, No.5, (May 2000), pp. 98-104, ISSN 0163-6804

Kaminow, I.P.; Li, T.; Willner, A.E. (2008). *Optical Fiber Telecommunications V B: Systems and Networks*, Elsevier Inc., ISBN 978-0-12-374172-1, San Diego, United States of America

Mukherjee, B. (2006). *Optical WDM Networks*, Springer Science+Business Media Inc., ISBN 978-0387-29055-3, New York, United States of America

Mestagh, D. et al. (2000). Zipper VDSL -A Solution for Robust Duplex Communication over Telephone Lines. *IEEE Communications Magazine*, Vol.38, No.5, (May 2000), pp. 90-96, ISSN 0163-6804

Oksman, V.; Werner J.-J. (2000). Single-Carrier Modulation Technology for Very High-Speed Digital Subscriber Line. *IEEE Communications Magazine*, Vol.38, No.5, (May 2000), pp. 82-89, ISSN 0163-6804

Róka, R. (2002). Theoretical and practical limits of transmission channels used by the ADSL technology in the metallic lines environment in the access network in Slovakia. *Journal of Electrical Engineering - EČ*, Vol. 53, No. 3-4, (March 2002), pp. 91-96, ISSN 1335-3632

Róka, R.; Cisár, R. (2002). The Analysis of Negative Influences in the Environment of Homogeneous Symmetric Lines at the Signal Transmission by Means of the ADSL

Technology. *Journal of Electrical Engineering - EČ*, Vol.53, No.9-10, (September 2002), pp. 241-249, ISSN 1335-3632

Róka, R. (2004). Environmental Influences on the Power Spectral Densities of VDSL Signals. *Journal of Electrical Engineering – EČ*, Vol.55, No.1-2, (January 2004), pp. 18-24, ISSN 1335-3632

Róka, R.; Dlháň, S. (2005). Modeling of transmission channels over the low-voltage power distribution network. *Journal of Electrical Engineering – EČ*, Vol. 56, No. 9-10, (September 2005), pp. 237-245, ISSN 1335-3632

Róka, R.; Urminský, J. (2008). Experimental Measurements for Verification of the Parametric Model for Reference Channels in the Real PLC Environment. *Journal of Electrical Engineering – EČ*, Vol. 59, No. 3, (May 2008), pp. 146-152, ISSN 1335-3632

Róka, R. (2009). Modeling of Environmental Influences at the Signal Transmission by means of the VDSL and PLC Technologies. *International Journal of Electrical Communication Networks and Information Security – IJCNIS*, Vol. 1, No. 1, (April 2009), pp. 6-13, ISSN 2073-607X

Schiff, M. (2006). *Introduction to Communication Systems Simulation*, Artech House Inc., ISBN 1-59693-002-0, Norwood, United States of America

Shieh, W.; Djordjevic, I. (2010). *OFDM for Optical Communications*, Elsevier Inc., ISBN 978-0-12-374879-9, San Diego, United States of America

Werner, J. J. (1991). The HDSL Environment. *IEEE Journal on Selected Areas in Communications*, Vol.SAC-9, No.6, (August 1991), pp. 785-800, ISSN 0733-8716

Xiong, F. (2000). *Digital Modulation Techniques*, Artech House Inc., ISBN 0-89006-970-0, Norwood, United States of America

Zimmermann, M.; Dostert, K. (2002a). Analysis and Modeling of Impulsive Noise in Broadband Powerline Communications. *IEEE Transactions on Electromagnetic Compatibility*, Vol.44, No.1, (February 2002), pp. 249 – 258, ISSN 0018-9375

Zimmermann, M.; Dostert, K. (2002b). Multipath Model for the Powerline Channel. *IEEE Transactions on Communications*, Vol.50, No.4, (April 2002), pp. 553-559, ISSN 0090-6778

4

Co-Simulation Procedure for PID and Fuzzy Logic Active Controls Strategies Applied to a Sprayers Boom Suspension

Cristiano Okada Pontelli and Mario Francisco Mucheroni
São Paulo University
Brazil

1. Introduction

The boom sprayers are responsible for applying chemical products on cultures in order to maximize agricultural production. The spray is the fractionation of liquid droplets in order to distribute uniformly over the target. So smaller is the liquid volume to be distributed through the area, so smaller is the required drop diameter. The sprayers are designed just to generate drops and throwing them over the target with the required uniformity.

The spray distribution uniformity of sprayers boom is given by the assembly and operation conditions such as, nozzle spacing and opening angle, boom distance from soil, liquid pressure and dynamic stability of the boom. The liquid volume distributed along the boom should be as constant as possible, Sinfort (1994).

The vertical boom oscillations caused by irregularities in the terrain modifies the distance between each nozzle and the target, distorting the distribution. Moreover, when the oscillations are excessive the tips of the boom can touch the ground, causing damages. These oscillations may increase with walking speed of the tractor vehicle, Musillami (1977). The horizontal boom oscillations also change the sprays uniformity, but in a smaller proportion than the vertical ones.

Another fairly common problem that can also change the application uniformity is the error in the juxtaposition of culture bands covered by the spray. Insufficient or excessive spacing between these bands can cause a variation in liquid volume used up to 100%.

Various methods to study the quality of spray distribution under the dynamical aspects of the movement are known. These methods differ in the way of exciting the sprayer. One of them uses the excitation by a vehicle walking on a standard grass track prepared (POCHI et al., 2002, MILLER et al., 1989), or translating on a track prepared with artificial obstacles (CHAPLIN and WU, 1989). Other methods develop and use a shake driver to simulate a track with obstacles (SINFORT et al., 1997).

Herbst and Wolf (2001) developed a servo-mechanism to perform excitations on sprayers. They measured the sprays of various equipments, pulled sprayers and tractor mounted sprayers from different manufacturers. In these experiments they found coefficients of variation from 5 to 22%, depending of the boom length, the walking speed and excitation method used. According to these researchers a coefficient of variation in order of 15% would be an acceptable value for the usual ground conditions founded.

One procedure to minimize the coefficient of variation of spray distribution is to design and use mechanisms to stabilize the boom within acceptable parameters. These mechanisms are known as boom suspensions for sprayers.

On many sprayers there are control of spray mean height and systems of boom movement management with passive boom suspensions. The active controls are still less used. However unstable movements have been characterized as a great limitation for chemical products applications with precision and good uniformity, (RAMON and BAERDEMAEKER 1997, POCHI and VANNUCCI, 2001).

Womac et al. (2001) investigated the effect of nozzle height and the equipment walking speed in the uniformity of chemical products application in field conditions. The coefficient of variation founded stays from 5% to 17% for boom static conditions and 6% to 37% for boom in motion (6 to 26 $km.h^{-1}$).

Sinfort and Herbst (1996) studied the boom movement and the spray pattern in terms of practical use. The movements of the spray boom were evaluated by a simulator with hydraulic cylinders and the spray pattern was simulated by software. It is concluded that the roll motions are responsible for major non-uniformity of liquid application.

Ramon et al. (1997) developed a polynomial model to predict the distribution of a single spray nozzle that moves on a channels table 15 meters long. The difference founded between the measured and the simulated values was below 7%. They observed also that the boom downward movements affect the liquid distribution more than the boom upward movements.

Speelman and Jansen (1974) determined that the amount of vibrations on the sprayer boom is influenced by the structure of the boom, ground surface irregularities and walking speed. Using an initial condition of 0.5 meters spray height, they observed that as amplitudes of boom vertical motion increase, the uniformity of spray distribution decreases.

On cereals spraying, Nation (1980) determined that the spray deposit variation is proportional to the movement of the sprayer boom end. He also observed that random vertical movements of the sprayer boom are more influenced by roll movements than vertical translation motions of the boom.

Considering a boom as rigid body subjected to sinusoidal inputs, Iyer and Wills (1978) proved that the bigest source of the spray distribution variation comes from the own movement of the boom

Langenakens et al. (1999) founded that increasing the vehicle translation speed, the boom oscillation amplitude also increases. They obtained for applied liquid volume coefficients of variation from 2% to 173%, caused mainly by boom rolling movement resulting from vehicle translation.

2. Models, simulations and results comparisons

We used a calibrated virtual model that was developed for some simulations to test control strategies. The performances of these strategies are compared with the performance of a passive suspension model. Following a brief description of the models and all the simulations are presented.

2.1 Description of the models used in simulations

This part will show the main configurations of the models used in simulations with the rigid body software (ADAMS).

2.1.1 Passive model

Figure 2.1 shows a trapezoidal type passive boom suspension model with its main dimensions.

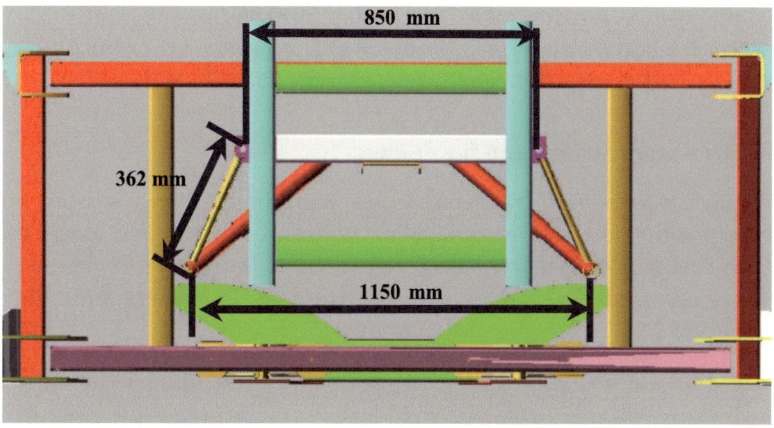

Fig. 2.1. Passive suspension model with its main dimensions.

2.1.2 Model with sensor fusion and proportional control

We used a boom suspension of trapezoidal type with the same dimensions listed in Figure 2.1. We used three position measurement sensors uniformily distributed along the length of the boom. The sensor 1 was placed at 4 meters from the center of the equipment, the sensor 2 at 8 meters from the center and the sensor 3 at 12 meters from the center, as illustrated in Figure 2.2.

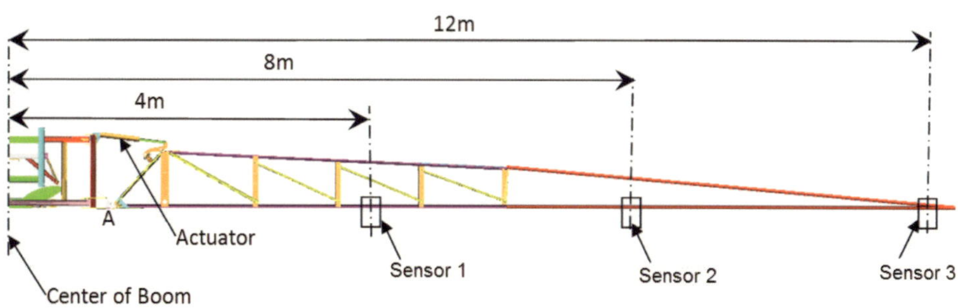

Fig. 2.2. Boom model with 3 sensors for fusion and proportional control.

The control strategy we used takes information from three position sensors making an weighted average with coefficients related to the distance from the center of the equipment. These coefficients increase from sensor 1 to sensor 3 to give more weight on rolling motion, because the boom pivoted at the point A. To keep the boom at a constant height of 500 mm from the ground is the main target. Therefore the control equation, using the force variable, is:

$$Fa = -Fe + k\left[-500 + \left(\frac{1}{6}\right) sensor\,1 + \left(\frac{1}{3}\right) sensor\,2 + \left(\frac{1}{2}\right) sensor\,3\right] \tag{1}$$

where:

Fa: actuator force (N);
Fe: actuator static force relative to the weight of the boom (N)
k: gain
sensor 1: ground position measurement (mm) - 4 m from equipment center
sensor 2: ground position measurement (mm) - 8 m from equipment center
sensor 3: ground position measurement (mm) - 12 m from equipment center

2.1.3 Model with sensor fusion and fuzzy logic

We used a boom suspension of trapezoidal type with the dimensions listed in Figure 2.1. We used three position measurement sensors uniformly distributed along the length of the boom. The first sensor is placed at 4 meters from the center of the equipment, the second at 8 meters from the center and the third at 12 meters from the center, as illustrated in Figure 2.2.

Here we used a procedure identified as a co-simulation method between ADAMS and MATLAB softwares, with the goal of the model of interacting rigid body capabilities of Adams software with the control plant capabilities of fuzzy system simulations in Matlab software. This procedure is showed schematically in Figure 2.3.

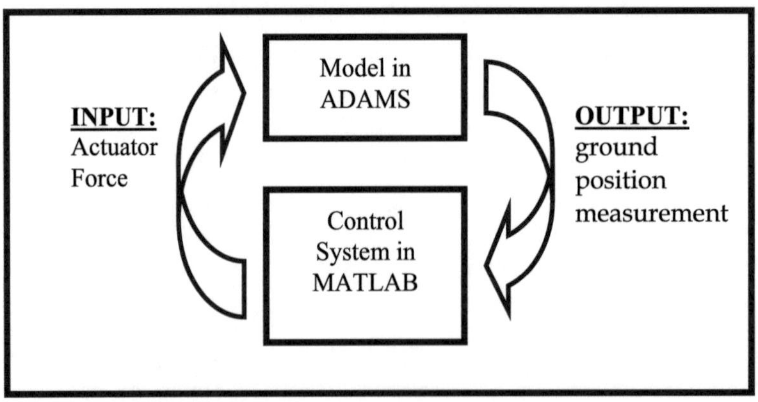

Fig. 2.3. Co-Simulation between ADAMS and MATLAB software.

Figure 2.3 is a simple diagram that shows how co-simulation is performed. The output variables of the model of Adams are exported to the plant control in Matlab. The actuator forces are calculated according to strategy and then applied to a control designed into the Adams. The first step is to define what are the input and output variables for the Adams model. Here the input variable is the force law and force the actuator to the actuator left. The output variables are the right sensor position 1, the right sensor position 2, the right sensor position 3 (at the boom right tip), the left sensor position 1, the left sensor position 2, the left sensor position 3 (at the boom left tip).

The second step is to create these variables in the Adams; so we need to create one variable for each state variable. To create a new state variable we need to select in the menu, following the instructions: Build, System Elements - state variability - New. Then insert the name and it will measure this variable, as shown in Figure 2.4.

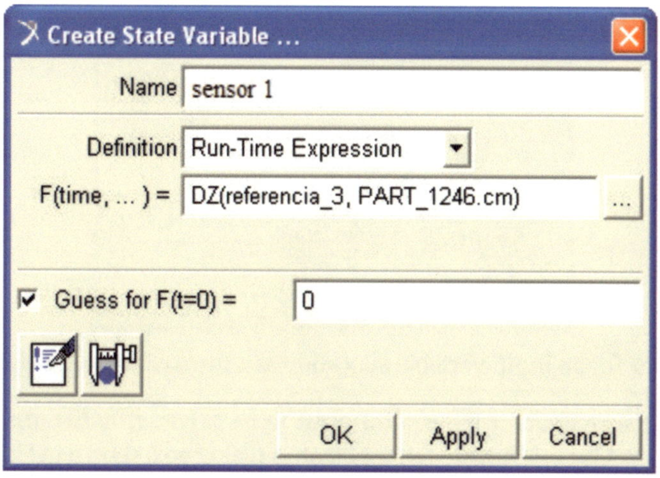

Fig. 2.4. Box dialog for creating an input state variable.

For the output variables follow the same steps except that F (time ,...) should be maintained the zero default value, as shown in Figure 2.5.

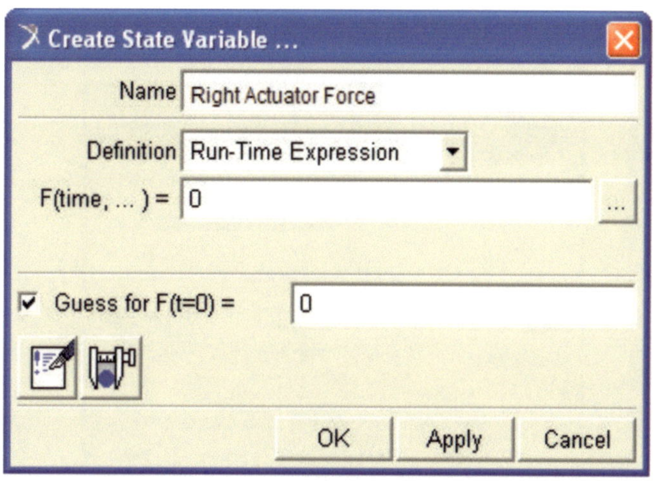

Fig. 2.5. Dialog box for creating an output state variable.

With the input and output variables defined, the values of input variables obtained from Simulink must to be applied (referenced) in the model components of the Adams. In this case, the intensity of the actuator force obtained in Simulink must be referenced to its respective force in the Adams model. To reference the input variable, we should select the menu Edit - Modify and open the right force variable. This will open a dialog box as shown in Figure 2.6.

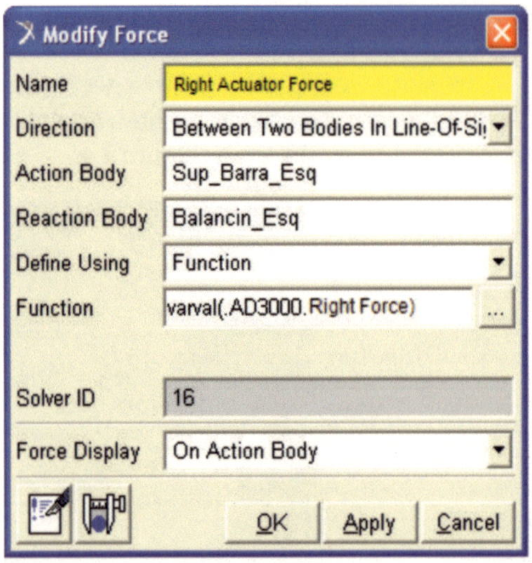

Fig. 2.6. Dialog box for an input variable allocation as a force component of the Adams.

The next step is the creation of the control plant to be exported to Simulink. To export the model, we select the Controls menu - Export Plant. A dialog box, shown in Figure 2.7, opens.

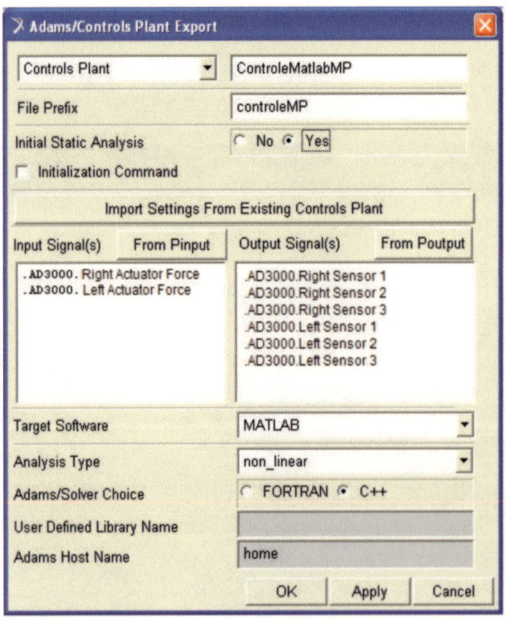

Fig. 2.7. Dialog box for export control plant to Adams.

The input and output variables are listed in the same order in which the respective connecting pins will appear in the control block. It is necessary that input and output pins are connected correctly each other to assure the proper simulation of the control systems applied to the boom.

This export process will show three kinds of files, each one with a prefix defined in the dialog box of Figure 2.7. In this case we can see the files controleMP.adm, controleMP.cmd and controleMP.m. These files will be saved in the working directory of the Adams.

The next step is to connect the block generated at the Adams model to the Simulink control plant. To adjust the control system with the Adams model we must first open the Adams block diagram in Matlab. To do this we must start Matlab and change the Matlab working directory to the same one used by Adams, that is, at the same location where the files are generated in the previous step. Once this is done we should write at the Matlab prompt the extension of the file we have created, in this case controleMP. This initializes the Adams input and output variables as Matlab variables. The next command used is Adams_sys, that opens a window with a block diagram of Adams as shown in Figure 2.8.

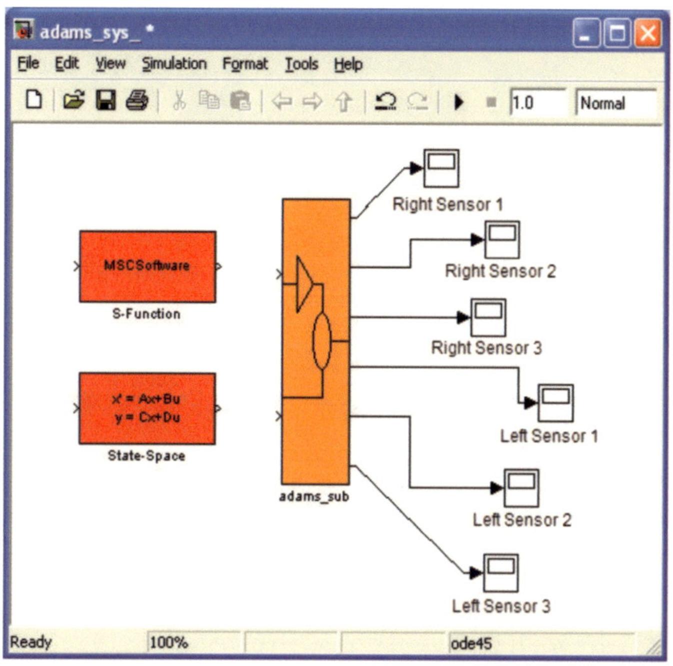

Fig. 2.8. Block diagram of Adams in the Simulink.

A double click on the block subsystem at Adams_Sub opens a new window that shows the available components, as seen in Figure 2.9.

A double click on the block plant at Adams opens a dialog box with the parameters that must be adjusted. The communication interval field specifies how often the Adams communicates with Simulink and the number of communications between them for each step of writing output. The animation mode field can be adjusted to be interactive, that is, the simulation can be shown graphically as the model is computed. These parameters can be seen in Figure 2.10.

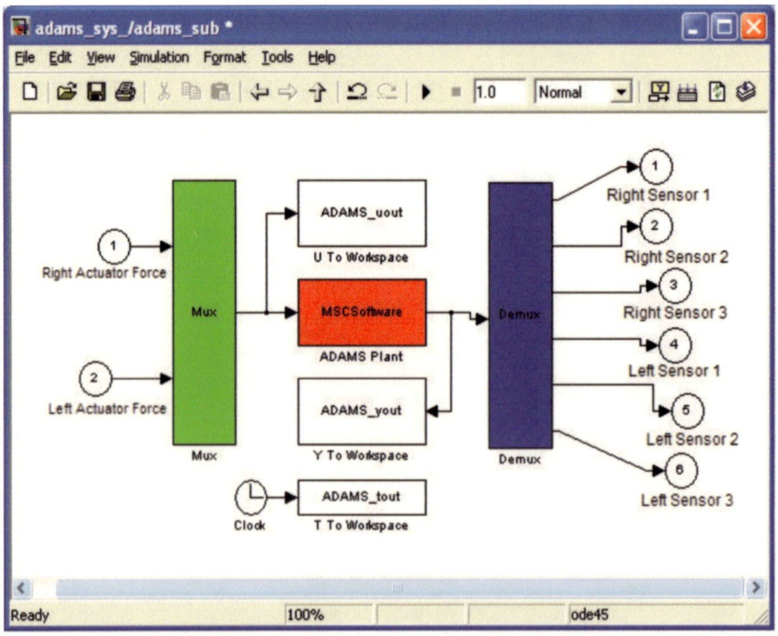

Fig. 2.9. Subsystem model in Adams.

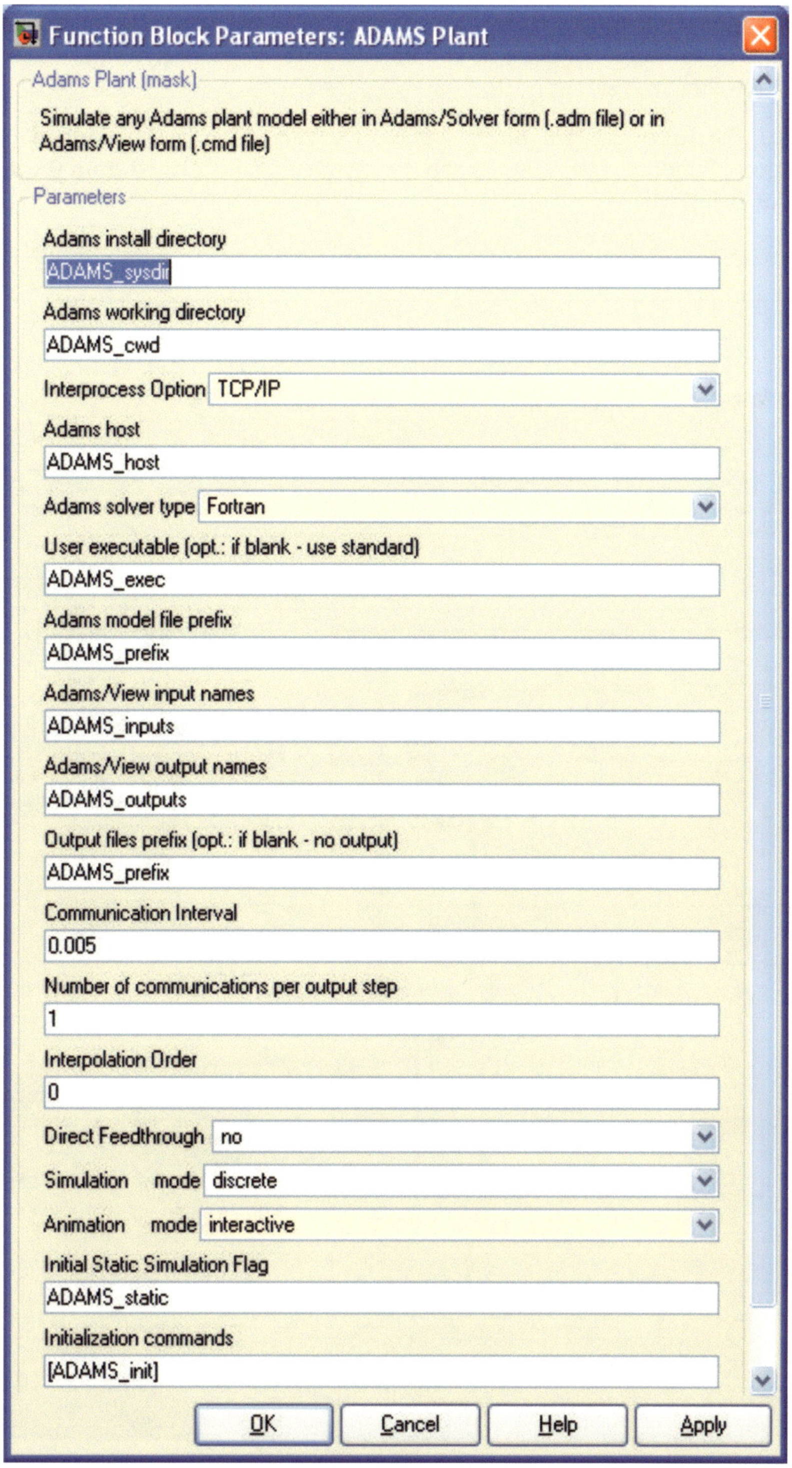

Fig. 2.10. Dialog box of function block parameters.

After the necessary adjustments they should be copied into the block Adams_sub plant control Simulink and then connect the inputs and outputs properly. Figure 2.11 shows an overview of the control system.

To construct the fuzzy system block we used a model with the method of centroid defuzzification Mamdani type. The weighted average height obtained from the sensors was used as input as follows:

$$A = \left[-500 + \left(\frac{1}{6}\right) sensor1 + \left(\frac{1}{3}\right) sensor2 + \left(\frac{1}{2}\right) sensor3 \right] \tag{2}$$

where:
A: value of weighted average height from the three sensors [mm].

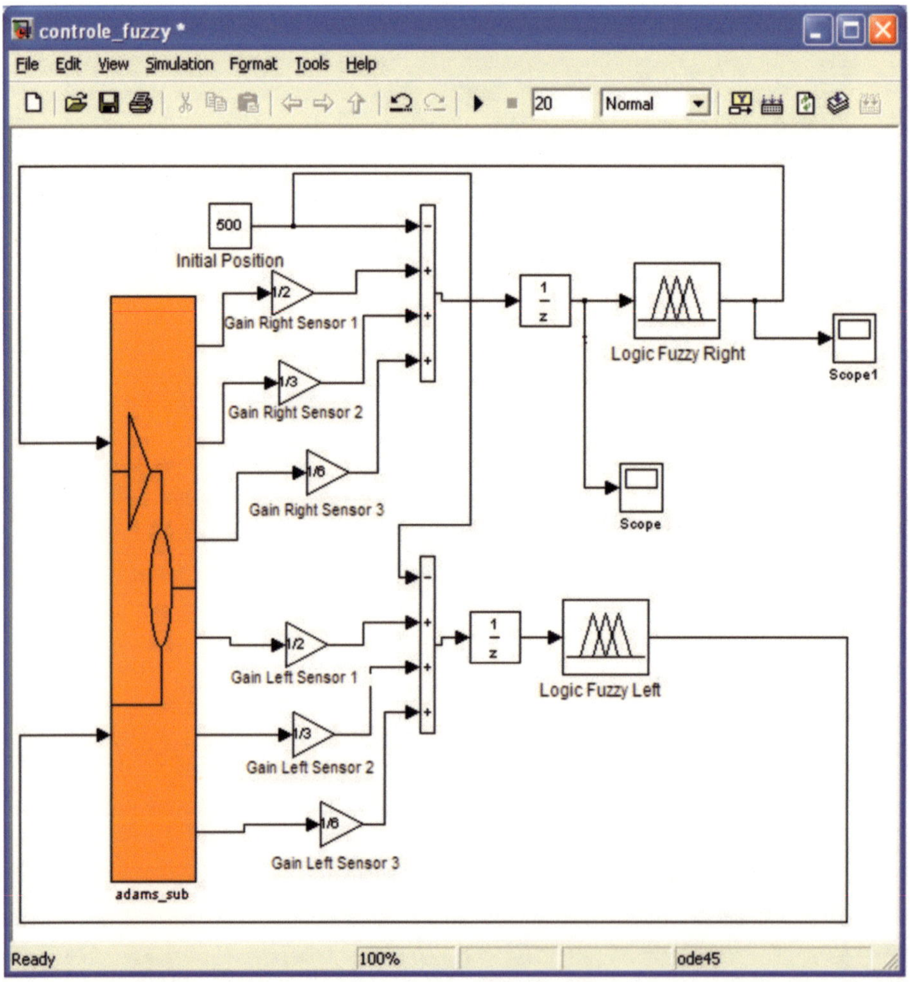

Fig. 2.11. Fuzzy control system integrated with Adams.

The Figure 2.12 shows a graphic of input inference, where the variable is the weighted average height obtained from equation 2.

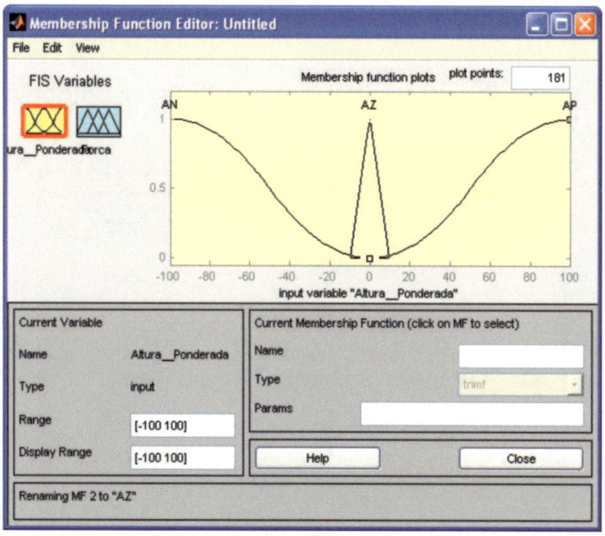

Fig. 2.12. Input inference of weighted average height.

The input linguistic variables are:

AN: Negative Height;
AZ: Zero Height;
AP: Positive Height;

The Figure 2.13 shows a graphic of output inference, where the variable is the force applied to the system.

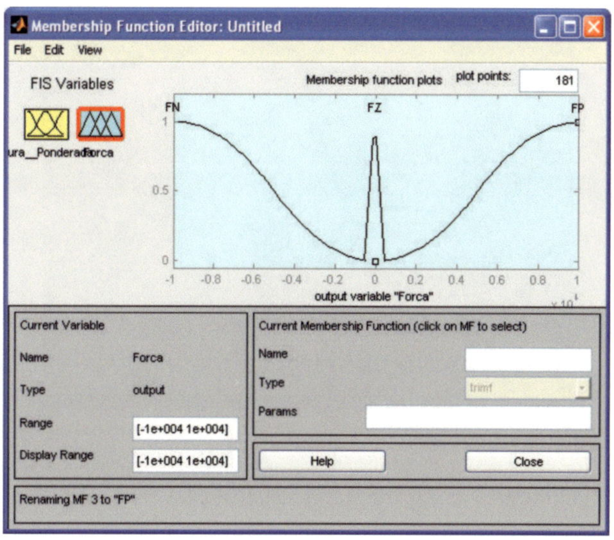

Fig. 2.13. Force output inference.

The output linguistic variables are:

FN: Negative Force;
ZP: Zero Force;
FP: Positive Force;

We find the rules for defuzzification of the input variables on output variables though the bos shown in Figure 2.14.

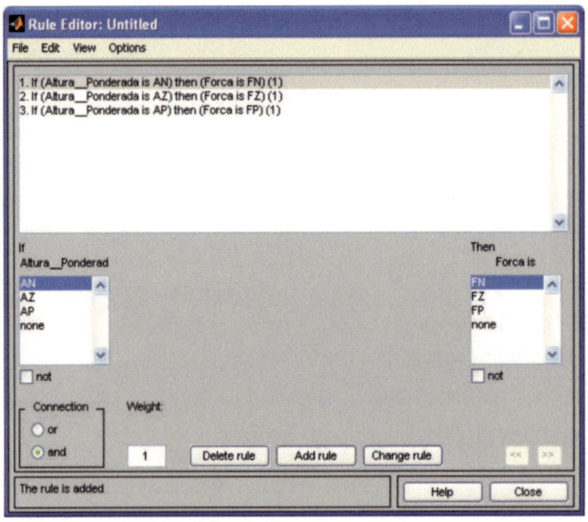

Fig. 2.14. Box of fuzzy rules used in the equipment model.

We can also define the curve of relationship between output and input using the rules previously established, as shown in Figure 2.15.

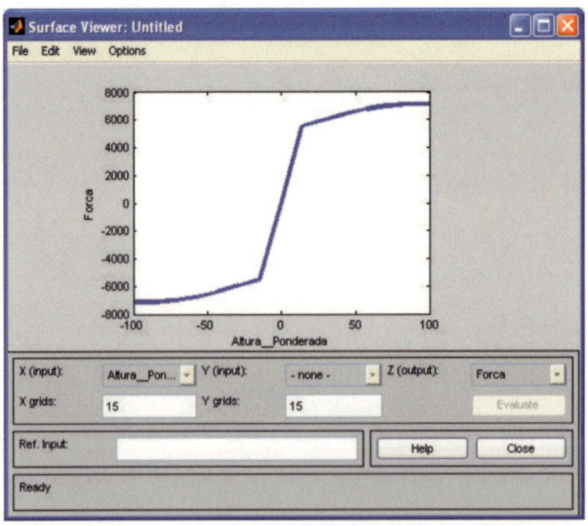

Fig. 2.15. Input versus output curve.

Therefore the control equation, using the fuzzy control power variable is:

$$Fa = -Fe + f(fuzzy) \tag{3}$$

where:

Fa: actuator force (N);
Fe: actuator static force relative to the weight of the boom (N)
f (fuzzy): the function obtained by defuzzification of the fuzzy model shown in Figure 2.15.

2.2 Simulations

The simulations were conducted in order to evaluate the three kinds of suspension in analysis, that are a passive suspension, an active PID control suspension and active Fuzzy control suspension.

The input conditions were grouped into three sets: the first set corresponds to step type input, the second to harmonic type input and the third to random type of input.

In the first set of inputs, we used two step sizes. With this kind of analysis we expected to evaluate the system overshoot, settling time and the power consumed for each type of control.

In the second set of inputs, we used two amplitudes and two frequencies in order to be able to measure the conditions of the boom oscillations and the power consumed by each type of control.

In the third set of inputs, we used random signals, taking from tractors standards (ASABE / ISO 5008, 2002) to evaluate the conditions of boom oscillation and power consumed for each type of control.

2.2.1 Step inputs

In this first set of simulation analysis we used a step type input with angle amplitudes of 5 and 10 degrees, which corresponds to the equipment transposing a 160 and 320 mm step obstacles, respectively, with a 1800 mm distance between tires, as shown in Figure 2.16.

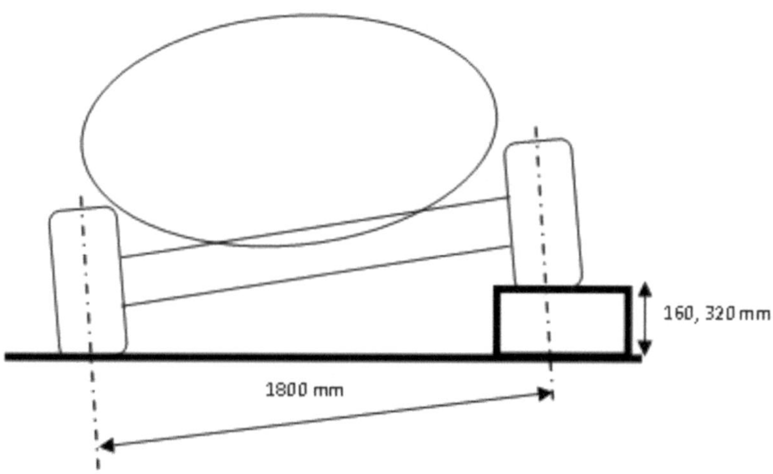

Fig. 2.16. Model for step type input.

The Figure 2.17 shows the displacement behavior of the three positions of the boom right side with the passive system, active PID system and active Fuzzy system, all subjected to a step type input with an angle amplitude of 5 degrees. It is also shown the power consumed by each suspension system used.

From the analysis of Figure 2.17 it is possible to note a great advantage of active systems when compared with passive system considering boom displacements, independently of the sensor position.

The Figure 2.18 shows the behaviors of active systems. We can observe that the Fuzzy active system stabilizes the boom quicker than the active PID system, but it has a larger overshoot signal for all the three sensors than PID. The RMS power value of active PID system is 0.30 kW and for Fuzzy active system is 0.32 kW.

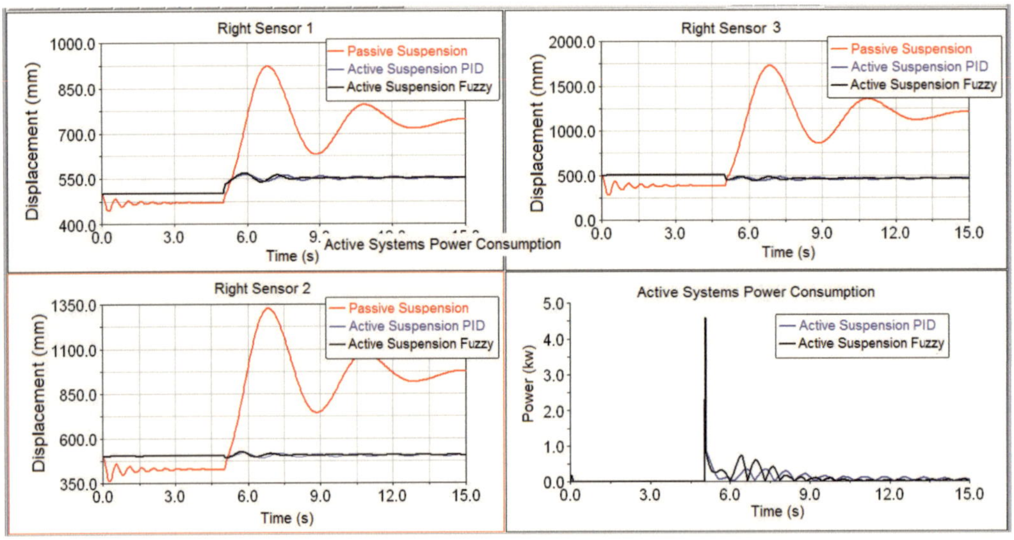

Fig. 2.17. Behavior of suspension systems subjected to a step input amplitude of 5 degrees.

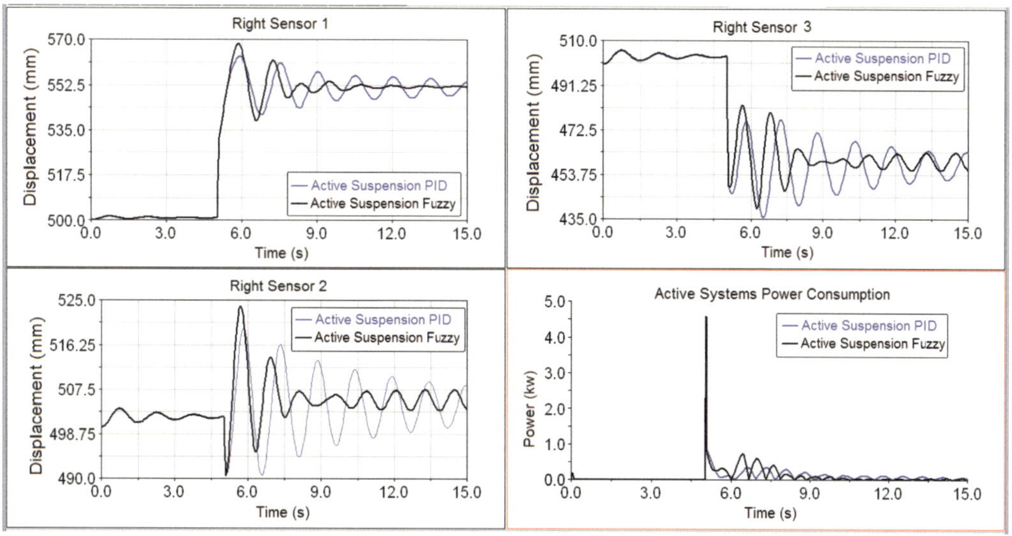

Fig. 2.18. Behavior of active systems subjected to a 5 degrees step input amplitude.

The Figure 2.19 shows the displacement behavior of the three positions of the boom right side of the passive system, active PID system and active Fuzzy system subjected to a step type input with angle amplitude of 10 degrees. It is also shown the power consumed by each suspension system used.

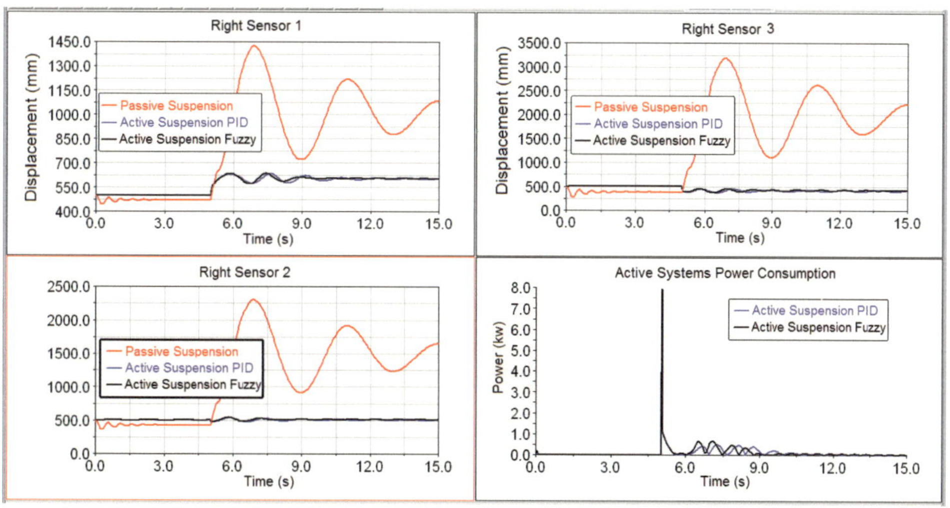

Fig. 2.19. Behavior of suspension systems subjected to a step input amplitude of 10 degrees.

From the analysis of Figure 2.19 it is possible to note the great advantage of active systems when compared with passive system considering boom displacements, independently of the sensor position.

Figure 2.20 shows the behaviors of active systems. We can observe that the active Fuzzy system stabilizes in less time interval than the active PID system but has a larger overshoot signal for all three sensors. The RMS power value of the active PID system is 0.49 kW and for Fuzzy active system is 0.50 kW.

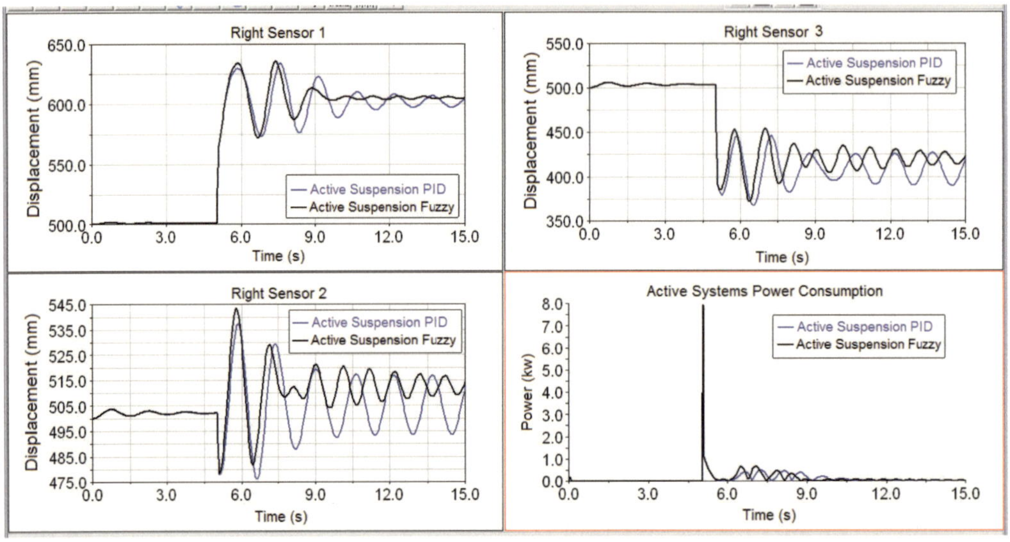

Fig. 2.20. Behavior of active systems subjected to a 10 degrees step input amplitude.

2.2.2 Harmonics inputs

The following Table 2.1 shows the harmonic parameters of the simulation signal used. We use two amplitudes and two frequencies for sinusoidal signals. Therefore four sinusoidal inputs were used in the systems simulations developed, as shown in Table 2.1.

Simulations	Amplitude (degree)	Frequency (Hz)	Simulation Code
1	5	0,1	A5F0,1
2	5	2,0	A5F2
3	10	0,1	A10F0,1
4	10	2,0	A10F2

Table 2.1. Amplitudes and frequencies of 4 sinusoidal inputs.

The Figure 2.21 shows the displacement behavior of the three positions of the boom right side of passive system, active PID system and active Fuzzy system subjected to a harmonic input with amplitude of 5 degrees and frequency of 0.1 Hz. It is also shown the power consumed by each suspension system used.

From the analysis of Figure 2.21 it is possible to note the great advantage of the active systems when compared with the passive system considering boom displacements, independently of the sensor position.

In Figure 2.22 we can see that there are no significant differences between the active system PID and fuzzy active system behavior for any simulated positions.

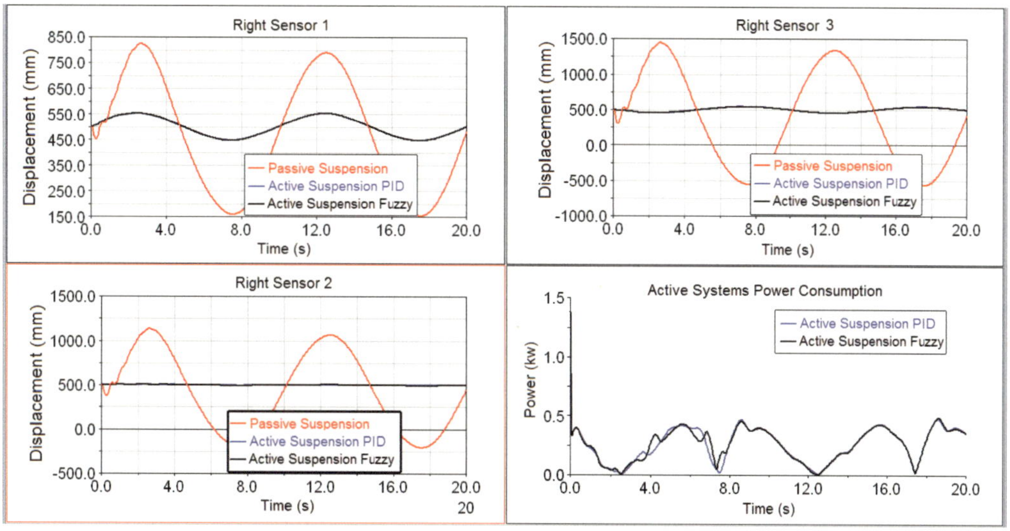

Fig. 2.21. Behavior of suspension systems subjected to harmonic input with 5 degrees amplitude and 0.1 Hz frequency.

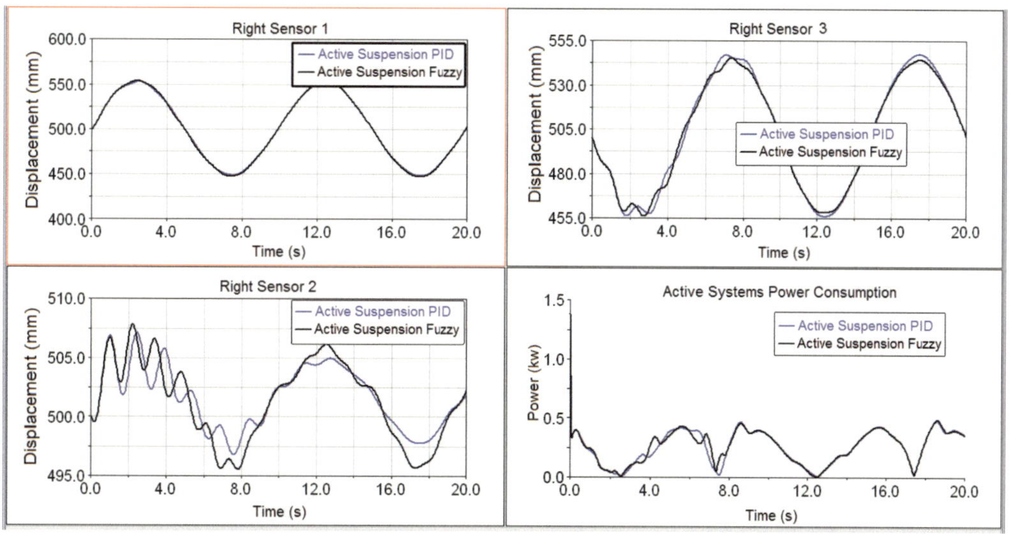

Fig. 2.22. Behavior of active suspension systems subjected to harmonic input of 5 degrees amplitude and 0.1 Hz frequency.

Figure 2.23 shows the displacement behavior of the three positions of the boom right side of the passive system, active PID system and active Fuzzy system subjected to a harmonic input with amplitude of 5 degrees and frequency of 2 Hz. It is also shown the power consumed by each suspension system used.

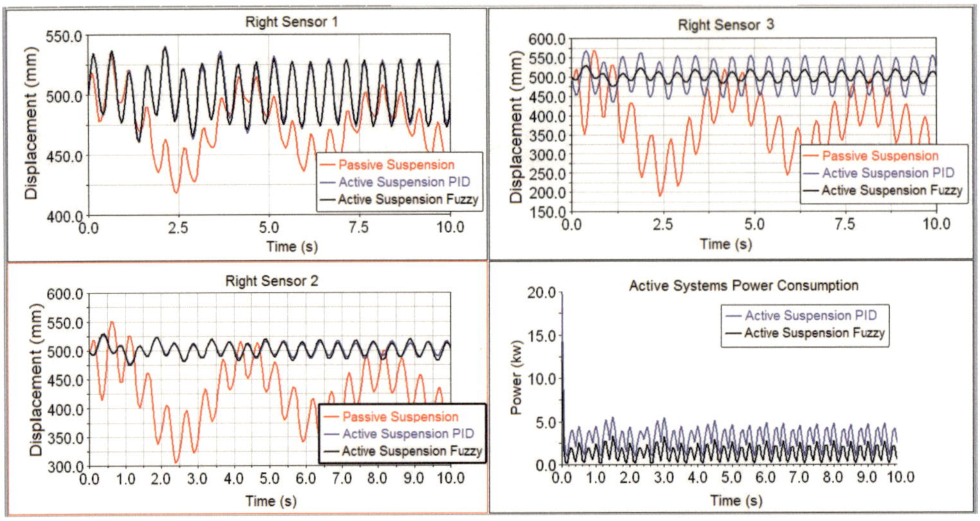

Fig. 2.23. Behavior of suspension systems subjected to harmonic input with 5 degrees amplitude and 2 Hz frequency.

From the analysis of Figure 2.23 we can see that active control systems are more efficient than passive system for all positions simulated.

From Figure 2.24 we can see that there are significant differences between active PID system and active Fuzzy system at position 3, the tip of the boom. The RMS value of power consumed by the active PID system is 3.32 kW while the RMS value of power consumed by active Fuzzy system is 1.57 kW.

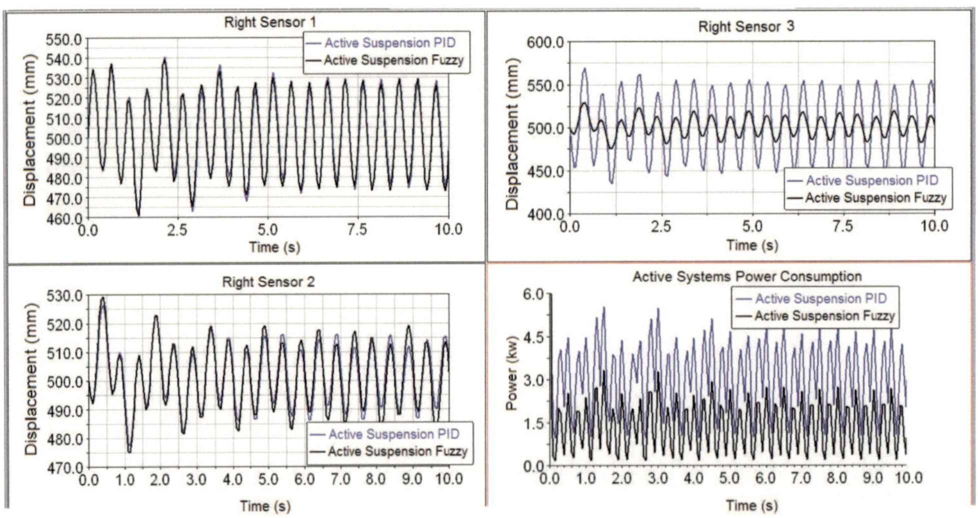

Fig. 2.24. Behavior of active systems subjected to harmonic input with 5 degrees amplitude and 2 Hz frequency.

Figure 2.25 shows the displacement behavior of the three positions of the boom right side of passive system, active PID system and active Fuzzy system subjected to a harmonic input with amplitude of 10 degrees and a frequency of 0.1 Hz. It is also shown the power consumed by each active system used.

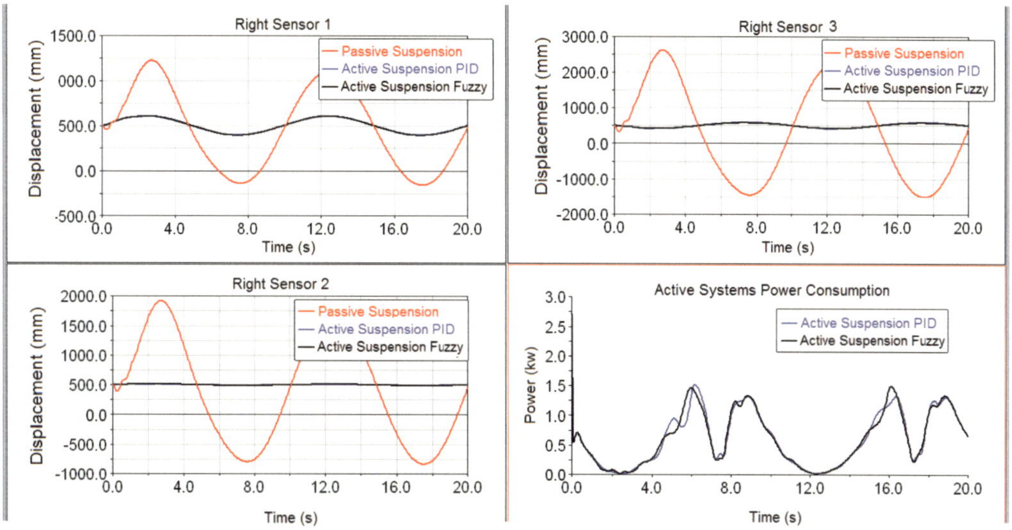

Fig. 2.25. Behavior of suspension systems subjected to harmonic input with 10 degrees amplitude and 0.1 Hz frequency.

From the analysis of Figure 2.25 is possible to note the great advantage of active systems when compared with passive system considering boom displacements, independently of the sensor position.

In Figure 2.26 we can see that there are no significant differences between active PID system and active Fuzzy system for any position simulated.

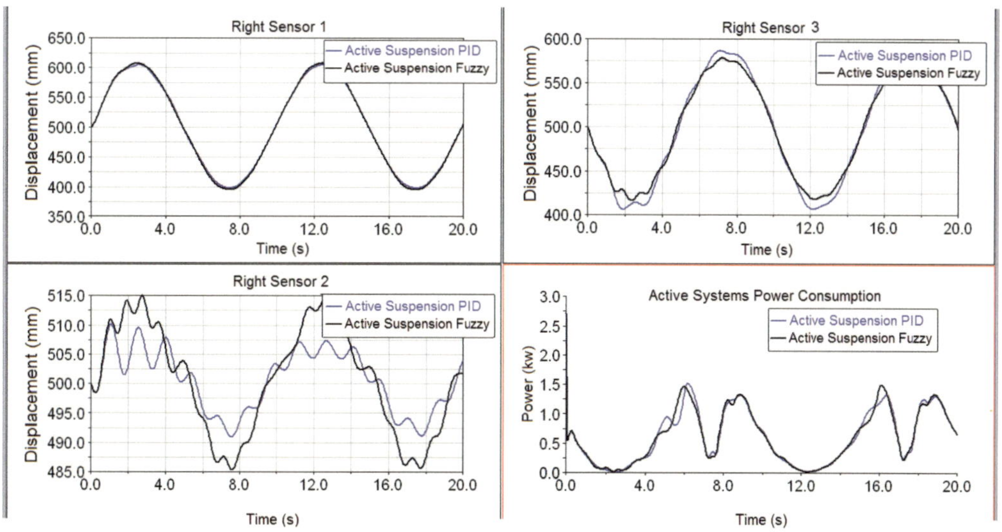

Fig. 2.26. Behavior of active systems subjected to harmonic input with 10 degrees amplitude and 0.1 Hz frequency.

From the analysis of Figure 2.27 it is possible to see the best performance of active systems when compared with passive system considering boom displacements, independently regardless of sensor position.

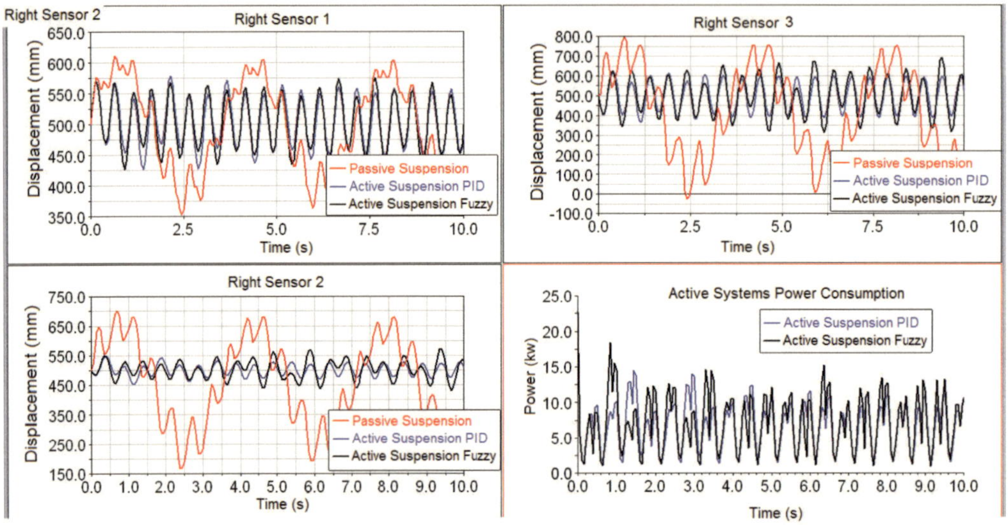

Fig. 2.27. Behavior of suspension systems subjected to a harmonic input of 10 degrees amplitude and frequency of 2 Hz.

In Figure 2.28 we can see that there are no significant differences between active PID system and active Fuzzy system for any position simulated.

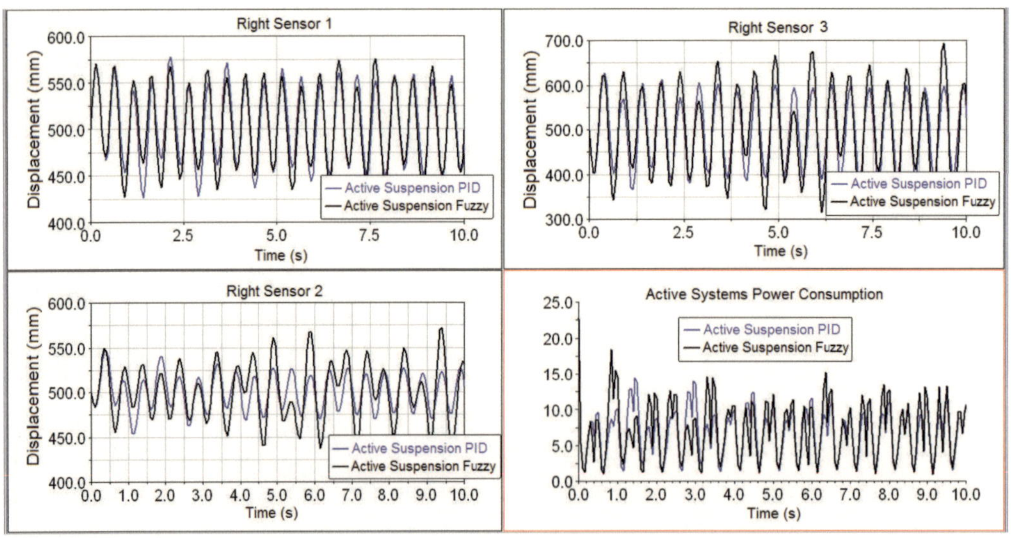

Fig. 2.28. Behavior of active systems subjected to a harmonic input range of 10 degrees amplitude and 2 Hz frequency.

2.2.3 Random inputs

For this simulation set, we use input signals from a vibration analysis of tractors standard (ASABE / ISO 5008, 2002). This standard establishes two pavement types (smooth and rough), and gives the Cartesian coordinates for each type of track. These coordinates are put through ADAMS software and then the simulations can be run.

Figure 2.29 shows the smooth pavement condition with equipment travel speed of 5 km/h. It also shows the boom displacement at the three sensor positions (1, 2 and 3).

From the analysis of Figure 2.29 it is possible to note the efficiency of active control to keep constant the distance between the boom and the ground.

In Figure 2.30 it is possible to note the equivalence of both active control systems, ie, there are no significant differences in maintaining the height of the boom from the ground.

Figure 2.31 shows the smooth condition of pavement with equipment travel speed of 7.5 km/h. It also shows the boom displacement at the three sensor positions (1, 2 and 3).

From the analysis of Figure 2.31 it is possible to note the efficiency of active control to keep constant the distance between the boom and the ground.

In Figure 2.32 it is possible to note the equivalence of both active control systems, ie, there are no significant differences in maintaining the height of the boom from the ground.

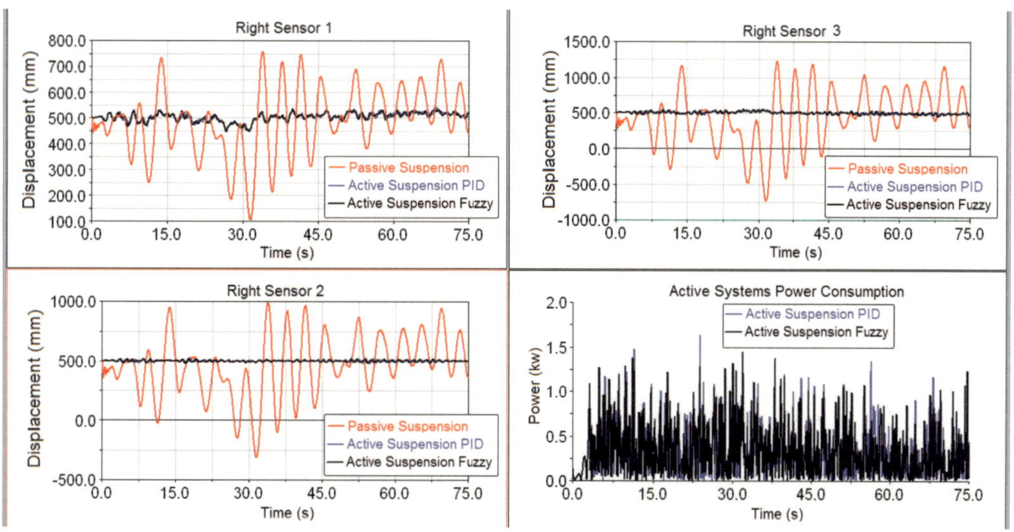

Fig. 2.29. Suspension systems submitted to a smooth track at 5 km/h.

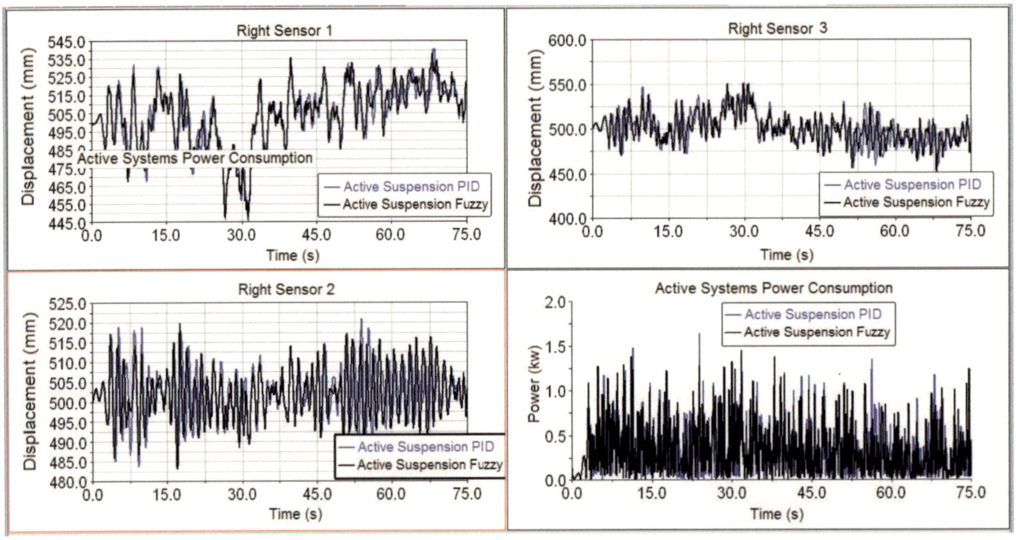

Fig. 2.30. Active suspension systems submitted to a smooth track at 5 km/h.

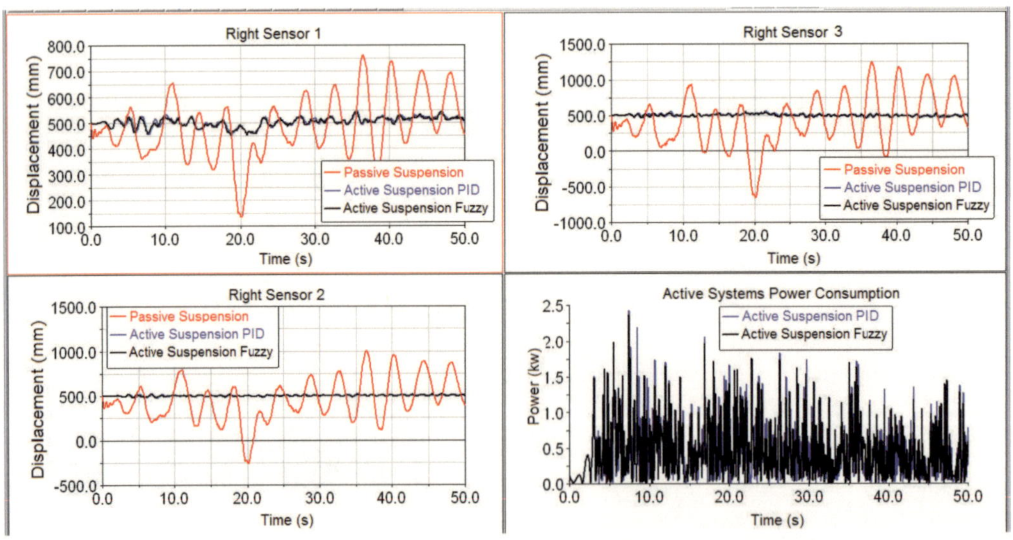

Fig. 2.31. Suspensions submitted to a smooth track at 7.5 km/h.

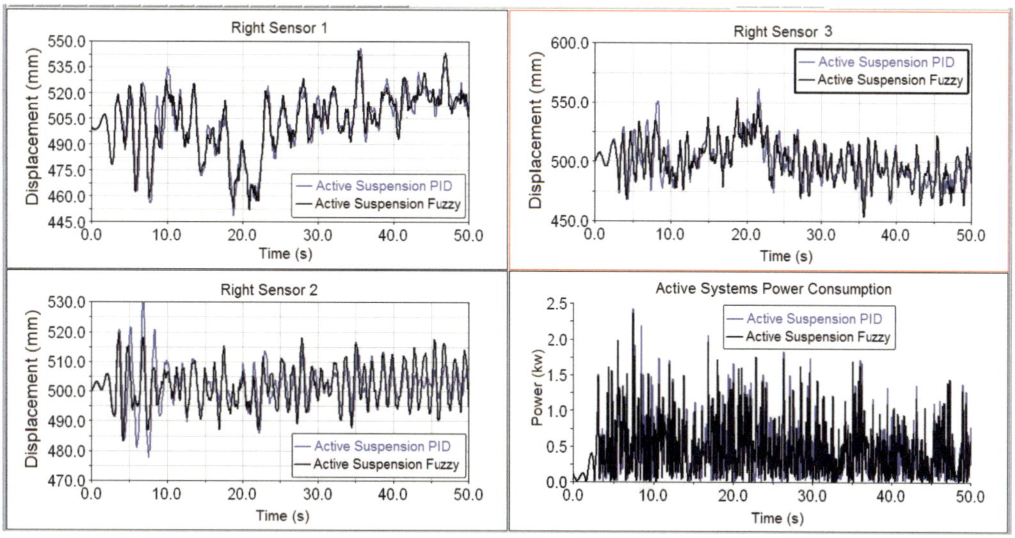

Fig. 2.32. Active suspension systems submitted to a smooth track at 7.5 km/h.

Figure 2.33 shows the smooth condition of pavement with equipment travel speed of 10 km/h. It also shows the boom displacement at the three sensor positions (1, 2 and 3).

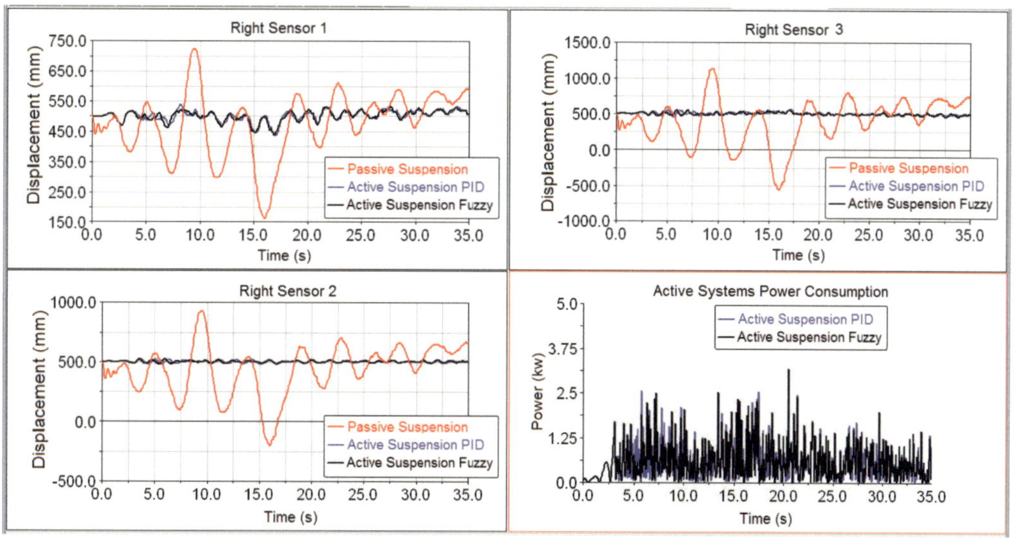

Fig. 2.33. Suspension systems submitted to a smooth track at 10 km/h.

From the analysis of Figure 2.33 it is possible to note the efficiency of active control to keep constant the distance between the boom and the ground.

In Figure 2.34 it is possible to note the equivalence of both active control systems, ie, there are no significant differences in maintaining the height of the boom from the ground.

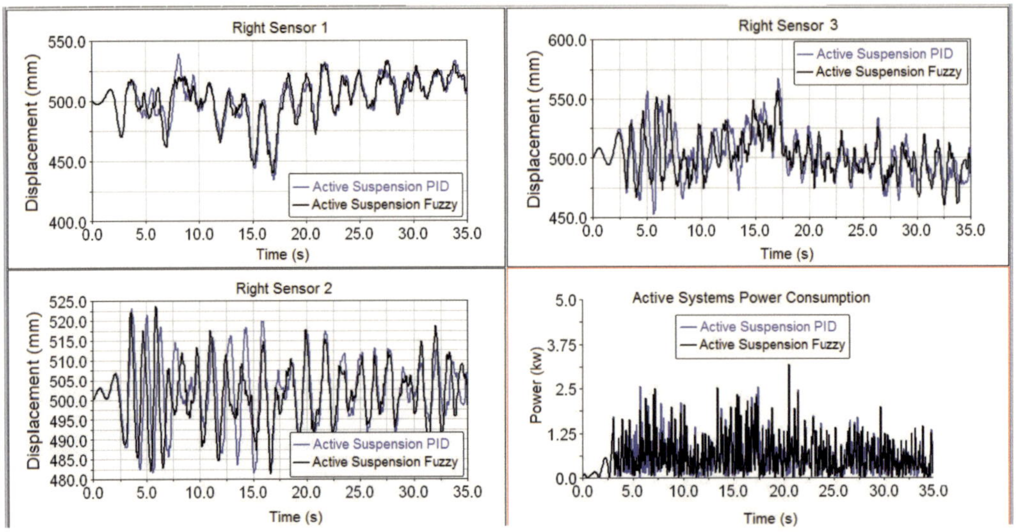

Fig. 2.34. Active suspension systems submitted to a smooth track at 10 km/h.

Figure 2.35 shows the rough condition of pavement with equipment travel speed of 5 km/h. It also shows the boom displacement at the three sensor positions (1, 2 and 3).

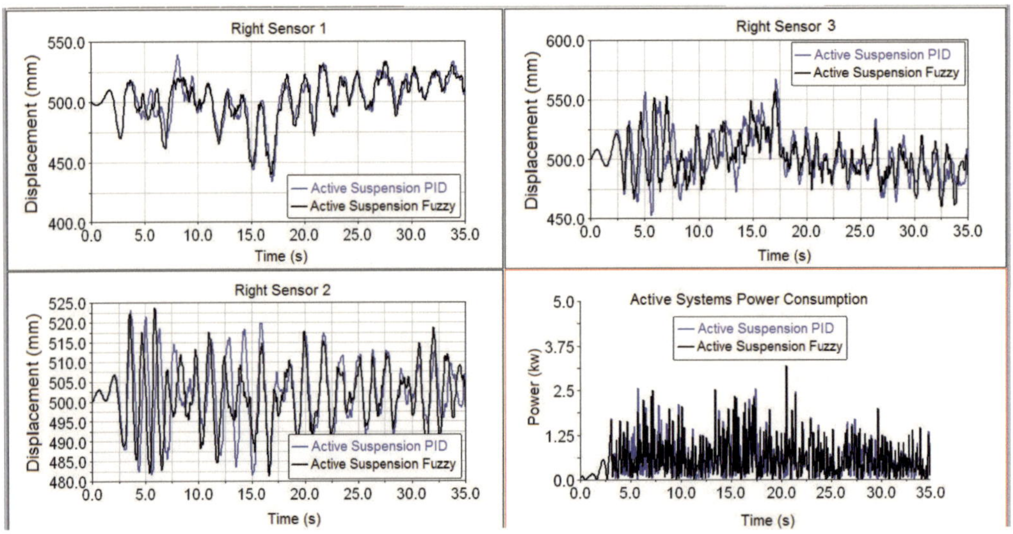

Fig. 2.35. Suspension systems submitted to a rough track at 5 km/h.

From the analysis of Figure 2.35 it is possible to note the efficiency of active control to keep constant the distance between the boom and the ground.

In Figure 2.36 it is possible to note the equivalence of both active control systems, ie, there are no significant differences in maintaining the height of the boom from the ground.

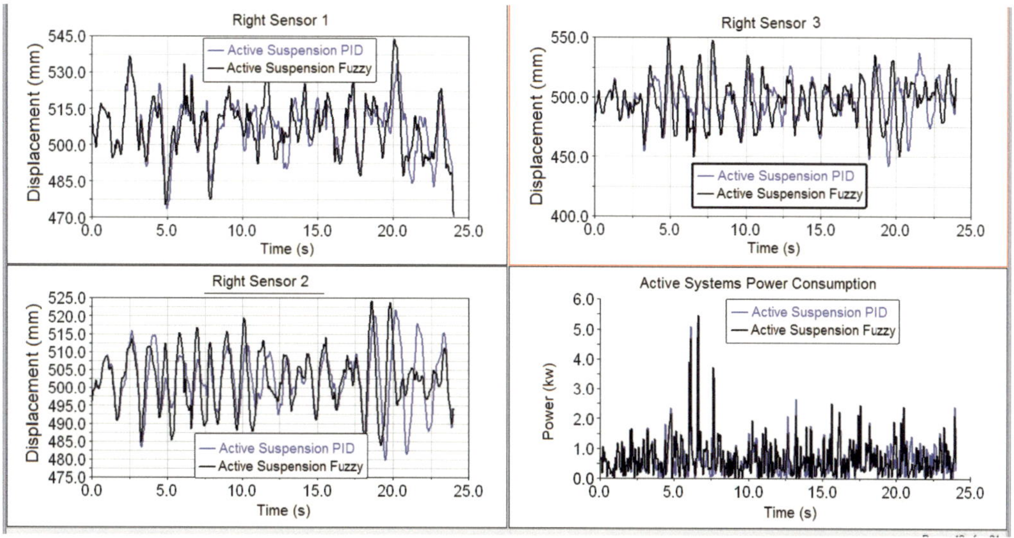

Fig. 2.36. Active suspension systems submitted to a rough track at 5 km/h.

Figure 2.37 shows the rough condition of pavement with equipment travel speed of 7.5 km/h. It also shows the boom displacement at the three sensor positions (1, 2 and 3).

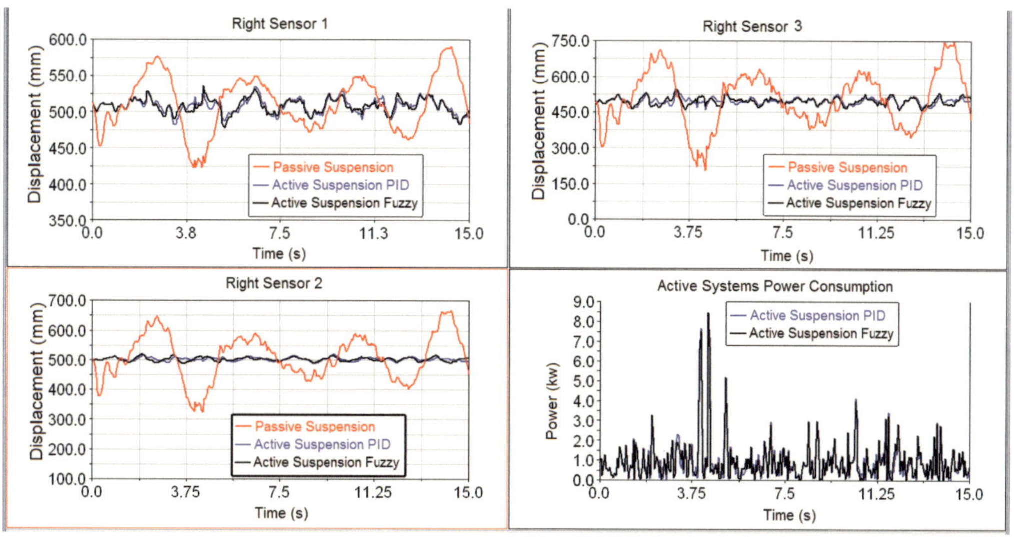

Fig. 2.37. Suspension systems submitted to a rough track at 7.5 km/h.

From the analysis of Figure 2.37 it is possible to note the efficiency of active control to keep constant the distance between the boom and the ground.

In Figure 2.38 it is possible to note the equivalence of both active control systems, i.e., there are no significant differences in maintaining the height of the boom from the ground.

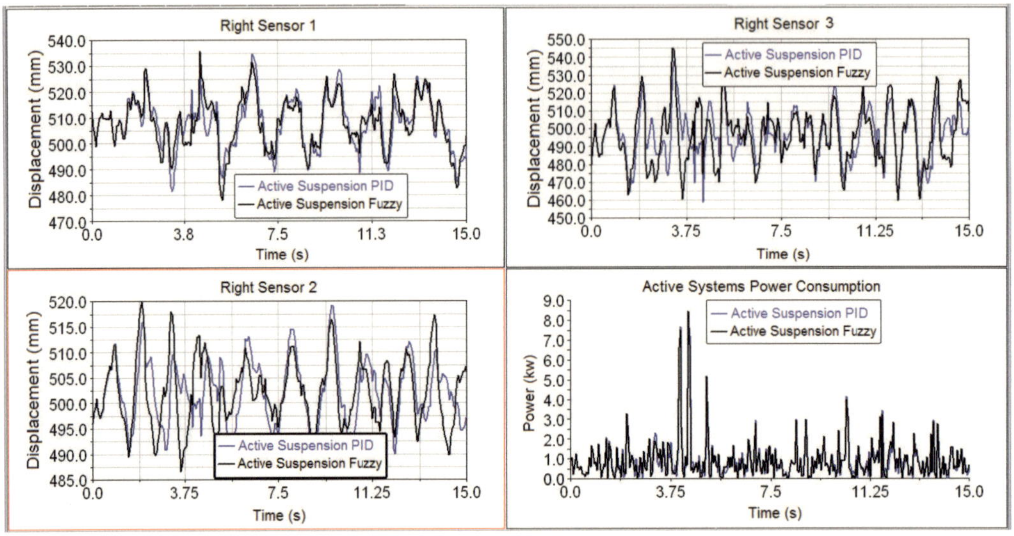

Fig. 2.38. Active suspension systems submitted to a rough track at 7.5 km/h.

Figure 2.39 shows the rough condition of pavement with equipment travel speed of 10 km/h. It also shows the boom displacement at the three sensor positions (1, 2 and 3).

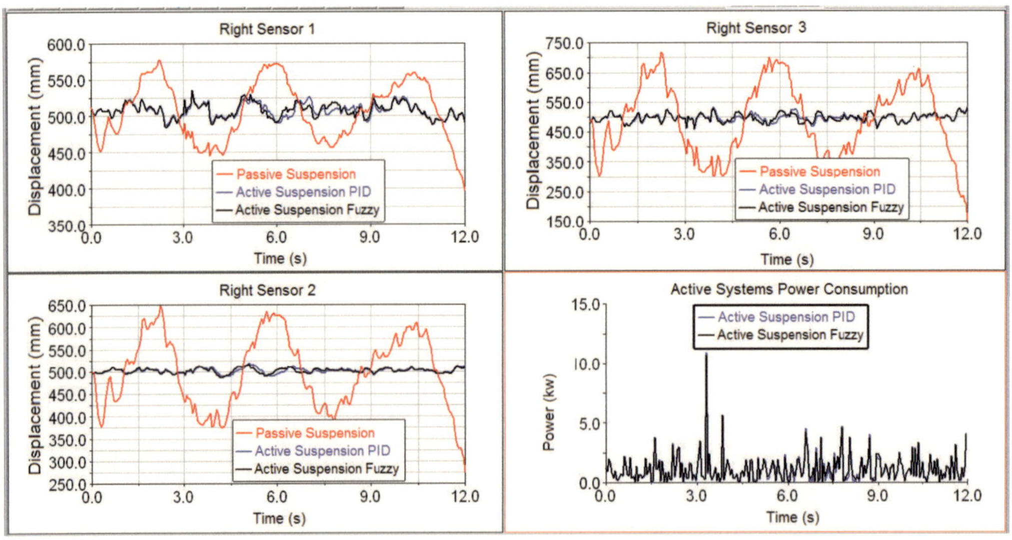

Fig. 2.39. Suspension systems submitted to rough track at 10 km/h.

From the analysis of Figure 2.39 it is possible to note the efficiency of active control to keep constant the distance between the boom and the ground.

In Figure 2.40 it is possible to note the equivalence of both active control systems, i.e., there are no significant differences in maintaining the height of the boom from the ground.

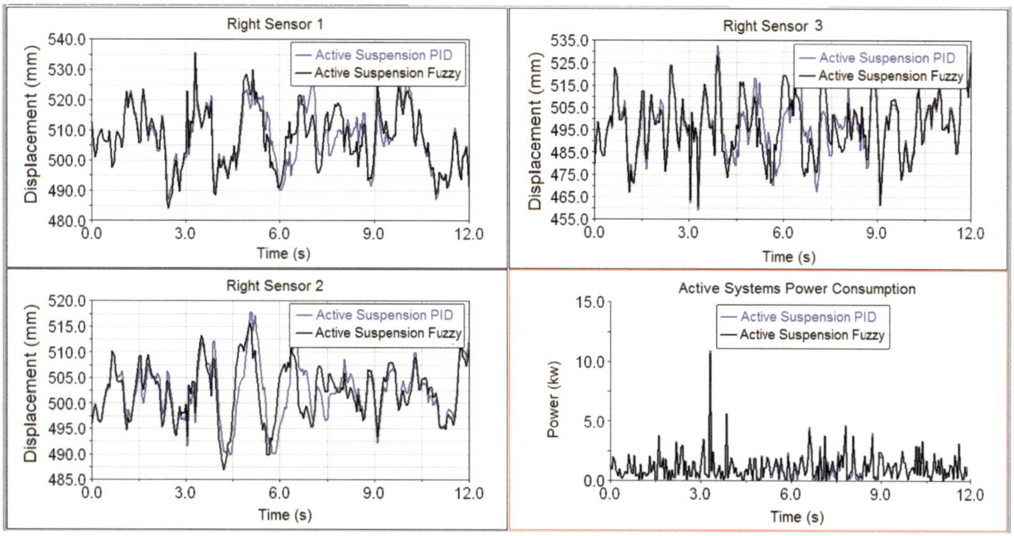

Fig. 2.40. Active suspension systems submitted to a rough track at 10 km/h.

3. Conclusion

We can conclude that independently of control strategy adopted, PID or Fuzzy control, the input signals are significantly attenuated if compared to a passive suspension.

The PID control strategy has a practical advantage of being more easily implemented than the Fuzzy control strategy in sprayer booms.

The power consumed by the active Fuzzy system was slightly lower than the PID controller, what presents no significant advantage in our practical design.

4. References

Musillami, S. (1977). Les mouvements des rampes de pulverization pour culture basses, a fixation classique, etudiés a travers les repartitions au banc a gouttieres. CNEEMA.

Sinfort, C.; Miralles, A.; Sevila, F.; Maniere, M. (1994). Study and development of a test method for spray boom suspensions. Journal of Agricultural Engineering Resource, 59, 245-252.

Pochi D; Vannucci D. (2002). A system with potentiometric transducers to record spray boom movements under operating conditions. Biosystems Engineering, 84(4), 393-406.

Miller, P.C.H. Mawer, C.J. (1989). Effect of roll angle and nozzle spray pattern on the uniformity of spray volume distribution below a boom. Crop Protection. Vol.8: 217-222.

Chaplin, J.; Wu,C.(1989). Dynamic modelling of field sprayers, Transactions of the ASAE 32 (1989) (6), pp. 1857-1863.

Sinfort, C.; Lardoux, Y.; Miralles, A.; Enf.alt, P.; Alness, K., Andersson, S. (1997). Comparison between measurements and predictions of spray pattern from a moving boom sprayer. Aspects Applied Biology, 48.

Herbst, A., and P. Wolf. (2001). Spray deposit distribution from agricultural boom sprayer in dynamic conditions. Paper Number: 011054, ASAE, St. Joseph. Mich.

Ramon, H. and J. De Baerdemaeker. (1997). Spray boom motions and spray distribution: part 1, derivation of a mathematical relation. Journal of Agricultural Engineering Research, 66(1): 23-29.

Pochi, D. and D. Vannucci. (2001). Laboratory evaluation and angular potentiometer for measuring spray boom movement. Journal of Agricultural Engineering Research. 80(2): 153-161.

Womac, A. R. R.; Etheridge, A.; Seibert, D.; Hogan, ; Ray, S. (2001). Sprayer speed and venturi-nozzle effects on broadcast application uniformity. Transactions of the ASAE, 44(6): 1437-1444.

Sinfort, C.; Herbst, A. (1996). Evaluation of the quality of spray distribution from boom sprayer in practical condition, Bulletin OEPP/EPPO (European and Mediterranean Plant Protection Organization) 26: 27-36.

Ramon, H., B. Missotten, and J. De Baerdemaeker. (1997). Spray boom motions and spray distribution: part 2, experimental validation of the mathematical relation and simulation results. Journal of Agricultural Engineering Research, 66(1): 31-39.

Speelman, L.; Jasen, J.W. (1979). The effect of spray-boom movement on the liquid distribution of field crop sprayers. Journal of Agricultural Engineering Resource, 19, 117-129.

Nation, H.J. (1980). The performance and stability of spray boom. Journal Agricultural Engineering Resource, 27(1), 61-70.

Iyer, A.M. and B.M.D. Wills. (1978). Factors determining the design of tractor-mounted sprayer boom–spray nozzle characteristics. Journal of Agricultural Engineering Research. 23(1): 37-43.

Langenakens Jan J; Clijmans L; Ramon H; De Baerdemaker J. (1999). The effects of vertical sprayer boom movements on the uniformity of spray distribution. Journal of Agricultural Engineering Research, 74, 281–291.

ASABE/ISO 5008. (2002). Agricultural wheeled tractors and field machinery - measurement of whole-body vibration of the operator.

5

S-Function Library for Bond Graph Modeling

B. Umesh Rai
Indian Institute of Science, Bangalore
India

1. Introduction

S-functions are short for system-functions. They are used for extending the capabilities of Simulink®. S-functions allows us to add our own algorithms to Simulink models. The process of creating S-function blocks is quite simple. Simulink provides a S-function API which can be used to write a S-function routine observing a set of laid down rules. The compiled routine is enclosed inside a Simulink block, which can be subsequently customised by masking. A library of customised S-function blocks are created for an application specific task. This library can be subsequently distributed to work in MATLAB® environment.

1.1 How is S-function useful?

S-function can also be described as a computer language description of the Simulink block. S-function is written in any one of the popular languages viz C, C++, Fortran or Ada besides MATLAB's own M programming language and compiled as MEX files, where MEX stands for *MATLAB Executable*. S-functions use a special calling syntax called the S-function API that interacts with the Simulink engine. This interaction is very similar to the interaction that takes place between the engine and built-in Simulink blocks.

In MATLAB S-functions, the S-function routines are implemented as MATLAB functions. In C MEX S-functions, they are implemented as C functions. All the S-function routines available to MATLAB S-functions exist for C MEX S-functions as well. However, Simulink provides a larger set of S-function routines for C MEX S-functions.

S-function routines can be written for continuous, discrete or hybrid systems. A set of S-function blocks created by us can be placed in a tool box or library and distributed for working in MATLAB environment. S-functions allow creation of customised blocks for Simulink. By following a set of rules, any block algorithms can be implemented in an S-function. It can also be deployed for using an existing C code into a simulation. After compiling the S-function, the run time file has to be placed in an S-function block. User interface can then be customised by using masking. An advantage of using S-functions is that a general purpose block can be built that can be used many times in a model, varying parameters with each instance of the block.

The most common usage of S-functions is for creating a set of custom Simulink blocks for an application. Existing C code in the application is easily encapsulated into S-function block and used as a separate Simulink block. This is used alongside the other blocks of Simulink.

If the system model has been already modeled as a set of mathematical equations, it becomes easy to convert each equation into a S-function block, and and develop the system model in Simulink.

1.2 Vectors in S-function

In a Simulink block, a vector of input, u, are processed by a vector of states, x to output a vector of output, y (Fig. 1) (Mathworks, 2011). The state vector may consist of continuous states, discrete states, or a combination of both.

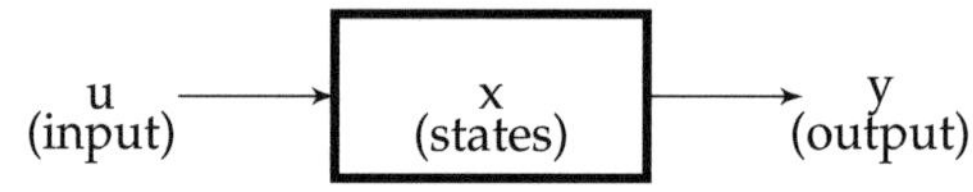

Fig. 1. Generalised Simulink block

In S-functions written in the MATLAB programming language, the MATLAB S-function, Simulink partitions the state vector into two spaces. The first part of the state vector is occupied by the continuous state, and the discrete states occupy the second part. But in the other programming language written S-function, MEX-file S-functions, there are two separate state vectors for the continuous and discrete states.

2. Steps in simulation

Routines have to be written in S-function to carry out the simulation steps required by the Simulink engine. To cross-reference the routine required for the simulation step, two different approaches are used. For an MATLAB S-function, Simulink passes a flag parameter to the S-function. The flag indicates the current simulation stage. Routines in M-code calls the appropriate functions for each flag value. For a C MEX S-function, Simulink calls the S-function routines directly. This is done by following a naming convention for the routines.

2.1 Steps in S-function block simulation

Simulink engine first calls the S-function Routine to perform initialisation of all S-functions block in the model. Later, the engine makes repeated calls during simulation loop to each S-function block in the model, directing it to perform tasks such as computing its outputs, updating its discrete states, or computing its derivatives. Finally, the engine invokes a call to each S-function Routine for a termination task (Fig. 2). The tasks required at various stages, include:

- Initialization: Simulink initializes the S-function as a first step. The tasks are:
  - Initialising the SimStruct, a structure that contains information about the S-function.
  - Setting the number and size of input and output ports.
  - Setting the block sample times.
  - And allocating storage areas and the sizes array.
- Calculation of next sample hit - for a variable step integration routine, this stage calculates the time of the next variable hit, that is, it calculates the next stepsize in the variable step.
- Calculation of outputs in the major time step. After this call is complete, all the output ports of the blocks are valid for the current time step.

- Update discrete states in the major time step. In this call, all blocks should perform once-per-time-step activities such as updating discrete states for next time around the simulation loop.
- Integration: This applies to models with continuous states and/or nonsampled zero crossings. If S-function has continuous states, Simulink calculates the derivative of the continuous state at minor time steps. Simulink computes the states for S-function. If S-function (C MEX only) has nonsampled zero crossings, then Simulink will call the output and zero crossings portion of S-function at minor time steps, so that it can locate the zero crossings.

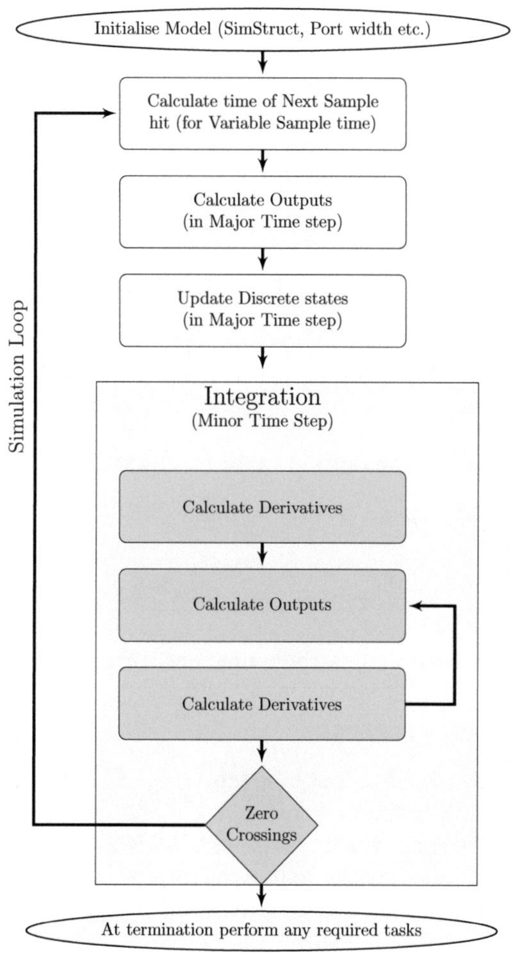

Fig. 2. S-function simulation cycle

2.2 Flags in MATLAB S-function

An MATLAB file that defines an S-Function block must provide information about the model. Simulink needs this information during simulation. The MATLAB S-function has to be of the following form:

$$[sys, x0, str, ts] = f(t, x, u, flag, p1, p2, ...)$$

where f is the name of the S-function. Simulink passes t, the current time, x, state vector, u, input vector, integer flag in argument to S-function. In an MATLAB S-function flags are used for indicating the current simulation stage. S-function code calls the appropriate functions for each flag value. Table 1 lists the simulation stages, the corresponding S-function routines, and the associated flag value for MATLAB S-functions.

Simulation Stage	S-Function	Routine Flag
Initialization	mdlInitializeSizes	flag = 0
Calculation of derivatives of continous state variables	mdlDerivatives	flag = 1
Update discrete states, sample times	mdlUpdate	flag = 2
Calculation of outputs	mdlOutputs	flag = 3
Calculation of next sample hit (Only when discrete-time sample time specified)	mdlGetTimeOfNextVarHit	flag = 4
End of simulation tasks	mdlTerminate	flag = 9

Table 1. M-File flags

An MATLAB S-function returns an output vector having the following elements:

- sys - the values returned depend on the flag value (for flag = 3, sys contains the S-function outputs).
- x0 - the initial state values at flag = 0 (otherwise ignored).
- str - reserved for future use.
- ts - two-column matrix containing sample time and offset.

2.3 C MEX S-function callback methods

As with MATLAB S-functions, Simulink interacts with a C MEX-file S-function by invoking callback methods that the S-function implements. C MEX-file S-functions have the same structure and perform the same functions as MATLAB S-functions. In addition, C MEX S-functions provide more functionality than MATLAB S-functions. C MEX-files can access and modify the data structure that Simulink uses internally to store information about the S-function. This gives it an ability to handle matrix signals and multiple data types.

C MEX-file that defines an S-Function block provides information about the model to Simulink during the simulation. Unlike MATLAB S-functions, no explicit flag parameter is associated with C MEX S-function routine. But the routines have to follow the naming convention. Simulink then automatically calls each S-function routine at the appropriate time during its interaction with the S-function. It defines specific tasks which include defining initial conditions and block characteristics, and computing derivatives, discrete states, and outputs.

Simulink defines in a general way the task of each callback and their sequence (Fig.3) (Mathworks, 2011). The green box in Fig.3 are the compulsorily present routines and the blue box are the optional routines. The S-function is free to perform any task according to the functionality it implements. For example, Simulink specifies that the S-function's mdlOutput method must compute that block's outputs at the current simulation time. It does not specify what those outputs must be. The callback-based API allows to create S-functions, and hence custom blocks, of any desired functionality. The contents of the routines can be as complex and any logic can reside in the S-function routines as long as the routines conform to their required formats.

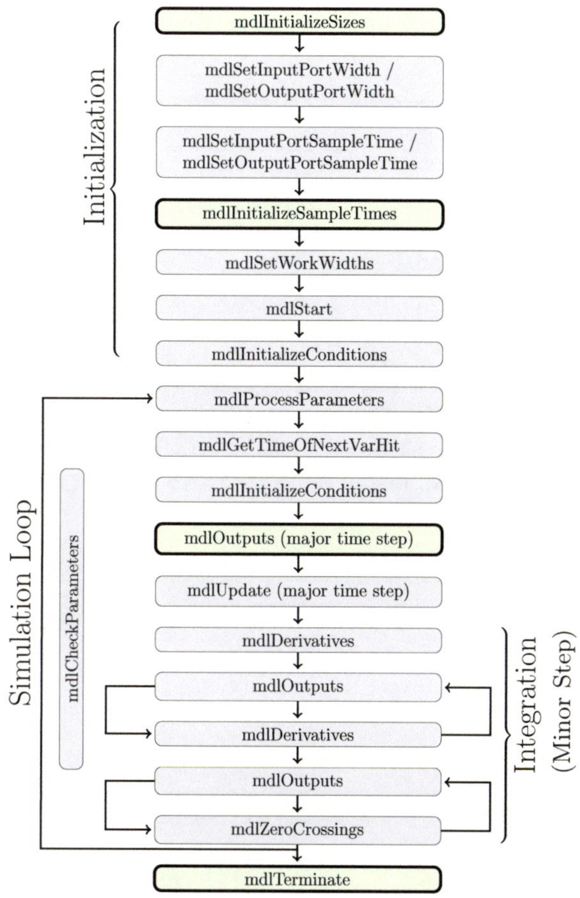

Fig. 3. Calling sequence of C MEX S-function Blocks

2.4 MEX versus MATLAB S-functions

Both the approaches of MATLAB and MEX S-functions development have some inherent advantages due to their origin in the programming language they are coded in. The advantage of MATLAB S-functions is speed of its development. Developing MATLAB S-functions avoids the time consuming compile-link-execute cycle required when developing in a compiled language like C. MATLAB S-functions also have easier access to MATLAB toolbox functions and can utilize the MATLAB Editor/Debugger. MEX S-functions are more appropriate for integrating legacy code into a Simulink model. For more complicated systems, MEX S-functions may simulate faster than MATLAB S-functions because the MATLAB S-function has to call the MATLAB interpreter for every callback routine.

3. S-function examples

The ease of writing an S-function is demonstrated here by taking a simple example. Both MATLAB file and C Mex approaches will be demonstrated. A block '*timestwo*' is implemented in S-function. This simple block has no states. Functionally, the block takes an input scalar signal, doubles it and outputs to a connected device (Fig.4).

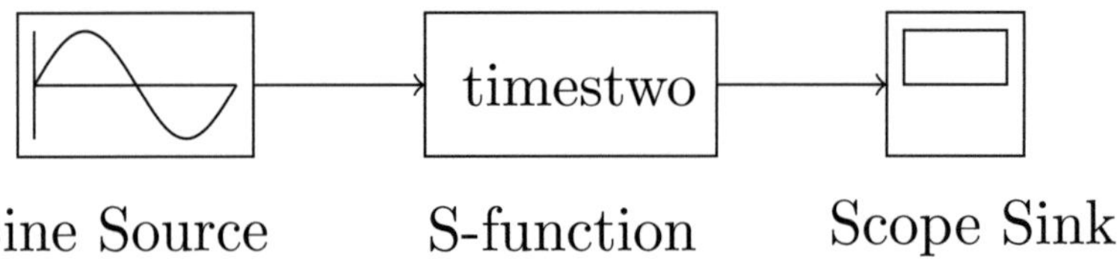

Fig. 4. timestwo S-function in model

3.1 MATLAB S-function implementation of timestwo

The S-function will be defined with four input arguments from Simulink. They are, the current time *t*, state *x*, input *u*, and flag *flag*. The output vector contains the variable listed in Sec.2.2. For the simple example chosen, two routines will be sufficient. A routine for initialisation and another for calculating the output. Below is the MATLAB code for the *timestwo.m* S-function:

```
function [sys,x0,str,ts] = timestwo(t,x,u,flag)

 % Dispatch the flag. The switch function controls the calls to
  % S-function routines at each simulation stage.
  switch flag,

    % Initialization
    case 0
       [sys,x0,str,ts] = mdlInitializeSizes;

    % Calculate outputs
    case 3
       sys = mdlOutputs(t,x,u);

    % Unused flags
    case { 1, 2, 4, 9 }
       sys = [];

    % Error handling
    otherwise
```

```
        error(['Unhandled flag = ',num2str(flag)]);

    end;
% End of function timestwo.
```

The routines that are called by *timestwo.m* are *mdlInitializeSizes* and *mdlOutputs*. The routine *mdlInitializeSizes* passes on the block information to the *size* structure. The information on number of outputs, inputs, continuous and discrete states, sample times and whether direct feed through is present, is passed on to the structure variable. The output variables, *x0*, *str* and ts are also set to the desired values. The second routine *mdlOutputs* just doubles the input scalar.

```
%===============================================================
% Function mdlInitializeSizes initializes the states, sample
% times, state ordering strings (str), and sizes structure.
%===============================================================

function [sys,x0,str,ts] = mdlInitializeSizes

% Call function simsizes to create the sizes structure.
sizes = simsizes;

% Load the sizes structure with the initialization information.
sizes.NumContStates= 0;
sizes.NumDiscStates= 0;
sizes.NumOutputs=1;
sizes.NumInputs=1;
sizes.DirFeedthrough=1;
sizes.NumSampleTimes=1;

% Load the sys vector with the sizes information.
sys = simsizes(sizes);

%
x0 = []; % No continuous states
%
str = []; % No state ordering
%
ts = [-1 0]; % Inherited sample time

% End of mdlInitializeSizes.



%===============================================================
% Function mdlOutputs performs the calculations.
```

```
%==============================================================
function sys = mdlOutputs(t,x,u)

sys = 2*u;

% End of mdlOutputs.
```

The timestwo MATLAB S-function can now be used in the Simulink model, by first dragging an S-Function block from the User-Defined Functions block library into the model. Then entering the name *timestwo* in the S-function name field of the S-Function block's Block Parameters dialog box (Fig. 5).

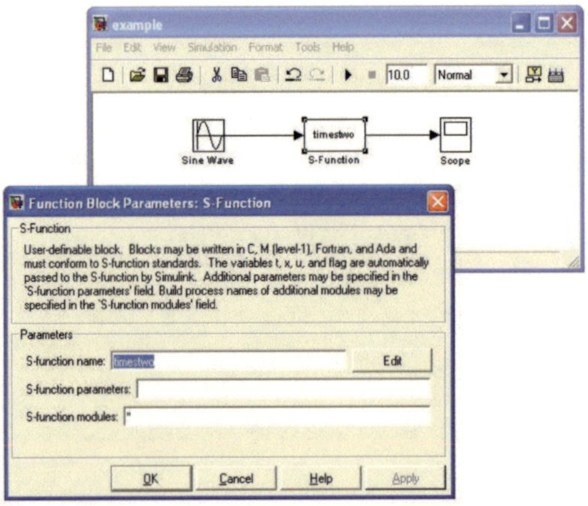

Fig. 5. timestwo S-function in Simulink model file

3.2 C MEX S-function implementation of timestwo

C MEX S-function will contain the callback methods mdlInitializeSizes, mdlInitializeSampleTimes, mdlOutputs and mdlTerminate. The simulation steps will have setting of intial condition by the first two blocks, the simulation loop in the third block and final termination by the last block (Fig.6). The code is reproduced below:

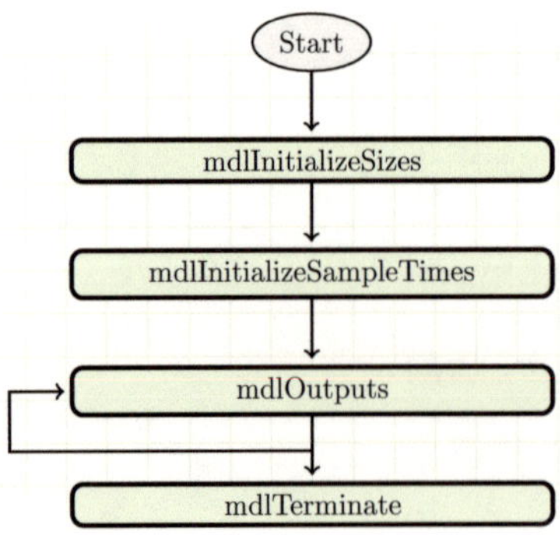

Fig. 6. C MEX S-function timestwo Blocks

```
#define S_FUNCTION_NAME timestwo /* Defines and Includes */
#define S_FUNCTION_LEVEL 2

#include "simstruc.h"

static void mdlInitializeSizes(SimStruct *S) {
  ssSetNumSFcnParams(S, 0);
  if (ssGetNumSFcnParams(S) != ssGetSFcnParamsCount(S)) {
    return; /* Parameter mismatch reported by the Simulink engine*/
  }
  if (!ssSetNumInputPorts(S, 1)) return;
  ssSetInputPortWidth(S, 0, DYNAMICALLY_SIZED);
  ssSetInputPortDirectFeedThrough(S, 0, 1);
  if (!ssSetNumOutputPorts(S,1)) return;
  ssSetOutputPortWidth(S, 0, DYNAMICALLY_SIZED);
  ssSetNumSampleTimes(S, 1);
  ssSetOptions(S, SS_OPTION_EXCEPTION_FREE_CODE);
}

static void mdlInitializeSampleTimes(SimStruct *S) {
  ssSetSampleTime(S, 0, INHERITED_SAMPLE_TIME);
  ssSetOffsetTime(S, 0, 0.0);
}

static void mdlOutputs(SimStruct *S, int_T tid) {
  int_T i;
  InputRealPtrsType uPtrs = ssGetInputPortRealSignalPtrs(S,0);
  real_T *y = ssGetOutputPortRealSignal(S,0);
  int_T width = ssGetOutputPortWidth(S,0);
  for (i=0; i<width; i++) {
    *y++ = 2.0 *(*uPtrs[i]);
  }
}

static void mdlTerminate(SimStruct *S){}

#ifdef MATLAB_MEX_FILE/*Is this file being compiled as a MEX-file?*/
#include "simulink.c" /* MEX-file interface mechanism */
#else
#include "cg_sfun.h" /* Code generation registration function */
#endif
```

3.3 Explanation of C MEX timestwo code

We start by two define statements, and give the name to our S-function and tell the Simulink engine that the code is written in Level 2 format. Later we include the header file *simstruc.h,* which is a header file that defines a data structure, called the SimStruct, that the Simulink engine uses to maintain information about the S-function. A more complex S-function will include more header files.

The callback routine *mdlInitializeSizes* tells the Simulink engine that the function has no parameters, has one input and output port. It also declares that only one sample time will be specified later in *mdlInitializeSampleTimes*. Simulink is also informed that the code is exception free code. This declaration speeds up the execution time. The next callback routine *mdlInitializeSampleTimes* declares the sample time to be inherited i.e the block executes whenever the driving block executes.

The callback routine *mdlOutputs* calculates outputs at each time step. The input and output port signals is accessed through a vector of pointers. The width of the output port which is defined to be dynamically set is then read and the program loops for the width while calculating the output signal to be two times the input signal. The final callback mandatory routine *mdlTerminate* performs the end of the simulation task, which in the present case is a *NIL* set. following this routine the mandatory trailer code for compiler is present. Its absence will lead to compile errors.

The C MEX S-function has to be now compiled. Simulink gives a choice of C compiler to be used. We can use either the built in MEX compiler or any other C compiler already loaded in the system. The following command at the command line

```
mex -setup
```

allows us to locate all the compilers available in the system and the option to use one for compiling and linking in the MATLAB environment. Later the command

```
mex timestwo.c
```

compiles and links the timestwo.c file to create a dynamically loadable executable for the Simulink software to use. The resulting executable is referred to as a MEX S-function. The MEX file extension varies from platform to platform. For example, on a 32-bit Microsoft Windows system, the MEX file extension is .mexw32. The compiled run time file is then put into the S-function block similer to MATLAB S-function file (Fig. 5).

4. Bond graph modeling

4.1 Analogous behaviour of physical systems

The bond graph approach to physical system modeling was conceptualized by Hank Paynter on April 24, 1959 (Paynter & Briggs, 1961), inspired by the earlier work of Gabriel Kron (Kron, 1962). Bond graph language is a port based graphical approach for modeling energy exchange between subsystems. This technique was further developed by Karnopp and Rosenberg (Karnopp et al., 1990; 2006; Karnopp & Rosenberg, 1968; Rosenberg & Karnopp, 1983). Several books, special issues and articles on bond graph technique have popularised it for growing usage (Borutzky, 2009; Borutzky et al., 2004; Breedveld, 1984; 1991; 2004; Breedveld et al., 1991; Cellier et al., 1995; Dauphin-Tanguy, 2000; Gawthrop, 1995; Gawthrop & Smith, 1996; Mukherjee & Karmakar, 2000; Thoma, 1990; Thoma & Perelson, 1976).

Energy domain	f flow	e effort	q Generalised momentum	p Generalised displacement
Electromagnetic	i, [A] current	v, [V] voltage	q, [C] charge	λ, [V-s] linked flux
Mechanical translation	V, [m/s] Velocity	F, [N] Force	x, [m] Displacement	p, [N-s] Momentum
Angular translation	ω, [rad/s] Velocity	T, [N m] Torque	θ, [rad] Angle	p_ω, [N-m-s] Momentum
Hydraulic	φ, [m^3/s] Volume flow	P, [N/m^2] Pressure	V, [m^3] Volume	Γ, [N-s/m^2] Momentum of flow tube
Thermal	T, [K] Temperature	F_S, [J/K/s] Entopy flow	S, [J/K] Entropy	
Chemical	μ, [mol/s] Molar flow	F_N, [J/mol] Chemical potential		N, [mol] Number of moles

Table 2. Flow and effort variables in different domains

Behaviour of a physical system is constrained, either implicitly or explicitly by laws of physics viz. mass and energy conservation, laws of momentum and positive entropy production. Furthermore, various physical domains are each characterized by a particular quantity that is conserved. Each of these domains have analogous ideal behaviour with respect to energy (Table 2). This analogy led to the concept of energy port, the building block of bond graph modeling language. Here, the interaction between physical systems is through energy port and is always bidirectional. There will be an input signal and a consequent output signal (*'back effect'*) and their product will signify the *'power that is transacted'*. From a computational point of view, the effort could be computed by 'Port 1', while the flow is computed in 'Port 2'. It could be the other way around as well. Apriori the computational direction of signal is not known, except the fact that they are in opposite direction (Fig.7).

4.2 Bond graph elements

Bond graphs are labelled, directed graphs. The vertices of a bond graph denote subsystems, system components or elements, while the edges, called power bonds or bonds for short, represent energy flows between them. The nodes of a bond graph have power ports where energy can enter or exit. As energy can flow back and forth between power ports of different nodes, a half arrow is added to each bond indicating a reference direction of the energy flow. The amount of power, *P(t)*, at each given time, *t*, is given by the product of the two conjugate variables, which are called effort, *e*, and flow, *f*, respectively.

$$P(t) = e(t) \cdot f(t) \tag{1}$$

There can be five groups of physical behaviour by elements handling energy:

1. **Storing** of energy.
2. **Supply** on demand.

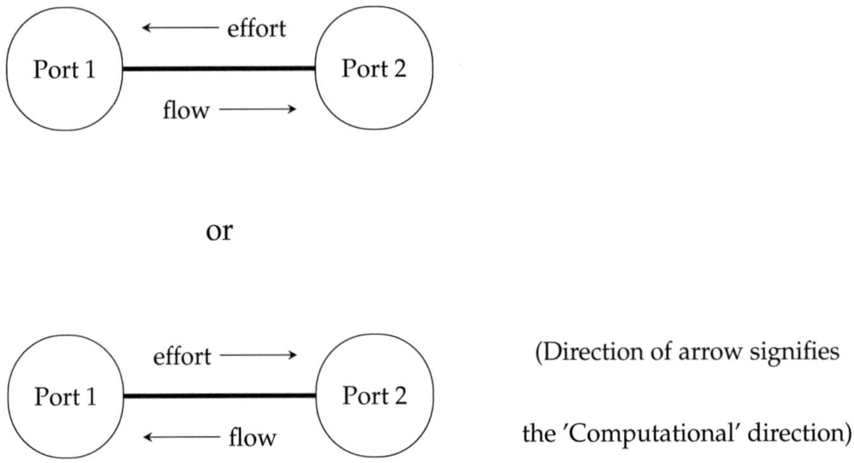

Fig. 7. Computational direction of flow and effort between ports

3. **Reversible** transformation (including inter-domain transfers).
4. **Irreversible** transformation (positive entropy production).
5. **Distribution** to connected ports.

These five behaviour are represented by nine basic elements.

- Two types of *storage* elements, effort or *Capacitive*- storage and flow or *Inductive* - storage.
- Two types of *sources*, *Source - effort* and *Source - flow*.
- Two types of Reversible transformators, non-mixing, reciprocal *Transformer* or **TF**-type transducer and mixing anti- reciprocal *Gyrator* or **GY**-type transducer.
- Irreversible transducer is an energy *Dissipater* or can be also classified as entropy producing **R**-type transducer.
- Distributor junction are also in dual form, **0**-junction and **1**-junction. The 0-junction represents a generalised domain independent Kirchoff current law and similarly a 1-junction represents a generalised domain independent Kirchoff voltage law.

The elements can also be segregated based on their port structure:

- Five one-port elements: $C, L(orI), R, S_e, S_f$.
- Two two-port elements: *TF, GY*.
- Two n-port junctions: *0-junction, 1-junction*.

4.3 Constitutive relations

A constitutive relation with a constant parameter characterises each element. For sources, the imposed variable is independent of the conjugate variable, and for the rest of elements, the relationship is algebraic between its conjugate variables. The storage elements are classified as *memory* elements. The preferred constitutive equation is integration with respect to time.

If differentiation with respect to time is used, the information on initial condition or *history* is lost. If sensors are included in the bond graph modeling and used for determining the factor of the algebraic relationship between the conjugate variable, we rename the bond as *modulated* bond with prefix M for the modulated element name.

Element	Effort causal	Flow causal
Resistor, R	$\xrightarrow[f]{e}\mid R:R$ $f=\frac{e}{R}$	$\mid\xrightarrow[f]{e} R:R$ $e=f\cdot R$
Capacitor, C	$\xrightarrow[f]{e}\mid C:C$ $f=C\frac{de}{dt}$	$\mid\xrightarrow[f]{e} C:C$ $e=\int\frac{f}{C}\cdot dt$
Inductor, I	$\xrightarrow[f]{e}\mid I:L$ $f=\int\frac{e}{L}\cdot dt$	$\mid\xrightarrow[f]{e} I:L$ $e=L\frac{df}{dt}$
Source, $S_{e/f}$	$S_e:V\xrightarrow{e}\mid$ $e=V$	$S_f:I\mid\xrightarrow[f]{}$ $f=I$

Table 3. One-port elements

Element	Effort causal	Flow causal
Transformer, TF modulating parameter = M	$\xrightarrow[f_1]{e_1}\mid \overset{M}{TF} \xrightarrow[f_2]{e_2}\mid$ $e_2=M\cdot e_1;\ f_1=M\cdot f_2$	$\mid\xrightarrow[f_1]{e_1} \overset{M}{TF}\mid\xrightarrow[f_2]{e_2}$ $e_1=\frac{e_2}{M};\ f_2=\frac{f_1}{M}$
Gyrator, GY modulating parameter = M	$\xrightarrow[f_1]{e_1}\mid \overset{M}{GY}\mid\xrightarrow[f_2]{e_2}$ $f_1=\frac{e_2}{M};\ f_2=\frac{e_1}{M}$	$\mid\xrightarrow[f_1]{e_1} \overset{M}{GY}\xrightarrow[f_2]{e_2}\mid$ $e_1=M\cdot f_2;\ e_2=M\cdot f_1$

Table 4. Two-port elements

5. Computational causality

Each bond connects two power ports of different primitive elements and carries two power variables as can be seen in Fig.7. One of the two power variables may be determined by one of the two sub-models, while the other is determined by the other model. A short stroke, called *causal stroke*, perpendicular to the bond is placed at one of its ends of the bond. This indicates the computational direction of the effort variable. Consequently the other *open* end is the decider of the flow variable. The nine basic elements with their constitutive relationships that are dependent on their causal stroke are shown in Table 3,4 and 5

Element	Symbol	Governing Law
0-junction	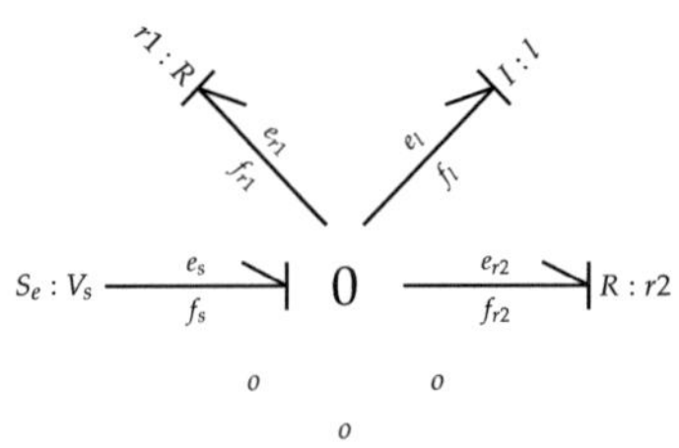	*Effort Law* General equation $\sum_{i=1}^{m} f_i = 0$ and $e_1 = e_2 = e_3 = ... = e_m$ For bond graph model at left $f_s - f_{r1} - f_l - f_{r2} - ... = 0$ and $e_l = e_{r1} = e_{r2} = ... = e_s$ The element having causal bar toward the junction decides the effort for all bonds associated with the junction.
1-junction	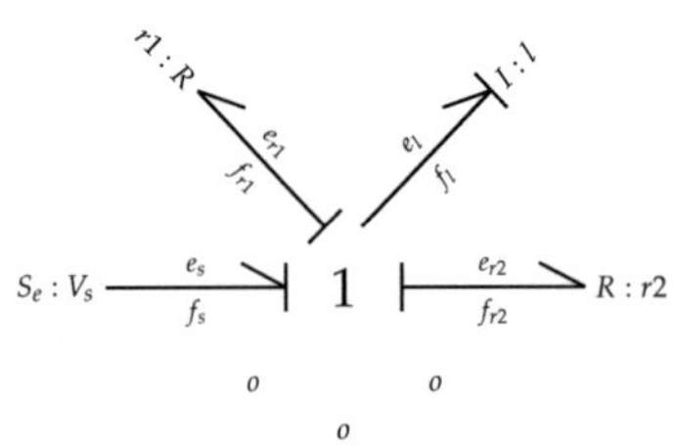	*Flow Law* General equation $\sum_{i=1}^{m} e_i = 0$ and $f_1 = f_2 = f_3 = ... = f_m$ For bond graph model at left $V_s - e_{r1} - e_l - e_{r2} - ... = 0$ and $f_s = f_{r1} = f_{r2} = ... = f_l$ The element having causal bar away from the junction decides the flow for all bonds associated with the junction.

Table 5. Junction elements

5.1 S-function implementation for C bond

We will now use the C MEX S-function code to develop a continuous state Simulink block. An One-port element which stores energy is chosen for illustration. Effort causal Capacitor C element in Table 3 is one such element. The code, which is an extension of code at Sec. 3.2 (added routines for continuous state) is given below:

```
#define S_FUNCTION_NAME  C_complex_bond
#define S_FUNCTION_LEVEL 2

#define NUM_INPUTS           1 /* Input Port  0 */
#define IN_PORT_0_NAME       u0
#define INPUT_0_WIDTH        DYNAMICALLY_SIZED
#define INPUT_0_FEEDTHROUGH 0

#define NUM_OUTPUTS          1 /* Output Port  0 */
#define OUT_PORT_0_NAME      y0
#define OUTPUT_0_WIDTH       DYNAMICALLY_SIZED

#define NPARAMS              2 /* Parameter  Capacitance */
#define PARAMETER_0_NAME     C /* Capacitance Value*/
#define PARAMETER_1_NAME     bias /* Initial Charge */
```

```
#define SAMPLE_TIME_0       CONTINUOUS_SAMPLE_TIME
#define NUM_CONT_STATES     2
#define CONT_STATES_IC      [0]

#include "simstruc.h"

#define PARAM_DEF0(S) ssGetSFcnParam(S, 0)
#define PARAM_DEF1(S) ssGetSFcnParam(S, 1)

static void mdlInitializeSizes(SimStruct *S) {
    ssSetNumSFcnParams(S, NPARAMS);

    if (ssGetNumSFcnParams(S) != ssGetSFcnParamsCount(S)) {
        return; /* Parameter mismatch will be reported by Simulink */
    }
    ssSetNumContStates(S, NUM_CONT_STATES);

    if (!ssSetNumInputPorts(S, NUM_INPUTS)) return;
    ssSetInputPortWidth( S, 0, INPUT_0_WIDTH);
    ssSetInputPortComplexSignal( S, 0, COMPLEX_INHERITED);
    ssSetInputPortDirectFeedThrough(S, 0, INPUT_0_FEEDTHROUGH);
    ssSetInputPortRequiredContiguous(S, 0, 1); /*direct input signal
    access*/

    if (!ssSetNumOutputPorts(S,NUM_OUTPUTS)) return;
    ssSetOutputPortWidth(S, 0, OUTPUT_0_WIDTH);
    ssSetOutputPortComplexSignal(S, 0, COMPLEX_INHERITED);

    ssSetNumSampleTimes(S, 1);
}

static void mdlInitializeSampleTimes(SimStruct *S) {
    ssSetSampleTime(S, 0, SAMPLE_TIME_0);
    ssSetOffsetTime(S, 0, 0.0);
}

static void mdlInitializeConditions(SimStruct *S) {
   real_T *xC    = ssGetContStates(S);

    xC[0] =  0;
    xC[1] =  0;
}

static void mdlOutputs(SimStruct *S, int_T tid) {
    boolean_T   yIsComplex = ssGetOutputPortComplexSignal(S, 0) ==
    COMPLEX_YES;
```

```
    real_T            *y0    = ssGetOutputPortRealSignal(S,0);
    const real_T      *xC    = ssGetContStates(S);
    const real_T      *C     = mxGetData(PARAM_DEF0(S));
    const real_T      *B     = mxGetData(PARAM_DEF1(S));

    y0[0] = *B + xC[0] / (*C);
    if(yIsComplex){ /* Process imag part */
         y0[1] = *B + xC[1] / (*C);
    }
}

static void mdlDerivatives(SimStruct *S) {
    const real_T    *u0   = (const real_T*) ssGetInputPortSignal(S,0);
    real_T          *dx   = ssGetdX(S);

    dx[0]=u0[0] ;
    dx[1]=u0[1] ;
}

static void mdlTerminate(SimStruct *S) {}/* mdlTerminate */

#ifdef MATLAB_MEX_FILE
#include "simulink.c"
#else
#include "cg_sfun.h"
#endif
```

6. Junction algorithm

In a bond graph model a set of elements is connected at the junction. One of the elements in the set takes up the role of *decider* bond. Remaining bonds in the set *per-se* take up the role of *non-decider* bonds. The junction algorithm is illustrated by taking O-junction as an example. The 0-junction block is a common effort junction (Fig.8). The effort is decided by a decider bond attached to it and having the causal bar towards the junction. Similarly for a 1-junction, decider bond will have its causal bar away from the junction, thus complementing the 0-junction behaviour. In the figure, J_{in}'s are the input from the non-decider bonds into the junction, and J_{sum} is the output of the junction.

The governing law of the 0-junction, *Effort Law (or KCL)*, states that the flow of the decider bond is the sum of the flows of all the non-decider bonds. In Fig.8, the decider bond of the junction has J_{sum}, the sum of all J_{in}, as its causal (flow) variable. Value of the conjugate variable (effort) of the decider bond, J_{out} is decided by the bond's constitutive equation. The second part he governing law of the 0-junction, states that the all the bonds connected to the junction share a common effort. Thus the effort of the decider bond becomes the causal variable for all the non-decider bonds. For each non-decider bond, its non-causal variable

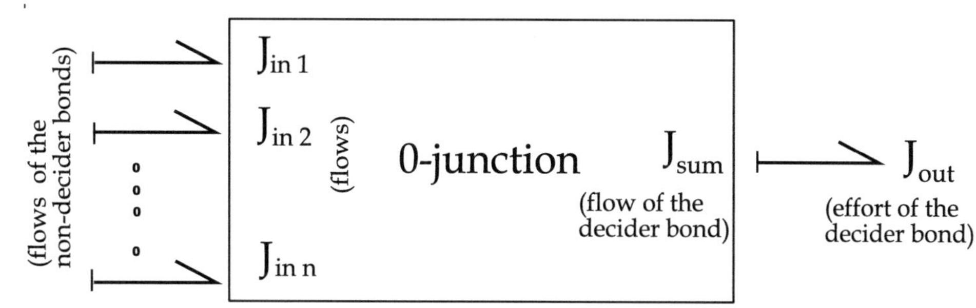

Fig. 8. 0-junction

flow into the junction as individual J_{in}. This completes the cycle for junction. Table 6 tabulates the algorithm for one-port elements.

Element	Decider		Non-decider	
	Causal	Non-causal	Causal	Non-causal
	⇀		⇀	
R,C,L	J_{sum}	J_{out}	J_{out}	J_{in}
S_e, S_f		J_{out}		J_{in}

Table 6. One-port element variables

It can be seen that for an element connected to a junction, the causal variable can take either of the two values, J_{sum} or J_{out}, depending on whether the connection bond is a decider or a non-decider, respectively. Similarly the non-causal variable can have either the value of J_{out} or J_{in}, again depending on whether the connection bond is a decider or a non-decider.

A two-port is connected to two junctions at either end. These junction could be either 0-junction or 1-junction. But as a two-port element allows only two combinations of causality out of available four, there will be only 2×2 alternatives for a variable. Looking at the two-port junction in Fig.9, if the element is decider bond for junction J_1, and the junction is 0-junction, then the flow at input port will be J_{1sum}. And if junction is a 1-junction the effort will be J_{1sum}. Similarly for the output junction connected to J_2. Note that the direction of two-port half arrows is reversed in the two junctions. Thus if two-port element with flow causal at input port is decider bond for the first junction, the junction has to necessarily be an 0-junction, but flow casual at output port as decider bond indicates a 1-junction. The modulus of the two-port element decides the value of the variable on the conjugate port, while the junction decides the conjugate variable value of the port. In a similar manner for all combination of causality and decider bond, the variables can be listed out. The algorithm is summarised in Table 7 (Umarikar et al., 2006).

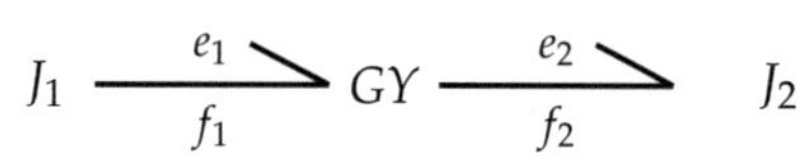

Fig. 9. Algorthim for 2 port element

Port	Input Port				Output Port			
	$J_1 \xrightarrow[f_1]{e_1} TF$				$\xrightarrow[f_2]{e_2} J_2$			
	Decider		Non-decider		Decider		Non-decider	
	e_1	f_1	e_1	f_1	e_2	f_2	e_2	f_2
TF (flow causality)	J_{1out}	J_{1sum}	J_{1in}	J_{1out}	J_{2sum}	J_{2out}	J_{2out}	J_{2in}
TF (effort causality)	J_{1sum}	J_{1out}	J_{1out}	J_{1in}	J_{2out}	J_{2sum}	J_{2in}	J_{2out}
	$J_1 \xrightarrow[f_1]{e_1} GY$				$\xrightarrow[f_2]{e_2} J_2$			
GY (flow causality)	J_{1out}	J_{1sum}	J_{1in}	J_{1out}	J_{2out}	J_{2sum}	J_{2in}	J_{2out}
GY (effort causality)	J_{1sum}	J_{1out}	J_{1out}	J_{1in}	J_{2sum}	J_{2out}	J_{2out}	J_{2in}

Table 7. two-port element variables

7. Linking elements

A bond graph model on paper does not explicitly use a connector as in block diagram model, to link one element to another element. To retain the look and feel of a paper model when transferred to computer terminal, the connection between the elements has to be invisible. The masking properties of the Simulink block is utilised for this purpose in the tool box. A junction is considered as a node, to which the elements are connected. The bond graph element, as in paper model, is placed next to its associated junction. The link to the junction is made by entering the junction label in the mask parameter box. *Shared Memory'* algorithm is then used to implicitly connect the element.

In bond graph modeling two or more elements will be linked to a junction. Their data have to be shared. Shared data structure is used in the toolbox. The memory locations are earmarked for a junction by assigning it a unique label by *character aggregation'* during its first run. An S-function's initialisation callback method is used for memory allocation as this callback is used only once during the simulation run. The associated elements using the notation listed out in Table 6 and Table 7, share their respective memory address, thereby their data.

The elements in the tool box are masked and have screen interfaces. For a one-port element the following details need to be entered.

1. Name of the element.
2. Parametric value.
3. Whether decider bond or not.
4. Associated junction name.

For a two-port element the extra information of the second port is also entered. Similarly a junction screen interface will have all entries of the elements that are linked to it, along with their energy flow direction signs.

7.1 Propagation of data

The propagation of data from one element to the next is by reading and writing into a common block address (Fig.10). The input element, designated as *Provider*, produces the data through its constitutive equation and writes it on to the labelled memory address. The label, as discussed earlier is unique to a junction. The next element in hierarchy, designated as *Consumer*, in turn reads the data and by using its constitutive equations, *Produces* the next set of data which is written on to the next labelled memory address. There can be many *Consumer* of the data but there is only one unique *Provider*. An analogy to bond graph junction concept of one decider and many non-decider can be clearly seen here. It is also seen that a *Consumer* element of previous step becomes the *Provider* element in the next step. As the model is hierarchical, all the elements are in turn *Provider* and *Consumer* to their respective memory address block in one integration step. The memory location is released and freed when the data is not needed.

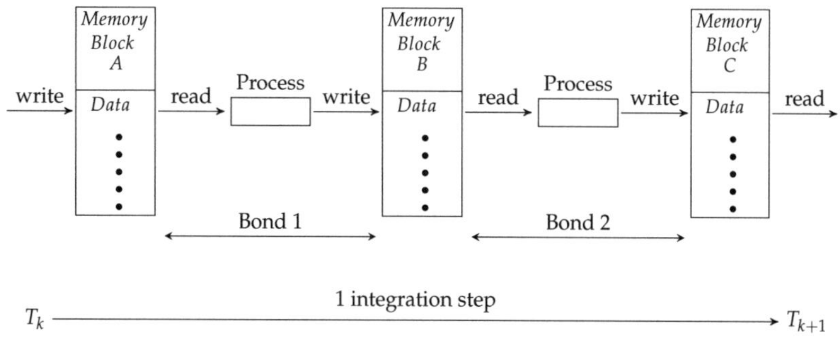

Fig. 10. Propagation of data in a integral time step

7.2 S-function implementation for shared memory link

The port of the bond graph element as discussed above is the pointer to the shared memory address. When we specify a input/output port for a bond graph element, we have to supply three parameters to the S-function. They are:

- The bond graph element name.
- Whether the element is a decider bond or not for the producer - consumer correspondence to the input - output port to be decided.
- The name of the junction to which it is connected.

The complete C MEX S-function code for input junction of a bond is given below:

```
#define S_FUNCTION_NAME  inPort
#define S_FUNCTION_LEVEL 2

#define NPARAMS              3
#define PARAMETER_0_NAME       decider
#define PARAMETER_0_DTYPE      boolean_T
#define PARAMETER_1_NAME       element
#define PARAMETER_2_NAME       junction

#include "shm_com.h"
#include "windows.h"
```

```
#include "mex.h"
#include <malloc.h>
#include "simstruc.h"

#define PARAM_DEF0(S) ssGetSFcnParam(S, 0)
#define PARAM_DEF1(S) ssGetSFcnParam(S, 1)
#define PARAM_DEF2(S) ssGetSFcnParam(S, 2)

#define IS_PARAM_DOUBLE(pVal)
  (mxIsNumeric(pVal) && !mxIsLogical(pVal) &&\
!mxIsEmpty(pVal) && !mxIsSparse(pVal) && !mxIsComplex(pVal)\
   && mxIsDouble(pVal))

static void mdlInitializeSizes(SimStruct *S) {
  ssSetNumSFcnParams(S, NPARAMS);/* Number of expected parameters*/
  if (ssGetNumSFcnParams(S) != ssGetSFcnParamsCount(S)) {
      return; /* Parameter mismatch will be reported by Simulink */
  }
  ssSetNumContStates(S, 0);
  ssSetNumDiscStates(S, 0);
  if (!ssSetNumInputPorts(S, 0)) return;
  if (!ssSetNumOutputPorts(S, 1)) return;
  ssSetOutputPortWidth(S, 0, DYNAMICALLY_SIZED);
  ssSetOutputPortComplexSignal(S, 0, COMPLEX_YES);
  ssSetNumSampleTimes(S, 1);
  ssSetNumRWork(S, 0);
  ssSetNumIWork(S, 0);
  ssSetNumPWork(S, 4);
  ssSetNumModes(S, 0);
  ssSetNumNonsampledZCs(S, 0);
  ssSetOptions(S, 0);
}

static void mdlInitializeSampleTimes(SimStruct *S) {
  ssSetSampleTime(S, 0, CONTINUOUS_SAMPLE_TIME);
  ssSetOffsetTime(S, 0, 0.0);
}

static void mdlStart(SimStruct *S) {
  const boolean_T *decider  = mxGetData(PARAM_DEF0(S));
  void *shared_memory_loc  = NULL;
  void *ishared_memory_loc = NULL;
  HANDLE hMapObject  = NULL;  // handle to real data file mapping
  HANDLE ihMapObject = NULL;  // handle to file mapping
  char_T str[sizeof("fbnbn00")];
  char_T temp[sizeof("fbnbn00")];
```

```
char_T istr[sizeof("fbnbn00")];
mxGetString(PARAM_DEF1(S),str,sizeof(str));  //element name
mxGetString(PARAM_DEF2(S),temp,sizeof(str));  //junction name
if(*decider){
  strcpy(str,temp); //junction name
  strcat(str,"sum");
} else {
  strcpy(str,temp); //junction name
  strcat(str,"out");
}
strcpy(istr,"j"); // prefix 'j'
strcat(istr,str);
hMapObject = CreateFileMapping(
  INVALID_HANDLE_VALUE, // use paging file
  NULL,                 // no security attributes
  PAGE_READWRITE,       // read/write access
  0,                    // size: high 32-bits
  sizeof(struct shared_struct),          // size: low 32-bits
  str);     // name of map object
ssSetPWorkValue(S,0, hMapObject);

shared_memory_loc = MapViewOfFile(
  hMapObject,     // object to map view of
  FILE_MAP_WRITE, // read/write access
  0,              // high offset:  map from
  0,              // low offset:   beginning
  0);             // default: map entire file
if (shared_memory_loc == NULL )   {
  CloseHandle(hMapObject);
  return;
} else {
  ssSetPWorkValue(S,1, shared_memory_loc);
  memset(shared_memory_loc, '\0', sizeof(struct shared_struct));
}
ihMapObject = CreateFileMapping(
  INVALID_HANDLE_VALUE, // use paging file
  NULL,                 // no security attributes
  PAGE_READWRITE,       // read/write access
  0,                    // size: high 32-bits
  sizeof(struct shared_struct),          // size: low 32-bits
  istr);     // name of map object
ssSetPWorkValue(S,2, ihMapObject);

ishared_memory_loc = MapViewOfFile(
  ihMapObject,     // object to map view of
  FILE_MAP_WRITE, // read/write access
```

```
    0,              // high offset:  map from
    0,              // low offset:   beginning
    0);             // default: map entire file
  if ( ishared_memory_loc == NULL)   {
    CloseHandle(ihMapObject);
    return;
    } else {
    ssSetPWorkValue(S,3, ishared_memory_loc);
    memset(ishared_memory_loc, '\0', sizeof(struct shared_struct));
  }
}

static void mdlOutputs(SimStruct *S, int_T tid) {
  boolean_T   yIsComplex=ssGetOutputPortComplexSignal(S, 0)
    ==COMPLEX_YES;

  real_T  *y  = ssGetOutputPortRealSignal(S,0);
  struct shared_struct *shared_stuff, *ishared_stuff;
  shared_stuff = (struct shared_struct *)ssGetPWorkValue(S,1);
  ishared_stuff = (struct shared_struct *)ssGetPWorkValue(S,3);
  y[0] = shared_stuff->some_data;
  y[1] = ishared_stuff->some_data;
  CloseHandle((HANDLE)ssGetPWorkValue(S,0));
  CloseHandle((HANDLE)ssGetPWorkValue(S,2));
}

static void mdlTerminate(SimStruct *S) {
  struct shared_struct *shared_stuff, *ishared_stuff;
  HANDLE c = (HANDLE) ssGetPWork(S)[0]; // retrieve and destroy C++
  HANDLE ic = (HANDLE) ssGetPWork(S)[2]; // retrieve and destroy C++
  shared_stuff = (struct shared_struct *)ssGetPWorkValue(S,1);
  ishared_stuff = (struct shared_struct *)ssGetPWorkValue(S,3);
  free(c);
  if(ic != NULL) {
    free(ic);
  }
  free(shared_stuff);
  if(ishared_stuff !=NULL) {
    free(ishared_stuff);
  }
}

#ifdef  MATLAB_MEX_FILE    /* Is this file being compiled as
    a MEX-file? */
#include "simulink.c"      /* MEX-file interface mechanism */
#else
```

```
#include "cg_sfun.h"        /*Code generation registration function*/
#endif
```

8. S-function library for bond graph elements

Bond graph modeling is an emerging field especially in electrical, mechatronics and electro-mechanics, and a bond graph engineer may feel the necessity to define his own element while making a model. With the set of callback routine and function available to MEX files, any complex constitutive equation can be written for a new element. To provide support for complex variables and vectors in Bond Graph, a tool library using C-MEX S-functions with data propagation through shared memory, is developed. The MEX file for the library has been written in C/C++. After compiling and debugging, C/C++ MEX S-Function are masked with bond graph icons to distinguish between different elements.

Each element of the bond graph library has two common input/output blocks along with with a middle block (Fig.11). The code for the middle block is specific to the element it implements. After placing the three S-functions block in the subsystem, the subsystem is masked. The element's mask screen has a help at the top and parameter entry text boxes, below. There is a check box to specify whether the bond is decider (Fig.12). The parameters entered in the mask screen are manipulated by the S-functions underneath to initialise the element before the simulation cycle starts.

The capability of S-functions to support arbitrary input dimensions is exploited in the tool box. The actual input dimensions can be determined dynamically when a simulation is started by evaluating the dimensions of the input vector driving the S-function. This feature allows the same element to handle a scalar or a vector input as the case may be, without declaring it apriori.

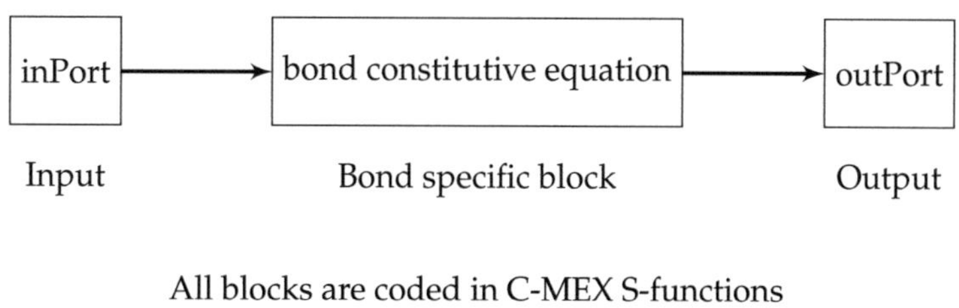

Fig. 11. Typical blocks under the mask of a bond graph element

The library is available in the standard format of simulink (Fig:13). The required elements can be had for *Pick and Place* from library after navigating down (Fig:13(a) and Fig:13(b)). The tools available in the mask's - icon graphics support, is utilised to give a natural iconic representation to the element subsystem.

8.1 Examples of tool box

Using the tool box, the circuit in Fig.14(a) is modeled in bond graph (Fig.14(b)). The simulation results are given in Fig.14(c) and Fig.14(d). As can be observed the library is able to handle complex quantities quite accurately.

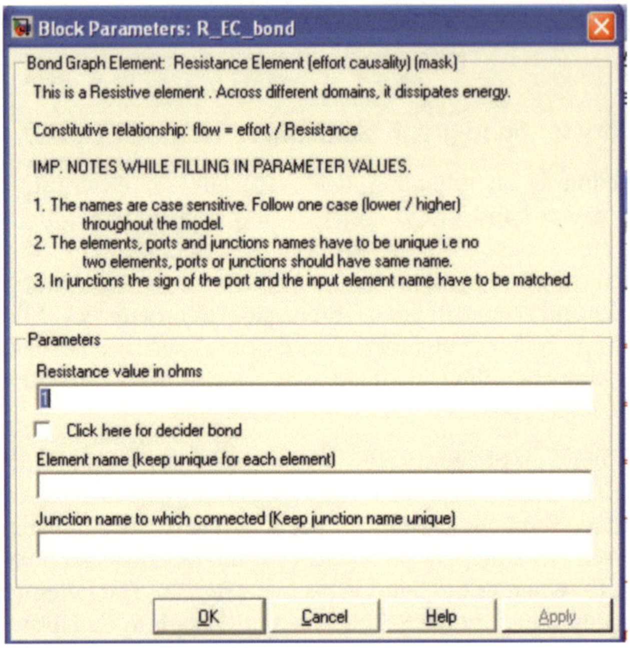

Fig. 12. Input mask screen

For another example of switched junction, one model of the switched mode power converter in Fig.14(f) is used. The circuit is of a boost converter. There are two switches S_1 and S_2 driven by complementary signals. This ensures that only one switch is on at any given time. The circuit is modeled in bond graph using the switched junction as shown in Fig.14(e). The simulation result of the effected state variable is shown in Fig.14(g).

8.2 Simulation results for IM model

A rotating electrical machine can be viewed as a machinery which converts one form of energy into another. More specifically it converts electrical energy into mechanical energy or vice-versa. Magnetic energy is used as a conversion medium between electrical and mechanical energy.

8.2.1 Axis rotator element

This generalised concept for electrical machine modeling needs 'Axis Rotator', a new bond graph element (Umesh Rai & Umanand, 2008; 2009a;b) to mathematically model a electrical commutator (Fig.15). The constitutive relationship for the flow and effort in the bonds is given by Eqn.(2) and Eqn.(3).

$$f_i = \frac{d}{dt}\left(\Lambda_m\left(\sum_{k=1}^{n} e_k \cos\alpha_{(i,k)}\right)\right) \quad \textit{where,} \quad \alpha_{(i,k)} = \alpha_i - \alpha_k \tag{2}$$

$$\sum_{k=1}^{n} e_k f_k = P_m \tag{3}$$

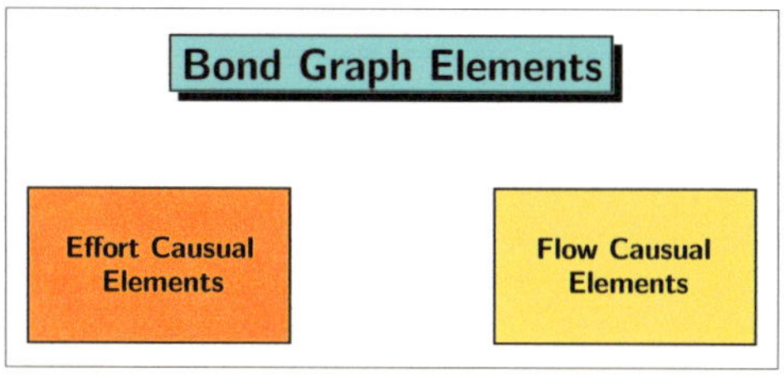

(a) Bond Graph tool Box level 1

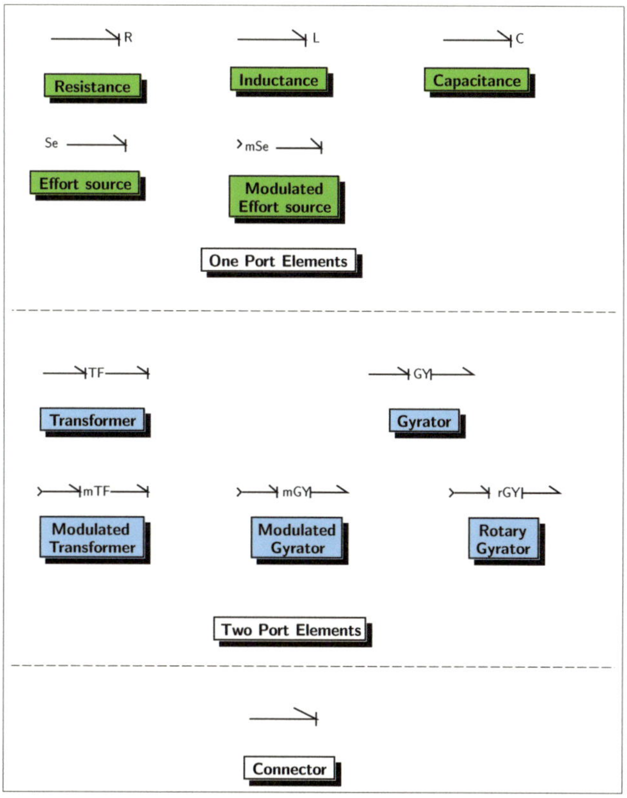

(b) Effort Causual Elements at level 2

Fig. 13. Bond Graph library

$\cos\alpha_{(i,k)}$ refers to the spatial angle between the kth winding's axis and the ith winding axis with respect to the bond under consideration. Λ_m is the mutual permeance (inverse of reluctance) of the magnetic core, P_m is the reactive power required to magnetise the core.

8.2.2 Induction motor model

A bond graph model of 3ϕ doubly fed induction motor using the Axis Rotator element is shown in Fig.16. There are six sets of electric energy input ports, three each for stator and rotor, in the model. The motor shaft represents a mechanical output port. The air gap is represented by the AR with six connection bonds terminating at it, each representing a set of

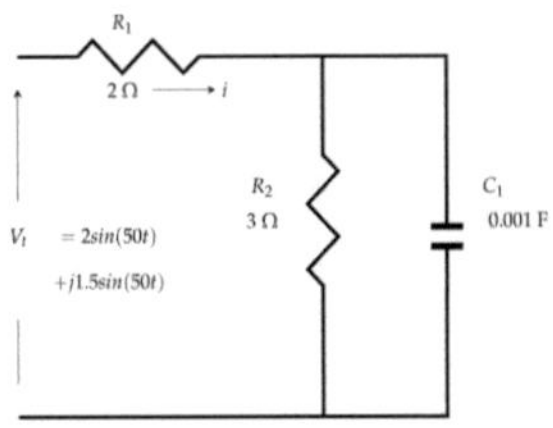

(a) RC circuit

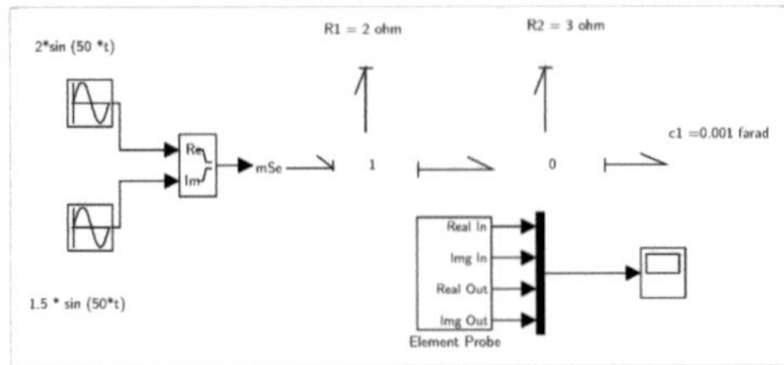

(b) Bond graph model of RC circuit

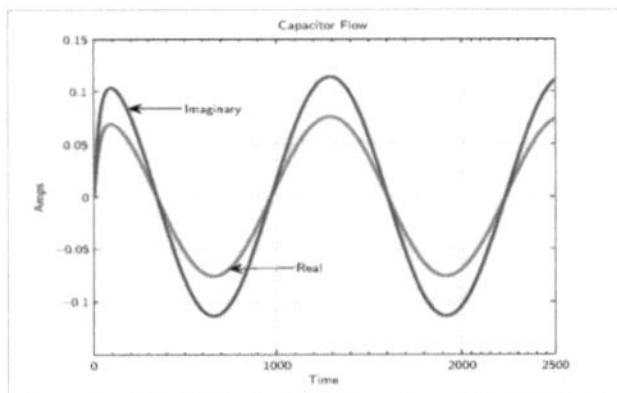

(c) Plots of C-bond flow

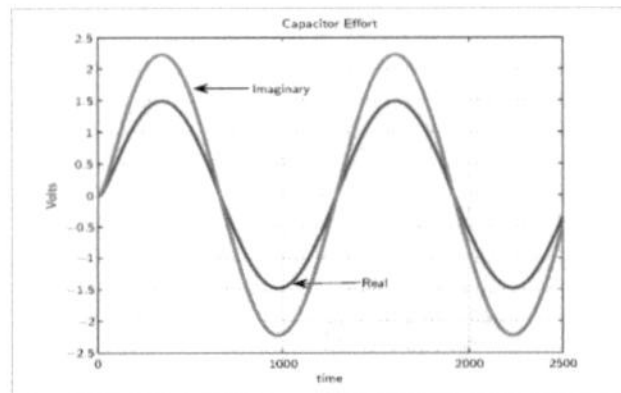

(d) Plots of C-bond effort

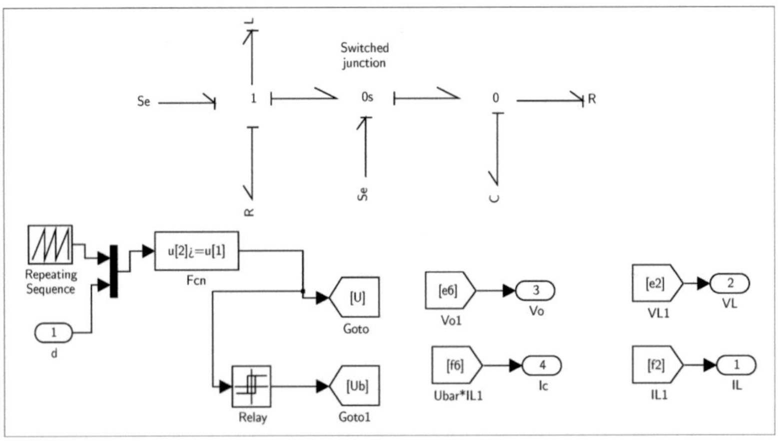

(e) Boost converter model built using switched junction

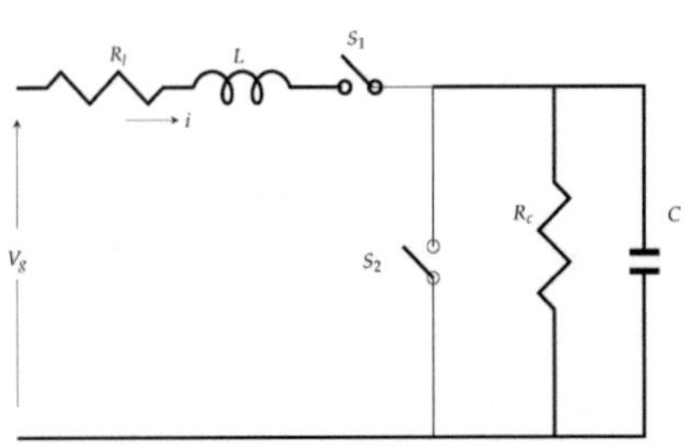

(f) A Boost converter

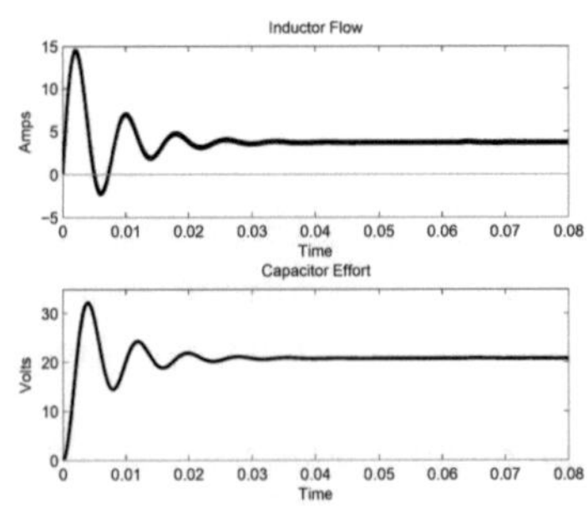

(g) Plot of effected state variables

Fig. 14. Bond graph tool box examples

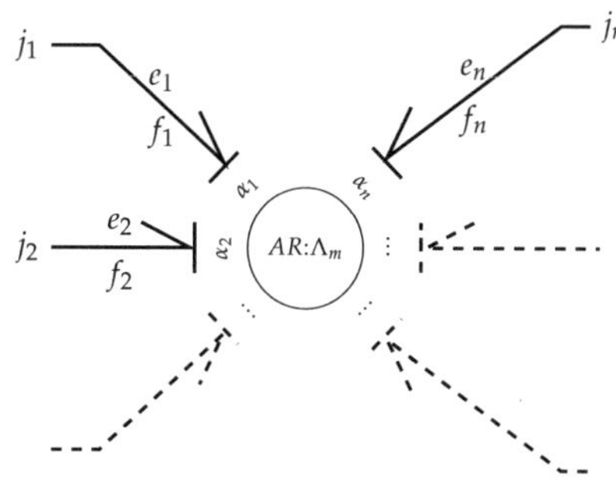

Fig. 15. Axis rotator connected with bonds representing windings

winding. The permeance parameter of the AR represents the mutual coupling effect of the flux. The iron loss is represented by the dissipative port. The stator and rotor energy ports are described with different set of port parameters.

The dissipative, entropy producing fields, R_{as}, R_{bs}, R_{cs}, R_{ar}, R_{br}, R_{cr} and R_i are non-equal non-linear resistances depending on the underlying physical system. R_i represents the iron losses of the core. In a similar manner, the model represents the permeances L_{asl}, L_{bsl}, L_{csl}, L_{arl}, L_{brl}, L_{crl} and L_m . There is no linearity restriction on the above parameters. They could be constants, functions or even a lookup table, without loss of generality. The value of the lumped parameters are different for different phases, dependent on the electric and the magnetic energy they represent. Similarly the energy sources feeding the different windings are represented by s_1, s_2 and s_3. For balanced supply voltages the voltage peaks and frequency would be same, with a phase difference of $(2\pi/3)$ to one another. The three domains of electrical, magnetic and mechanical are clearly brought out in Fig.16.

At the shaft the developed electromagnetic torque as a function of the stator, rotor currents and the angle between them is represented as an effort source. The electromagnetic torque provides the effort at the one junction against the inertial, frictional and load torque components. The feedback information on flow at this junction, which gives the measure of rotor speed is transmitted to the AR for calculating the instantaneous angle of the rotor windings.

8.2.3 S-function model of induction motor

The power of S-function is demonstrated by firstly implementing the complex AR element using C Mex S-function and making it a part of bond graph library. As discussed in the above section, there is no linearity or balance supply constraint on the model. The increased complexity can easily be handled by the bond graph library. The causal model implementation of squirrel cage induction motor is shown in Simulink (Fig.17). The machine starts from stall. A step load is applied to the motor at 0.5sec. The simulation results of speed curve for various step load are presented in Fig.18(a). Similarly the current curves and the torque curve for a specific load are at Fig.18(c) and Fig.18(e) respectively. The transition of rotor currents to slip frequency can be distinctly seen at Fig.18(c). The simulation results of the bond graph model in S-function co-related well with the speed curves obtained by d-q model of the induction motor implemented by functional block in Simulink (Fig.18(b), Fig.18(d) and Fig.18(f)).

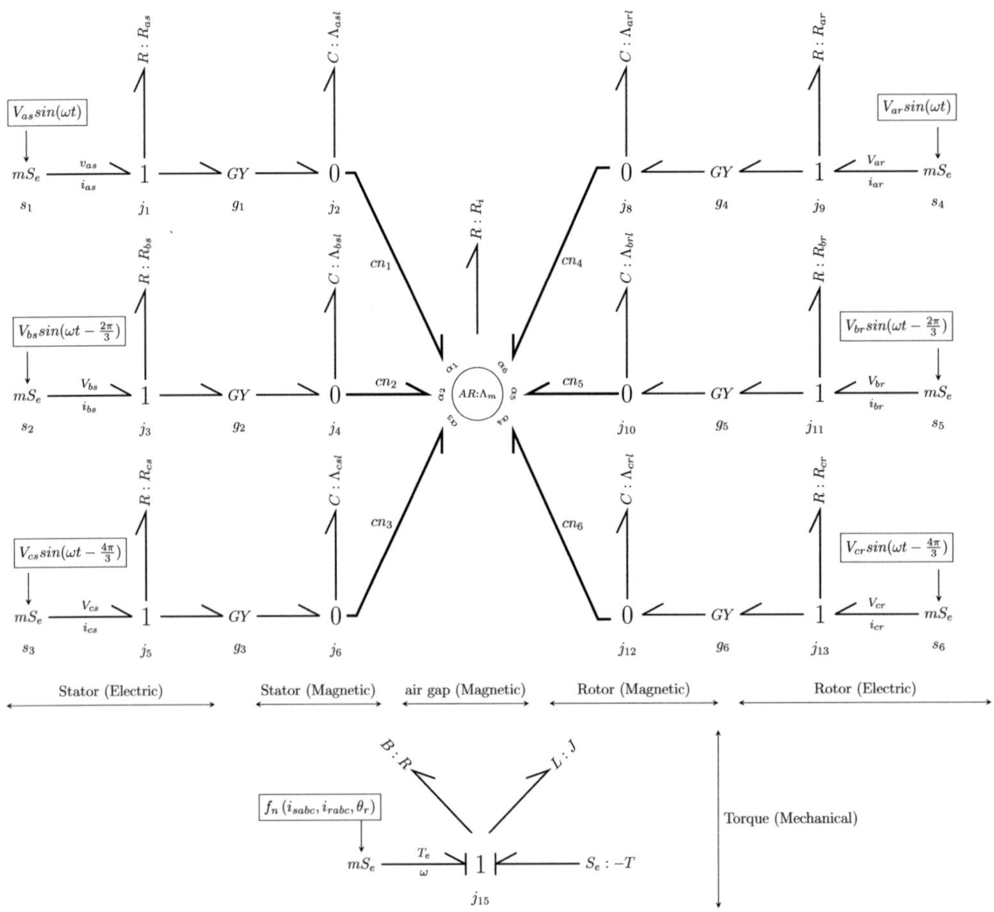

Fig. 16. 3ϕ *DFIM* bond graph model

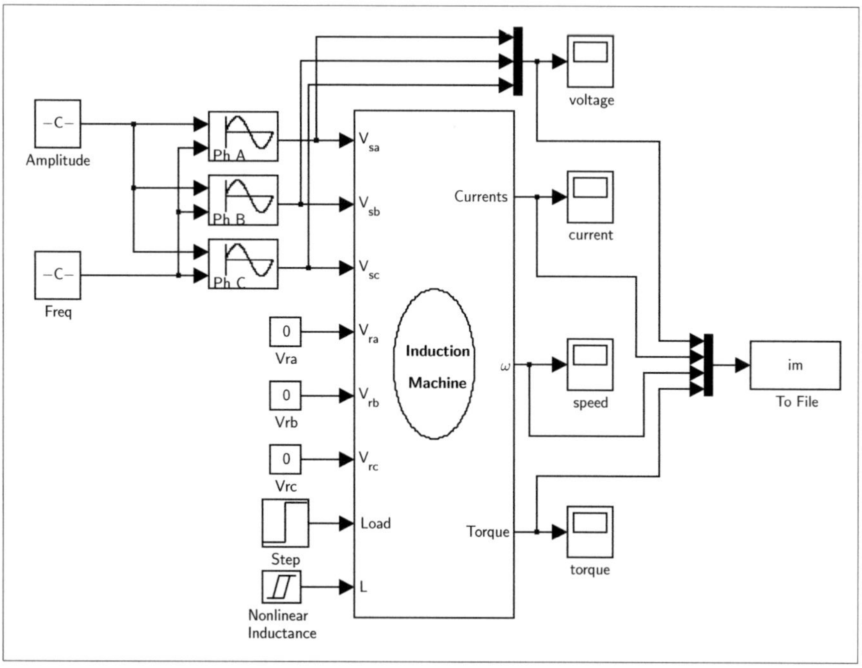

(a) Model in Solver

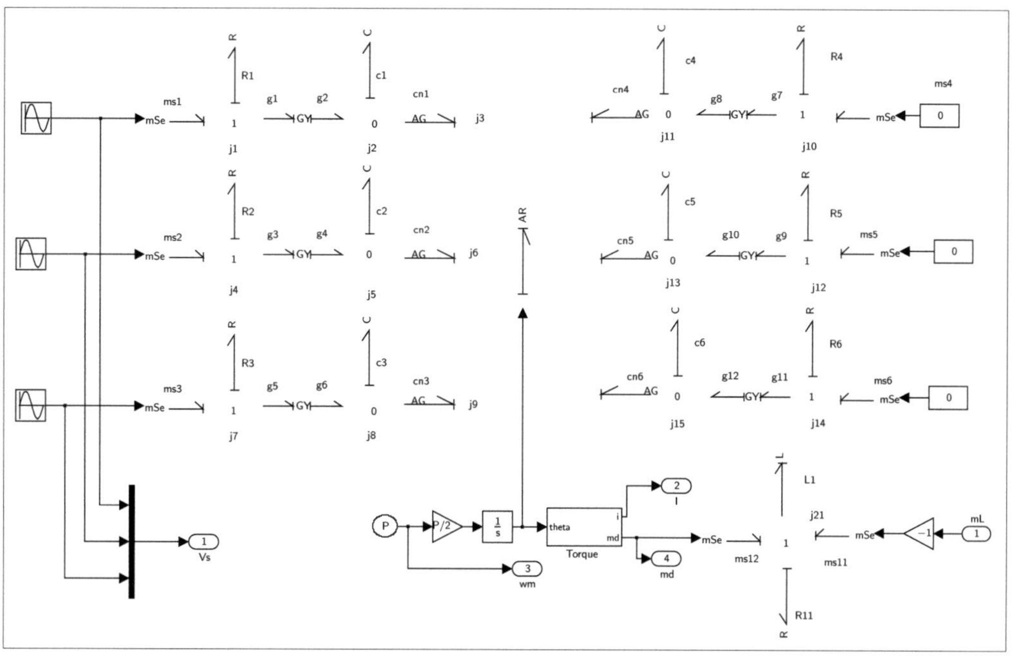

(b) Model in MATLAB/Simulink)

Fig. 17. 3ϕ Induction motor model in Matlab

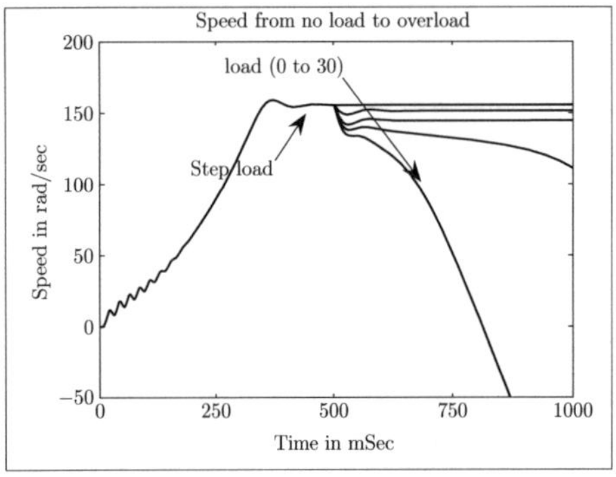

(a) Speed curves proposed model

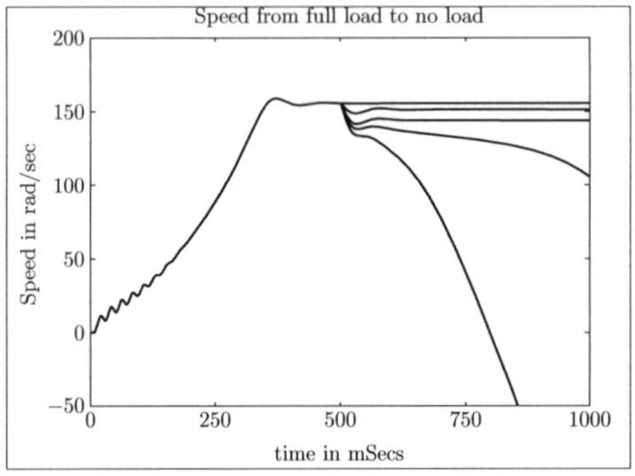

(b) Speed curves dq model

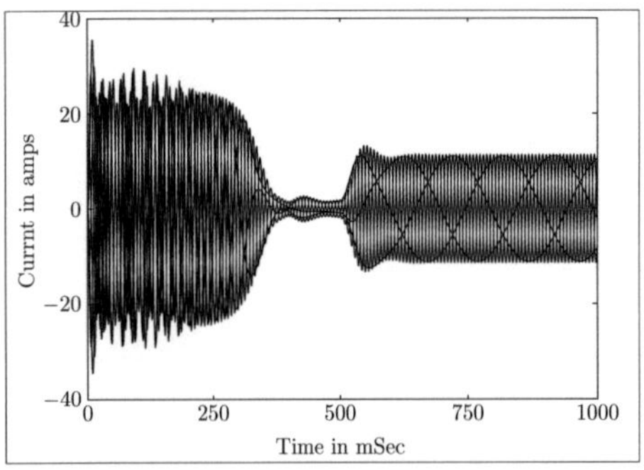

(c) Current curves proposed model

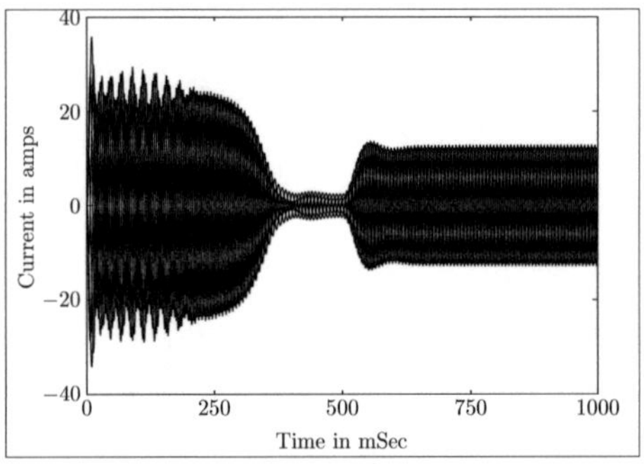

(d) Current curves dq model

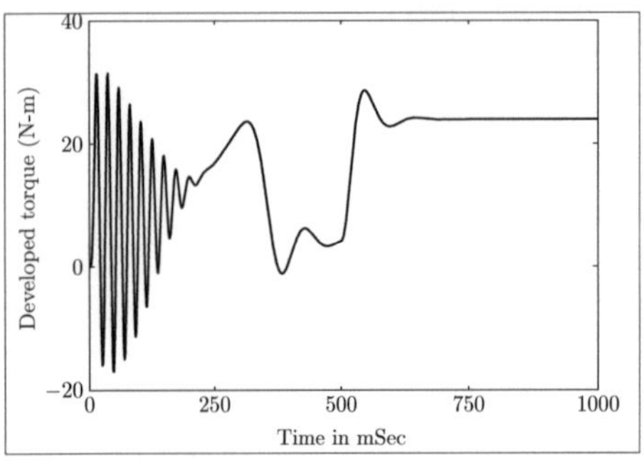

(e) Torque curves proposed model

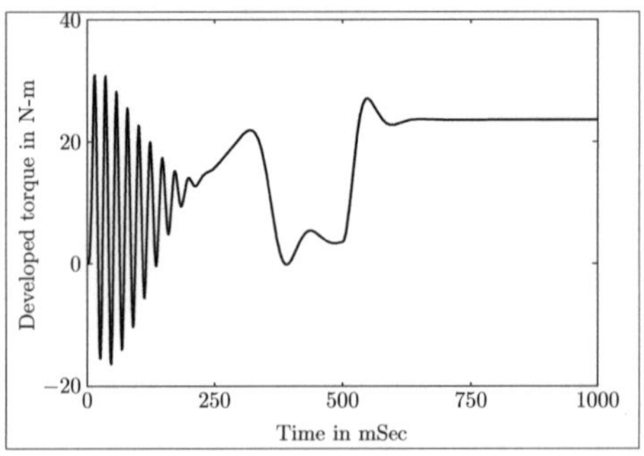

(f) Torque curves dq model

Fig. 18. Simulation results of the bond graph model

9. Conclusion

The power of S-function in customising MATLAB/Simulink® environment suitable for a specific modeling need is illustrated in this chapter. Two different approaches for implementing a customised Simulink element is then discussed with their advantages and disadvantages. Later the Bond graph approach of modeling is briefly introduced. Level 2 C MEX S-function technique is then used to develop a library of bond graph element.

This library of bond graph elements can handle both the scalar and vector or complex variables without declaring apriori, a distinct advantage. A new element - *Axis Rotator,* used for representing rotating magnetic field is included in the library. The ability to handle complex variables along with the rotation enables the elements in the library to be used for modeling rotating frames as that existing in an electric machine. The library also incorporates switched junctions, which allows for the modeling of switches in any circuit. In developing the library, the *Shared Memory Concept* is used. By using shared memory concept, the memory requirement comes down as only the pointer to the memory location are passed and not the data values.

10. References

Borutzky, W. (2009). *Bond Graph Modelling,* Simulation Modelling Practice and Theory.

Borutzky, W., for Modeling, S. & International, S. (2004). *Bond Graphs: A Methodology for Modelling Multidisciplinary Dynamic Systems,* SCS Publishing House e. V.: Society for Modeling and Simulation International.

Breedveld, P. (1984). *Physical Systems Theory in Terms of Bond Graphs,* THT-Afdelin Electrotechniek.

Breedveld, P. (1991). *Special Issue on Current Topics in Bond Graph Related Research,* Pergamon.

Breedveld, P. (2004). Port-based modeling of mechatronic systems, *Mathematics and Computers in Simulation* 66(2-3): 99–128.

Breedveld, P., Rosenberg, R. & ZHOU, T. (1991). Bibliography of bond graph theory and application, *Franklin Institute, Journal* 328(5): 1067–1109.

Cellier, F., Elmqvist, H. & Otter, M. (1995). Modeling from physical principles, *The Control Handbook* pp. 99–108.

Dauphin-Tanguy, G. (2000). *Les bond graphs,* Hermès science publications.

Gawthrop, P. (1995). Physical model-based control: A bond graph approach, *Journal of the Franklin Institute* 332(3): 285–305.

Gawthrop, P. & Smith, L. (1996). *Metamodelling: for bond graphs and dynamic systems,* Prentice Hall International (UK) Ltd. Hertfordshire, UK, UK.

Karnopp, D., Margolis, D. & Rosenberg, R. (1990). *System Dynamics: A Unified Approach,* John Wiley & Sons, Inc., NY.

Karnopp, D., Margolis, D. & Rosenberg, R. (2006). *System Dynamics: Modeling and Simulation of Mechatronic Systems,* John Wiley & Sons, Inc. New York, NY, USA.

Karnopp, D. & Rosenberg, R. (1968). *Analysis and Simulation of Multiport Systems: The Bond Graph Approach to Physical System Dynamics,* MIT Press.

Kron, G. (1962). *Diakoptics: The Piecewise Solution of Large-scale Systems,* Macdonald.

Mathworks (2011). *Developing S-Functions,* The MathWorks, Inc.
URL: *www.mathworks.com*

Mukherjee, A. & Karmakar, R. (2000). *Modelling And Simulation of Engineering Systems Through Bondgraphs*, Alpha Science Int'l Ltd.

Paynter, H. & Briggs, P. (1961). *Analysis and Design of Engineering Systems*, MIT Press.

Rosenberg, R. & Karnopp, D. (1983). *Introduction to Physical System Dynamics*, McGraw-Hill, Inc. New York, NY, USA.

Thoma, J. (1990). *Simulation by bondgraphs*, Berlin and New York, Springer-Verlag, 194 p.

Thoma, J. & Perelson, A. (1976). Introduction to Bond Graphs and Their Applications, *Systems, Man and Cybernetics, IEEE Transactions on* 6(11): 797–798.

Umarikar, A., Mishra, T. & Umanand, L. (2006). Bond graph simulation and symbolic extraction toolbox in MATLAB/SIMULINK, *J. Indian Inst. Sci* 86: 45–68.

Umesh Rai, B. & Umanand, L. (2008). Bond graph model of doubly fed three phase induction motor using the Axis Rotator element for frame transformation, *Simulation Modelling Practice and Theory* 16(10): 1704–1712.

Umesh Rai, B. & Umanand, L. (2009a). Bond graph model of an induction machine with hysteresis nonlinearities, *Nonlinear Analysis: Hybrid Systems* 4(3): 395–405.

Umesh Rai, B. & Umanand, L. (2009b). Generalised bond graph model of a rotating machine, *International Journal of Power Electronics* 1(4): 397–413.

6

From Control Design to FPGA Implementation

Marcus Müller, Hans-Christian Schwannecke and Wolfgang Fengler
Ilmenau University of Technology
Germany

1. Introduction

As a modelling and simulation tool, MATLAB/Simulink plays a significant role in industrial control design. To allow the deployment of the designed control solutions a number of code generation facilities have been developed, that aim on implementing PC-based control units or embedded controllers based on micro-controllers or digital signal processors (DSP). This has enabled MATLAB/Simulink to cover the model-based development process from conceptual design over simulative validation to rapid-prototyping (Krasner (2004)). Although not a new technology per se, since the first commercial field-programmable gate array (FPGA) has been released by Xilinx in 1985, recent development in the field of reconfigurable hardware has created FPGAs, the capabilities of which apply to the requirements of industrial control in a growing number of application domains (Monmasson & Cirstea (2007)). Therefore, also code generation facilities targeting FPGAs have emerged, that link the modelling level to the level of hardware description languages (HDL), from which the lower-level descriptions (RTL) and chip-specific implementations are derived using hardware synthesis tool chains.

MATLAB/Simulink manages to incorporate the processes of high level control design, system modelling on various levels of abstraction and, the availability of respective tool boxes provided, the target-specific code generation. Yet, there is a semantic gap between the control system model, and the model describing an implementation of the controller. The former is a platform-independent simulation model, an executable specification for a controller design, that fulfills the control task within the given simulation scenario. From such a model various implementations can be derived, but not without a step via a platform-specific model, that, to a certain extend, has to incorporate the characteristics of the target platform. An important issue to consider at this point is, that the modelling semantics changes from a functional view to the execution view. The question is no longer "What is being computed?", but "How is it computed?" - a question, that has even more impact on models aimed on generating hardware designs, than on those targeting software generation.

Especially models targeting HDL code generation and hardware synthesis have to undergo an explicit change of the abstraction level, i.e. *model refinement*, towards a hardware-specific implementation model. The Simulink model has to very closely resemble the hardware structure as well as the behaviour of the data flowing through the chip.

This chapter will illustrate the characteristics of this semantic gap and demonstrate a number of techniques on how to make a consistent transition. An overview of control system modelling using Simulink as well as the HDL Coder code generation flow will be given. As an example the model of a 3D trajectory tracking controller for deployment in high-precision positioning and measuring stages will be introduced. The main parts of this chapter regard the structural and behavioural changes, that create a HDL-compatible implementation model from a given simulation model in a top-down manner.

In conclusion a modelling flow is proposed, that - in the course of a model-based top-down development process - precedes the utilization of MATLAB-associated HDL code generation facilities and describes the transition from a platform-independent control system model to a hardware-specific implementation model of the controller. This flow incorporates all discussed modelling activities in a consistent manner, aims on minimizing redesign iterations and allows a simulative validation during all design steps.

2. Control design using Simulink

The extent of MATLAB/Simulink allows the design of control systems on various levels of abstraction. A *system* model is comprised of:

- a model of the controlled process/plant,
- environment and instrumentation, and
- the controller, the *device under development*.

While the plant model can be of a very abstract form, only describing the transfer function or functional behaviour of the controlled process, the controller model is the part, that undergoes the model-based development from control design over refinement to implementation.

The *control design* incorporates the functional design of the controller with regard to the requirements of the plant. As a result, a controller structure and parametrization is achieved, that fulfills the required control task and quality, which can be validated by simulation. This model is called a *platform-independent model* (PIM) of the controller.

When aiming on deploying this solution to the real world, the subsequent step would be the generation of an executable implementation for a processing platform. MATLAB/Simulink provides a variety of possibilities to generate software for PC-based or embedded targets using the MATLAB tool boxes Real-Time Workshop and Embedded Coder plus several vendor-specific extensions, that require no or little additional modelling effort to build a compatible model - a *platform-specific model* (PSM). All code generation facilities provide an abstraction of the targeted processing platform in form of a platform-specific block library and the according tools to transform the blocks in adequate code fragments. For single-processor targets this is quite straight-forward. More difficult is the targeting of multi-processor hardware, since the inter-processor communication has to be incorporated on modelling level (Müller et al. (2009)), and embedded hardware, that often includes the addressing of peripherals.

Figure 1 depicts a Simulink-based development flow tailored for an FPGA implementation of the controller. Regarding the *Target platform abstraction libraries and tools* for HDL, two methods of tool integration can be distinguished, that greatly ease the transition from model to HDL code and the implementation on hardware. First, there are the tool boxes provided by hardware vendors, like the Altera Corporation (2011) DSP Builder and the Xilinx, Inc. (2011) System Generator for DSP, that provide proprietary block sets as additional Simulink libraries and access the respective synthesis tools. Second, there is the HDL generation process via The

Mathworks (2011b) Simulink HDL Coder, which has undergone an extensive development during recent MATLAB revisions, and conducts the HDL code generation from a growing subset of Simulink library blocks (Auger (2008)), allowing a more hardware-independent design approach. Similar within all approaches is the final utilization of the vendor-specific implementation tool chains, that conduct the synthesis and FPGA implementation of the generated HDL code and provide the option to conduct a further validation step on code level via HDL simulation.

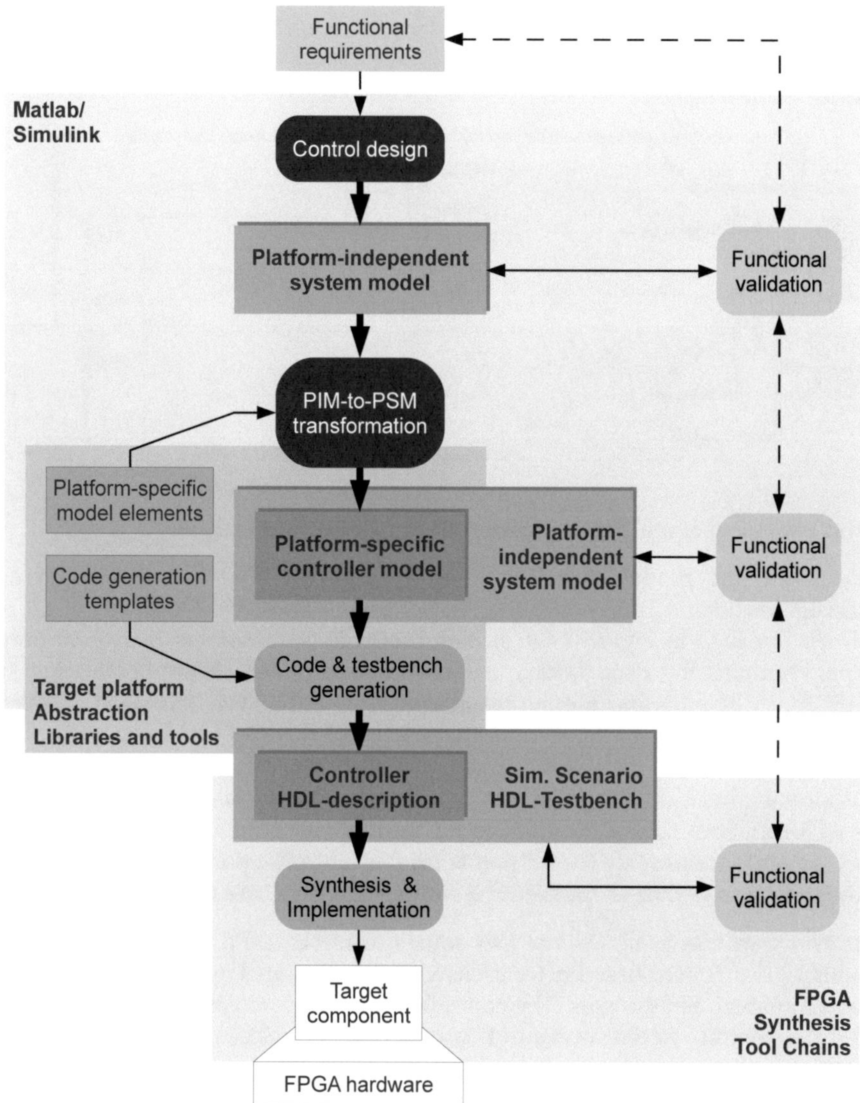

Fig. 1. Overview of the Simulink-based controller development flow targeting FPGA hardware.

Result of Simulink control system modelling is a controller design that fulfills the specified control task and quality, which has been validated by simulation within the bounds of the given scenario. The critical activity is the *transformation of the PIM into the PSM* - the creation of a model, that conforms to the characteristics of hardware execution and fulfills all the requirements to seamlessly run the respective HDL code generators. Therefore, the given controller design and behaviour serves as specification, against which the derived and refined HDL-compatible implementation model has to be validated.

Before the Simulink model characteristics, that may not conform with HDL code generation and/or hardware implementation, are discussed, the example system will be introduced, which will provide the *device under development* for this contribution.

2.1 Example control system

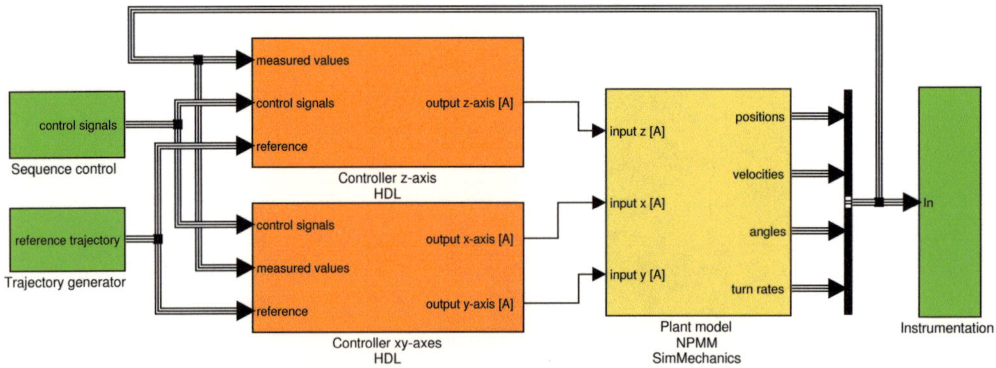

Fig. 2. Top level view of multi-axis trajectory control system model.

As an example the model of a 3D trajectory tracking controller for deployment in high-precision positioning and measuring stages, as presented by Zschäck et al. (2010), will be used. As depicted in Figure 2 the system model is comprised of three partitions. The yellow part contains the *Plant Model*, a SimMechanics model of the positioning stage of a nano-metre positioning and measuring machine, short NPMM. The stage receives input currents to power the electro-magnetic actuators for all three spacial axes, while the lateral positions and velocities as well as the angles and turn velocities of the stage leave the plant model as measured values. The green partition, the *Environment and Instrumentation* partition, consists of a sequence control to manage the system's general modes of operation and a trajectory generator to provide the set points for the controller partition. The control sample rate of the process is 10kHz, so the model is simulated with a base sample time of $100\mu s$.

The *Controller* partition itself, coloured in orange, consists of PID controllers coupled with Kalman filter disturbance observers for each axis, supplemented by additional controllers for angle correction between the axes. The controller is divided into separate modules for z-axis and x-y-plane control. In the course of this contribution a closer look will be taken on the x-axis controller, that is depicted in Figure 3.

In the x-axis controller module first the tracking errors of both position and velocity are determined, before both are subjected to the *P* and *D* gains, respectively. From the position error a nonlinear *I* gain is obtained from a look-up table, after which the values are submitted to the actual discrete integrator. A limiting block after the summation of the P, I and D components and an integrator anti-windup function complete the PID controller. A *Kalman filter* block serves as a disturbance observer for the non-measurable effects - in this application

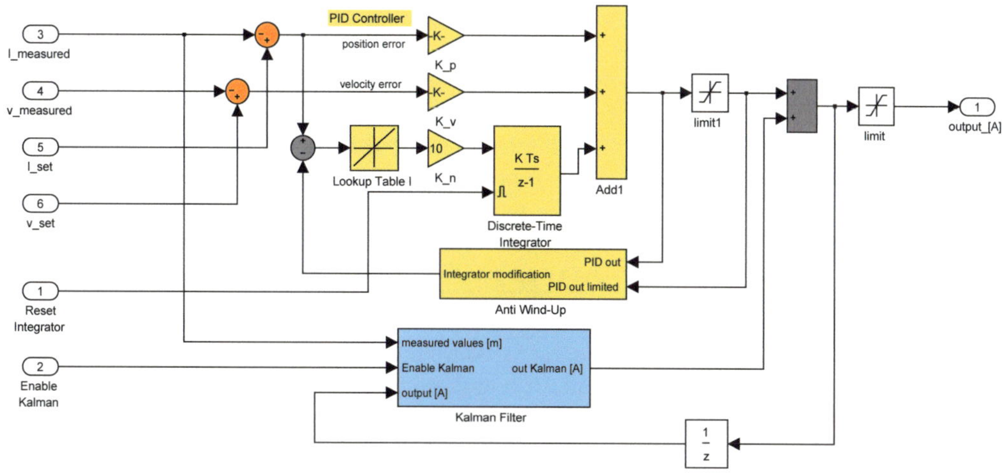

Fig. 3. Internal view of a single axis controller module.

domain, these are mainly friction forces, as described by Amthor et al. (2008). The filter works on the current measured position and velocity values, as well as on the last control step's accumulated output value, to correct its internal state and predict the current step's friction compensation value. The x-axis control output value is accumulated from the PID controller's and Kalman filter's outputs and represents a current to drive a linear electromagnetic actuator.

2.2 Controller partition and the embedded hardware realization

Since the purpose of this model is to design a controller for the specified plant and control task, the properties of the hardware interface and the future implementation hardware are omitted. In this model, digital measurement and set point values are submitted to the controller at discrete points in time without any delay - a behaviour, that in a physically realized control unit requires the passing of peripheral hardware, including A/D and D/A converters, before the actual controller function can be processed.

The developer targeting an FPGA as processing resource for the controller has to be aware of the questions, how far towards the platform-specific properties the controller implementation model can be refined, and how the resulting generated component has to be integrated into the embedded platform.

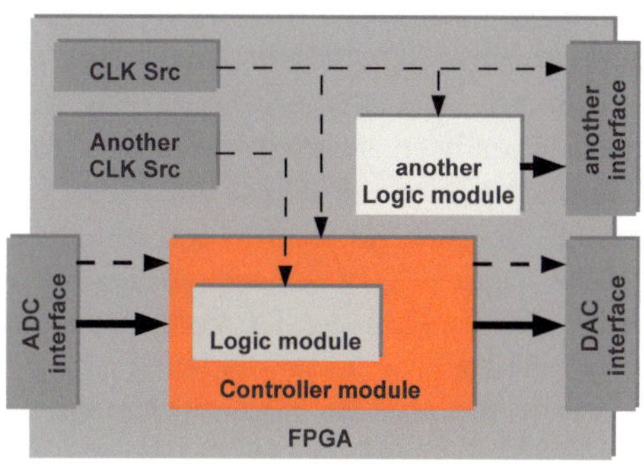

Fig. 4. A generated controller component embedded in a possible FPGA design.

As stated e.g. in Xilinx, Inc. (2011), some parts of a chip design require a level of design control, that cannot easily abstracted from and therefore cannot be adequately dealt with on modelling level. This includes the connection to restricted on-chip resources like peripheral and memory interfaces and the clock management. Figure 4 illustrates the generic structure of an FPGA design, which includes a component generated from a model. This component is likely to reside on the chip with other logic modules, side by side or in hierarchical relations - each will have to be connected to a clock source, but there might exist different clocks driving different components. The modules may also be connected to predefined interfaces to off-chip resources, with which they exchange data and synchronisation signals like triggers.

In some cases it might be possible to manage the complete chip design from the modelling level, but the general case will be to generate a component to be integrated in a chip design. This integration, however, will be the more seamless, the more the model of the controller component is refined to correspond to the structural and behavioural requirements of the embedding design.

2.3 Simulink model properties and HDL code generation

At this point a closer look will be taken at a couple of properties of a Simulink model, that need special consideration when aiming on generating HDL code from this model and implementing this HDL description on a chip.

A Simulink "time-based block diagram" model resembles a synchronous data flow graph, the signal outputs and states of which are computed every simulation time step. One simulation time step defines the time interval in which a significant change of values is to be recorded. In principle, simulation modes with variable time steps can be used in order to decrease the time intervals in cases of rapidly changing values, so that the discretization error can be minimized. For details on the block diagram and time simulation semantics the reader is referred to The Mathworks (2011a) Simulink User Guide. For this control design, the simulation time resolution is determined by the fixed sample period of the time-discrete controller, which here will be referred to as `T_Control` with $100\mu s$. For a hardware-oriented model, the simulation time interval resembles the fixed period of the clock signal (`T_Clk`) driving the generated logic. Due to this fact, the notion of time resolution has to be changed - from the sample time of the controller, the interval, in which new input values are acquired, to the execution cycle period, the time interval a logic stage computes one cycle.

MATLAB and Simulink allow heterogeneous modelling and the integration of models with different levels of functional abstraction. This is majorly supported by the MATLAB functions and Simulink blocks being polymorph. That means, they work on scalar, vector and matrix data alike, as well handle different data types transparently to the engineer. The library functions/blocks are designed to easily create complex models from reusable, parametrizable blocks, hiding the actual implementation details. But these details are significant when considering a hardware design, because some function, as e.g. division operators, cannot be trivially mapped to binary logic. As a consequence, only a subset of the Simulink libraries feature corresponding synthesizable HDL constructs. For any non-synthesizable blocks adequate substitute constructs have to be modelled or the block has to be treated as an abstract black-box, that is to be replaced by a pre-implemented external HDL-component during code generation.

By default, MATLAB uses the data type DOUBLE for all its algorithm descriptions, be it in MATLAB script language or Simulink block models. DOUBLE represents a 64 bit wide floating-point number, which covers a range of up to $\pm 2^{1024} \approx 2 \times 10^{308}$ and a precision of up to $2^{-52} \approx 2 \times 10^{-16}$, which is supposed to cover the needs of any modelling and simulation task. Any code generation without interference would map the model signals to variables of a supported floating-point type. Difficulties could arise when trying to deploy this code to a processing hardware - floating-point units are quite complex and comparatively slow in general-purpose processors, some support only single-precision (32 bit), some micro-controllers and DSPs do not even feature any, and in custom hardware designs they can only be used in very limited numbers. So double-precision floating-point arithmetic has to be time-intensively emulated, limited hardware units have to be reused in a time-multiplexed fashion, requiring a complex execution flow, or the arithmetic functionality cannot be realized at all. The hardware description language VHDL supports the double-precision floating-point data type REAL, which allows direct code generation from Simulink. The VHDL simulation of floating-point arithmetic is possible, but the REAL data type is not synthesizable, as stated e.g. by Rushton (2011). Therefore, any platform-specific Simulink model, that is intended to resemble a hardware description, has to feature integer or fixed-point arithmetic.

The following sections will exemplify several activities to create a HDL compliant and hardware implementable model from the controller design introduced above. Since the 2010 version of MATLAB introduced the HDL Workflow Advisor for the Simulink HDL Coder, a tool is featured that guides the code generation, and via utilization of vendor-specific synthesis tools, also allows the rapid-prototyping synthesis and FPGA implementation of Simulink models. The model transformations will be described with regard to the Simulink HDL Coder, since no change in the basic block set will be required. First, structural changes to the data path of the model will be discussed, followed by behavioural modifications, that transform the model behaviour to the hardware execution behaviour.

3. Data path design

The structural changes to a model in order to facilitate both successful HDL code generation and successful hardware implementation, that are considered in this section, include

- the insertion of HDL-compatible substitutes,
- the utilization of black-box blocks to incorporate predefined HDL components, and
- the fixed-point data type conversions.

3.1 HDL-Coder supported substitute constructs

The substitution of blocks is necessary, since only a subset of the modelling blocks and block configurations available in Simulink supports the generation of HDL code. The blocks that do are compiled into the so called "Supported Blocks Library" by the hdllib command - refer to The Mathworks (2011b) HDL Coder user guide for details. Still some blocks can feature modes or configurations, that are not synthesizable. Common examples are the arithmetic function blocks that polymorphically work on scalars, as well as on vectors and matrices. Since matrix operations are not supported these blocks have to be substituted by explicit constructs.

Regarding the controller model displayed in Figure 3, the first block to consider is the *Discrete Integrator* block. This block can be configured to a mode of computation, e.g. Forward-Euler,

Backward-Euler, etc. In this case the integrator is required to be resettable, since the internal value has to be set to zero in case of de- and reactivation of the controller module. The *resettable* feature is documented as not being HDL compatible, so the block has to be substituted by the self-tailored subsystem, that is depicted in Figure 5. It resembles a forward-Euler integrator with the discrete sample time interval of `T_Control`, the internal state of which can be reset by an external signal.

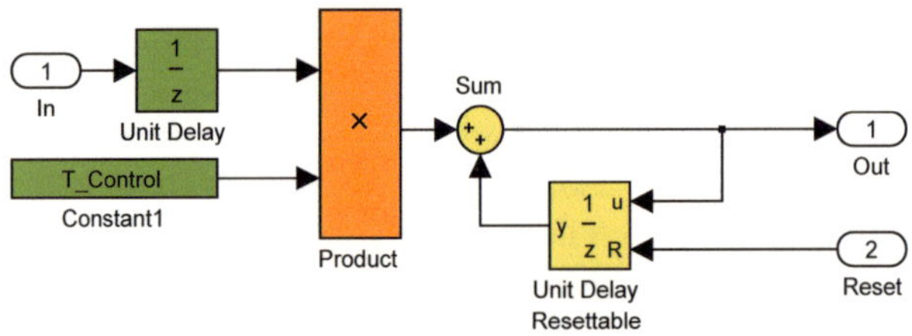

Fig. 5. Substitute for the Forward-Euler Discrete Integrator block with external reset.

A further aspect for consideration is the use of *Look-up tables* (LUT), like the one determining the variable *I*-gain in Figure 3. Simulink LUT blocks can be configured to determine an output value according to a set of sampling points and an interpolation method, like in this case linear *Interpolation/Extrapolation*.

Starting with MATLAB Release 2011a the HDL Coder supports the code generation from LUTs configured to linear interpolation, but only based on evenly distributed sampling points. For certain LUT mappings the minimal distance between sampling points would require a large number of them to cover the input data value range, resulting in a large memory requirement for the on-chip LUT implementation.

A method to substitute a Simulink look-up table with linear interpolation/extrapolation between sparsely and arbitrarily distributed sampling points is presented in Figure 6. Here, the input value range is subdivided into intervals according to the sampling points. The input value x is compared to the interval boundaries, the comparison results are accumulated to an index value. A switch assigns a respective set of coefficients A, B to the actual linear interpolation $y = Ax + B$.

3.2 Fixed-point conversion

To effectively implement an algorithm into hardware, it is advised to utilize an integer or fixed-point representation of both data and algorithm. Since the initially designed executable specification model uses double-precision floating-point data representation, a conversion to fixed-point data types has to be performed.

The key steps are to determine the maximum/minimum values to be covered, and the minimal discretization step width. From these information, the fixed-point format consisting of *sign bit*, *word length* and *position of radix point* can be derived, which in MATLAB is denoted as e.g. `fixdt(1,16,4)`[1].

MATLAB features the Fixed-Point Tool and the Fixed-Point Advisor process, documented by The Mathworks (2010), to aid the determination of the respective fixed-point formats. The

[1] for a 16 bit wide signed number with the four least significant bits being fraction bits

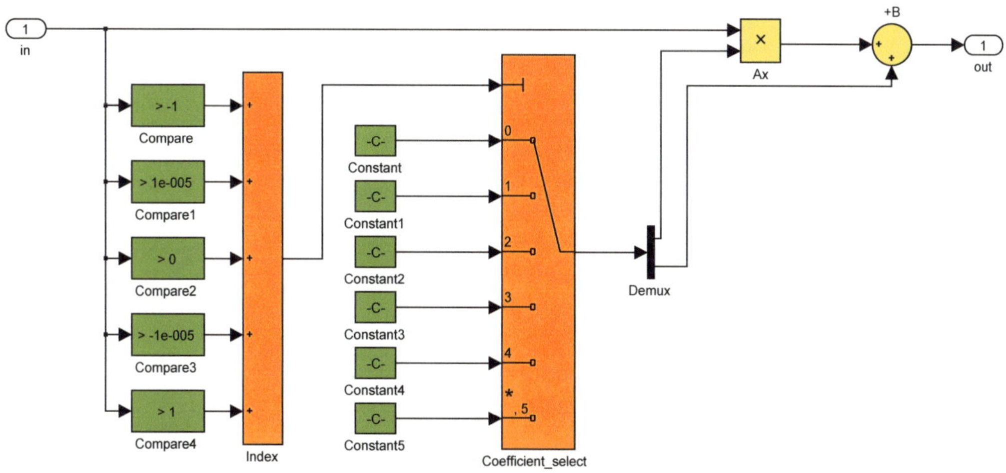

Fig. 6. Substitute for Simulink Look-up table block with linear *Interpolation/Extrapolation* between arbitrarily distributed sampling points.

automated Fixed-Point Advisor conversion process relies on the default data type definitions for *classes* of values, even if the hardware implementation option is set to `FPGA/ASIC`. So, globally fixed word lengths for all the input values, constant values and internal outputs, respectively, have to be set by the designer. Based on the globally set word length definitions the fixed-point tools move the radix point to achieve the maximum precision while covering the maximally necessary value range. Only afterwards can be determined, if the resulting precision meets the specified precision requirements, usually leading to an iterative process of re-adapting the word lengths.

For FPGA implementations there are per se no such restrictions as globally predefined operand word lengths. On the contrary, for each operation the operand and result widths can be determined with bit accuracy, therefore allowing to tailor the word lengths exactly to the algorithms' requirements, especially regarding the fact, that the specified precision can be used as a-priori information.

Regarding this, it should be noted, that a decimal fraction cannot easily be expressed using a binary fraction, since each additional fraction bit only enhances precision to the next negative power of two, resulting in a decimal precision with a maximum numerical error ϵ. Based on the approach presented by Carletta & Veillette (2005), the required positions for the most significant bit (MSB) and the least significant bit (LSB) in a binary representation of the decimal value x with a desired decimal precision ϵ can be computed by $P_{MSB}(x) = \lfloor log_2|x| \rfloor + 1$, and $P_{LSB}(x)s = \lceil log_2(\epsilon * |x|) \rceil - 1$, respectively. The required binary word length L is given by $L = P_{MSB} - P_{LSB}$ plus the sign bit, if required.

A successive fixed-point conversion is conducted based on the minimal fixed-point expression of all inputs, constants and coefficients, and on the following rules:

- for binary Addition of two operands: $L_{result} = max_i(L_{operand\_i}) + 1$,
- for binary Multiplication of two operands: $P_{MSB}(result) = \sum P_{MSB}(operand_i)$ and $P_{LSB}(result) = \sum P_{LSB}(operand_i)$

The Simulink block parametrization option `Data type inheritance via internal rule` works similarly, but can not resolve feed back loops without major restrictions. In those cases definitely manual parametrization based on good knowledge of the process parameters is expedient.

The operand bit widths can be regarded as a measure for chip area utilization, since they influence the complexity of the synthesized register and routing structures on the target chip. The use of the Fixed-Point Advisor will produce valid solutions for hardware implementation, which therefore makes it a valuable tool for rapid prototyping, but the advantage of a manual minimization of the fixed-point representation and its effect on chip resource utilisation becomes obvious.

3.3 Excluding externally provided black-box blocks

The utilization of black-box components is a means to include externally available implementations as substitutes for Simulink modelling blocks, that are not or not feasibly synthesizable. The model element regarded as black box will still be simulated, but neglected during HDL code generation, where an interface-compatible predefined HDL component will be referenced instead. For details on the declaration of a black box subsystem refer to The Mathworks (2011b) HDL Coder documentation.

For the presented controller design these circumstances will be illustrated by the example of the Kalman filter, the design of which has been presented by Amthor et al. (2008). For this Simulink module no feasible hardware implementation could be generated using a model-driven HDL generation process. This is not at least caused by the fact, that for the high-precision application domain this filter has no feasible fixed-point solution in terms of required data widths and resulting chip area requirements. So, the computation of this function on the hardware is conducted using a highly optimized VHDL-designed core, based on the floating-point processing architecture presented by Pacholik et al. (2011). According to its specification, the IP[2] component executing the Kalman filter function has the following properties, which are of significance for the model integration:

- clock port for internal clock (up to 120 MHz),
- latency: 215 clock cycles @ 120 MHz $\approx 1.8\mu s$,
- clock port for external clock (to allow synchronisation with the surrounding design),
- execution triggered on rising edge of `Trigger` signal,
- result availability signalled by `Valid` signal (pulse with width of one external clock period).

In order for the IP component to be correctly referenced during the synthesis process the Simulink black-box subsystem requires the exact replication of the IP components interface and motivates the following adaptions in the HDL-oriented Simulink model.

Figure 7 shows the configuration of the Kalman filter subsystem as a black-box component. A closer look reveals that the data ports of the Simulink subsystem block have been supplemented with a `CLK_120MHz`, a `Trigger` and `Valid` port. The dialog shows options to configure the appearance of the interface of the HDL instance - in addition to the data

[2] "Intellectual property" cores describe pre-designed logic blocks to be reused for FPGA/ASIC design

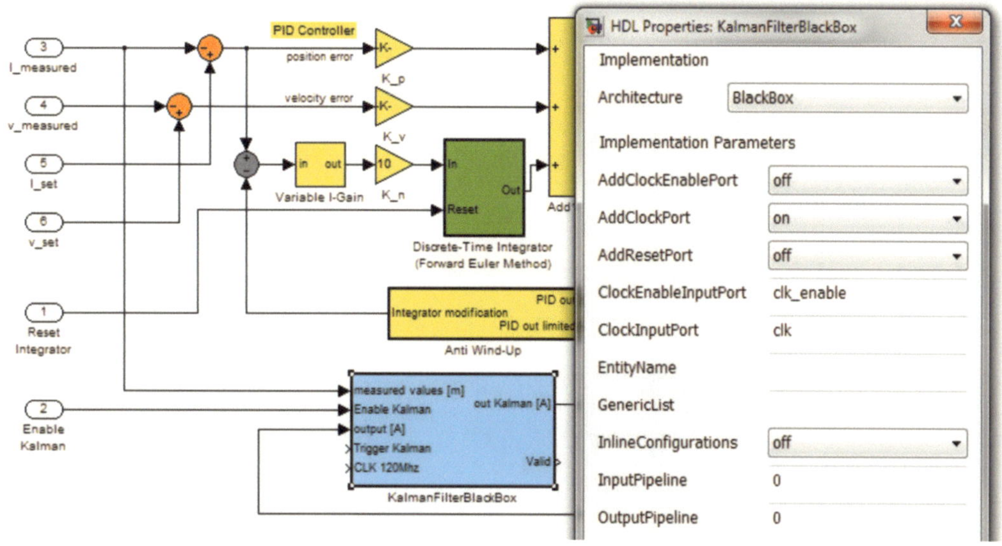

Fig. 7. Declaring a black-box component.

ports from the Simulink block - to fit the predefined component interface, as documented in The Mathworks (2011b) HDL Coder guide. The clock port `clk`, that is added, matches the hardware port connected to the clock of the surrounding design, which completes the replication of the referenced component's interface. At this point the black-box declared subsystem ensures both, the correct simulation using the platform-independent filter model, and the structurally correct instantiation and therefore seamless integration of the Kalman filter component at code level.

3.4 Resulting model

The model of the x-axis controller module after the completed data path design steps is depicted in Figure 8. It includes the substituted discrete integrator and look-up table blocks, the black-box interface of the Kalman block, as well as additional compatibility issues like the resolved bus signals, and shows the resulting fixed-point data widths for the operands. At this point the HDL Coder compatibility check should complete successfully.

4. Behavioral design

The behavioural changes the model has to undergo during its transformation into an implementation model are mainly characterized by a changed notion of time[3]. In the simulation model the base sample rate describes the interval, in which the change of relevant physical values is observed - the control system sample time `T_Control`. The computation of the outputs of the controller and the reaction of the plant is done "timelessly" at one point in simulation time. In reality, as illustrated in Figure 9, the begin of the time interval `T_Control` marks the time, when measured values are acquired (DAQ), before they are submitted to the controller module and the computation of the controller function can begin. The computation

[3] Prerequisites for behavioural compatibility to the HDL Coder code generation process are set by the `hdlsetup` command - refer to the The Mathworks (2011b) HDL Coder documentation.

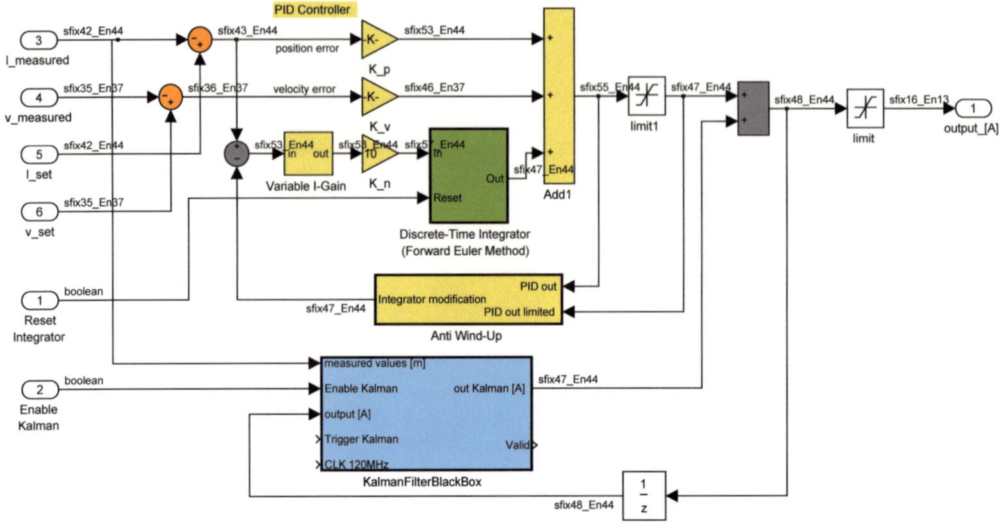

Fig. 8. Structurally HDL compatible controller model.

of the controller function and the control output have to be completed within one period of `T_Control` in order to fulfill the real-time execution restriction for the discrete-time controller design (Caspi & Maler (2005)).

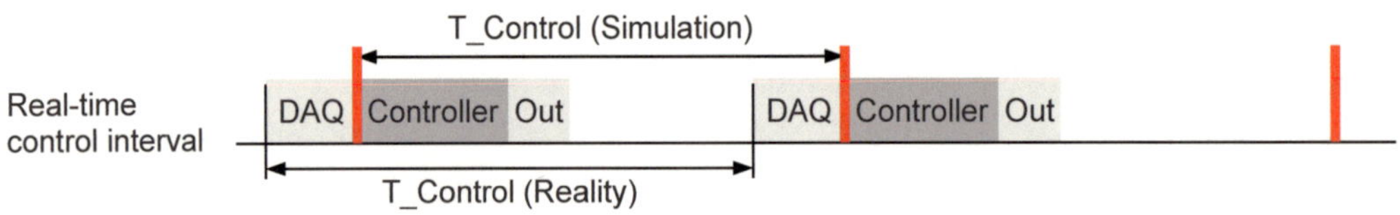

Fig. 9. Execution cycle of a real-time control system in reality and simulation.

Since the platform-independent model abstracts from the DAQ and output behaviour, from the model-based design point of view, the beginning of the `T_Control` interval has to be regarded as the point in time, when the state of the plant has been captured and the controller simulation/computation is initiated. For the platform-specific controller model the question arises, how to regard the hardware execution of the controller and its delay in relation to the real-time interval and how to model it.

In this section first a hardware implementable model is directly derived from a `T_Control`-cycle oriented model to analyze its hardware execution semantics. Afterwards a model with advanced clocking and trigger structures necessary to ensure consistent hardware execution are introduced. Along with the required modifications to the model structure and the simulation semantics the advantages and disadvantages of each modelling and implementation variant are discussed.

4.1 Control cycle oriented design

When applying the HDL Workflow Advisor directly to the model shown in Figure 8 a valid HDL entity of the controller model including the referenced HDL component for the black box will be generated. The data paths from the inputs through the internal arithmetic functions of this entity will be transformed into *combinational logic*. The unit delays in the feedback path, see Figure 8, and in the integrator block, see Figure 5 storing the control cycle state will be realized as *registers*. The update of these registers will be triggered by a rising edge of the clock signal connected to this entity.

At this level of abstraction, although the Kalman filter subsystem is still simulated as an abstract black box, the integration of the underlying HDL component in the logic path has to be prepared. This includes the connection to a 120 MHz clock source, which is best designed at chip level. Therefore, the according clock port `CLK_120MHz` is linked to the controller component's interface to the top level. Furthermore, the Kalman filter component has to be triggered at a point in time defined by outside prerequisites, which requires the connection of the `Trigger` port to an outside source. Both modifications are shown in Figure 10.

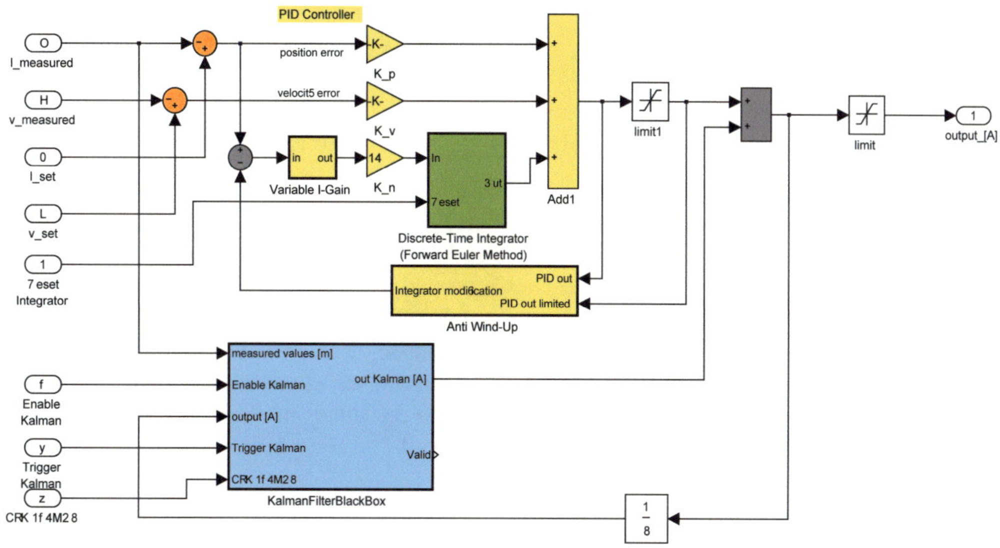

Fig. 10. Model of the controller with an externally clocked Kalman filter component.

Prototyping the implementation with the HDL Coder Workflow Advisor and using the back-annotation feature allows to examine the computational delays of the combinational path of the resulting hardware implementation of the controller. For the example design this value is $45ns$. Regarding the $1.8\mu s$ execution delay of the Kalman filter, which on the FPGA is computed in parallel, it is certain, that the computation is completed well within the `T_Control` $= 100\mu s$ real-time interval.

During code generation the HDL Coder will generate an entity, that, aside from the ports defined in the Simulink model, declares the port `clk` to connect to an on-chip clock source. As the simulation model computed one step per sample interval `T_Control`, the controller implementation will conduct one computation step, if the `clk` port is driven by a clock source with the period of the simulation base sample time, i.e. clock frequency $f = 1/T\_Control$.

But it has to be noted, that the only safe assertion, that can be made for hardware design derived from this model, is that at each rising clock edge the output and integrator values are stored in the respective registers. Due to the combinational logic, the design is sensitive to the *input/output behaviour* of the surrounding hardware design. All value changes of the signals will be directly propagated through the circuit, only subject to gate delay - an effect that cannot be expressed in the Simulink model with a time resolution of `T_Control`. This makes it very difficult to determine, e.g. when all current input data will be available and stable in relation to the clock edge, when to trigger the Kalman filter component on valid input data and when to submit the result values to the surrounding circuitry.

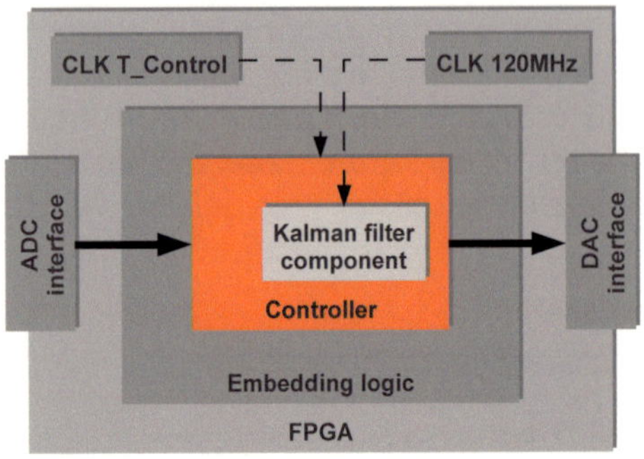

Fig. 11. Integration of the generated controller and Kalman filter components in an FPGA design.

If the logic embedding the controller component, as depicted in Figure 11, is known to provide the required clock and trigger signals, to guarantee for the stability of the input values for the computation time and to correctly time the take-over of the result values, the utilization of a combinationally integrated component should not pose a problem. Nevertheless, the correct design of the embedding logic and the behavioural validation of both, the component and the overall implementation are efforts, that cannot be undertaken on modelling level. To provide a more robust component implementation and to ease the integration of the component in a chip design a more advanced modelling approach should be considered.

4.2 Execution cycle oriented clocked design

Guidelines for good design practice regarding the creation of reusable IP components have been formulated by Keating & Bricaud (2002). A key feature is the independence from the influence of embedding logic regarding the data propagation timings, especially when the timing behaviour is unknown or cannot be guaranteed at component design time.

The method to ensure the simultaneous submission of input values to the component design and the stability of those inputs for a defined time period is to provide input registers. These registers are triggered to store the input values at defined points in time, when the validity of the values can be assumed. This decouples the timing of the component from any surrounding issues, so the internal behaviour of the component can be designed based on this trigger event.

On modelling level the Simulink controller design has to be equipped with input registers, that are triggered to store the input values at the sample points defined by `T_Control`. Additionally, the output has to be provided with a register to submit a stable and valid value to the embedding logic after the computation has been completed. These port registers are modelled by additional *Enabled Unit Delays*, as depicted in Figure 12.

Now the data propagation along the forward path of the data flow has been divided in multiple logic stages and is therefore delayed by multiple simulation cycles. Still, the simulation of the controller has to be accomplished within the period `T_Control`, i.e. within

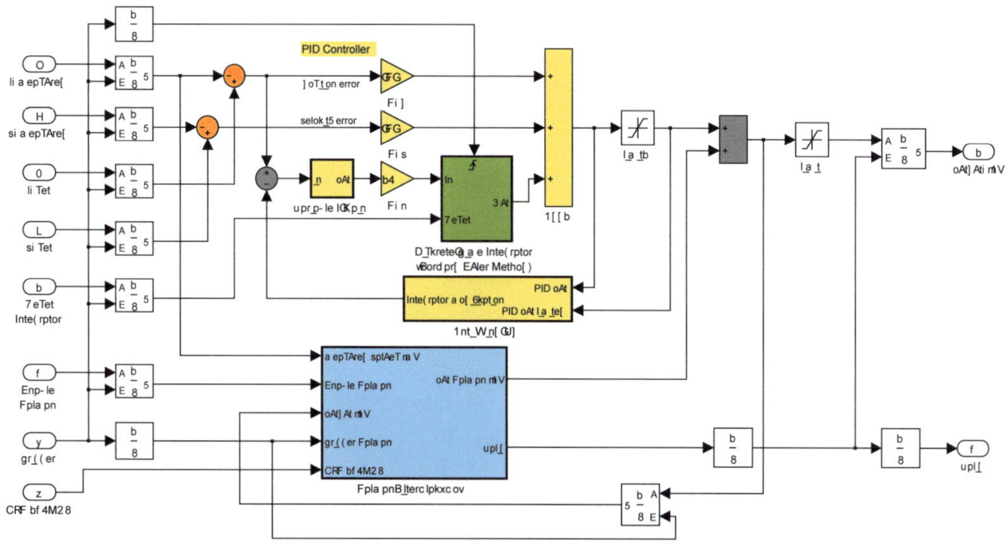

Fig. 12. Model of a controller design with registered I/O ports.

one simulation interval of the plant and environment model. This requires the introduction of a *new simulation base sample time* with a resolution high enough to fit the respective controller simulation cycles. In the following, this simulation sample period will be referred to as `T_Clk`.

The controller design shown in Figure 12 is now simulated with `T_Clk` - each unit delay only adds one `T_Clk` latency. Still, there are values, that have to be updated only once every `T_Control`. Since this can no longer implicitly accomplished by using unit delays based on `T_Control`, it has to be expressed by unit delays enabled for one `T_Clk` every `T_Control` interval by an explicitly modelled trigger signal. The relation of the control interval `T_Control`, the execution cycle interval `T_Clk`[4] and the trigger signal, representing the beginning of the control cycle in the execution time domain, is displayed in Figure 13.

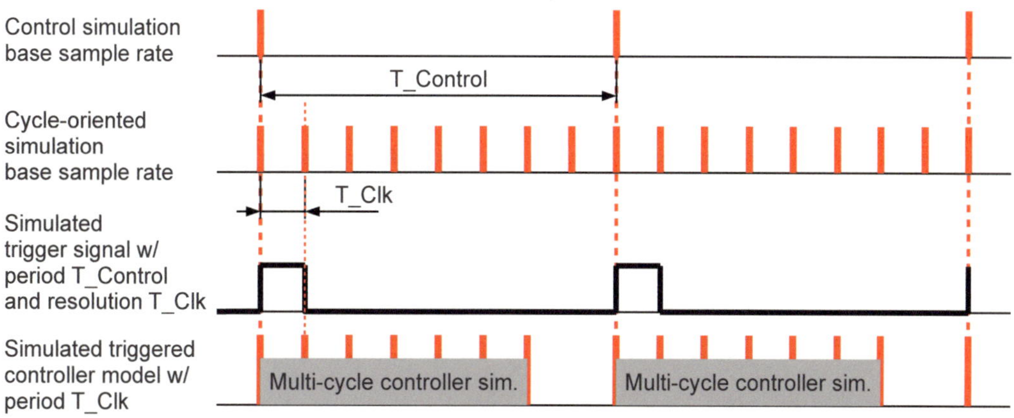

Fig. 13. Simulation rate multiplication for computation cycle oriented simulation.

[4] Simulation solver restrictions still require `T_Control` being an integer multiple of the base sample time `T_Clk`

This trigger signal is used to enable the following elements for one cycle of `T_Clk` in order to store a value at the beginning of each `T_Control` interval. First, the controller's input unit delays take over the current input values. Second, the unit delay storing the feedback output value is enabled. Third, the Discrete Integrator block has to store the last accumulated value. For this purpose, the integrator block from Figure 5 has been turned into a triggered subsystem. Until the next enable phase these values will be kept stable by the registers. Within one `T_Clk` the results are propagated through the design and on a further trigger submitted to the output register. Since the result depends on the output of the Kalman filter component, the trigger for the output register is derived from the `Valid` signal of this component.

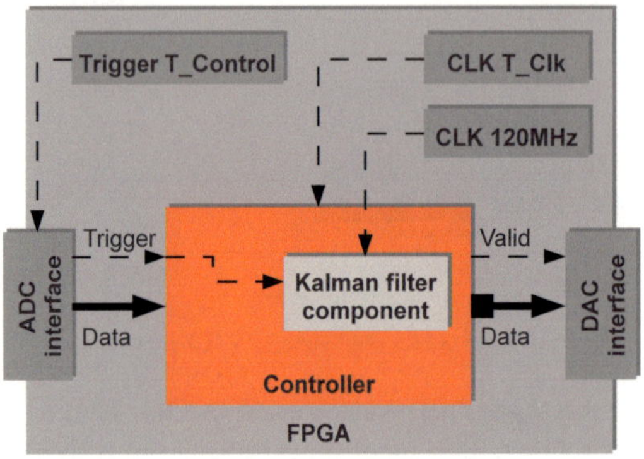

Fig. 14. Integration of the generated synchronized controller into an FPGA design.

Figure 14 depicts the integration of the I/O-synchronized controller into an FPGA design. The component is independent from surrounding logic, except the clock sources. Thanks to the registered I/Os and the trigger signal, the execution of the controller can be started upon the event of input data availability. This is best signalled by an upstream component like an ADC, which in turn relays its own trigger signal with period `T_Control`. The execution flow is continued in a deterministic way further downstream to trigger the output, constituting a real-time behaviour as illustrated in Figure 9.

The introduction of `T_Clk` as simulation base sample time allows to simulate all significant controller computation steps within the control system sample period. An decrease of the simulation sample period always increases the simulation complexity and duration, since now also the plant and environment would have to be simulated with increased rate, although they only produce a significant value change with a period of `T_Control`. To minimize this effect, the construction of a *multi-rate model* is recommended, allowing to simulate the controller partition with `T_Clk` while only executing the plant model once every `T_Control`, as in the platform-independent model.

Figure 15 shows a section of the model surrounding the x-axis controller module, illustrating the interface adaptions necessary to accommodate a HDL compatible, cycle-oriented partition. The data lines for values coming from the plant and environment model have been supplemented with *Data type conversions* (Convert) to provide the fixed-point values and *Rate transitions* (RT) to transition from the `T_Control` to the `T_Clk` time domain. Furthermore, the pulse generator block producing the execution trigger pulse with a width of `T_Clk` and period `T_Control` is shown.

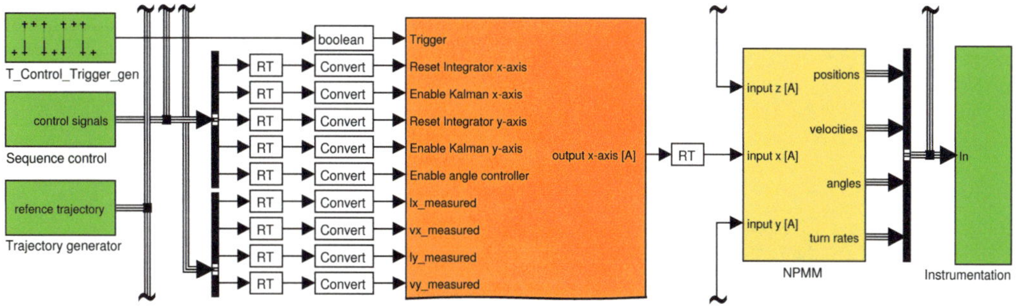

Fig. 15. Section of the multi-rate model containing the controller design simulated with higher time resolution.

4.3 Remarks

This section introduced two different implementable designs of the example controller - first, a largely combinational design with feedback registers to be clocked with `T_Control`; and second, an I/O registered design to be clocked with at least `T_Clk` and triggered with period `T_Control`. Both represent different styles of hardware implementation, depending on the grade of robustness, decoupling, universality or reusability, that is required for the component under development with regard to the system it is to be embedded in.

The introduction of the sample time `T_Clk` allows to simulate the controller execution cycles within the control system sample steps. In principle, `T_Clk` does not need to be more fine-grained, than necessary to simulate the N designed computation steps - i.e. $T\_Clk \leq 1/N \times T\_Control$. Of course, on the chip the component will be clocked with a much higher frequency, but a true cycle-accurate simulation of a multi-MHz clocked controller design is not feasible in the early design and validation stages of a control design with a sample rate of some kHz. Scaling up the resolution of `T_Clk` with continuing refinement of the execution path and logic stages is a way to find the balance between behavioural validation - "as accurate as necessary" - and simulation time - "as short as possible".

The controller model with registered I/O resembles only the first step into the direction of *synchronous component* design. In principle it is possible to insert registers after each operation step, thus assuming the total control over the execution of the algorithm in terms of timing and determinism. The subdivision of the data path by registers shortens the combinational paths and allows to drive the hardware design with a higher clock - in turn, the overall latency will increase due to the higher cycle count. Aiming on either, the smaller overall latency of combinational designs, or the higher frequency of synchronous designs, is possible by adapting advanced hardware design principles on modelling level, but exceeds the focus of this chapter.

5. From simulation model to implementation model

To summarize the activities discussed in this chapter, Figure 16 shows a detailed view of the *PIM-to-PSM transformation* as a part of the Simulink-based development flow from the introduction. Based on a controller partition embedded in a plant and environment model the refinement process towards a platform-specific execution model starts with the *data path design*. This iterative process substitutes the algorithmic blocks with constructs supported by the code generation facilities. Additionally, all signals carrying the data are converted to fixed-point representations with as minimal bit widths as possible.

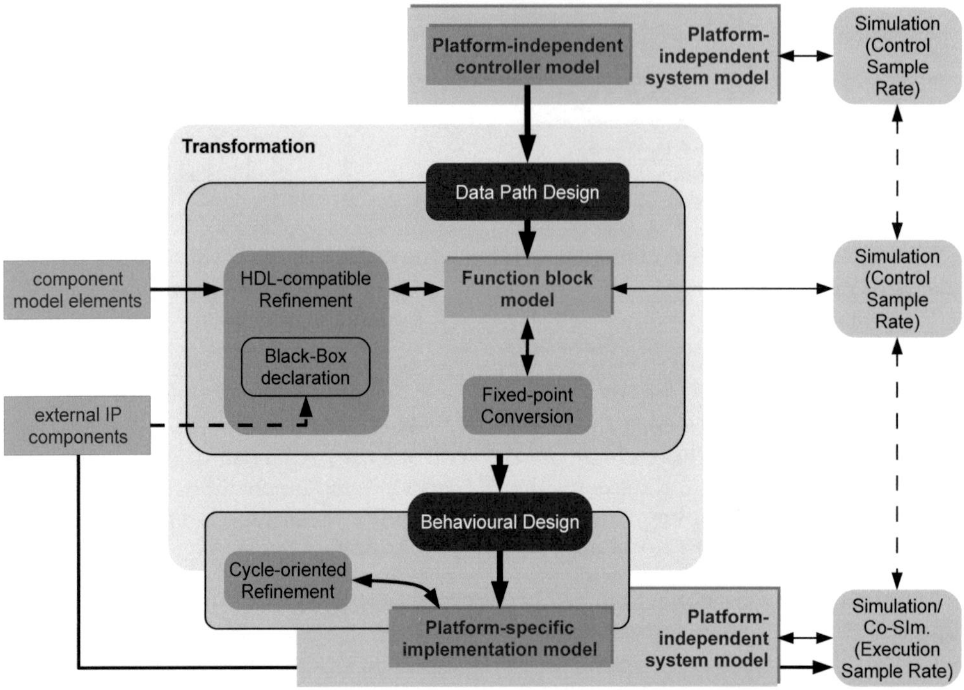

Fig. 16. The platform-specific controller modelling and validation flow in detail.

The substitutions and conversions necessary to fulfill the HDL-compatibility can produce deviations from the behaviour of the specified controller design. Therefore, a *simulative validation* of each modification towards a more platform-specific representation against the initial platform-independent specification is necessary, which might motivate an iteration of the initial controller design and parametrization. Validation of the fixed-point solution is a critical factor. Both the automated conversion using the Fixed-Point tools as well as the manual conversion rely on the specified data ranges for all operations. For operators with a-priori unknown output data ranges, the tools offer the option to determine the minima and maxima from the simulation results. Obviously, the consistency of this solution is based on the completeness of the simulation scenario - not covering the real minima/maxima of certain values will result in falsely scaled fixed-point representations. As a side note, as pointed out by The Mathworks (2011b), MATLAB has a restriction on simulation data widths of 128 bit, for larger word lengths a bit-accurate simulation is not possible, and the simulation results will deviate from the actual execution results.

The data path design approach also applies to the utilization of the vendor specific tools Xilinx, Inc. (2011) System Generator or Altera Corporation (2011) DSP Builder. But, when using these tools, from some point onwards during refinement process the model will have to be completely (re-)designed using the vendor-specifc block sets to create a platform-specific model, that is compatible to the respective code generation tool chains.

The activity of *behavioural design* applies for all mentioned tools in a similar fashion and concerns the design of the execution behaviour of the algorithm on the hardware.

Two possible designs have been introduced along with their properties concerning chip integration. Depending on the number of logic stages incorporated in the design, the platform-specific model has to be simulated with a more fine-grained simulation time resolution. The Mathworks (2011b) HDL Coder provides the possibility to create a cycle-accurate model of the HDL code derived from Simulink blocks configured to more advanced architectural implementations, which might introduce additional execution cycles not reflected in the original model. In those cases the execution control path of platform-specific model has to be further refined, regarding both the logic stages and the, simulation time resolution, to cycle-accurate simulation.

The simulative validation of the platform-specific model including a black-box component can also be conducted using HDL co-simulation, via links to external HDL simulators, like e.g. ModelSim. This method allows to analyse the behaviour of the black-box implementation and its interaction with the surrounding controller design on a cycle-accurate level. HDL co-simulation is also supported by the Xilinx System Generator. Without the HDL co-simulation option the validation of the black-box behaviour can be conducted only after leaving the modelling level by simulating the complete HDL generated design with instantiated black-box component with an HDL simulator. This course of action is aided by the HDL Coder by giving the option to generate an HDL testbench from the recorded Simulink simulation scenario. A method for validation of the implemented chip-design within the environment of the simulated plant model is the hardware-in-the-loop (HIL) simulation, that is supported by the vendor-specific tools DSP Builder and System Generator.

6. Conclusion

In conclusion it can be stated that MATLAB/Simulink supports the seamless top-down development flow for control designs with the intention of implementing the digital real-time controller on a reconfigurable logic platform. Within the extends of the Simulink block set and associated tools, and under consideration of the issues discussed in this chapter, the engineer can conduct the process of data path design by successive refinement and transformation of the controller model under constant validation against the surrounding plant model. The construction of the correct control flow of the algorithm's execution is a decisive engineering step, but it is well supported by the model-based approach. From a certain level of refinement, the usage of the HDL Coder supported block set or the the FPGA vendors' block sets provide the ability to construct and validate a hardware-oriented execution model. While the former allows a more integrated top-down modelling process, and the latter provide more platform-specific design and validation abilities, either tool facilitates in closing the gap between model-based design, automatic code generation and FPGA synthesis.

7. Acknowledgements

The work presented here is related to the research within the Collaborative Research Centre 622 "Nano-Positioning and Nano-Measuring Machines", funded by the German Research Council (DFG) under grant SFB 622 / CRC 622.

8. References

Altera Corporation (2011). DSP Builder Handbook Volume 1 : Introduction to DSP Builder.

Amthor, A., Zschack, S. & Ament, C. (2008). Position control on nanometer scale based on an adaptive friction compensation scheme, *2008 34th Annual Conference of IEEE Industrial Electronics*, IEEE, Orlando (USA), pp. 2568–2573.

Auger, D. (2008). Programmable hardware systems using model-based design, *2008 IET and Electronics Weekly Conference on Programmable Hardware Systems* .

Carletta, J. & Veillette, R. (2005). A methodology for FPGA-based control implementation, *IEEE Transactions on Control Systems Technology* 13(6): 977–987.

Caspi, P. & Maler, O. (2005). From control loops to real-time programs, *Handbook of networked and embedded control systems*, Birkhäuser, pp. 395–418.

Keating, M. & Bricaud, P. (2002). *Reuse Methodology Manual*, 3rd edn, Springer.

Krasner, J. (2004). Model-based design and beyond: Solutions for today's embedded systems requirements, *Analyst report, American Technology International* (January): 1–12.

Monmasson, E. & Cirstea, M. (2007). FPGA Design Methodology for Industrial Control Systems - A Review, *IEEE Transactions on Industrial Electronics* 54(4): 1824–1842.

Müller, M., Fengler, W., Amthor, A. & Ament, C. (2009). Model-driven development and multiprocessor implementation of a dynamic control algorithm for nanopositioning and nanomeasuring machines, *Journal of Systems and Control Engineering* 223: 417–429.

Pacholik, A., Klöckner, J., Müller, M., Gushchina, I. & Fengler, W. (2011). LiSARD: LabVIEW Integrated Softcore Architecture for Reconfigurable Devices, *2011 International Conference on Reconfigurable Computing and FPGAs (ReConFig '11), 30. Nov.- 02. Dec. 2011, Cancun (Mexico)*, IEEE Computer Society CPS, pp. 442–447.

Rushton, A. (2011). *VHDL for Logic Synthesis*, 3rd edn, John Wiley & Sons.

The Mathworks (2010). Simulink Fixed Point 6 User Guide.

The Mathworks (2011a). MATLAB/Simulink Online Documentation.
URL: *http://www.mathworks.com/help/toolbox/simulink/*

The Mathworks (2011b). Simulink HDL Coder User's Guide R2011b.

Xilinx, Inc. (2011). Xilinx System Generator for DSP User Guide.

Zschäck, S., Amthor, A., Müller, M., Klöckner, J., Ament, C. & Fengler, W. (2010). Integrated system development process for high-precision motion control systems, *2010 IEEE International Conference on Control Applications*, IEEE, pp. 344–350.

7

Describing Function Recording with Simulink and MATLAB

Krunoslav Horvat, Ognjen Kuljaca and Tomislav Sijak
Brodarski Institute
Croatia

1. Introduction

Describing function is an equivalent gain of nonlinear element, defined by the harmonic linearization method of nonlinear static characteristic (Novogranov, 1986, Slotine and Li, 1991, Schwarz and Gran, 2001, Vukic et al. 2003 and many others). It is a known method of analysis and synthesis when nonlinear system can be decoupled into linear and nonlinear parts (Fig. 1). If the linear part of the system has the characteristics of low-pass filter and if we apply periodical signal to the system, output signal will have the same base frequency as input signal with damped higher frequencies.

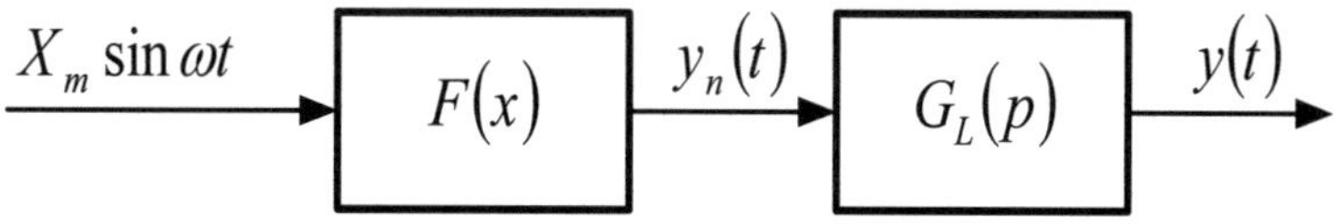

Fig. 1. Nonlinear system represented with decoupled nonlinear F(x, px) and linear parts $G_L(p)$, p=d/dt.

If the amplitudes of higher harmonics are relatively small when compared to the amplitude of the first harmonic, i.e. if filter hypothesis holds, output signal can be approximated by it's first harmonic. Mathematically, first harmonic of the output signal, for the sinusoidal input signal $X_m \sin\omega t$, can be expressed by the Fourier expressions:

$$y_N(t) \approx Y_{P1} \sin\omega t + Y_{Q1} \cos\omega t$$
$$y_N(t) \approx \mathrm{Im}\left\{\left(Y_{P1} + jY_{Q1}\right) e^{j\omega t}\right\} \tag{1}$$

$$Y_{P1} = \frac{1}{\pi} \int_0^{2\pi} F(X_m \sin\omega t) \sin\omega t \, d(\omega t) \tag{2}$$

$$Y_{Q1} = \frac{1}{\pi} \int_0^{2\pi} F(X_m \sin\omega t) \cos\omega t \, d(\omega t) \tag{3}$$

where Y_{P1} and Y_{Q1} are first Fourier coefficients.

Describing function is the ratio between first harmonic of the output signal and input signal in complex form:

$$G_N(X_m) = P(X_m) + jQ(X_m) = \frac{Y_{P1}}{X_m} + j\frac{Y_{Q1}}{X_m} \tag{4}$$

where $P(X_m)$ and $Q(X_m)$ are coefficients of the harmonic linearization (Novogranov, 1986, Slotine and Li, 1991, Schwarz and Gran, 2001, Vukic et al., 2003 and many others).

Determination of describing function boils down to the determination of integral expressions for the known static characteristic of the nonlinear part of the system.

There are many conventional nonlinearities for which static characteristics and describing functions are theoretically derived and given in analytical form.

The problem arises when the static characteristic of nonlinear system cannot be analytically expressed or integral expressions can not be solved. In that case describing function can be determined by experiment or simulation (Kuljaca et al., Sijak et al.k 2004, 2005, 2007a, 2007b) or some method of numerical integration (Schwarz and Gran, 2001).

2. Nonlinear elements in Simulink

Nonlinear elements are given in Simulink library Discontinuities. Twelve discontinuities given there are shown in Fig. 2.

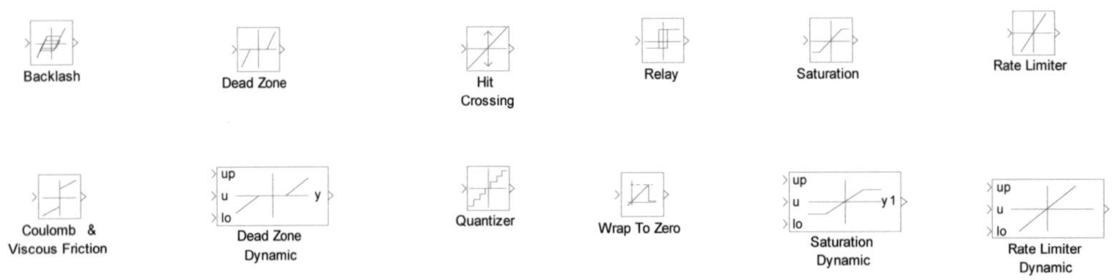

Fig. 2. Discontinuities (nonlinearities) given in Simulink.

We can see that there are three elements called "Dynamic" (Dead Zone Dynamic, Saturation Dynamic and Rate Limiter Dynamic). The term dynamic is considered at these elements with respect to change of nonlinearity limits (output values limits or rate change limits), not as dynamics in control systems sense (i.e. behavior in time domain). Never the less, we will not deal with such elements here. Describing function method analysis or synthesis is not suitable for systems with varying parameters.

One can see that Simulink gives only basic non-dynamic nonlinearities. More nonlinearities and their describing function can be found in work by Vukic et al., (2003). It is clear that one needs to build them out of basic Simulink models or write them as m or s functions. Since given functions don't have dynamics it is recommended to build them out of given Simulink blocks, or if that is not possible, then using type 2 s-functions. Even in that case some real time extension software for Simulink and Matlab might not be able to handle user designed s-functions.

3. Describing function by numerical integration

An interesting approach to obtaining describing function using Simulink is given by Schwartz and Gran. The approach is very simple, yet effective. In essence, equations (2) and (3) are directly applied in Simulink on nonlinear element outputs. A simulation scheme adapted from Schwartz is given in Fig. 3. In this case dead zone nonlinearity is analyzed. Instead of dead zone, any other nonlinearity can be included in model.

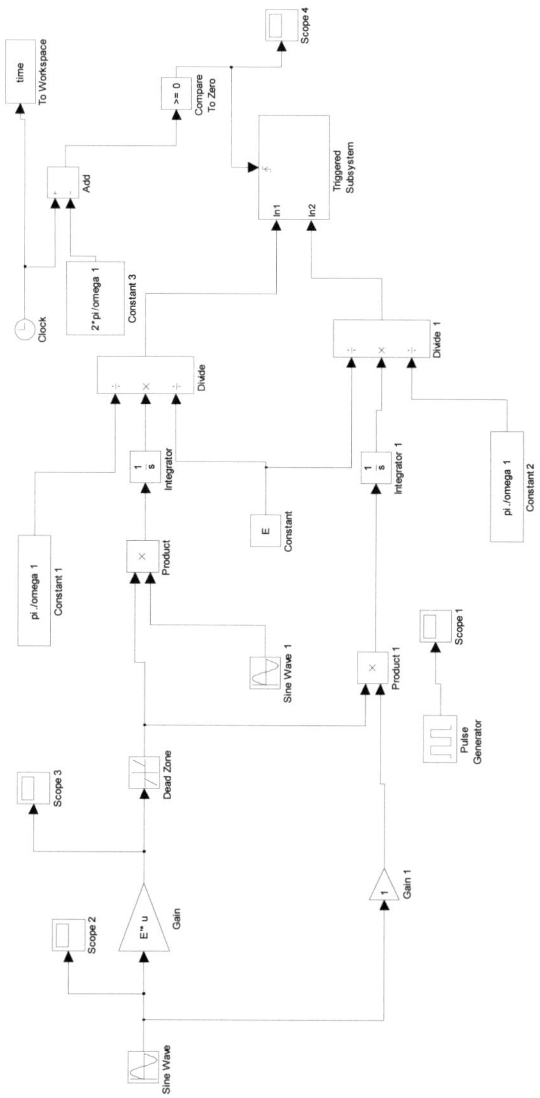

Fig. 3. Simulink model 'csm' for generating describing function (Schwartz)

Model is called from Matlab script (adapted form Schwartz and Gran as well) as shown in Fig. 4. simulation parameters are passed to Simulink schematic from Matlab script, as given in Fig. 5.

```
E=[[0.15:.01:0.25],[0.3:0.1:0.9],[1:.5:3]];%amplitudes
omega=[.5:.5:5 5.5:.1:6.2 2*pi 6.2:.1:7.5 7:.5:10];
%omega are frequencies
Nf=length(omega);
array=zeros(1,1,length(omega),length(E));
s=zeros(length(omega),length(E));
for j=1:Nf
omega1=omega(j);
sim('csm');
DF = (DFreal+sqrt(-1)*DFimag);
s(j,:)=DF;
array(1,1,j,:)=DF;
end
figure(1); surf(E,omega,abs(s))
shading interp
ylabel('Frequency (rad/sec)'); xlabel('Amplitude');
zlabel('Describing Function Gain')
title('Describing Function Amplitude vs. Frequency and
Amplitude of Input')
figure(2)
surf(E,omega,angle(s))
shading interp
ylabel('Frequency (rad/sec)'); xlabel('Amplitude');
zlabel('Describing Function Phase')
title('Describing Function Phase vs. Frequency and
Amplitude of Input')
```

Fig. 4. Matlab script for describing function generation

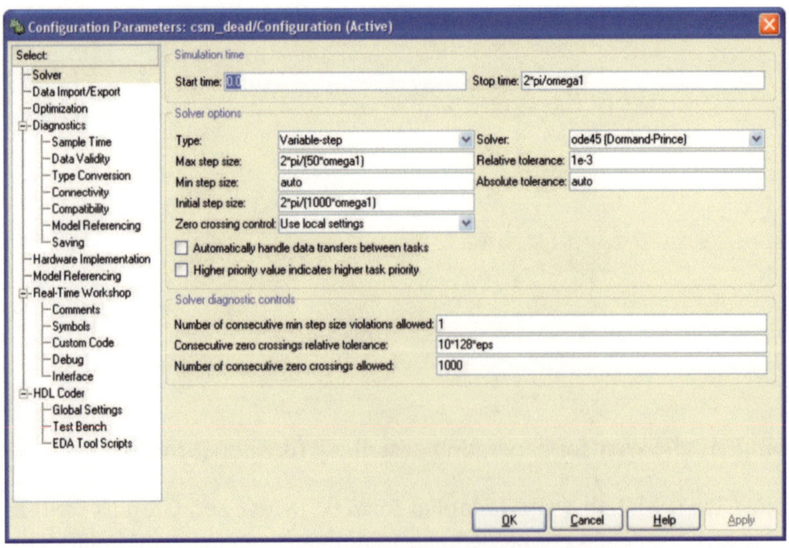

Fig. 5. Simulation configuration parameters – parameter omega1 is taken from Matlab script

Triggered subsystem is shown in Fig. 6. The whole file is built to stop simulation after one full period for a given frequency.

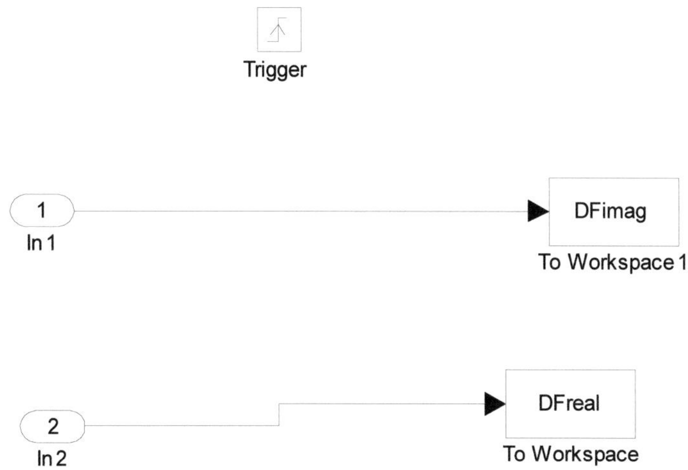

Fig. 6. Triggered subsystem

Let us now see how Simulink file with Matlab function will perform for a common nonlinearity, saturation with saturation limit 0.5. Saturation type nonlinearity is shown in Fig. 7.

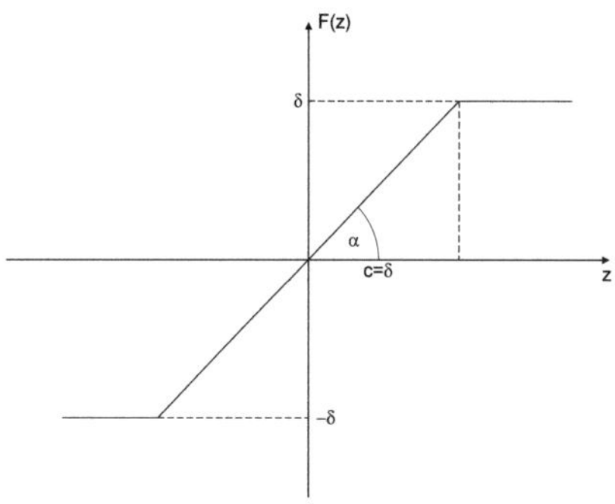

Fig. 7. Saturation

Saturation has known describing function given by (5). It can be seen that imaginary part of the gain is zero. That is a case with all symmetrical nonlinearities.

$$G = G(Z_m) = \frac{2 \cdot tg\alpha}{\Pi}\left(\arcsin\frac{c}{A_m} + \frac{c}{A_m} \cdot \sqrt{1 - \frac{c^2}{A_m{}^2}}\right); A_m > c \tag{5}$$

where A_m is amplitude of signal entering saturation.

Let us now see the results of running our simulation script in order to obtain describing function for saturation. Simulation results are shown in Fig. 8 and Fig. 9.

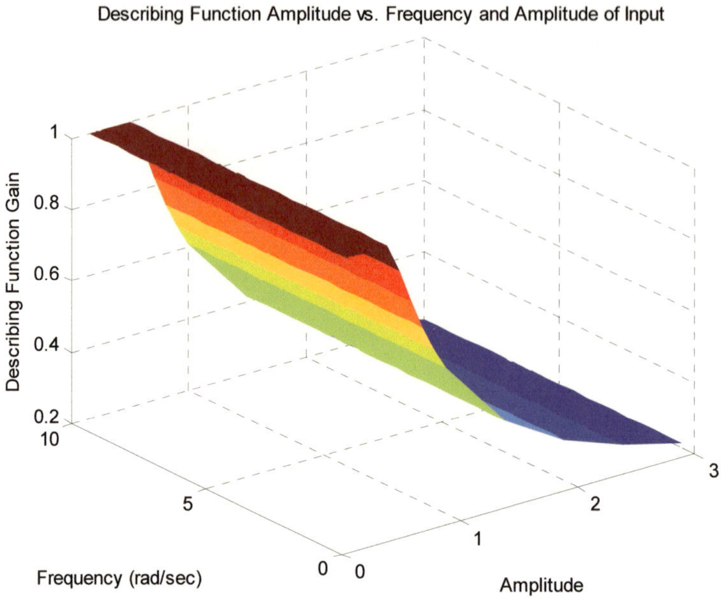

Fig. 8. Describing function gain as function of amplitude and frequency

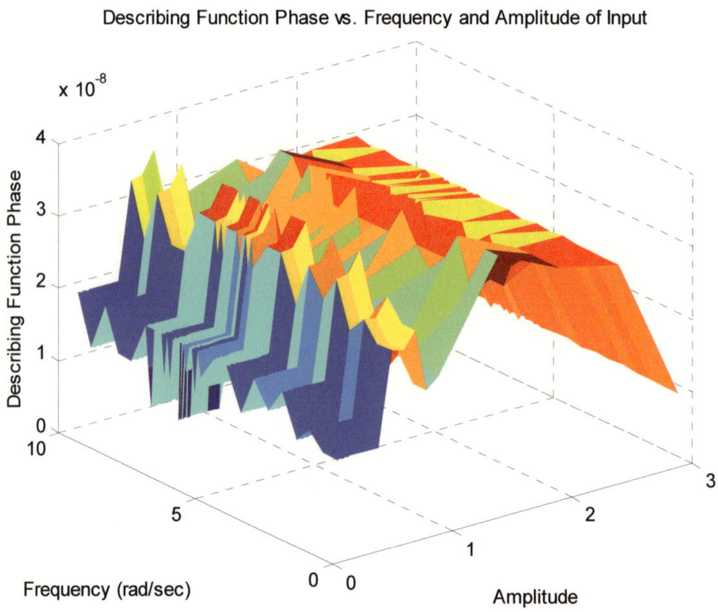

Fig. 9. Describing function phase as function of amplitude and frequency

It can be seen from Fig. 8 that describing function in this case is not dependent on frequency. Also, phase is zero since saturation is symmetrical nonlinearity. That can be seen from very small values of describing function phase as given in Fig. 9. These values are practically zero. Obtained result from simulation is given complex matrix s. In case like this, where there is no frequency dependency and phase is zero, there is no need for plotting describing function in three dimensions. To make function plot in two dimensions we run the following short script:

```
gdf=s(1,:);
plot(E,real(gdf)),grid, ylabel('Describing function gain');
xlabel('Amplitude');
```

Two dimensional describing function gain is shown in

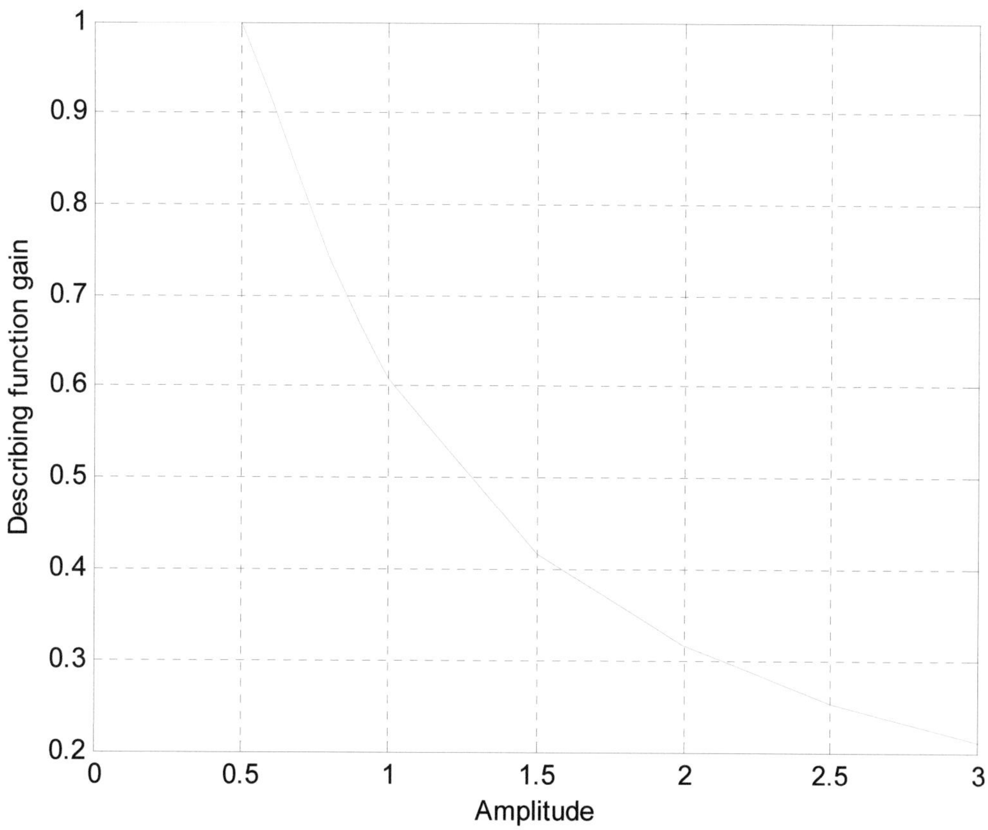

Fig. 10. Describing function gain – two dimensional representation

We will see in subsequent sections that this representation of symmetrical nonlinearities as gain dependent on amplitude of nonlinearity input signal is important for stability analysis.

This technique can be used to obtain describing functions of real nonlinearities by using Simulink model from Fig. 3 with appropriate real time additions with Real Time Window Target, xPc Target or other real time systems for use with Simulink. Of course, in that case amplitudes will have to be given one by one, not as here as one vector.

4. Fuzzy control systems and their describing functions in Simulink

Use of fuzzy control systems is today well known in control systems design. Unfortunately, while there are well developed methods for design or training of fuzzy systems, stability analysis remains problematic. If the fuzzy system is of Mamdani type, than its mathematical description can be very complicated and stability analysis is complicated as well. However, if we can obtain describing function of fuzzy system, then we can use known stability analysis methods developed for linear systems. One type of experimental method of obtaining describing function for fuzzy elements is given in (Kuljaca et al.) and (Sijak et al., 2005, 2007b). Here, we will use numerical integration in Simulink as given by Schwartz. Simulation file will have to be reworked since we cannot use vectors in this simulation due to fuzzy element.

Of course, there are different fuzzy controllers and elements, but describing function for all of them can be achieved using this method. One should note that here we are not talking about adaptive fuzzy controllers, but about fuzzy controllers with fixed membership functions and rule base.

Let us first look on one example of fuzzy controller, as shown in Fig. 11 (Kuljaca et al., Sijak et al. 2007a), where k_p and k_d are gains.

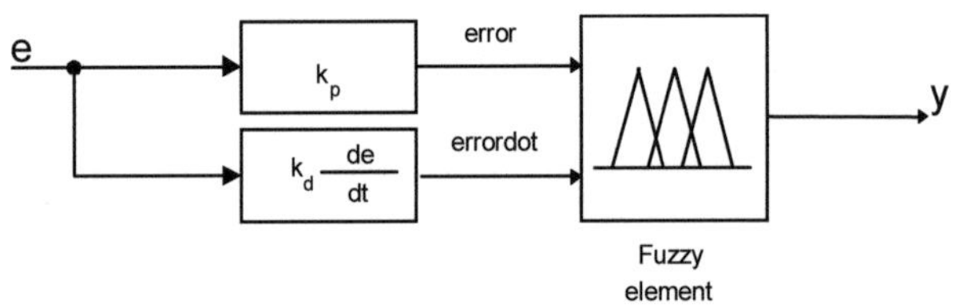

Fig. 11. The block diagram of fuzzy controller

First of all, it can be seen that fuzzy element here has two inputs. Fuzzy elements in general can have more inputs and outputs than here, but, this structure is most often in control systems (either as given here with derivative of the error or with integral of the error). When more inputs are used it becomes extremely complicated to tune the controller.

Numerical integration Simulink model (Schwartz) with fuzzy controller will look like in Fig. 12, without vector inputs for amplitudes since fuzzy block in Simulink cannot handle such input type. This is also much closer to real measurement, since in real measurement we would not able to use vector inputs. Meaning of this is that we need to use adjusted script to run the Simulink model. Adjusted script is given in Fig. 13.

Fuzzy Logic controller Simulink block is regular block from Simulink Fuzzy Logic toolbox library.

Fuzzy element itself is developed using FIS editor from Matlab Fuzzy Logic Toolbox.

This is an illustrative example; however, it is quite useful in giving an insight in use of describing function for fuzzy controllers. The given method can give a graphic representation of any fuzzy controller based on error and derivatives of error signal. In most cases fuzzy controllers are also symmetrical, thus subsequent stability analysis will be simpler. Amplitudes and frequencies are to be chosen to satisfy expected operational environment of controller.

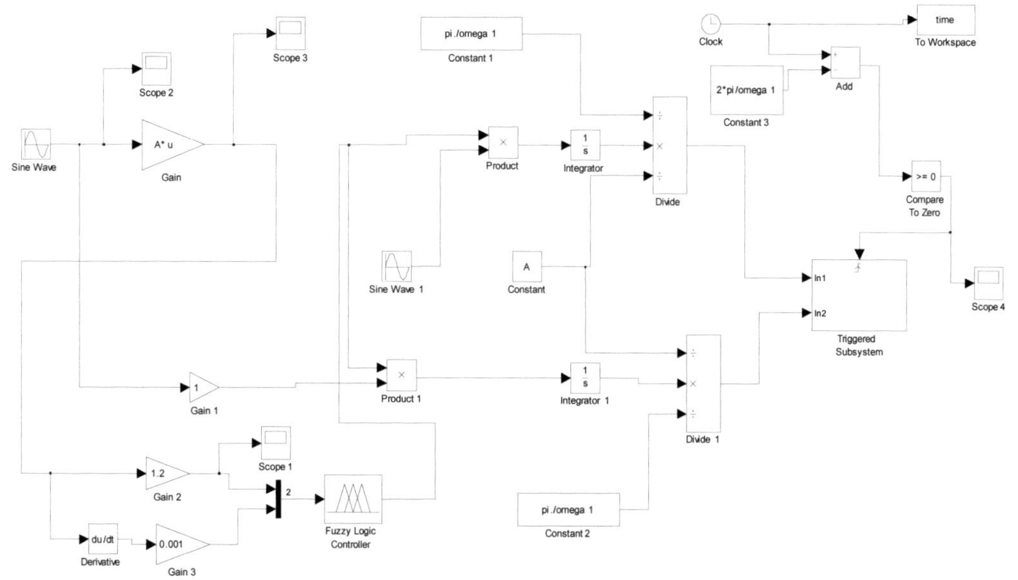

Fig. 12. Numerical integration model 'csm_fuzzy'- describing function recording

```
E=[[0.15:.01:0.25],[0.3:0.1:0.9],[1:.5:3]];
omega=[.5:.5:5 5.5:.1:6.2 2*pi 6.2:.1:7.5 7:.5:10];
for ke=1:max(size(E))
    A=E(ke);
    for kw=1:max(size(omega))
        omega1=omega(kw)
          sim('csm_fuzzy')
        s(ke,kw) = (DFreal+sqrt(-1)*DFimag);
    end
end
figure(1); surf(omega,E,abs(s))
shading interp
xlabel('Frequency (rad/sec)'); ylabel('Amplitude');
zlabel('Describing Function Gain')
title('Describing Function Amplitude vs. Frequency
and Amplitude of Input')
figure(2);surf(omega,E,angle(s))
shading interp
xlabel('Frequency (rad/sec)'); ylabel('Amplitude');
zlabel('Describing Function Phase')
title('Describing Function Phase vs. Frequency and
Amplitude of Input')
```

Fig. 13. Matlab script for running 'csm_fuzzy' model

In example given here gains k_p and k_d are set to 1.2 and 0.001 respectively, min-max and centroid defuzzification Mamdani type fuzzy controller membership functions are given in Fig. 14 and rulebase is given in Fig. 15.

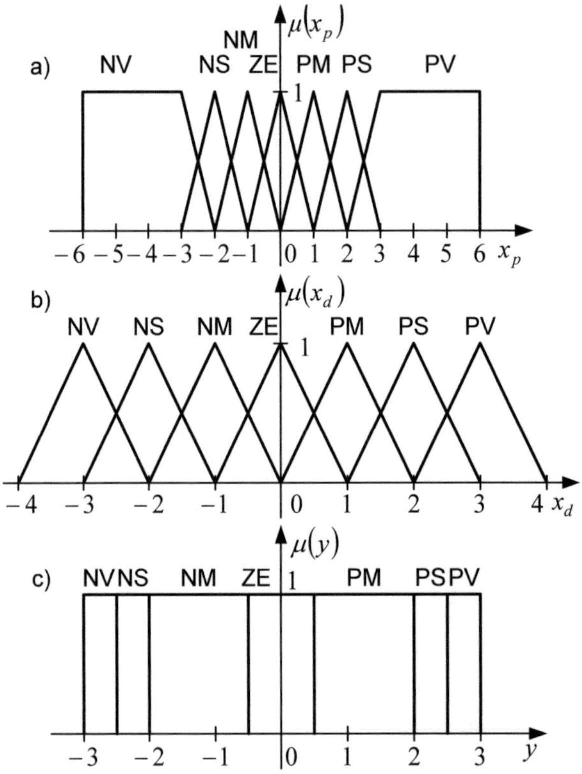

Fig. 14. Membership functions of the fuzzy element: a) proportional input, b) derivative input and c) output

x_d \ x_p	**NV**	**NS**	**NM**	**ZE**	**PM**	**PS**	**PV**
NV	NV	NV	NV	NV	NS	NM	ZE
NS	NV	NV	NV	NS	NM	ZE	PM
NM	NV	NV	NS	NM	ZE	PM	PS
ZE	NV	NS	NM	ZE	PM	PS	PV
PM	NS	NM	ZE	PM	PS	PV	PV
PS	NM	ZE	PM	PS	PV	PV	PV
PV	ZE	PM	PS	PV	PV	PV	PV

Fig. 15. Rulebase of the fuzzy element

Describing function for given fuzzy controller is given in Fig. 16 and Fig. 17. It can be seen from Fig. 16 that describing function gain is function of amplitude and it really does not depend on frequency in this case.

Describing function phase as function of amplitude and frequency shown in Fig. 17 shows very small values and for all practical purposes can be considered to be zero. Since our fuzzy controller design is symmetrical one that is in compliance with theoretical expectations.

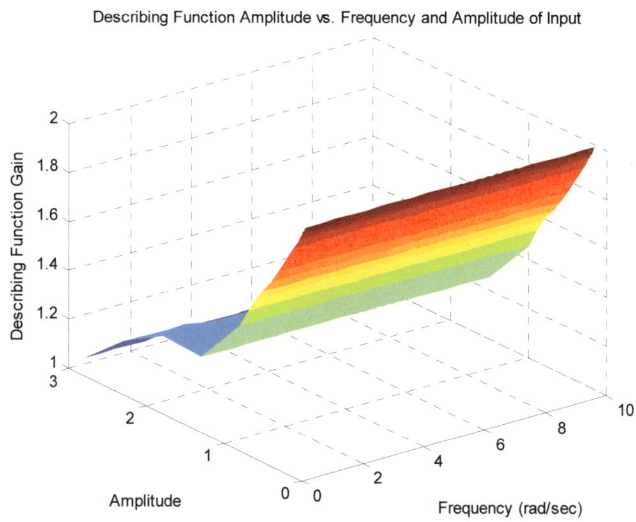

Fig. 16. Describing function gain as function of amplitude and frequency

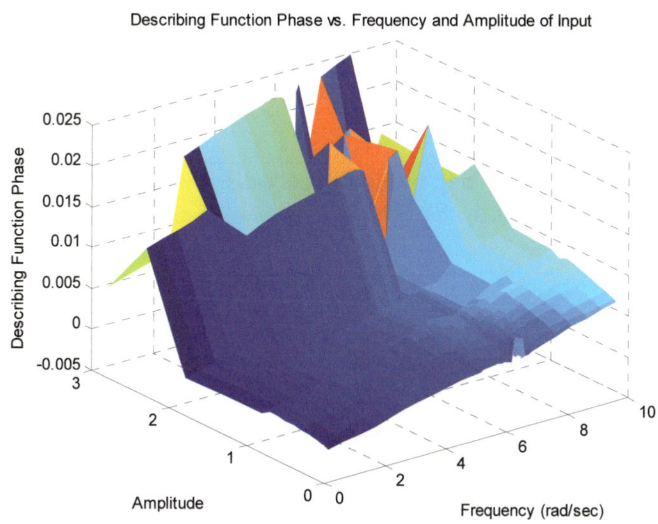

Fig. 17. Describing function phase as function of amplitude and frequency

5. Stability analysis with describing functions in Simulink – Case study

Once describing function is obtained, it could be used for stability analysis. We will use a simplified secondary frequency control model of the isolated thermo power system with generation rate constraint (Sijak et al.,2001). Control model is shown in Fig. 18.

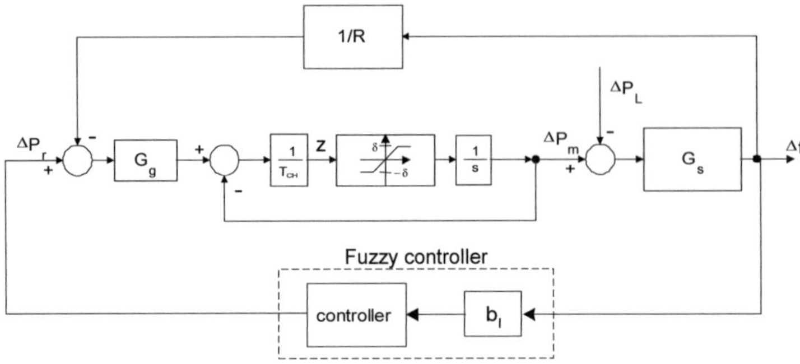

Fig. 18. Power system secondary load-frequency control model

where:

$G_G = \dfrac{1}{1+sT_G}$ - the transfer function of the turbine governor

T_{CH} - the steam turbine time constant

ΔP_m – the change of the mechanical power of the turbine

ΔP_L – the change of the power system load

ΔP_r – the power system active power reference change

Δf – the power system frequency change

$G_s = \dfrac{K_s}{1+sT_s}$ - the power system transfer function

R - the static speed droop of the uncontrolled system

$F(z)$ - the power system generation rate constraint, static characteristic of saturation nonlinearity.

The system given in Fig. 18 consists of nonlinear parts divided by linear parts for which the filter hypothesis is satisfied. Such system can be represented as in Fig. 19.

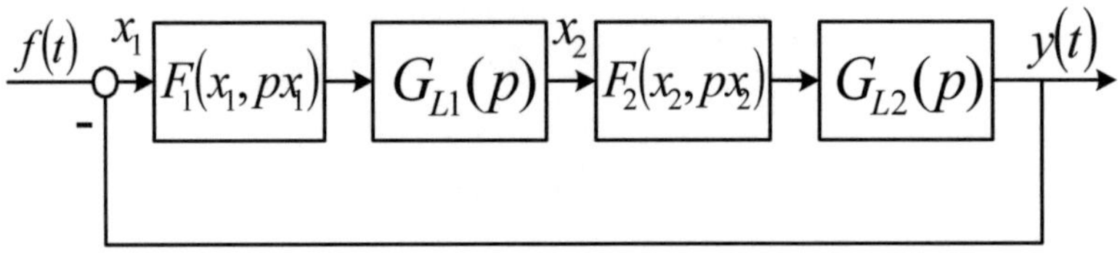

Fig. 19. The structure of the nonlinear system and fuzzy controller

where:

$F_i(x_i, px_i), p = \dfrac{d}{dt},$ - nonlinear parts of the system

$G_{Li}(s)$ - transfer functions of the linear parts of the system

Assuming that the filter hypothesis is valid for $G_{Li}(p)$, the nonlinearities can be harmonically linearized and their describing functions used instead (Vukic et al., Netushil et al.).

$$F_i(x_i, px_i) \approx F_i(X_{im}, \omega), x_i = X_{im}\sin(\omega t) \tag{6}$$

Harmonically linearized system is shown in Fig. 20.

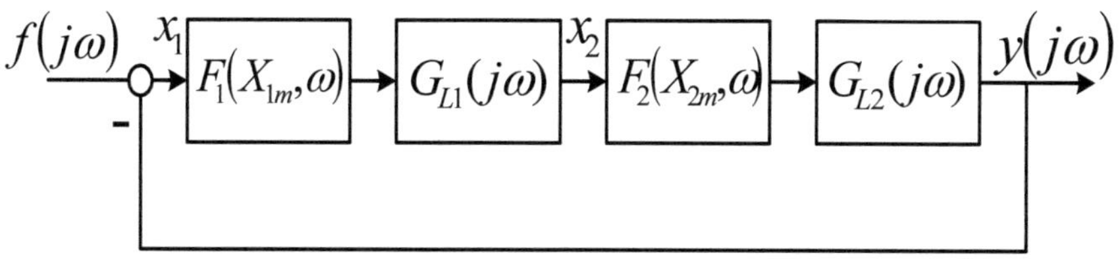

Fig. 20. The structure of the harmonically linearised nonlinear system and fuzzy controller

The self-oscillations (limit cycles) of the system in Fig. 20 are described by solution of:

$$1 + F_1(X_{1m}, \omega)G_{L1}(j\omega)F_2(X_{2m}, \omega)\, G_{L2}(j\omega) = 0 \tag{7}$$

Assuming that $F_1(X_{1m}, \omega)$ and $F_2(X_{2m}, \omega)$ are describing functions of the fuzzy controller and nonlinear part of the plant respectively, then the stability analysis of the system can be conducted using the solution of complex equation (7).

Let us now deal with nonlinearities. Generation rate constraint is saturation type nonlinearity shown in Fig. 21. Describing function for such nonlinearities is known and it is given in (8).

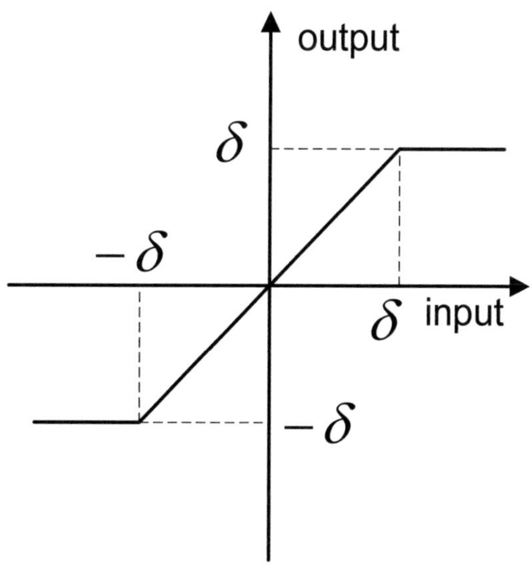

Fig. 21. Generation rate constraint

$$G_N(Z_m) = \frac{4}{\pi}\left(\frac{\alpha}{2} - \frac{\sin 2\alpha}{4} + \frac{\cos\alpha}{Z_m/\delta}\right), \alpha = \arcsin\frac{\delta}{Z_m} \tag{8}$$

The parameters of the system are: $T_G = 0.08$ s, $T_{CH} = 0.3$ s, $\delta = 0.0017$, $K_s = 120$ Hz/p.u., $T_s = 20$ s, R = 2.4 Hz/p.u., $b_l = 1$. With given parameters, describing function of generation rate constraint is shown in Fig. 22.

Fuzzy controller represents a bit more complex problem. We do not have its describing function in analytical form and we need to obtain it by experimental method. The method is described in Section 5 and describing function gain is plotted in Fig. 16 in three dimensional representation. Phase changes are zero, thus there is no complex component of describing function.

Representation in three dimension in this case is not required since there is no dependency of describing function gain on frequency. After running simulation script given in Section 5, one should run the following Matlab code in order to obtain two-dimensional representation of fuzzy controller describing function:

```
gdf=s(:,1);
plot(E,real(gdf)),grid, ylabel('Describing function gain');
xlabel('Amplitude');
```

Describing function in two dimensional representation is given in Fig. 23.

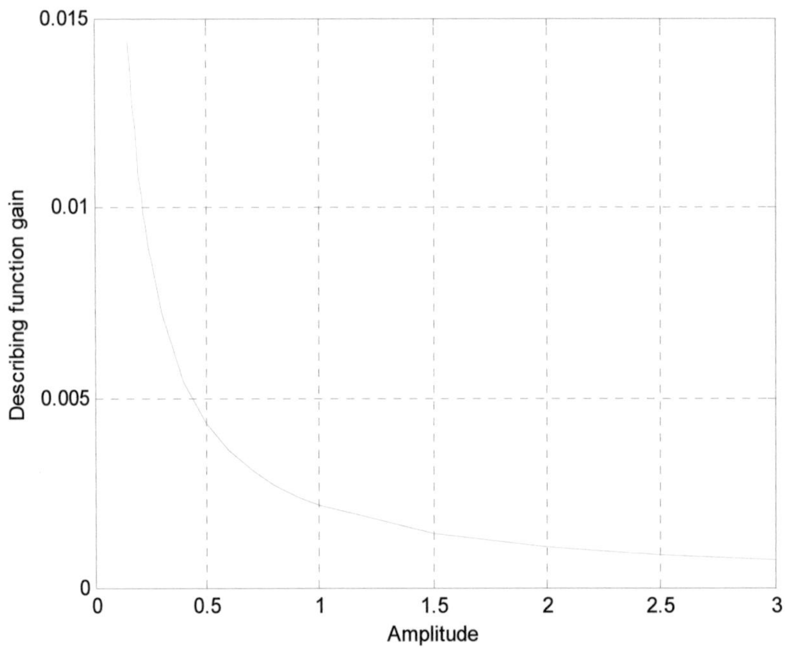

Fig. 22. Generation rate constraint describing function

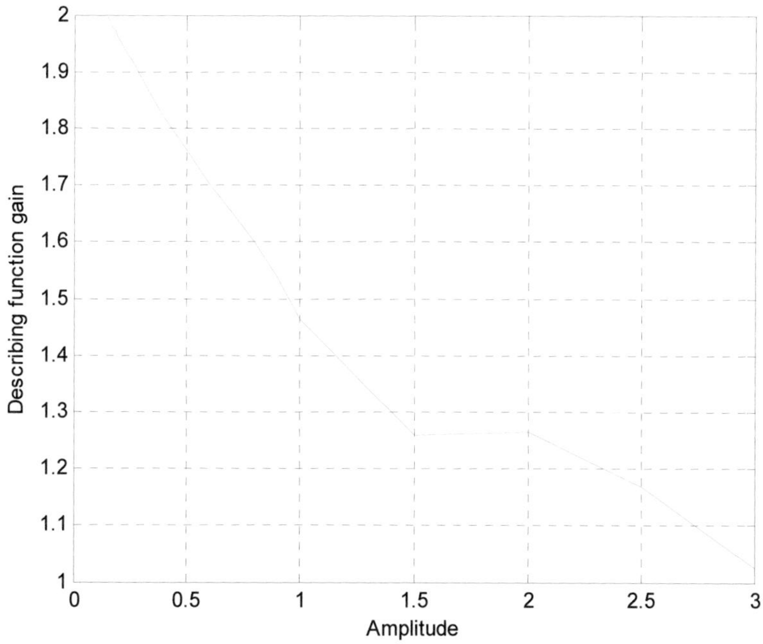

Fig. 23. Describing function of fuzzy controller in two dimensional representation

The static characteristics of the fuzzy regulator, i.e. its describing functions, shows that harmonically linearized fuzzy regulator can be regarded as input dependent variable gain element. Consequently, the stability analysis can be conducted in the plane $G_{NF} = f(G_{NZ})$, where

- $G_N(X_m) = G_{NF} = G_N(\Delta F_m)$ - describing function of the fuzzy regulator ,
- $G_{NZ} = G_N(Z_m)$ - describing function of the power system generation rate constraint.

The stability of the equilibrium point for the system given in Fig. 18 can be determined from the characteristic polynomial of the closed loop harmonically linearised equation (Kuljaca et al., Sijak et al., 2007):

$$T_{CH} + \left(K_0 + b_l G_{NF}\right) \cdot \frac{K_s}{1 + s \cdot T_s} \cdot \frac{1}{1 + s \cdot T_G} \cdot \frac{G_{NZ}}{s} + \frac{G_{NZ}}{s} = 0 \tag{9}$$

where: $K_0 = \dfrac{1}{R}$

From (9) the closed loop characteristic equation of the controlled system can be obtained:

$$\begin{aligned} &T_{CH} T_s T_G s^3 + \left[T_G T_s G_{NZ} + T_{CH}\left(T_G + T\right)_s\right] s^2 + \\ &\left[T_{CH} + \left(T_G + T_s\right) G_{NZ}\right] s \\ &+ G_{NZ} + (K_o + b_l G_{NF}) K_s G_{NZ} = 0 \end{aligned} \tag{10}$$

By applying Hurwitz stability criterion the following inequality is obtained:

$$\begin{aligned}&\left[T_G T_s G_{NZ} + T_{CH}\left(T_G + T_s\right)\right]\left[T_{CH} + \left(T_G + T_s\right)G_{NZ}\right] - \\ &T_{CH} T_s T_G\left[G_{NZ} + (K_0 + b_l G_{NF}) K_s G_{NZ}\right] > 0\end{aligned} \tag{11}$$

The system is stable as long as (11) is positive. Thus, the stability boundary can be derived as:

$$\begin{aligned}G_{NF} = &\frac{\left(T_G + T_S\right)G_{NZ}}{b_l T_{CH} K_s} + \frac{T_{CH}\left(T_G + T_s\right)^2 - T_G T_s T_{CH} K_0 K_s}{b_l T_{CH} T_s T_G K_s} \\ &+ \frac{T_{CH}\left(T_G + T_s\right)}{b_l T_s T_G K_s G_{NZ}}\end{aligned} \tag{12}$$

With the parameters used for simulation, the stability boundary function $G_{NF} = f(G_{NZ})$ can be evaluated. The function $G_{NF} = f(G_{NZ})$ is shown in Fig. 24.

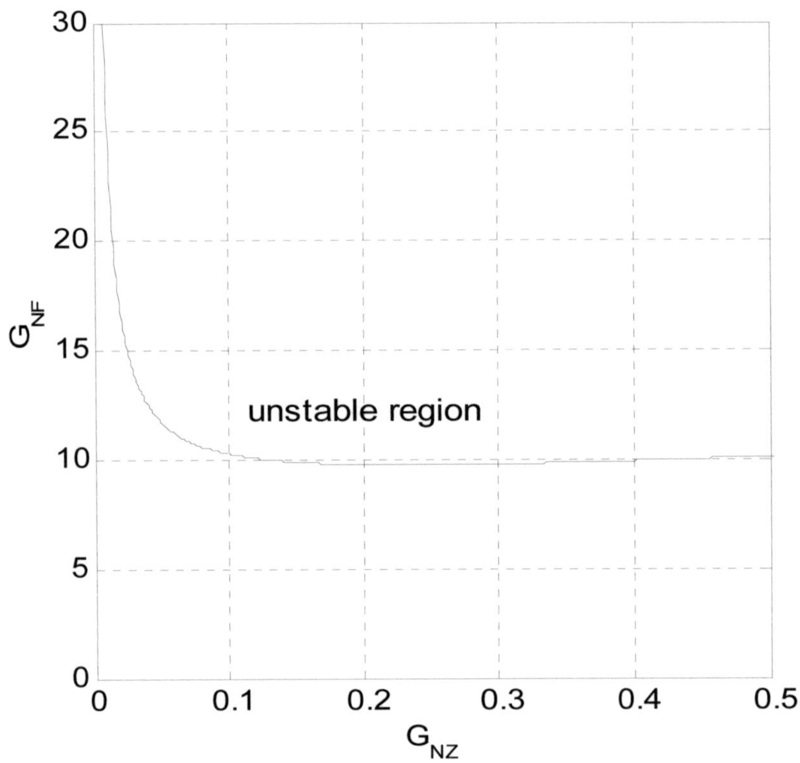

Fig. 24. Function $G_{NF} = f(G_{NZ})$

With given values system is stable in operating region of interest.

6. Conclusion

Chapter deals with use of Simulink for obtaining describing function for different elements. Described method of numerical simulation performed in Simulink is suitable for obtaining describing function of any single input single output non-dynamic nonlinearity. Method used for conventional static nonlinearities is then adjusted to work with fuzzy systems (and other systems that cannot handle vector based batch simulation in Simulink). Matlab scripts required to run given Simulink model are also given in Chapter. This method can be also used to obtain describing function for single input single output static neural networks. Finally, an example from use describing function for stability analysis is given.

Described method can be used with practical controllers with Matlab real time tools.

7. References

Kreyszig, E. (1993). *Advanced Engineering Mathematics (7),* John Wiley and Sons, New York, USA

Novogranov, B.N. (1986). *Determination of Frequency Domain Characteristics of Nonlinear Systems (in Russian),* Masinostroenie, Moskow, Russia

Kuljaca, O., Tesnjak, S., Vukić, Z. (1999). Describing Function of Mamdani Type Fuzzy Controller with Input Signals Derived From Single System Input and Singleton Ouput Membership Functions, *Proceedings of the 1999 IEEE Hong Kong Symposium on Robotics and Control,* Volume I, HKSRC '99, Hong Kong, 1999.

Sijak, T., Kuljaca, O., Antonic, A., Kuljaca, Lj., (2005). Analytical Determination of Describing Function of Nonlinear Element with Fuzzy Logic, *Proceedings of the IEEE International Symposium on Industrial Electronics 2005,* ISBN 0-7803-8739-2, Dubrovnik, Croatia, June 2005

Sijak, T., Kuljaca, O., Kuljaca, Lj. (2004). Describing function of generalized static characteristic of nonlinear element, *Proceedings of REDISCOVER 2004, Southeastern Europe, USA, Japan and European Community Workshop on Research and Education in Control and Signal Processing,* ISBN 953-184-077-6, Cavtat, Croatia, June 2004

Sijak, T., Kuljaca, O., Kuljaca, Lj., (2007). Engineering Procedure for Analysis of Nonlinear Structure Consisting of Fuzzy Element and Typical Nonlinear Element, *Proceedings of the 15th Mediterranean Conference on Control and Automation,* Athens, Greece, July 2007

Sijak, T., Kuljaca, O., Kuljaca, Lj., (2007). Computer Aided Harmonic Linearization of SISO Systems Using Linearly Approximated Static Characteristic. *Proceedings of EUROCON 2007 The International Conference on Computer as a Tool.* ISBN 1-4244-0813-X, Warsaw, Poland, September 2007.

Sijak, T., Kuljaca, O., Tesnjak, S. (2001). Stability analysis of fuzzy control system using describing function method, *Proceedings of 9th Mediterranean Conference on Control and Automation,* ISBN 953-6037-35-1, Dubrovnik Croatia, June2001

Slotine, J.J.E., Li, W. (1991). *Applied Nonlinear Control,* Prentice Hall, ISBN 0-13-040890-5, Engelwood Cliffs, New Jersey, USA

Schwartz, C., Gran, R. (2001). Describing Function Analysis Using MATLAB and Simulink. *IEEE Control Systems Magazine,* Vol. 21, No. 4, (August 2001), pp. 19-26, ISSN 1066-033X

Vukic, Z., Kuljaca, Lj., Donlagic, D., Tesnjak, S. (2003). *Nonlinear Control Systems*, Marcel Dekker, ISBN 0-8247-4112-9, New York, USA

Netushil at al. *Theory of Automatic Control*, Mir, Moscow 1978

8

Performance Evaluation of a Temperature Control Stage Used on a Semiconductor Gas Sensor 3D Electro-Thermal Model Through Simulink®

E.N. Vázquez-Acosta[1], S. Mendoza-Acevedo[1], M.A. Reyes-Barranca[1], L.M. Flores-Nava[1], J.A. Moreno-Cadenas[1] and J.L. González-Vidal[2]

[1]*CINVESTAV-IPN, Electrical Engineering Department*

[2]*Universidad Autónoma Del Estado de Hidalgo, Computing Academic Area*

Mexico

1. Introduction

Actually, the use of CAD-CAE is a widespread activity for design and evaluation purposes. Hence, several programs can be found for simulation and optimization of systems described with 3D graphic representation, giving the morphology of the model (Muñoz et al., 2008). Also, suites can be found that can simulate and prove some kind of controls being described with transfer functions (TFs), differential equations (DE), space states or ASIC models (Goering, 2004).

In general, the design begins creating the file of the solids that describe the geometry of the device through CAD tools and then exported to simulation and analysis environments (multi-physics). Thereafter, the results obtained are used in a multi-domain platform, where more complete results can be obtained for a system in consideration, taking advantage of modules that can link these environments. Now, one should have in mind that if complex dynamic models are to be considered, a serious limitation can be present if two or more variables of the system are mutually dependant. Therefore, it is suggested to export static models. In this case, the role of the modules is centred only to a basic interchange of data between the environments, having not a real and full interaction between the models considered. Then as a recommendation, it is convenient to include all the possible dynamics in the exported model, even as a part of it or as an external issue, such that the dynamic simulation can give more precise results. On the other hand, when a dynamic simulation is done based on a static model, there could be a dramatic increase in simulation time since a call to the static exported model will be done at each simulation time step. For instance, if a simulation is specified for a 1s lapse with 1ms steps, the exported model will be called 1000 times.

The particular case exposed in this paper is the analysis of a coupled thermo-electrical model designed to operate a micro hotplate (MHP) with a temperature control circuit, used in an integrated semiconductor gas sensor (SGS). The analysis should consider that the MHP will be physically located in a thin membrane created with MEMS technology. The complexity of this system is rather high since a thermo-electrical coupling must exist among devices that operate as a heat source and the different layers affected by the generated heat. Specifically, the case here studied treats the Joule Effect applied to the polysilicon material used in integrated circuits. Thus, it is necessary to combine somehow the analysis programs to obtain the required electro-thermal simulation results and to verify if the expected performance, i.e. temperature variation in time, is correct.

2. Description of the system

A SGS was designed based on layers available in standard CMOS technology, having two polysilicon layers and two metal layers. The layout of the prototype is shown in Fig. 1.

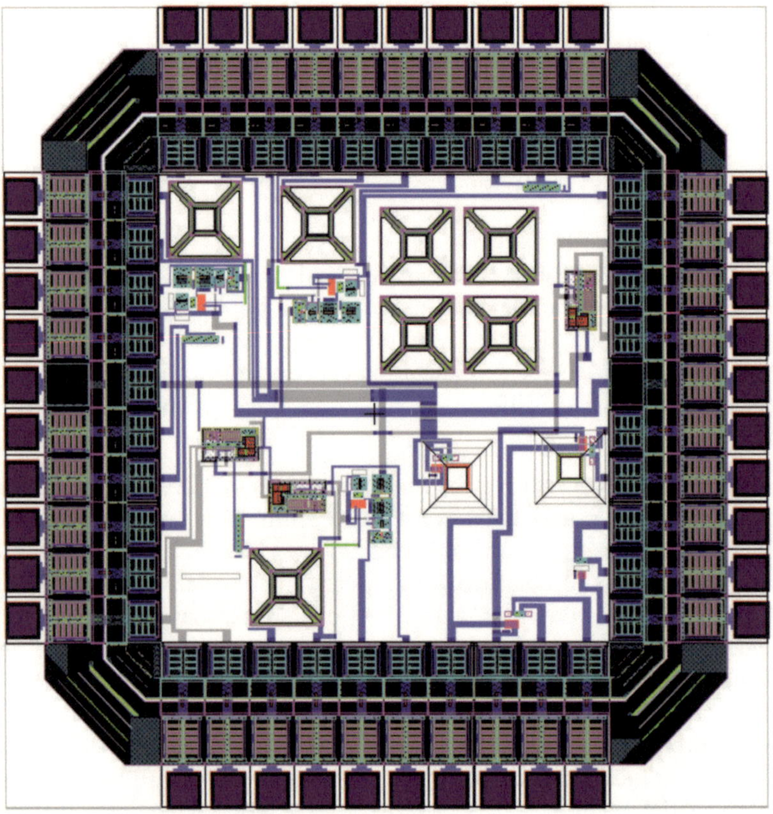

Fig. 1. Layout of the gas sensor prototype.

One advantage in using this kind of technology is its compatibility with MEMS micromachining processes made with anisotropic etching solutions as tetramethyl-ammonium hydroxide (TMAH), resulting in a preferential etching of the silicon substrate. This way, a very thin membrane is obtained containing the MHP (Fedder, 2005). The layout of the integrated sensor circuit is shown in Fig. 2, where the different blocks implemented for the system, are identified.

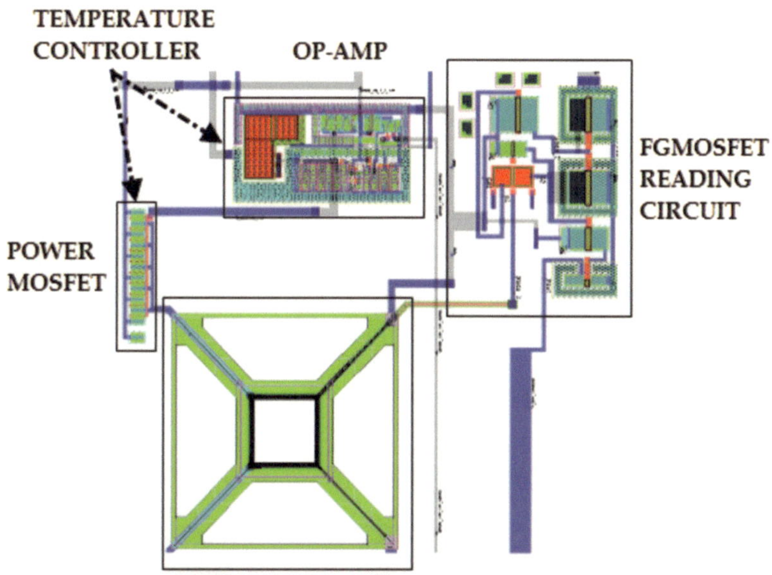

Fig. 2. Layout of the integrated gas sensor system.

This kind of gas sensor can be fabricated starting with a silicon substrate and includes a micro hotplate (MHP), whose structure stands as a mechanical support for the layers contained in the thin membrane ($SiO2$/Polysilicon/$SiO2$/Polysilicon/Metal Oxide). The thin film located above all these layers is a sensitive metal oxide layer that senses the gaseous species to be detected. Besides, the main purpose of the membrane is to isolate the heat generated in that zone and to uniformly distribute the temperature in the thin membrane.

The size of the MHP is 80μm x 80μm and will be suspended by four arms over the microcavity obtained after a bulk micromachining post-process usual in MEMS technology, giving an effective thermal isolation from the substrate. This way, the thermal mass of the MHP is reduced and as a consequence, its thermal inertia is decreased. Therefore, it is easy to attain an operation temperature range between 250°C and 350°C with low voltages applied (< 2.5V). This temperature promotes the chemical reaction between the thin metal oxide layer and the gas species (Afridi et al., 2002). Also, the MHP contains a micro temperature sensor (TS) and a microheater (MH) that is biased to raise its temperature due to the Joule Effect. Both will be fabricated with polysilicon and the proposed configuration is shown in Fig. 3.

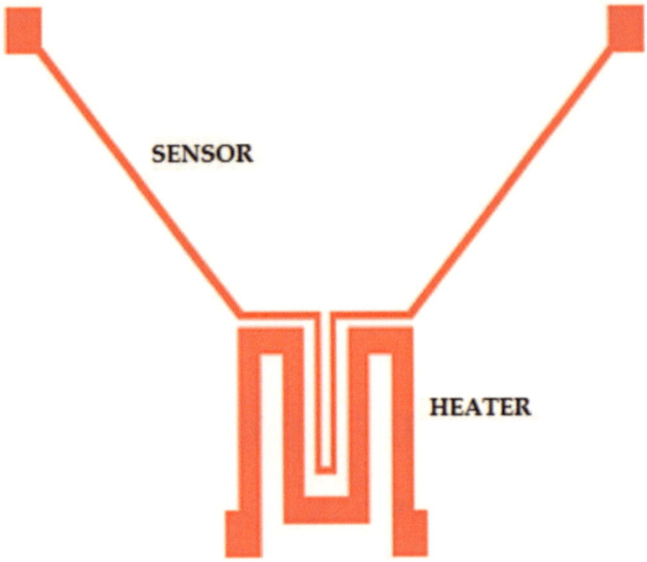

Fig. 3. Geometry of the microheater resistor and the temperature sensor.

When implemented as a resistor, polysilicon increases its resistance value proportionally with an associated temperature rise. This property is named Thermal Coefficient of Resistance (TCR) (Cerda et al., 2006). The relation of the resistance value with a temperature change is expressed with the following equation:

$$\frac{R - R_0}{R_0} = TCR\left(T - T_0\right) \tag{1}$$

where T0 is room temperature and R0 is the resistance value at room temperature. TCR and R0 can be experimentally determined. If the relation between temperature and resistance is known, it can be conveniently used to design a temperature control circuit if a constant current is passed through TS. If a DC voltage is applied across the microheater terminals, the resistance value of polysilicon increases as predicted by equation (1). Fig. 4 shows the variation of the resistance of TS and MH as a function of temperature from where TCR can be obtained.

TCR property sets a problem hard to solve from the simulation point of view when using traditional methods or programs like SPICE, since there is no possibility to consider at the same time the Joule Effect and the electro-thermal coupling between MH and TS. Also, it is difficult to properly consider the thermal inertia of the MHP's thermal mass using electrical simulators.

From Fig. 3, it is easy to deduce that the thermal coupling between the temperature sensor and the microheater is possible because of their proximity, so the fact that TS follows the temperature changes in MH can be used favourably. As it is well known, the thermal coupling behaviour depends on the properties of the materials used. For the structure here analysed, the materials involved are crystalline silicon, polysilicon, silicon dioxide and aluminium.

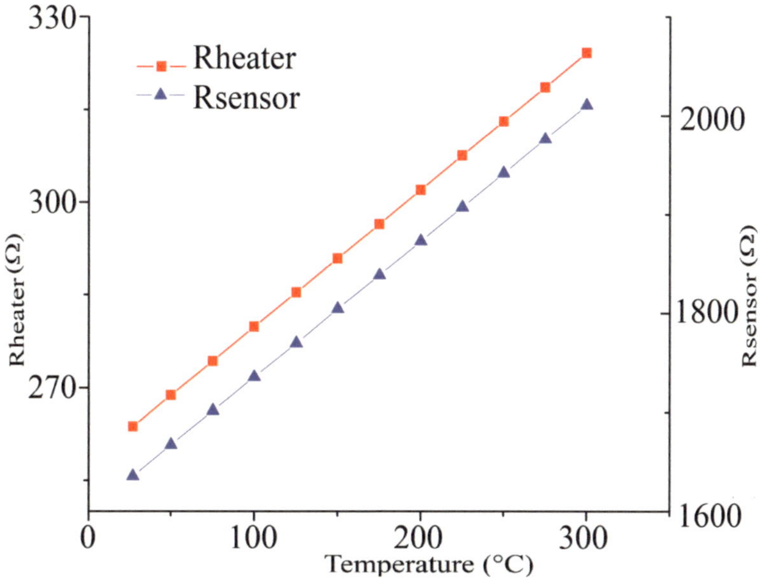

Fig. 4. MH and MS resistance value as a function of temperature.

Based on the later and the geometry drawn (Fig. 3), then the system will have a particular thermal response time for heating and cooling of the MHP. This is precisely the performance that is desired to be evaluated. Given the above background, the objectives of this work are: a) to propose a simulation and analysis strategy to find the dynamic behaviour of the model of the MHP driven by a temperature control circuit, based on the results obtained from the electro-thermal analysis, and b) to optimize the computing resources and simulation time. If the results are the expected, then the system can be fabricated with confidence. The following sections establish the proposed methodology.

3. Electro-thermal model

3.1 Simulation based on finite elements

Using specialized CAD software, a 3D solid model was created in order to propose the geometry of the structure needed for the electro-thermal analysis and simulation. This geometry should include the microcavity that is supposed to be made with the anisotropic etching after the fabrication of the chip. Once the geometry is finished, it can be exported to a multi-physics platform and proper sub-domains were assigned as well as boundary conditions (DC conductive media and heat transfer) to perform the analysis of the electro-thermal model. Also, to assure convergence with the finite elements analysis, a convenient mesh density should be selected. The analysis was made using an applied voltage sweep from 1V to 3V with 0.2V steps. The result is shown in Fig. 5, where the electro-thermal behaviour of the 3D geometric model of the gas sensor can be seen after the analysis with finite elements. Here it is confirmed that the heat is focused at the MHP as a result of the micromachining specified before. It should be noted that although the TS is not biased, it will have the same temperature induced by Joule Effect in the MH as a consequence of heat transfer by conduction across the silicon dioxide between them.

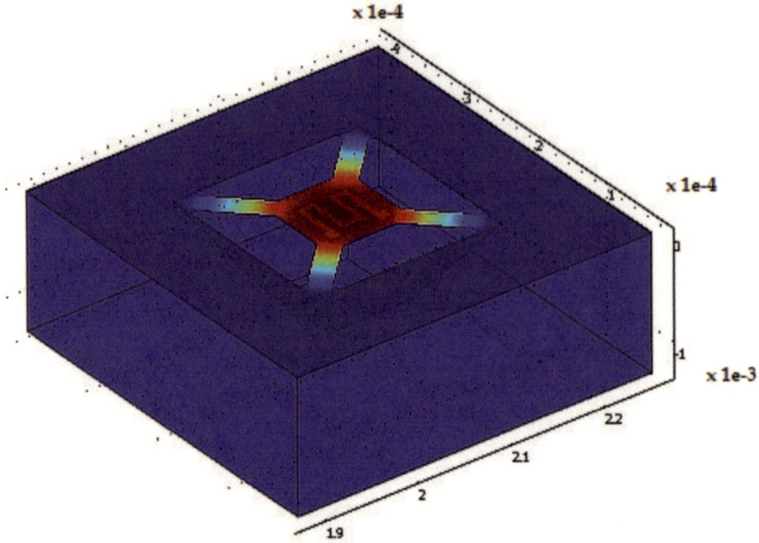

Fig. 5. 3D exported model from AutoCAD® after simulated with COMSOL Multiphysics®.

Using this same platform (multi-physics), the thermal response as a function of time having the applied voltage as a parameter was also obtained. Figs. 6 and 7 show the results for heating and cooling, respectively and it should be mentioned that a different response will be obtained for different geometries of MH and TS. This behaviour follows the change in resistance of polysilicon predicted by equation (1).

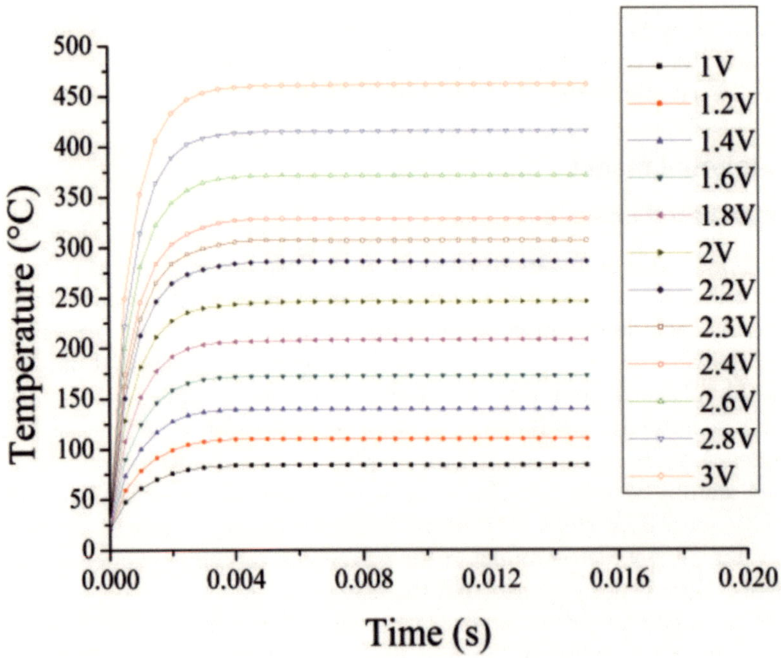

Fig. 6. MH heating response with applied voltage as a parameter.

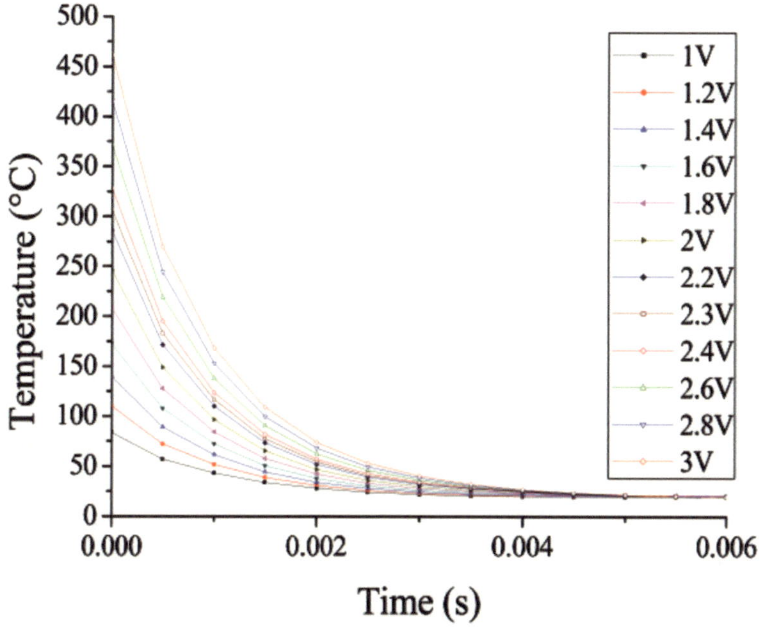

Fig. 7. MH cooling response with applied voltage as a parameter.

3.2 Simulation of the static model with the transfer function at the output

The model created in the multi-physics environment can be exported to a multi-domain environment using the existing modules specially created to link different software suits. Once the model is exported, one arbitrary exciting input and several reading outputs can be declared. In the case here exposed, the input is described as the voltage applied to MH. The value (or even the waveform) of this voltage can be modified along the simulation process in the multi-domain software. This is not possible to do with the multi-physics program. One of the outputs is declared as the reading of the temperature reached by MHP. The typical TCR of polysilicon can be easily calculated from this temperature reading.

Regardless of the possibilities and advantages that linking modules have, the model presents limitations when it is exported due to the mutual dependence of the variables as described by the electro-thermal coupling, therefore it is exported only as a static model.

Due to the above reason, transfer functions (TFs) must be added at the output of the simulation block of the exported system to consider dynamic features of the model. This makes possible to emulate the dynamic behaviour while heating or cooling, following the results obtained in Figs. 6 and 7. From now on, this model will be named as the exported model. For the case here reported, the TFs of interest can be obtained after making a series of heating and cooling cycles using the voltage range specified in Figs. 6 and 7. With the results obtained, an expression that nearly fits with the heating and cooling curves can be extrapolated. This can be done either with computational methods or by trial and error. Selection of the order of the expression of the TFs highly depends on the response of the system to a step input signal and to the desired accuracy. Since the system here analysed has no over damping, using a first order TF will simplify the task (Ogata, 1999).

The simplest expressions that fit approximately with the dynamics of the original system are the following:

- Cooling TF:

$$G_c(s) = \frac{1}{0.00077s + 1} \tag{2}$$

- Heating TF:

$$G_h(s) = \frac{1}{0.000095s + 1} \tag{3}$$

Fig. 8 shows the result after the simulation of the static model, together with the deduced TFs output when a voltage pulse was applied to the MH.

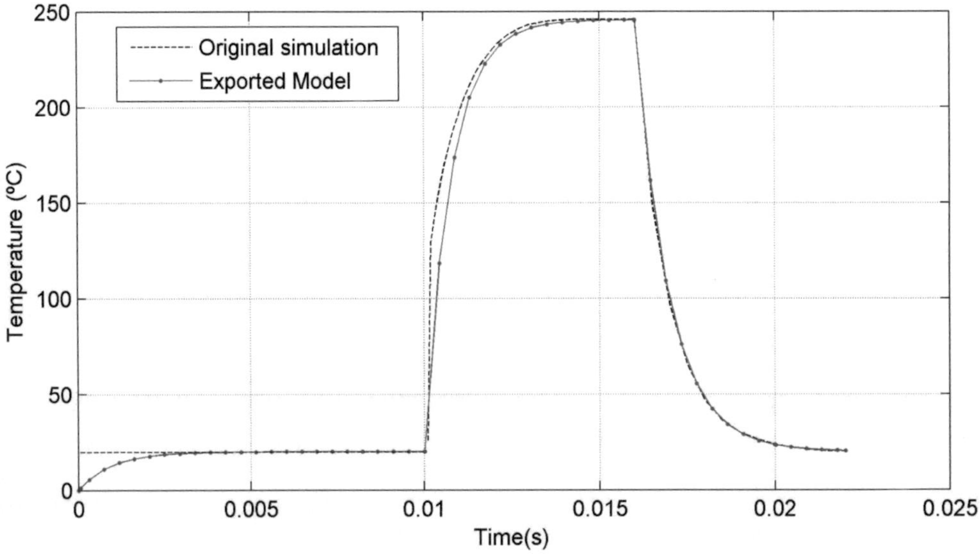

Fig. 8. Output of the static model when excited with an input step signal (continuous line) and the transfer function deduced from Figs. 6 and 7 (dashed line).

Once these TFs are included it is possible to apply arbitrary inputs to the system and read their corresponding dynamic outputs storing them as variables of the multi-domain software, with Simulink® of Matlab®, for instance. Also, it is possible to add and simulate some kind of temperature control block together with a signal processing or ASIC circuit. The later is not possible to do within the environment from where the created model was exported. Using the approximation with TFs it is possible to use certain blocks that call the exported model only when there are abrupt changes in the system's input. This helps to decrease the computing processing time (Hsu, 2002). Therefore, the suggested block diagram of the model that can be simulated with this alternative is shown in Fig. 9. This figure shows the block of the simulated electro-thermal system (COMSOL Subsystem), a signal generator block (Signal Builder), a block that calls the exported static model simulation (Pulsed COMSOL Sim), having the task to evaluate the model only when a change at the input signal is detected, saving this way time and computational resources. Here, existing modules that detect signal changes (Detect Change) are used together with a Boolean converter and a module that evaluates the exported model (COMSOL Triggered Simulation) followed by a Hold block that keeps the output value until there is a change at the input signal. All these modules are contained in the library of the multi-domain platform. Other supporting blocks included in Simulink® are a temperature unit converter (from K to °C), the Dynamic Adjust block that includes the heating and cooling TFs deduced before, and finally a block that displays the output waveform (Scope).

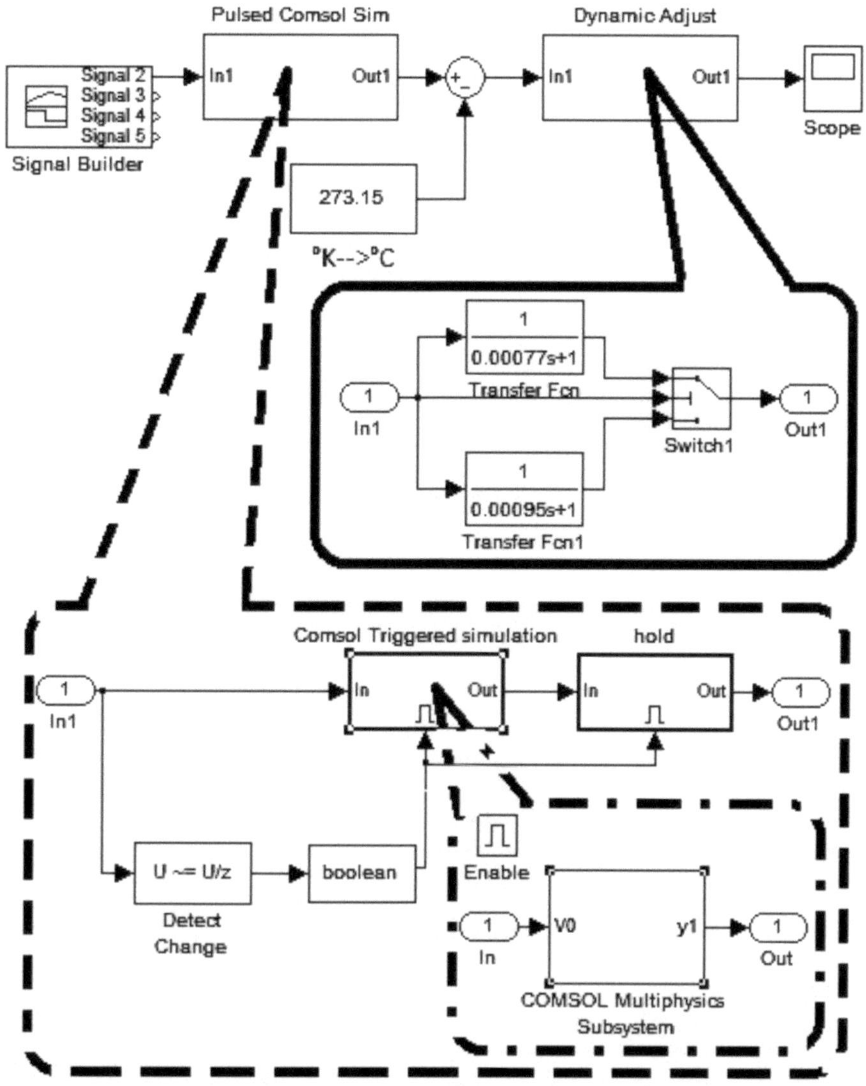

Fig. 9. Block diagram of Simulink® for the pulsed simulation.

3.3 Simulation with the approximated equation and transfer functions

The model illustrated in Fig. 9 presents great performance advantages if the applied inputs present abrupt changes in time like step signals. However it could be extremely slow if input signals have no abrupt changes during time like ramps or sine waveforms. So, if signals continuously changing in time are to be used, a more useful method to apply is based on the substitution of the block that calls the model (illustrated in Fig. 9), with an approximated equation that closely follows the temperature dependence of MH to the applied DC voltage, as obtained in the multi-physics platform. The kind of equation can be arbitrarily chosen while the parameters of it should be adjusted using the data obtained from the simulation of the exported model. Again, this can be done with the help of computational regression methods or by trial and error. Care should be taken to assure that the equation used is valid at least within the voltage sweep range of interest. The equation found for the case here presented is the following:

$$f(x) = 64x^{(1.938 - 0.0605x)} + 20 \tag{4}$$

where f(x) is the temperature output in K and x is the voltage applied to the MH in the exported model. Fig. 10 shows good agreement between the curve obtained after the static simulation of the exported model and the plot of equation (4).

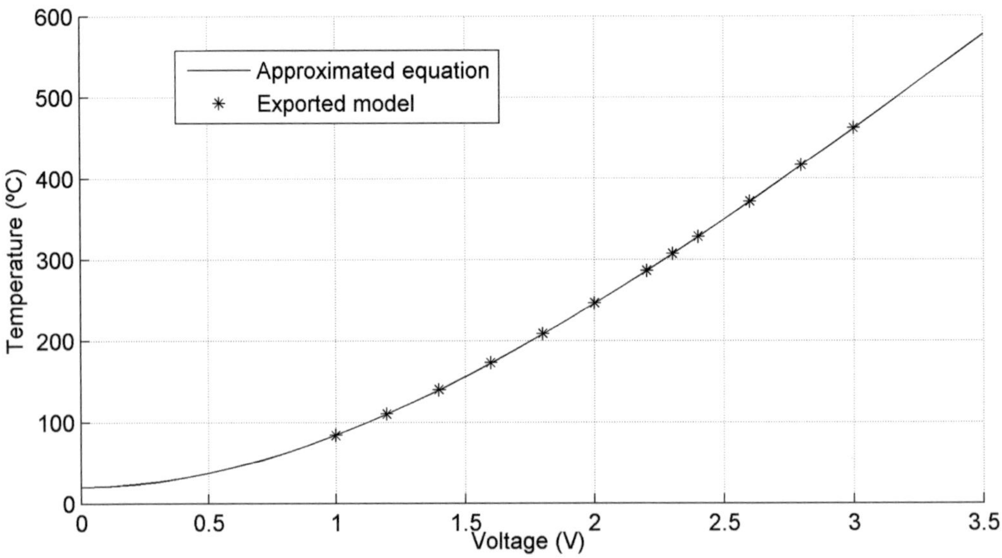

Fig. 10. Comparison between the static model and Eq. (4).

Therefore, this different alternative can be used properly in the desired dynamic simulation of the model. Once the approximated equation is obtained, it can be integrated into the simulation model instead of the module that invokes the pulsed exported model, using a function block as is shown in Fig. 11. Then, three options for the model simulation were presented: the exported model (3.1), the exported static model (3.2) and the approximated model (3.3). A series of simulations can be done to compare performance, validate the models and make a convenient choice among these methods. At first glance, a MH temperature range of 172.6 °C - 327.8°C (corresponding to a voltage range of 2V ± 0.42V) was used. The first test was done using a pulse train having arbitrary widths and magnitudes. The results are shown in Fig. 12.

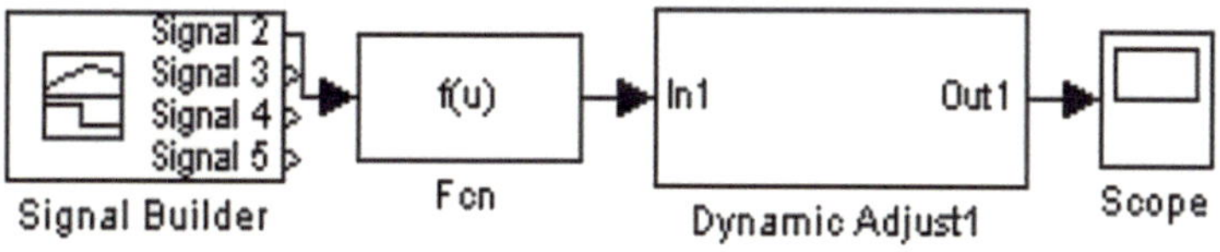

Fig. 11. Model with the approximated equation.

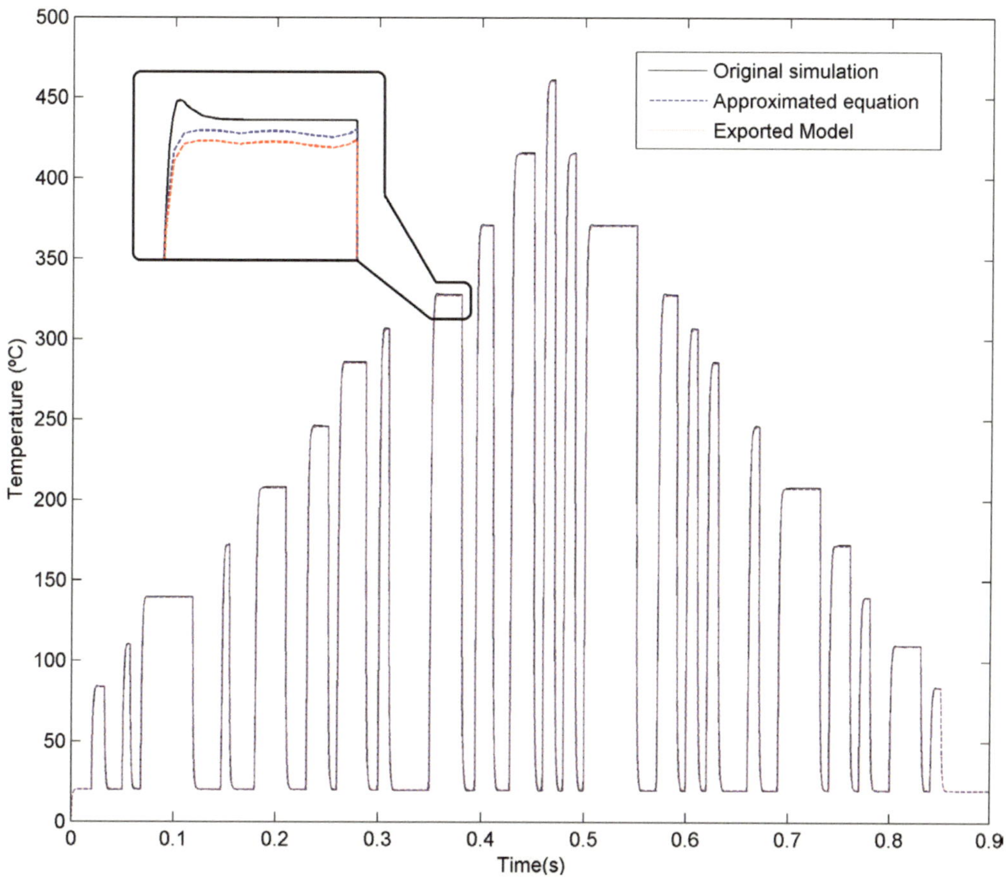

Fig. 12. Results from the simulation using the three analysing alternatives proposed, with an arbitrary pulse train as input.

As shown in Fig. 12, the three curves are quite similar among them. Deviation of methods 3.2 and 3.3 compared with 3.1 is only 0.22% in the worst case, meaning a variation of 1°C each 461.4°C. Hence it can be concluded that these options give similar results such that each of them can be used with confidence in the voltage range studied. However, it should be remembered that the exported model is limited to tests with simple on-off temperature controls and/or for abrupt inputs or with almost no changes in time. Otherwise, if inputs like a ramp or a sine waveforms are used, for instance, the static model will be invoked at each simulation step declared, increasing considerably the processing time. Since the objective is to optimize the simulation procedure, method 3.2 will be discarded from now on and only the original model (3.1) and the last one (3.3) will be considered in the following analyses. Comparative simulations between these two last methods were made, using the results of the original model obtained in the multi-physics environment and those obtained using the approximated model in the multi-domain platform. The results are shown in Figs. 13-15.

With these last results using arbitrary waveforms as input to the MH, heating and cooling can be effectively evaluated considering also heat dissipation due to the environment that is surrounding the system.

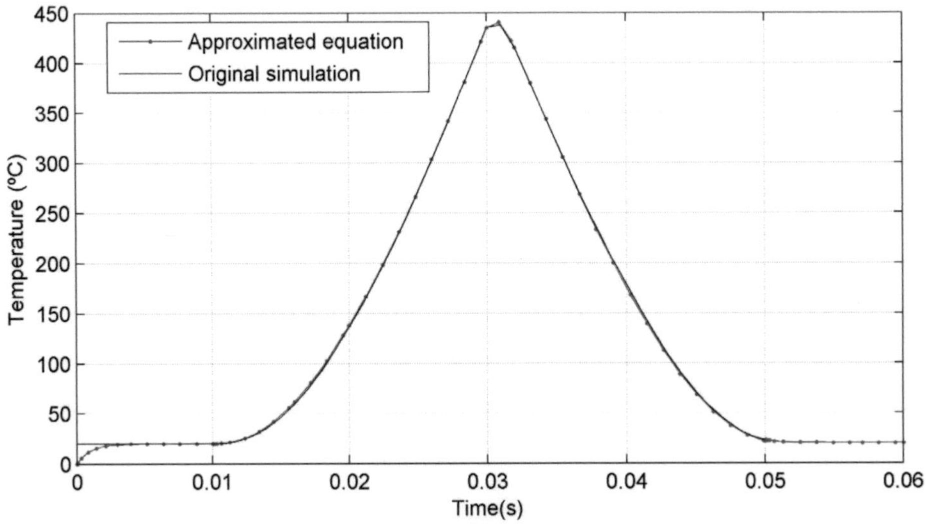

Fig. 13. Comparative with a saw tooth input signal.

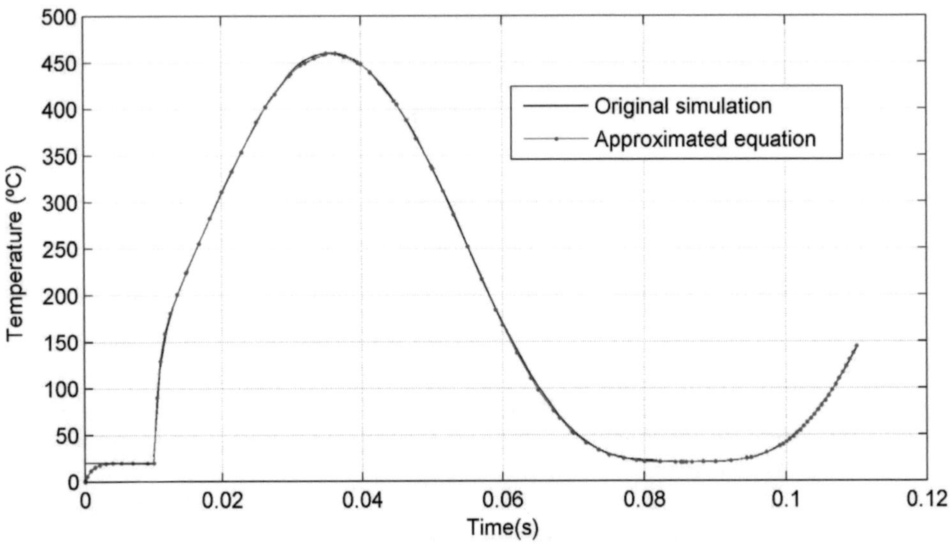

Fig. 14. Comparative with a sine waveform with a 3V amplitude and 10Hz frequency.

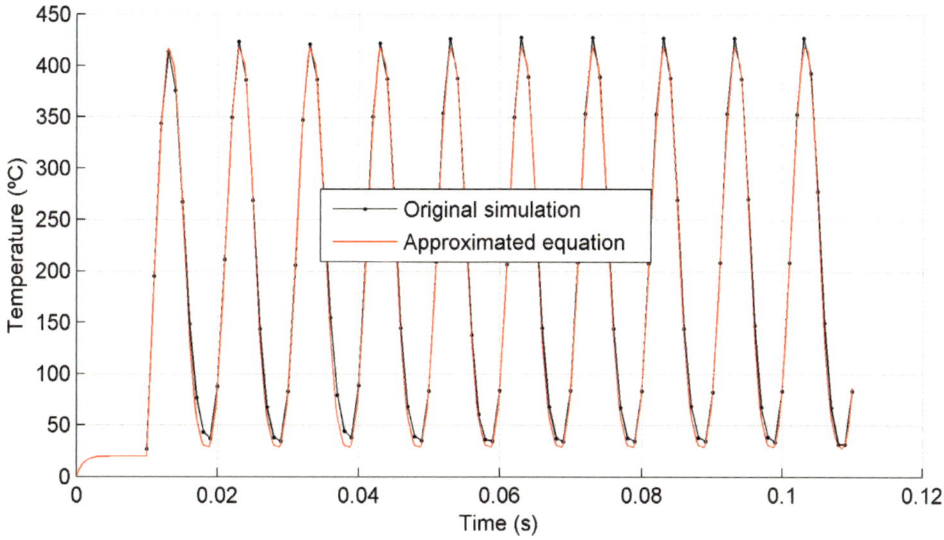

Fig. 15. Comparative with a sine waveform with a 3V amplitude and 100Hz frequency.

Near to real operating conditions can be considered this way. Also, it should be noted that the initial temperature considered in the multi-physics simulation is 20°C, as established in the boundary conditions, but the simulation results obtained with the approximated model (see Fig. 11) begin at 0°C, as shown in Fig. 16.

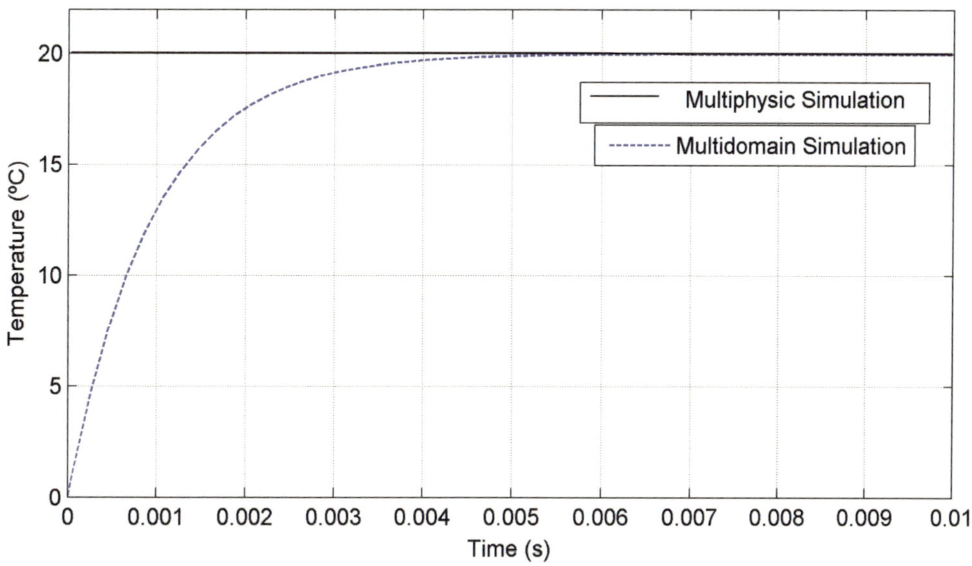

Fig. 16. Stabilization time to room temperature.

So in order to compare at same temperature points, the multi-domain simulation is first allowed to stabilize at 20°C, then the input signal is applied. Therefore, the considered waveform is started after 0.01s although the temperature stabilization time is shorter as is seen in Fig.16. Taking the temperature stabilization to times shorter than 0.001s may affect the simulation dynamics at the beginning.

Based on the above, it may be concluded that the outlined strategies have good performance and therefore they can be used to continue with the system design. Now the temperature control circuit will be included for the next analyses. So, after the validation of the models, the following step is to prove a temperature control, either using blocks from the library of the platform or using integration modules with other simulation programs. Once this is made, the designer can have a global idea about the performance of the system with the possibility to optimize the design.

4. Model of the temperature control system and simulation

For the temperature control of the micro hotplate obtained with post-processes compatible with CMOS technology described before, an analogue proportional control based on an operational amplifier (OP-AMP) is proposed (Barrentino et al., 2004). The schematic used for the basic simulations of the system is shown in Fig. 17.

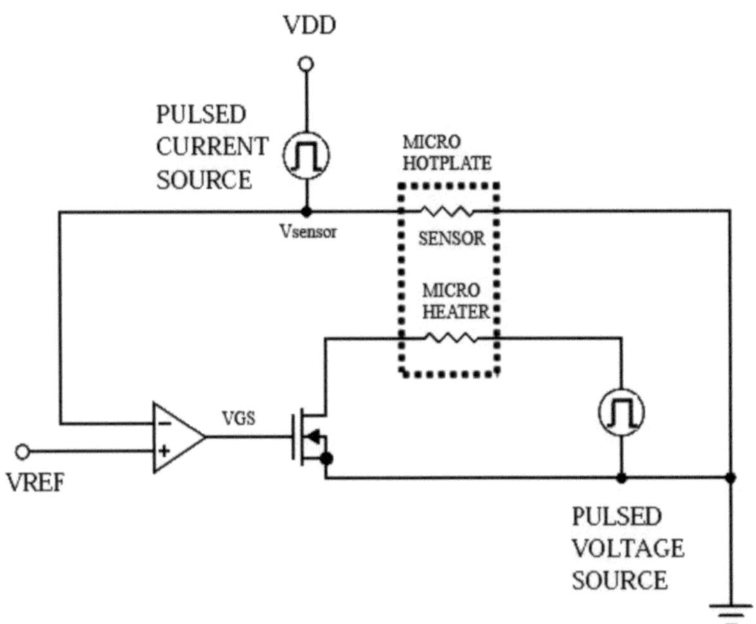

Fig. 17. Schematic of the temperature control circuit.

From the mentioned electro-thermal characteristics of polysilicon, MH and TS can be used as part of a temperature control circuit. When the temperature sensor is connected as a feedback from the output to the input of the operational amplifier, the voltage drop in it is compared with a reference voltage (VREF). If the voltage difference between both inputs is zero, a power MOS transistor used as a switch connected at the output of the OP-AMP, will interrupt the biasing to the MH. A regulated current source applying pulses with constant amplitude should be used to bias TS (note that this does not cause Joule Effect to TS). Due to heat transmission by conduction, the resistance in the TS will increase (see Fig. 4) and its voltage drop will be modified. This property makes feasible to apply the TS in a temperature control circuit. On the other hand, the MH should be biased with a pulsed voltage source to heat the MHP. The magnitude of the pulse depends on the desired temperature. Besides, a pulsed stimulus will help to reduce the power consumption of the system.

Hence, when the reference voltage is higher than the feedback voltage drop, the output of the OP-AMP is high making the MOS transistor to conduct allowing a current flow through the MH. So, due to Joule Effect the temperature will gradually rise from room temperature up to a temperature established by the applied voltage, VREF. At the same time the TS will follow the MH's temperature, changing also the voltage drop on it. At the moment when both voltages are equal, the OP-AMP output will go low turning off the MOS transistor and heating will stop. This cycle will be repeated according to the heating and cooling dynamic behaviour of the microheater, operating around the desired temperature. It is expected that the MH will keep this temperature until the set point is modified if a different temperature target within the physical and mechanical limits of the MHP is desired. Next, to ease the dynamic analysis of the controlling circuit, an equivalent circuit was used to consider the thermal coupling between the heater and the sensor as well as the time constant of the electro-thermal system. The MH was replaced with a voltage controlled voltage source and the TS with an RC circuit, where R and C are the thermal resistance and thermal capacitance of polysilicon, respectively. The corresponding time constant of this circuit should be consistent with the thermal behaviour of the 3D model of the MH considered.

From the finite element analysis made above, different time constants resulted for heating and for cooling (see Figs. 6 and 7). That is the reason why the equivalent circuit shown in Fig. 18 has two resistance elements corresponding to each value. The magnitude of R for heating is 770 Ω and 950 Ω for cooling. The capacitance value used to fit with each time constants is 1μF; the circuit was biased with VDD=1.5V. The transient behaviour of the system can be evaluated using the circuit shown in Fig. 18. The voltage drop in C is equivalent to the temperature reached by the system and is also the feedback voltage of the OP-AMP. Finally, the MOS transistor switch is replaced by two MOS transistors (PMOS and NMOS) to handle charge and discharge (heating and cooling, respectively) of the capacitor, as the output of the OP-AMP goes high or low. This is the reason why two resistors are used, so heating and cooling can be considered. The results of the transient analysis of the circuit show that there will be control over the current flow of the microheater until the voltage drop on TS reaches the reference voltage (1V for the case illustrated in Fig. 19). As soon as the voltage at the gate of the MOS transistor, VGS, equals the reference voltage, then biasing of the microheater stops. According to the cooling dynamics of the microheater, bias will be switching on and off to hold the temperature around the operating point as can be seen in Fig. 19.

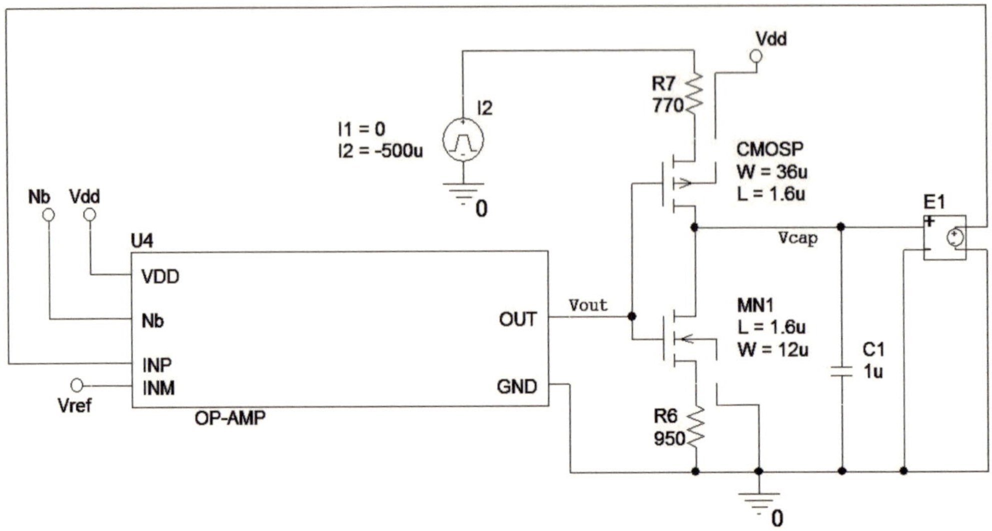

Fig. 18. Equivalent circuit of the temperature control circuit.

In order to have a complete analysis of the performance of the circuit, it was simulated also in SPICE with a temperature sweep (27°C to 300°C) applied to MH and TS and keeping all other circuit components at room temperature (27°C). The result is shown in Fig. 20, where it can be seen that the output of the OP-AMP goes low when the set point (1V) is reached. This is the expected behaviour for the control circuit but it should be noted that this simulation is independent to time, so it is not a dynamic analysis. Then, from Figs. 19 and 20 it can be considered, as a first approximation, that the system behaves as it should even for heating or cooling of MH.

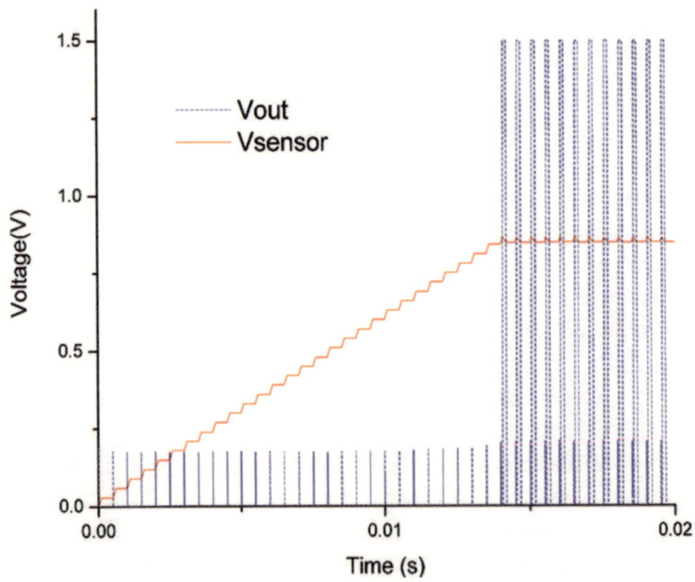

Fig. 19. Simulation results from the equivalent circuit shown in fig. 18 using SPICE.

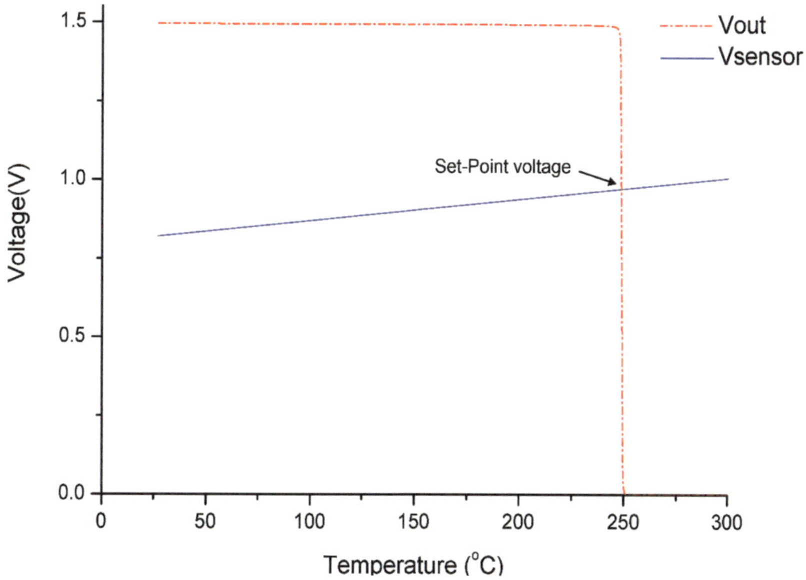

Fig. 20. Output of the OP-AMP when a temperature sweep is applied to MH and TS.

5. Simulation using Simulink®

It is important to remark that simulating the control circuit with SPICE presents a limitation since it is not possible to directly model the electro-thermal coupling between the microheater and the temperature sensor. Therefore, the simulation result shown in Fig. 19 does not take into account the heat transfer by conduction. As a consequence, the result obtained in that simulation is not fully consistent with the real behaviour of the system. Then to consider the thermal coupling, other tools are required such that an analysis of the system with conditions near to real can be done as a function of the elements and materials used in the electro-thermal system together with the temperature control circuit.

To simulate the dynamic performance of the circuit upon temperature changes over the MHP, it is necessary to follow a strategy that can take the SPICE model to a dynamic environment including random temperature changes in time. This is not a task that can be done exclusively with SPICE. Simulink® can help to achieve this using the SLPS integrating block and handling the electro-thermal feature of the micro hotplate with function blocks. It should be mentioned that the SLPS block allows interaction between models of the circuits described in SPICE and models found in Simulink®, whether they were designed using this platform or imported from some other environment. To make use of the SLPS block, it should be initialized from Matlab® as recommended by the supplier; once this is done functional blocks will be available in the library of Simulink. There, the desired interacting block can be loaded identifying the name of the circuit described in SPICE and the respective inputs and outputs are then selected. On one side, inputs are previously defined in SPICE as input voltage sources of the circuit, and on the other side, the output ports will drive a component or device simulated with SPICE. Nevertheless, the SLPS block has only one input and one output, both multiplexed since the use of MUX or DEMUX blocks must be used in Simulink® to read more than one input or output if this is the case.

Based on this, the circuit described with SPICE must be modified to work properly with the SLPS block. The proposal here reported gives good results if the temperature sensor resistor and its biasing current supply are eliminated, keeping only the OP-AMP, the MOS transistor switch and the microheater resistor, connecting them to voltage sources in SPICE, as is shown in Fig. 21. With this procedure, the SLPS block uses the simulation profile of SPICE and the output files from the corresponding simulation. The power supplies and the MHP model are external to this block in the Simulink® environment. The simulation will contain every element of the micro hotplate and the temperature control circuit must be adjusted to the previous simulation conditions. The values used in the voltage sources are shown in Table 1. They correspond to requirements like low power consumption, VDD=1.5V, a compensation voltage for the OP-AMP of Vnb=0.6V, a feeding voltage for the MH of Vtrans=3V and a reference voltage corresponding to 250°C, VREF=0.971V.

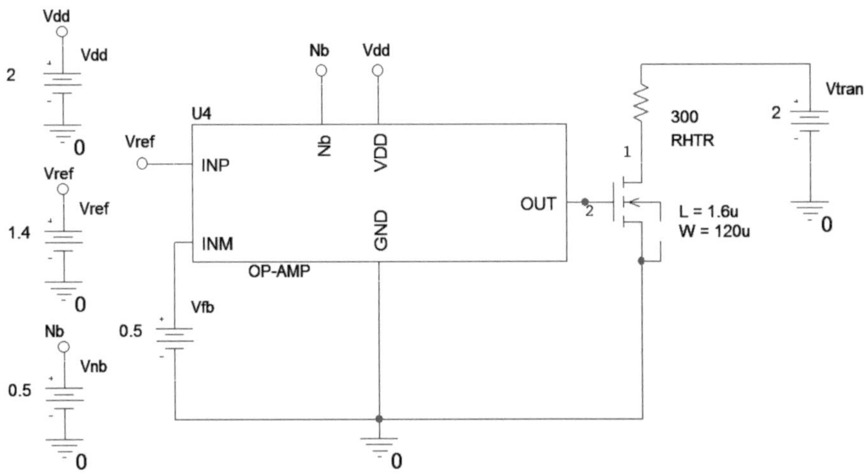

Fig. 21. SPICE circuit description for simulation with Simulink®.

6. Results and discussion

First, a simulation was done for an on-off control circuit using the function blocks that consider the electro-thermal model including TS and MH with their respective features like thermal coupling, temperature sensor morphology and its biasing current. This simulation helps to prove the models developed for the MHP and the dynamic performance. Fig. 22 shows the configuration used for this purpose. On the other hand, it is possible to use the SLPS block with the simulation profile together with the output files from SPICE to integrate the results from both simulations within only one process. Using the conditions specified in Table 1, the performance of the proposed control circuit can be evaluated.

Variable Values	
Vdd	1.5V
Vnd	0.6V
Vrans	3V
VREF	0.971V

Table 1. Variable values for simulation.

The block diagram is shown in Fig. 24. Random temperature variation affecting the system can be included in the descriptions shown in Figs. 22 and 24 with the objective to observe the response of the control circuit of the gas sensor system when temperature perturbations are added to the surrounding environment. Hence, any external factor that should alter the operating temperature of MHP will be considered.

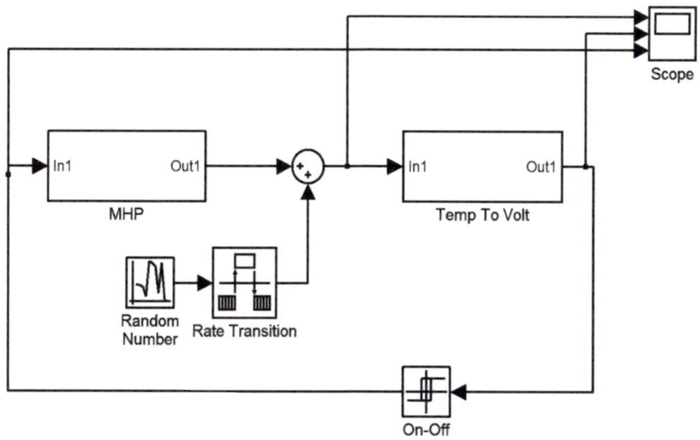

Fig. 22. On-Off Configuration.

When the diagram shown in Fig.22 is simulated, a plot of the temperature variation across time can be obtained showing the behaviour of the MHP connected to a temperature control. As soon as the MH reaches a given temperature established with the set point, the control system maintains this temperature as close as possible, through the control of the switch transistor with the output of the OP-AMP. Fig. 23 shows that a rather good temperature control is achieved around 250°C, as the proposed operating temperature.

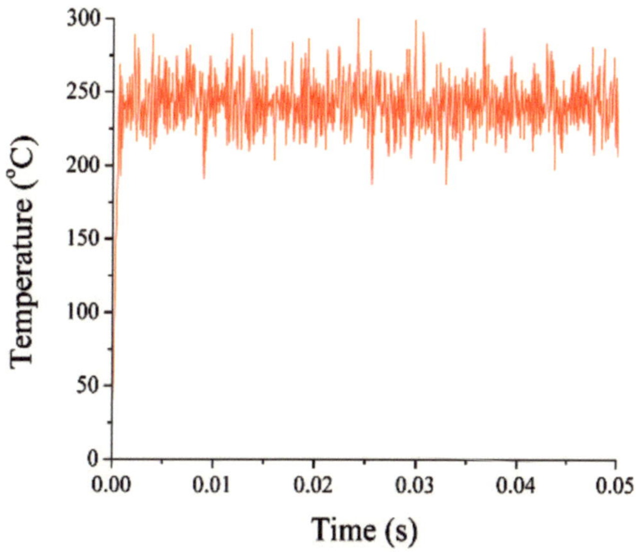

Fig. 23. Simulated operating temperature of MHP without SLPS and considering random temperature variations.

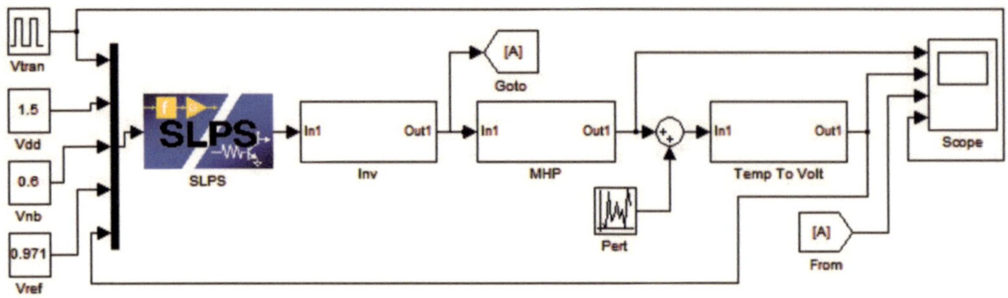

Fig. 24. Block diagram using Simulink®.

Later, including the SLPS block as indicated in Fig. 24, the same simulation as before was made and the results are similar to those presented in Fig. 23, oscillating too around 250°C, as can be seen in Fig. 25.

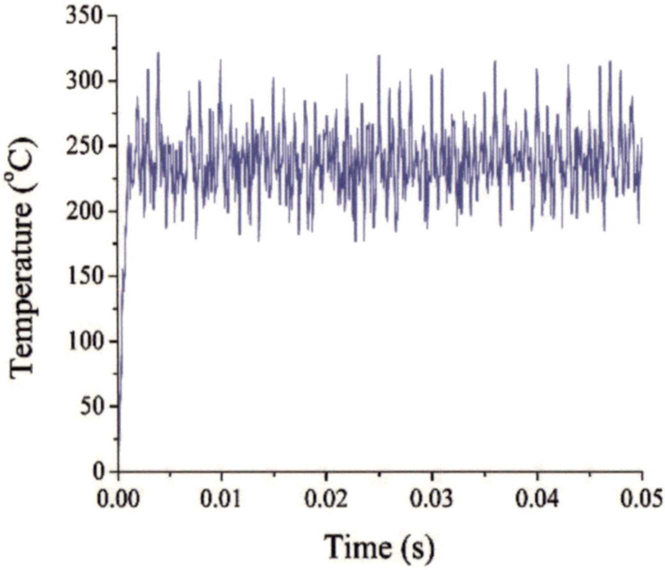

Fig. 25. Simulated operating temperature of MHP with the SLPS block included, considering random temperature variations.

Obviously the oscillations shown in Figs. 23 and Fig. 25 are different but there are two reasons for this: first, since random temperature variations were used, every simulation will generate different values that are not coincident each other; second, it should be remembered that the circuit simulated using SLPS, considered a pulsed current driver to decrease power consumption. Although it can be considered that real external temperature variations will not have such abrupt and rapid transitions, the temperature control circuit is able to hold the temperature around the desired set point. After these simulations, it can be said that the objectives of this study were achieved, this is, a proper design of a temperature control for the MHP that considers the electro-thermal coupling of the materials used for the SGS and with a particular geometry. As it was shown, both strategies can be used for evaluation and validation since they give reasonable results either using a simple on-off control block or with a more elaborate control circuit based on an OP-AMP. If a rapid evaluation of the performance is desired, a simple block with Simulink® can be used, which can give an approximated idea if the system is giving the expected results. This can be the basis for a more complete analysis using a more complex temperature control circuit based in the SLPS integrating block of Simulink®. It should be remembered that a single geometry for the MH and TS was studied in this work, but depending on the results obtained in the multi-physics environment, it should be optimized also to avoid heat concentration on borders and corners of MH that will damage the structure and to minimize as well the voltage applied in order to reach a given operating temperature. Besides, as this can be a time consuming process until a highly optimized design is obtained, it is convenient to have a strategy that helps to readily have the system design that can be fabricated with no fatal consequences. Finally, it was possible to couple different software environments to complete in short time the electro-thermal analysis of a 3D structure with its temperature control circuit included and with no huge computational resources. For example, the simulation performed to obtain the results shown in Fig. 12 took approximately from 4 to 6 hours to finish using a laptop loaded with a 3D solids engineering and analysis software based on finite elements, to generate the model. On the other hand, the simulation of the exported static model shown in Fig. 9, took from 1 to 2 hours to give the same results in the same machine. Finally, the approximated model illustrated in Fig. 11, gave also the same results in as much as 15 minutes. This is a dramatic difference and the criteria used in the present analysis can be used in turn, to extrapolate to other kind of systems or analyses.

7. Conclusions

The simulation with approximated models have excellent results in repetitive tests, since they reduce the use of hardware requirements, optimize simulation time and avoid interconnection as well as related problems among software programs. There may be cases in which models created in a multi-physics environment can be exported to Simulink® in a dynamic fashion, but the risk of no convergence may be present if there are inconvenient or unexpected changes in the simulation time step. In this case, the exported model will not be useful and the evaluation of the control stage cannot be done. Regardless the approximated model method is faster and allows driving signals as ramps or sine waveforms, results will depend on the equation accuracy and its range of validity. Therefore, the simulation option using approximated models can be the solution to accelerate tests and to apply controls to the model. Also, it can be considered a useful methodology for those users working with rather complex models and having no high capacity resources. However, it is recommended to always verify, if possible, the results with the original program and to try to find models using higher order TFs. There is no doubt that the CAD resources definitely support developing and design activities. Nevertheless, sometimes they may be limited to specific tasks so it is necessary to assess and to explore different alternatives. For some cases, partial results thrown by simulations can be considered good enough, but it will be preferable to have wide information about the behaviour of a system. Coupling compatible simulation environments can be a reliable strategy as was demonstrated for the case presented in this work, where satisfactory results were obtained at different stages. Good results were obtained for the operation of a temperature control circuit applied to a gas sensor system using two different methods.

8. Acknowledgements

This work was financed by CONACYT through the project number 57429. The authors thanks to Oliverio Arellano Cárdenas for his help in figures edition and formatting.

9. References

Afridi, M. Y.; Suehle, J. S.; Zaghloul, M. E.; Berning, D. W.; Hefner, A. R.; Cavicchi, R. E.; Semanick, S.; Montgomery, C. B. & Taylor, C. J. (2002). A monolithic CMOS microhotplate-based gas sensor system. *IEEE Sensors Journal, Vol.2*, pp. 644-655, ISSN 1530437X.

Barretino, D.; Graf, M.; Song, W. H.; Kirstein, K. U.; Hierlemann A. & Baltes, H. (2004). Hotplate-based monolithic CMOS microsystem for gas detection and material characterization for operating temperatures up to 500ºC. *IEEE Journal of Solid-State Ciruits*, Vol.39, pp. 1202-1207, ISSN 0018-9200.

Cerdà, J.; Manzano, J.; Arbiol, J.; Cirera, A.; Puigcorbé, J.; Vilà, A.; Sabaté, N.; Gràcia, I.; Cané, C. & Morante, J. R. (2006). Micromachined twin gas sensor for CO and O2 quantification based on catalytically modified nano-SnO2, *Sens. and Act. B: Chem.*, Vol.114, pp. 881-892, ISSN 09254005.

Fedder, G. K. (2005). CMOS-Based sensors. *Proceedings of the 4th IEEE Conference on Sensors Oct. 30-Nov. 3 2005, IEEE*, pp. 125-128, ISBN 0780390563, Irvine, CA, U.S.A. Oct. 30 - Nov. 3, 2005.

Goering, R. (2004). Matlab® Edges Closer to Electronic Design Automation World. In: *EE Times*. Last Accessed: Feb. 8, 2011. Available from: http://www.eetimes.com/electronics-news/4050334/Matlab-edges-closer-to-electronic-design-automation-world

Hsu, T. R., (2002), *MEMS & Microsystems* 1st Ed., Mc Graw Hill, ISBN 0-07-239391-2, New York, NY, U.S.A., 2002.

Muñoz, J. S., Valencia, R. and Nieto, C. (2008). COMSOL and MATLAB Integration to Optimize Heat Exchangers Using Genetic Algorithms Technique, *Proceedings of COMSOL Conference 2008*, Boston, U.S.A, 2008.

Ogata, K., (1999), *Problemas de Ingeniería de control utilizando Matlab® 1ª Ed.*, Prentice Hall Iberia, ISBN 84-8322-046-6, Madrid, España, 1999.

9

Matlab Simulink® Model of a Braked Rail Vehicle and Its Applications

Grażyna Barna
Rail Vehicles Institute "TABOR"
Poland

1. Introduction

When a braking force applied to the axle sets of a rail vehicle exceeds a critical value, which depends on the wheel-rail adherence, the wheels start to slide. If no corrective action is taken, in a very short time the wheels can be locked. Locking of the wheels or their excessive slide can result in increased braking distance and damage to the wheel rims (flat spots, also called "flats"). Wheel flats are sources of vibration and noise, they lower riding quality of a vehicle as well as passenger comfort, but first and foremost increasing of the braking distance directly impairs safety of the train staff and passengers and also of people nearby. In order to prevent excessive wheel slide and wheel lock, rail vehicles are equipped with Wheel Slide Protection (WSP) systems.

From the point of view of a WSP controller, the rail vehicle is a strongly non-linear and non-stationary plant. From the other hand there exist intuitive expert knowledge concerning the way the slide should be controlled. For these two reasons fuzzy logic controllers (FLC) are widely used in WSP systems (Caldara et al. (1996), Barna (2009)).

One of the basic problems concerning FLCs is lack of formal methods of design. Designing the rule bases of the fuzzy controllers is usually performed using a trial-and-error method, which in turn requires performing numerous tests of the controlled plant. When a controlled plant is a rail vehicle, possibilities of performing such tests are very limited due to high costs of tests and danger of damaging the wheels. A commonly used solution to this problem is employing a simulator of a braked rail vehicle, which can be used for preliminary design, optimization and tuning of the controllers. Tests on a real object are performed at the last stage of the design process in order to verify the designed controller.

The purpose of this chapter is to present the Matlab Simulink® model of a braked rail vehicle and its many applications, which comprise both designing and testing of the WSP systems. In the next two introductory sections the slide phenomenon as well as the structure and principle of operation of WSP systems are described in order to provide the readers who are not familiar with the WSP devices with some useful information which would facilitate reading of this chapter.

2. Slide during braking of a rail vehicle

During braking of a rail vehicle, a braking torque generated by a rail vehicle braking system is applied to the axle sets. When a value of this torque exceeds a boundary value, which depends on the instantaneous value of wheel-rail adherence, than the circumferential speed of the wheels starts to decrease (which is called sliding). If no corrective action is taken, in a very short time the wheels can be locked.

Locking of the wheels of a rail vehicle, as well as an excessive wheel slide have several negative consequences, out of which two are critical. First and foremost, due to decreasing of the adhesion coefficient, the braking force remains constant at a small value, which makes impossible effective braking of a vehicle and results in significant increasing of the braking distance. As an example, the braking distance of a 150A passenger car braked at 120 km/h amounts, according to both field and simulation tests approximately 480 m, while at braking with all the wheels locked at the beginning of braking it can be increased even up to 800 m. Increasing of the braking distance impairs the safety of passengers, train staff and people in proximity. Secondly, when locked wheels slide along the rails, flat spots (called "flats") can be produced on wheel treads. The depth of a wheel flat can amount up to several millimeters (Pawełczyk (2008)), especially in case of a prolonged slide. In Fig. 1 and Fig. 2 photographs of wheel flats of a passenger car wheels are shown.

Fig. 1. Flat spot on a wheel tread 1

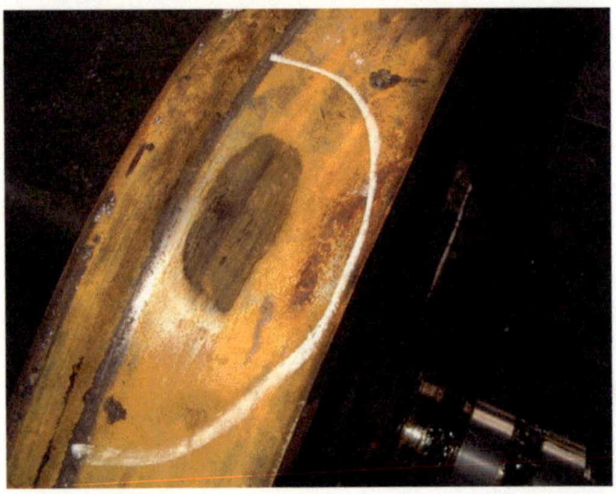

Fig. 2. Flat spot on a wheel tread 2

Increase of the temperature of the sliding wheel and rapid cooling of the outer wheel layer, caused by regaining speed after the wheel slide has ceased, may result in forming of martensite around the flat spot. Martensite is a form of steel, firm, but fragile, which is subjected to cracks and crumbling. It develops first of all at the surface, and then propagating far into the wheel material. It results in developing the loss of the material of the wheel treads (Jergéus (1998); Kwaśnikowski & Firlik (2006)).

Damage to the wheel treads may be caused not only by wheel lock, but also by excessive difference (above 30 km/h) between vehicle velocity and circumferential velocity of a wheel.

Vibrations also lower the comfort of the passengers and the trains staff, negatively influencing their mood and ability to work after the journey, and also their health. In Fig. 3 simulation characteristics are shown for both a vehicle with round wheels and a vehicle with one flat spot on one wheel, at speed 140 km/h. The influence of a flat spot is seen the most clearly for frequency of app. 13,5 Hz. Lowering of comfort, defined as increasing of the effective value of vertical acceleration in the middle of the body amounts in this particular case to app. 30 %, and it depends on the vehicle velocity (Ofierzyński (2008)).

The concern about wheel slide has increased, as rail vehicles began running at higher speeds, because not only braking torque which is necessary to brake a vehicle needs to be bigger, which increases the probability of the wheel slide, but also consequences of such event are more serious when it occurs at high vehicle velocities.

To prevent the described above situations, rail vehicles are equipped with Wheel Slide Protection (WSP) devices, which detect slide of the vehicle wheels and adequately control the braking torque, not only preventing wheels from being locked, but also increasing the adhesion coefficient value, thus making the braking distance as short as possible.

Because a safety critical system is a system the failure of which can result in severe consequences, e.g. death or injury of people, or significant damages to property or environment, thus it is evident that a WSP device is a safety critical system (Barna & Kaluba (2009)). Standard CEN (2009) and leaflet UIC (2005) contain specification of requirements for both structure and functions of WSP devices.

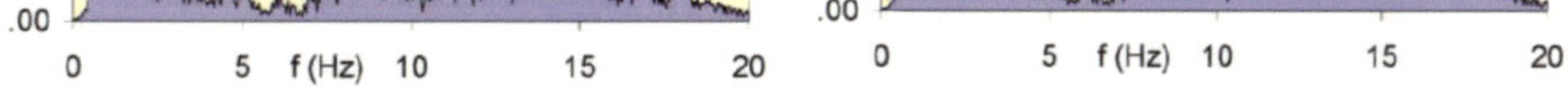

Fig. 3. Swing and frequency characteristics of vertical acceleration in the middle of the passenger car body, respectively without and with a wheel flat (Ofierzyński (2008))

3. Wheel Slide Protection systems

A WSP system consists of the following elements: wheel speed sensors, controller and dump valves. The block diagram of a WSP system for a two-axle bogie with block brake is shown in Fig. 4 (Barna (2009), UIC (2005), CEN (2009)).

A WSP controller on the basis on signals from speed sensors of all wheel-sets, performs calculation of circumferential wheel velocities and determines circumferential wheel

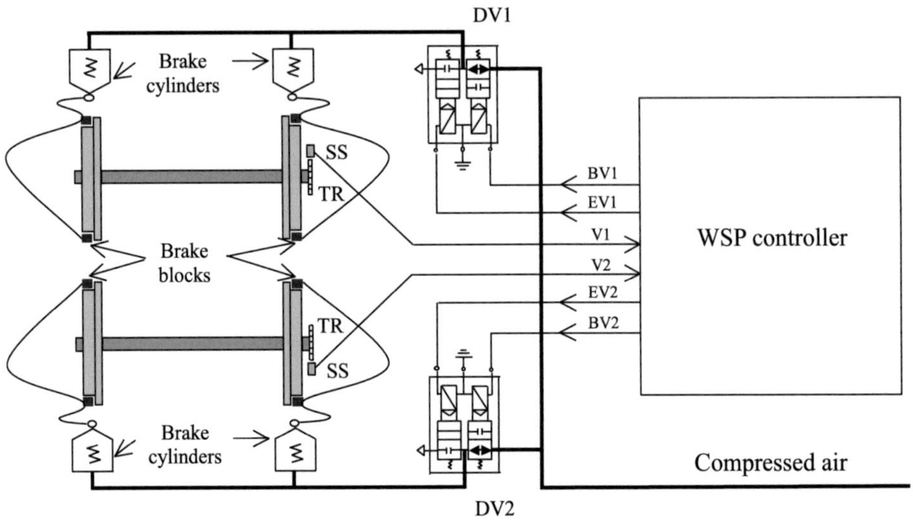

Fig. 4. Block diagram of a WSP system: DV1, DV2 - dump valves, V1, V2 - speed measurement signals, EV1, EV2, BV1, BV2 - dump valve control signals

accelerations and wheel slides, performs estimation of vehicle velocity (called the reference velocity), and then, on the basis of the obtained values appropriately controls the dump valves, in order to adjust the braking torque to the instantaneous adhesion conditions (Barna (2010a)). When a slide is detected, the braking torque should be adequately decreased by proper control of the dump valves; after recovery of adhesion the torque should be increased in order to provide effective braking of the vehicle.

Speed sensors make possible measuring the angular speeds of the wheels – they generate square-wave signals from which circumferential wheel speeds can be calculated, and which are main input signals for the WSP controller.

The WSP actuators are dump valves, mounted as close as possible to the brake cylinders. The valves can adopt one of the three states, which makes possible increasing, decreasing or maintaining the pressure value in the brake cylinders:

- filling of the cylinders (F)
- venting of the cylinders (V)
- cutting-off the air supply without venting (H).

Both filling and venting of the dump valves can be performed in one of the two following ways (Boiteux (1999)):

- *continuous*: applying either F or V state
- *graduated*: increasing or decreasing of the pressure are realized by applying repeated sequences of respectively F and H or V and H states.

In Barna (2009) seven levels of pressure change have been proposed, designated P1, P2, P3, U1, U2, U3, H. The levels are obtained by cyclical applying sequences of the three mentioned above states of the valves **P3**: P, **P2**: P H, **P1**: P **H**: H, **U1**: U H H, **U2**: U H, **U3**: U. Each of the states is applied for a defined period of time, e.g. 100 ms.

4. Characteristics of the WSP controllers

Wheel Slide Protection (WSP) devices control braking torque, not only preventing wheels from being locked, but also increasing the adhesion coefficient value, making the braking distance as short as possible. Thus the main task of WSP systems is *"to make the best use of available adhesion for all intended-operating conditions by a controlled reduction and restoration of the brake force to prevent axle sets from locking and uncontrolled sliding due to low adhesion"* (CEN (2009)).

The main difficulties concerning the control algorithm resulting from the characteristics of a braked rail vehicle as a controlled plant are listed below, the first two out of which are the most crucial:

- instantaneous value of the coefficient of adhesion between wheel and rail ψ cannot be measured
- translation vehicle speed v_T is usually not measured due to costs
- controlled plant is highly non-linear
  - characteristics $\psi = f(s)$ is non-linear (see Fig. 13)
  - characteristics $M_b = f(p_c)$ is characterized by hysteresis
  - dump valves behavior is non-linear
- controlled plant is non-stationary — parameters of characteristics $\psi = f(s)$ change in a way which is possible to comprehend in stochastic manner only
- direct control of a braking torque is not possible; actuators control the pressure values in the brake cylinders
- controlling of the brake cylinder pressures is performed indirectly and discretely
- instantaneous values of the cylinder pressures are not known.

The task of a WSP controller is to achieve the highest possible at the current adhesion conditions adhesion forces (forces transferred to the wheels of the axle sets), which is equivalent with achieving the shortest possible braking distance. This goal is achieved, as mentioned in Section 3 by proper control of the dump valves of each axle set.

In Fig. 5 a trajectory $\psi = f(s)$ for an optimally working controller has been shown, superimposed on a generalized adhesion versus slide curve. A WSP device equipped with such a controller, called in Boiteux (1999) a Second Generation WSP, realizes control in the neighbourhood of the point B of an adhesion curve and maintains a value of a relative slide s close to its optimum value s_B (see subsection 5.2.4).

A control system such as described above is called an *extremum regulation system*. The task of the extremum regulation system is maintaining a controlled signal as close as possible to the extremum value, which changes depending on disturbance signals (Kaczorek (1977)). In the case of a braked rail vehicle and a WSP controller this extremum value should be the instantaneous value of adhesion coefficient between wheel and rail ψ.

In Fig. 6 an overall block diagram of a WSP control system is shown, which is a base for practically realized control algorithms of WSP controllers.

A braked rail vehicle as a control plant is strongly non-linear and non-stationary, therefore the WSP controllers are usually designed using Fuzzy Logic and Expert

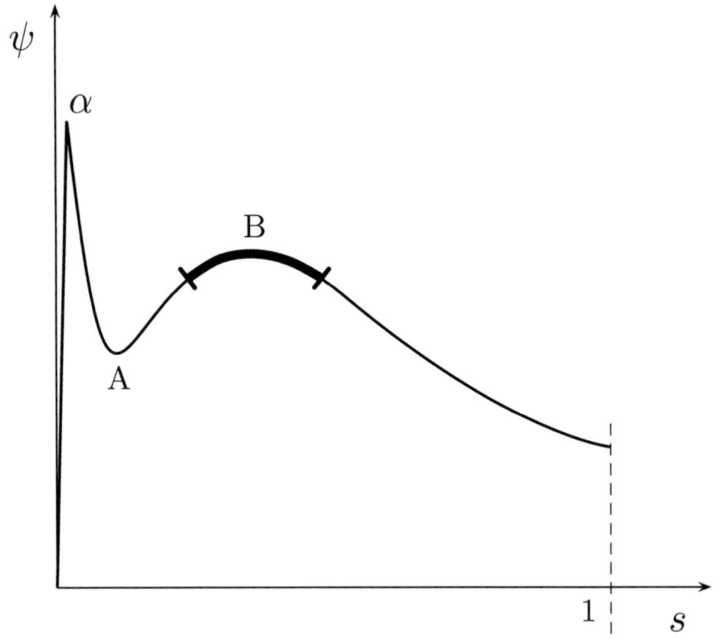

Fig. 5. The principle of operation of an optimal Wheel Slide Protection (Boiteux (1999))

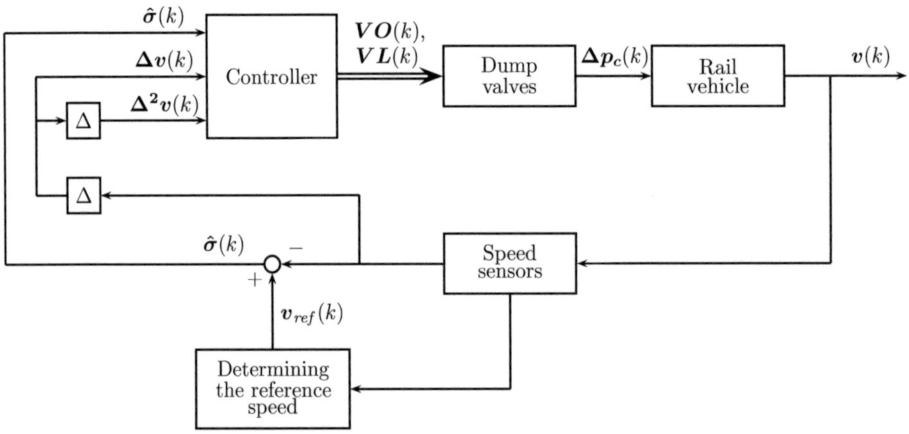

Fig. 6. Practical block diagram of WSP control system (Barna (2009))

Knowledge techniques (Caldara et al. (1996); Cheok & Shiomi (2000); Mauer (1995); Sanz & Pérez-Rodríguez (1997); Will & Żak (2000)).

The WSP control system using Fuzzy Logic controllers implemented in Matlab Simulink® is shown in Fig. 7. The control system is realized as Triggered Subsystem Simulink® block, triggered every 100 ms, which corresponds to a real controller program cycle time. The controller blocks for every axle are implemented with Fuzzy Logic Controller Simulink® blocks. The inputs for each FLC block are absolute axle slide σ [km/h] and axle acceleration a, which are calculated on the basis of the measured wheel circumferential velocities and vehicle reference velocity v_{ref}, as shown in Fig. 6. The measured wheel circumferential velocities are obtained by feeding the calculated continuous wheel velocities (see section 5.2.3) through a model of speed sensors. Fuzzy Logic Controllers are of PI type. The Simulink® subsystem determining the reference velocity v_{ref} is shown in Fig. 8. The output of each FLC is an integer in the range from −3 to 3, designating one of seven levels of pressure change (see section 3), which is then transformed in a post-processing block into signals controlling a dump valve.

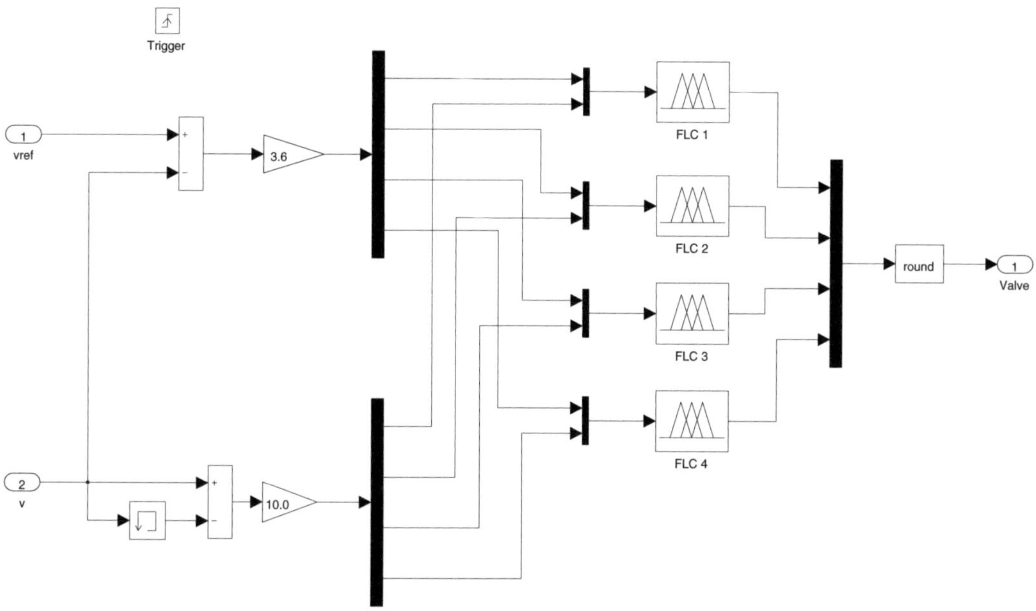

Fig. 7. Fuzzy Logic WSP control system implemented in Matlab Simulink®

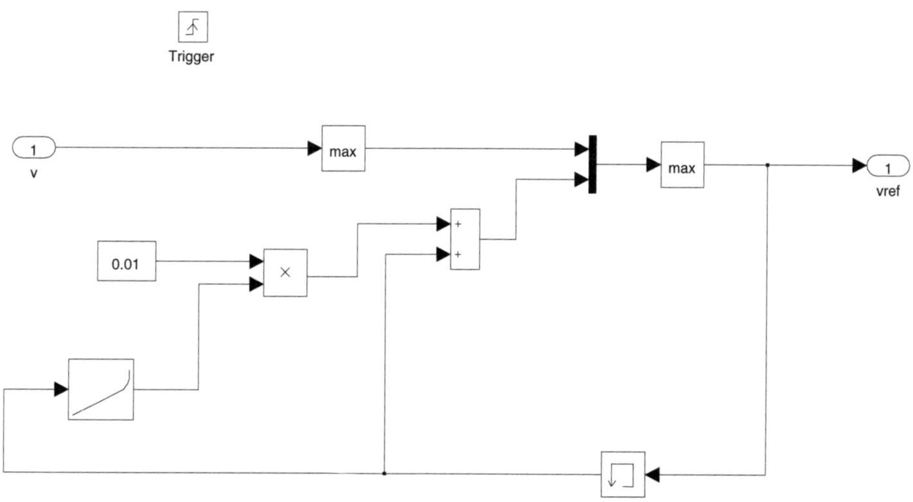

Fig. 8. Matlab Simulink® subsystem determining the reference velocity v_{ref}

5. Simulator of a braked rail vehicle

5.1 Introduction

Designing and testing of the FLC WSP controllers demands performing numerous experiments. Performing tests using a real rail vehicle is not feasible, because of high costs and possibility of damaging the object, therefore for designing and testing WSP controllers a test stand is indispensable. One of the most important elements of the test stand is a simulator of a braked rail vehicle.

The mathematical model of a braked rail vehicle, simulation model and various versions of a simulation stand are presented in this subsection.

5.2 Mathematical model of a braked rail vehicle

5.2.1 Introduction

The basis for a rail vehicle simulator is a mathematical model of a braked rail vehicle, taking into consideration the basic phenomena occurring during sliding and omitting the phenomena that are of no or slight significance.

The model has the following parameters:

- parameters describing properties of the vehicle (e.g. mass, number of axles, inertia of the axle sets)
- vehicle velocity in the moment of commencement of braking
- intensiveness of braking defined as the maximum pressure in the brake cylinders.

The inputs to the model are:

- state of dump valves generated by the WSP controller
- state of the rail (adhesion coefficient).

The purpose of the model is performing the simulations of braking of a rail vehicle at reduced adhesion. Therefore all the basic phenomena influencing the wheel speeds during braking must be modeled as faithfully as feasible. A special attention must be put to all the main non-linear subsystems of the system. The most important example is the wheel-rail adhesion coefficient.

Some simplifying assumptions have been adopted, which simplify the model, while do not significantly alter its functionality. One of these assumptions is considering the vehicle as a rigid body with the agglomerated mass.

The model consists of the following subsystems:

- model of a braking system
- model of a rotational motion of a wheel-set
- model of the adhesion curve
- model of a translation vehicle motion.

The subsystems of the model are described in the subsequent subsections.

5.2.2 Model of a braking system

The model of the braking system describes the relation between pressure in the brake cylinders of the axle set and its braking torque.

This model can be divided into the following three subsystems:

- model of the pneumatic system and the dump valves
- model of the lever system
- model of the friction elements.

5.2.2.1 Model of the pneumatic system and the dump valves

The pressure at the input of a dump valve can be described with the following equation (Kaluba (1999)):

$$p_{c_{in}} = p_{c_{max}} \left(1 - e^{-0.75t}\right). \tag{1}$$

The dump valves are a part of delivery of the WSP system. However, from the modeling point of view, because they are integrated into the pneumatic system of the vehicle, they are considered as part of this system.

The dump valve has been modeled as the inertia element of adjustable time constant independently for filling T_F and venting T_V.

The pressure in the brake cylinders supplied by the valve are given with one of the following equations:

for filling

$$p_c = p_0 + (p_{c_{in}} - p_0)\left(1 - e^{-\frac{t-t_z}{T_F}}\right), \tag{2}$$

for venting

$$p_c = p_0 e^{-\frac{t-t_0}{T_V}}, \tag{3}$$

and for holding

$$p_c = p_0. \tag{4}$$

5.2.2.2 Model of the lever system

The relation between the pressure of the friction linings of the brake blocks onto the wheel treads of the brake disks, which is exerted by the piston of the brake cylinder and the pressure in the brake cylinder is highly non-linear and is characterized by hysteresis, resulting from friction in the brake cylinder and in the joints of the clamp mechanism (Knorr (2002); Tao & Kokotovic (1996)). This relation is shown in Fig. (9). The two rays limiting the area are given with:

$$N_{k1} = (p_c A_k - F_f)\eta_s \eta_r i_p, \tag{5}$$

$$N_{k2} = (p_c A_k - F_f)(2 - \eta_s \eta_r) i_p. \tag{6}$$

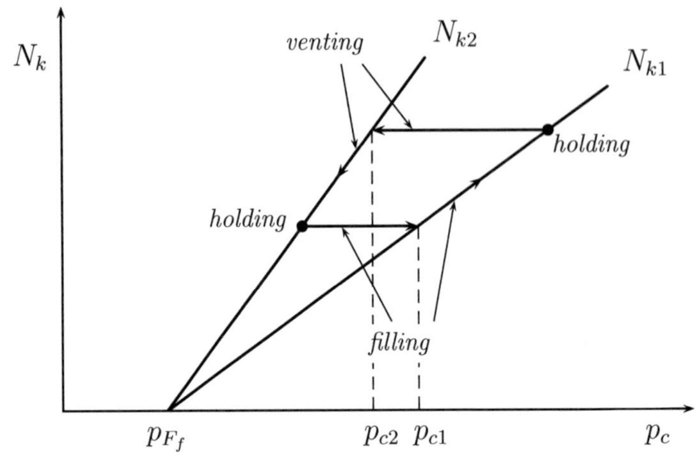

Fig. 9. Relation between the air pressure in brake cylinders and the brake blocks pressure

5.2.2.3 Model of the friction elements

Because some vehicles are equipped with disk brakes and some with block brakes, models of both types of brakes have been prepared.

For both types of the brakes the braking torque is given with:

$$M_b = N_k \mu r_b, \tag{7}$$

where r_h is the braking radius.

For the block brake, the braking radius r_h is equal to the wheel radius r, for the disk brake it is equal to the radius of the brake disk r_d.

The friction coefficient between the friction linings of the brake blocks and the wheel tread or the brake disk μ depends in a non-linear way on many factors, first of all on wheel velocity and pressure of the disk block.

A simplified value of the friction coefficient μ for a block brake is given with the empirical equation. In this model the equation given in Sachs (1973) has been adopted:

$$\mu = 0,16 \sqrt[3]{\frac{40,25}{v}} \sqrt[3]{\frac{2,461}{p_x}}, \tag{8}$$

while:

$$p_x = \frac{N_k}{A_x}. \tag{9}$$

In Fig. 10 a surface of the friction coefficient μ vs. circumferential speed of the vehicle wheel and the unitary pressure of the friction linings for a block brake is shown.

For the disk brake the friction coefficient μ has been determined on the basis of the results presented in Kaluba (1999). In Fig. 11 a surface of the friction coefficient μ vs. circumferential speed of the vehicle wheel and the sum of unitary pressure of the friction linings for a disk brake is shown.

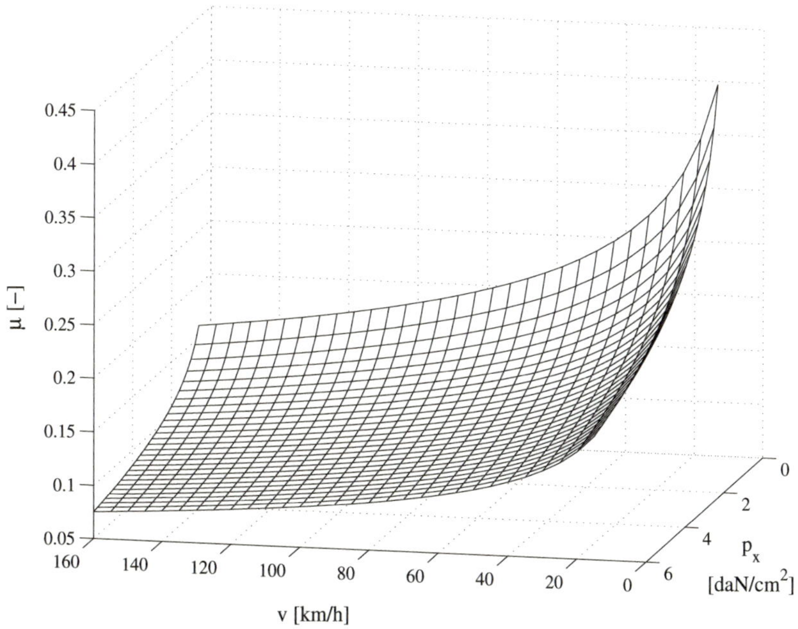

Fig. 10. A surface of the friction coefficient μ vs. circumferential speed of the vehicle wheel and the unitary pressure of the friction linings (Sachs (1973))

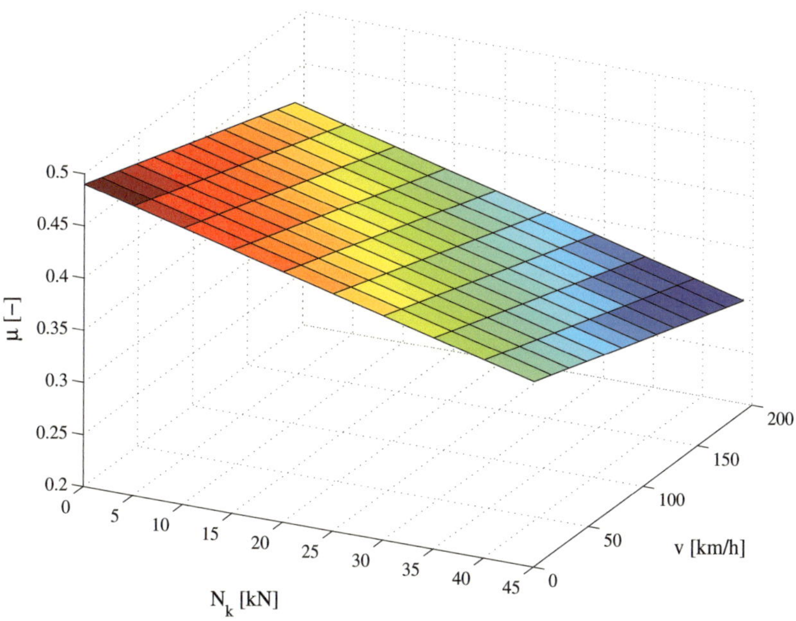

Fig. 11. A surface of the friction coefficient μ vs. circumferential speed of the vehicle wheel and the sum of unitary pressure of the friction linings for a disk brake (Kaluba (1999))

5.2.3 Model of a rotational motion of a wheel-set

A simplified diagram of forces acting upon a braked axle set is shown in Fig. 12.

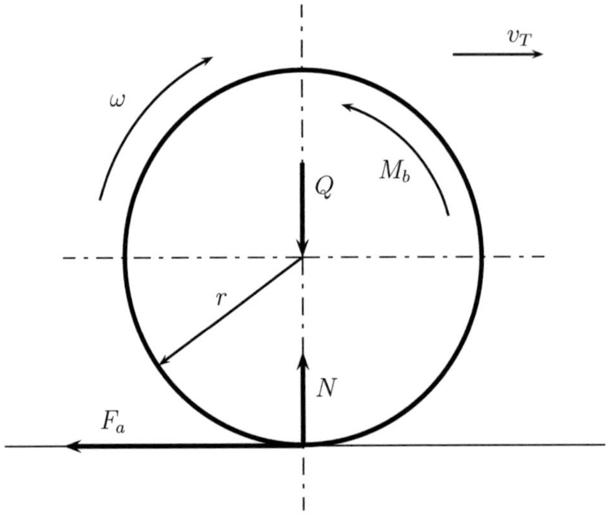

Fig. 12. A simplified diagram of forces acting upon a braked axle set

The dynamics of the axle set rotary motion is given with the following equation set:

$$J\frac{d\omega_i}{dt} = F_{ai}r - M_{bi}, \quad (10)$$

$$F_{ai} = \psi_i(s_i, \mathbf{p})Q_i, \quad (11)$$

$$s_i = \frac{v_T - v}{v_T}, \quad (12)$$

where (11) defines the adhesion force, and (12) defines the relative slide. The model of value of ψ is described in the following subsection.

5.2.4 Model of the adhesion curve

Generalized characteristics of instantaneous adhesion coefficient ψ versus relative slide s is shown in Fig. 13. Value of adhesion coefficient at point B (ψ_B) is called *maximum exploitable adhesion* and corresponding slide (s_B) is called *optimal slide* (Boiteux (1987)).

The parameters of the generalized curve are the following values:

- relative slide at point α s_α
- available adhesion coefficient ψ_α
- relative slide at point A s_A
- adhesion coefficient value at point A ψ_A
- optimum relative slide s_B
- maximum exploitable wheel-rail adhesion coefficient ψ_B
- adhesion coefficient value for wheel lock ψ_l.

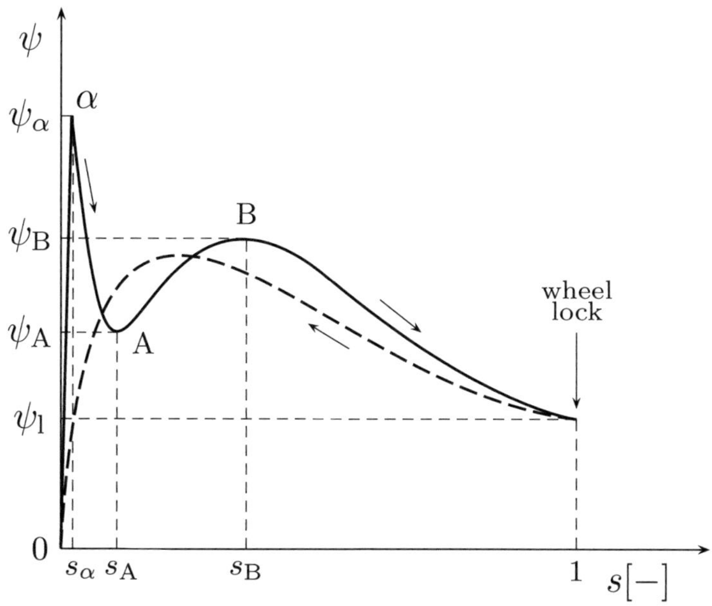

Fig. 13. Generalized characteristics of instantaneous coefficient of adhesion ψ versus relative slide s (ORE (1985))

The shape and parameters of the curve depend on many factors, most of which are difficult or impossible to establish. The most important factors are listed below (Boiteux (1987; 1990; 1998); ORE (1985; 1990)):

- state of the rail
- vehicle velocity v_T
- absolute wheel slide σ
- relative wheel slide s
- circumferential deceleration of the wheels d
- slide energy E developed in the wheel and a rail contact point.

The mathematical model of adhesion coefficient, based on Boiteux (1987; 1990; 1998); ORE (1985; 1990), is described in detail in Barna (2009).

As an example, according to Boiteux (1987), maximum exploitable wheel-rail adhesion coefficient ψ_B and optimum relative slide s_B can be estimated with the following equations:

$$\psi_B = k\sqrt{\frac{Q\,\psi_\alpha\,E_o}{2\,d_m}}, \tag{13}$$

and

$$s_B = \frac{1}{v_T}\sqrt{\frac{2\,E_o\,d_m}{Q\,\psi_\alpha}}. \tag{14}$$

One of the most important behavior of the adhesion curve, which has been taken into consideration is, that during the braking at low adhesion with efficiently operating WSP system, the value of the maximum exploitable wheel-rail adhesion coefficient ψ_B increases, so it can double or even triple within 10 s.

Simulated characteristics of adhesion coefficient ψ vs. time for a braking from the initial velocity of 120 km/h, showing increase of the maximum exploitable wheel-rail adhesion coefficient in the course of braking is presented in Fig. 14

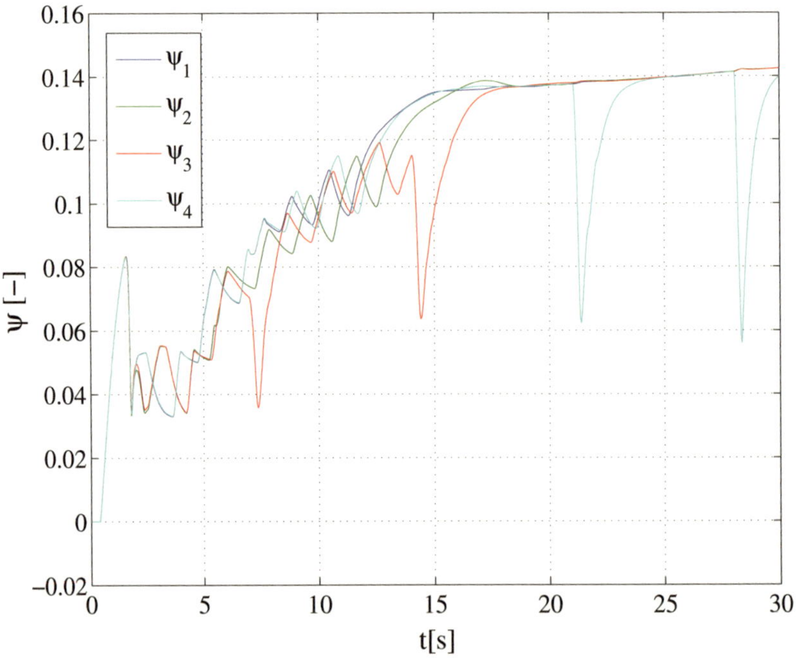

Fig. 14. Simulated characteristics of adhesion coefficient ψ vs. time, where ψ_i – adhesion coefficient for i-th axle set (Barna (2009))

5.2.5 Model of a translation vehicle motion

The model of a translation vehicle motion is described with:

$$m\frac{dv_T}{dt} + \sum_{i=1}^{n} \frac{J_i}{r}\frac{d\omega_i}{dt} = -F_{a\Sigma}, \tag{15}$$

where i is the number of axle sets of the vehicle.

5.3 Simulation model and a simulation stand

5.3.1 Requirements

In UIC (2005) and CEN (2009) there are contained requirements concerning the simulator of a braked rail vehicle. According to these normative documents the simulator should make possible simulating various conditions and scenarios concerning the wheel-rail adhesion as well as vehicle and track parameters:

- adhesion coefficient ψ between 0,02 (extremely poor adhesion) and 0,15 (dry rail)

- adhesion variation as occurs in real life
- sudden changes of adhesion as the ones occurring when a wheel encounters a spilled oil or dead leaves
- dynamic variation of wheel-rail adhesion coefficient vs. vehicle velocity and the slide controlled by WSP system
- maximum rail slope of 50‰
- drag braking test (when a vehicle is hauled at constant speed).

Simulator should make possible modeling the vehicles of the following parameters:

- vehicle velocity up to 240 km/h
- changes of parameters such as wheel diameter and inertia of axle sets, mass of the vehicle and particular bogies as well as location of the centroid, loading with passenger or cargo as well as braking force characteristics
- various brake positions with braking rate values λ being within the range 25% do 200% (for the braking systems independent of adhesion)
- braking systems which, apart from the friction brake are additionally equipped with the brake independent of adhesion, e.g. track brake

It is recommended, that for the traction vehicles it should be possible to simulate blending (electrodynamic brake cooperating with friction brake).

5.3.2 Simulation model

The simulation model of the braked rail vehicle integrated with the WSP system has been implemented in Matlab Simulink®. A simplified block diagram of the model is shown in Fig. 15. Validation of the model is basically performed by comparing the braking distances obtained from simulations performed with the experimental results (CEN (2009); UIC (2005)).

5.3.3 Simulation stands

In the Figures 16, 17 i 18 block diagrams showing various possibilities of realizing the laboratory test stand have been shown.

In Fig. 16 a stand described in UIC (2005) and CEN (2009) is shown, in which the computer simulation is minimized. This stand comprises a hardware model of a brake system with dump valves installed and pressure sensors mounted in brake cylinders. These pressure values are read by the analog inputs of the computer vehicle simulator, which calculates the adhesion forces and resulting wheel velocities. Fast analog output or counter output board of the computer vehicle simulator outputs pulse train simulating impulses from the WSP speed sensors.

A real WSP controlling device inputs the simulated speed signals from the computer vehicle simulator and outputs signals controlling dump valves in the hardware model of a brake system. The advantage of this stand is fidelity of simulating the pneumatic part of the vehicle braking system, which makes possible obtaining accurate values of brake cylinder pressures during WSP operation. The disadvantage is relatively high cost of the stand.

In Fig. 17 another version of a test stand is shown in which, comparing to the previous stand, also the pneumatic system is computer simulated. A reliable model of a pneumatic system

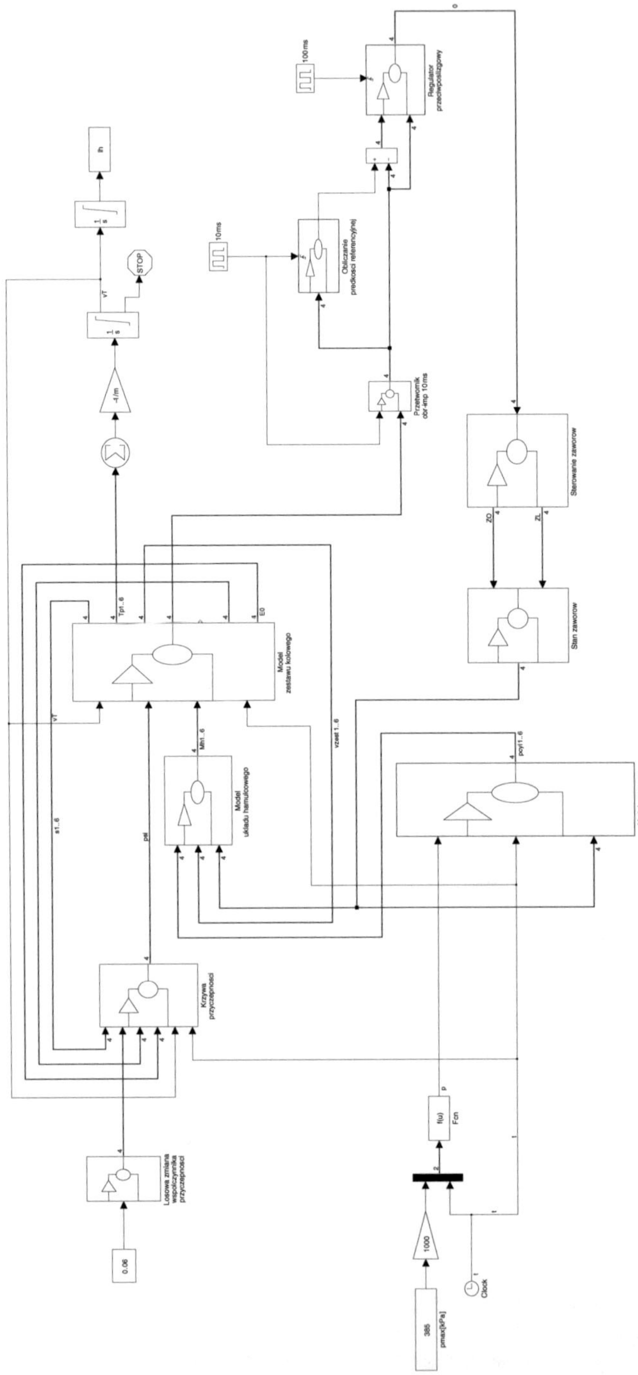

Fig. 15. A simplified block diagram of the braked rail vehicle integrated with the WSP system implemented in Matlab Simulink®

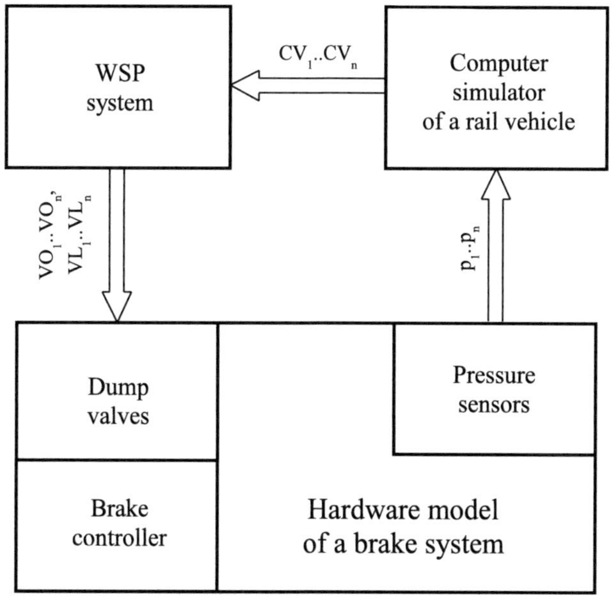

Fig. 16. Laboratory test stand using a hardware model of a brake system

and of the dump valves is additionally needed. The advantage of the stand is much lower cost. It is also much cheaper in operation, because it does not require supplying with the compressed air. However it cannot be used for homologation tests of WSP systems according to UIC (2005) and CEN (2009).

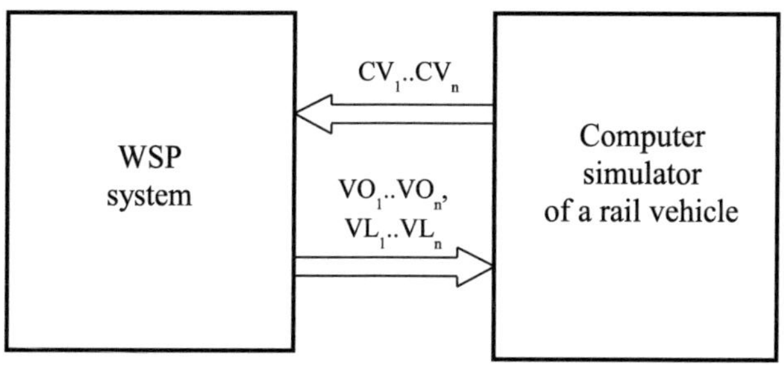

Fig. 17. Laboratory test stand with computer simulation of the pneumatic system

In Fig. 18 a third test stand is shown, in which a WSP controller is also computer simulated. Such stand can be realized if a control algorithm of a WSP system is known. The biggest difference comparing to the previous stand is, that the fast counters of the WSP system are also simulated. The stand is realized using only a computer with a Matlab Simulink® program, thus the advantage is a very low cost of the test stand. The stand is a good choice at the stage of development of WSP control algorithm, because the WSP developer can perform numerous tests of the WSP systems, examining various variants of the control algorithm. However, this stand does not allow for the testing of the ready WSP control device. One of the described above test stands should be used for such purpose. It is this variant of the test stand that is used for simulations described in this chapter.

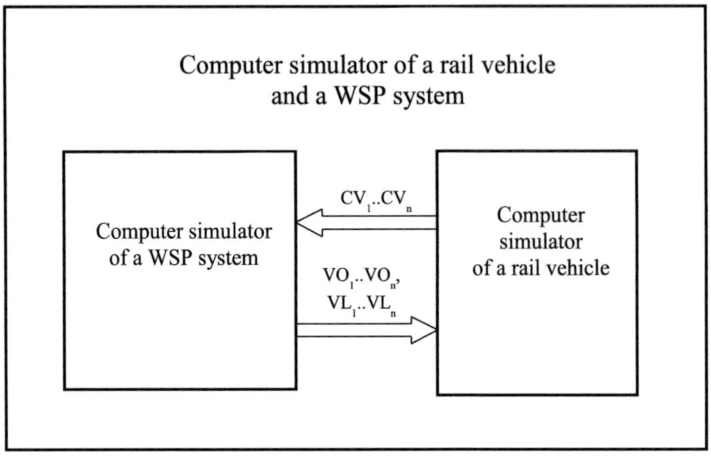

Fig. 18. Laboratory test stand with computer simulation of all the systems

6. Application and simulation results

6.1 Introduction

The simulator of a braked rail vehicle can be used for manifold purposes, which fall into two categories. The first one is developing WSP control algorithms, and it may comprise:

- acquiring the numerical data concerning the critical values used in the control algorithms
- establishing the influence of the changes of the control plant parameters
- establishing the influence of the changes of the controller parameters
- acquiring the reference data for design of the FLC WSP controllers
- tests of the WSP controllers.

The second category is preliminary testing of the WSP control algorithms or the designed WSP control devices or systems against the requirements given in CEN (2009) and UIC (2005).

In the remaining part of this section the three chosen examples of using the simulation stand for some of the mentioned above purposes are shown.

6.2 Acquiring reference data for designing the WSP control algorithms

By performing simulated brakings at both good and poor adhesion conditions, it is possible to acquire data, which can be used for designing both structure and parameters of WSP controllers. Several examples are given below.

In Fig. 19 the characteristic of vehicle acceleration for simulated braking from 120 km/h at maximum brake cylinder pressure $p_{c_{\max}}$ = 385 kPa at good adhesion is shown. Such data, acquired for various brake positions and initial test speed are especially valuable for developing algorithm of calculating the reference speed.

In Fig. 20 the results of simulated braking at poor adhesion conditions (initial value of $\psi_B \approx 0,06$) are presented. The initial test velocity was 160 km/h and the brake position was R ($p_{c_{max}}$ = 385 kPa). In the figure vehicle velocity, circumferential wheel velocity and circumferential

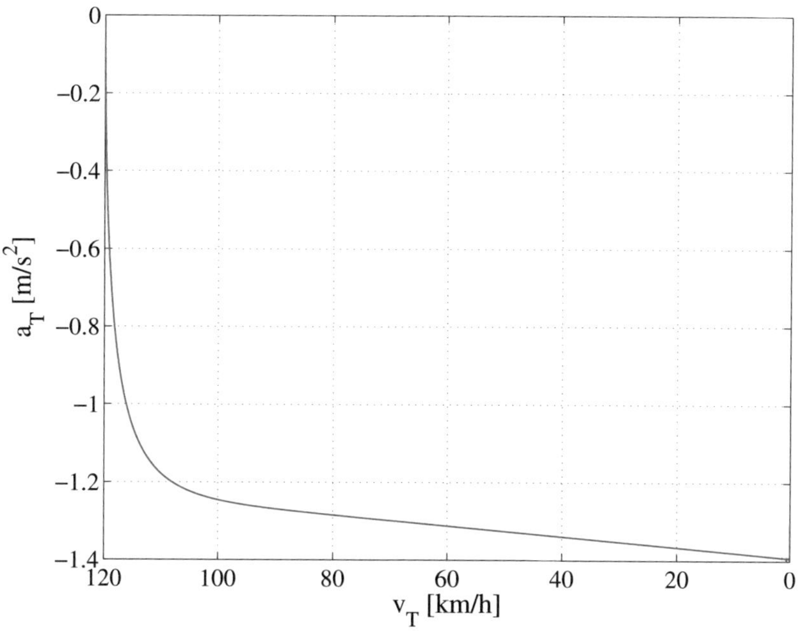

Fig. 19. Characteristic of vehicle acceleration a_T vs. vehicle velocity v_T for simulated braking from 120 km/h at maximum brake cylinder pressure $p_{c_{max}}$ = 385 kPa at good adhesion (Barna (2009))

wheel accelerations are shown. The numerical data can be used for setting and adjusting the parameters of the WSP control algorithms.

With a braked rail vehicle simulator it is also possible to perform simulations of braking at poor adhesion conditions aimed at acquiring data concerning the behavior of circumferential wheel speeds and accelerations, which can facilitate the process of developing the WSP control algorithms. In Fig. 21 the characteristics of vehicle velocity and circumferential wheel speed and acceleration during the first cycle of slide detection and suppression.

6.3 Designing the rule bases of FLC WSP

The rule bases of fuzzy controllers can be designed using expert knowledge and numerical simulation results, provided that such data is available and that the controller which has been used for obtaining the data has controlled the slide in an effective way. In Cheok & Shiomi (2000) a method of designing the fuzzy controller rule base has been proposed, which uses both expert knowledge and chosen numerical results obtained during operation of a PID controller. Basing on the numerical results some rules have been determined, and the lacking rules have been defined on the basis of expert knowledge concerning the slide control. In a simulator of a braked vehicle it is possible to access the signals, which are nor available during normal operation of the systems, i.e. wheel-rail adhesion coefficient and translation velocity of the vehicle. An advantage of having a simulator can be taken to create so called reference controllers which can be used for generating data for FLC WSP rule base design.

A block diagram of a WSP control system with a reference controller is shown in Fig. 22.

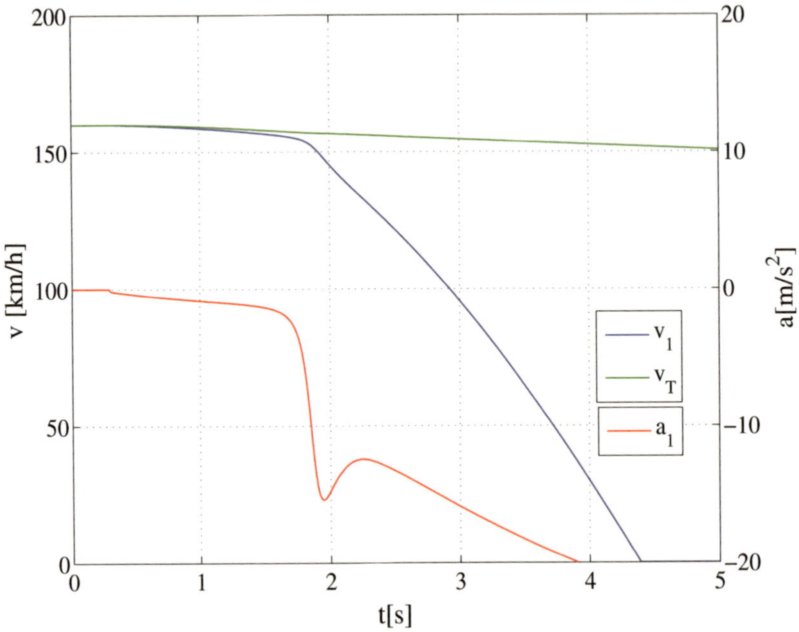

Fig. 20. Results of simulated braking at poor adhesion conditions (initial test velocity 160 km/h, initial value of $\psi_B \approx 0,06$, brake position R ($p_{c_{max}}$ = 385 kPa)) (Barna (2009))

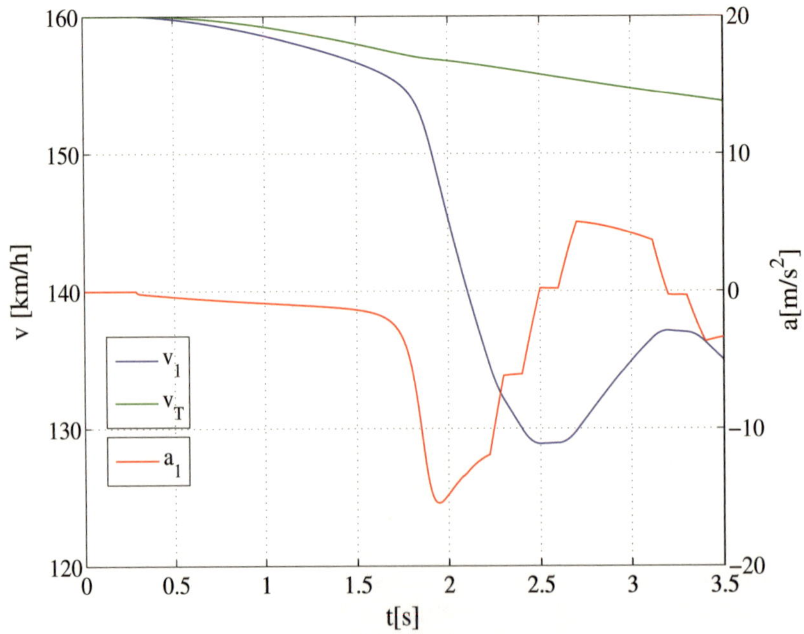

Fig. 21. Characteristics of vehicle velocity and circumferential wheel speed and acceleration for the first cycle of slide detection and suppression (Barna (2009))

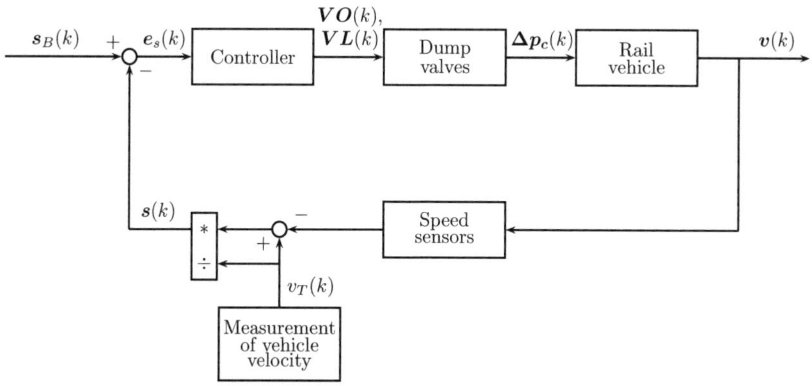

Fig. 22. Block diagram of a WSP control system with a reference controller (Barna (2009))

In Barna (2010b) a method of designing the rule bases of WSP fuzzy controllers for rail vehicles is presented. In this method results of simulation of two reference controllers are used, both of which use signals which are nor available during normal operation of the systems, i.e. optimal relative slide s_B and translation velocity of the vehicle v_T. Two types of reference controllers have been designed in order to obtain data for designing a real-life FLC WSP . One of them is a Fuzzy Logic controller, and the other is an expert knowledge based controller.

A block diagram of a Fuzzy Logic reference WSP control system implemented in Matlab Simulink® is shown in Fig. 23. It's structure is similar to a regular Fuzzy Logic WSP controller, but the reference value is the optimal relative slide s_B. A standard Mac-Vicar Whelan rule base has been adopted (Yager & Filev (1995)).

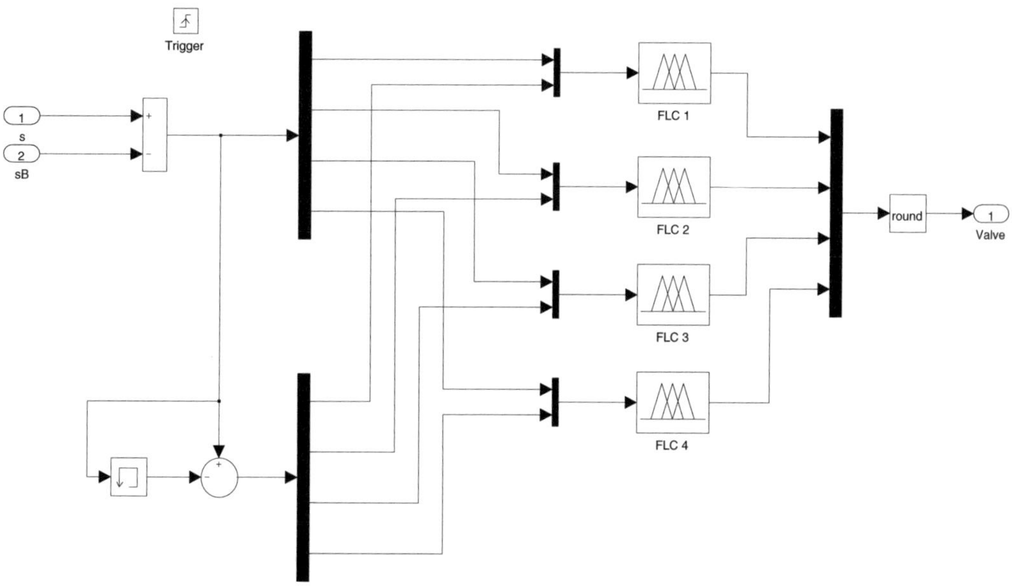

Fig. 23. Fuzzy Logic reference WSP control system implemented in Matlab Simulink®

A knowledge based algorithm is based on a MSG1 WSP controller made by Knorr-Bremse and presented in Boiteux (1999).

The input controller values for each axle set are:

- absolute wheel slide σ
- circumferential wheel acceleration a.

The output controller values are the same as in the Fuzzy Logic controllers described earlier. Three reference functions are defined, which divide the slide space into four ranges versus the reference velocity v_{ref}: $\Delta\sigma_1(v_{ref})$, $\Delta\sigma_2(v_{ref})$ and $\Delta\sigma_3(v_{ref})$. These functions are shown in Fig. 24.

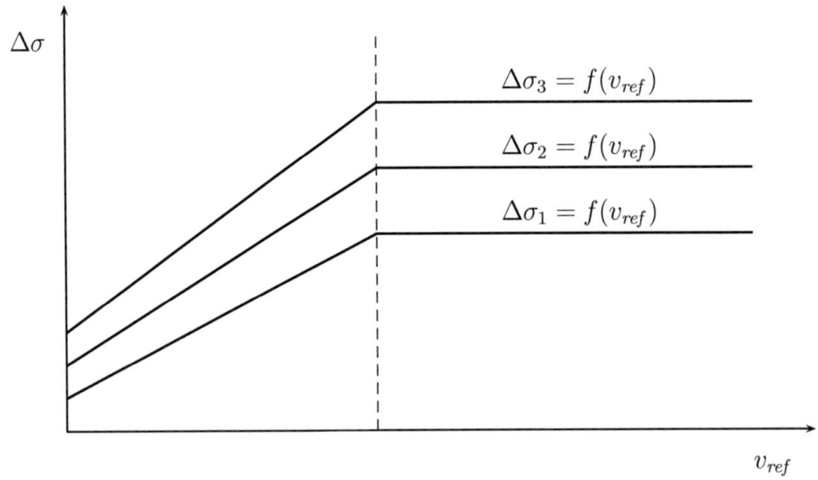

Fig. 24. Reference values of absolute slide used in control algorithm of MSG1 WSP system (Boiteux (1999))

Four values of circumferential wheel accelerations are also defined: a_1, a_2, a_3 oraz a_4. These values are demonstratively pictured in Fig. 25.

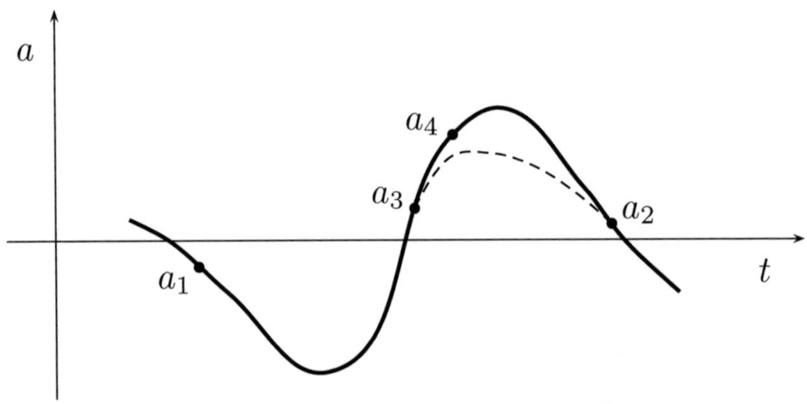

Fig. 25. Values of circumferential wheel accelerations used in control algorithm of MSG1 WSP system pictured demonstratively (Boiteux (1999))

The decision table of MSG1 WSP system control algorithm is presented in Table 1.

A block diagram of a knowledge based WSP control system implemented in Matlab Simulink® is shown in Fig. 26.

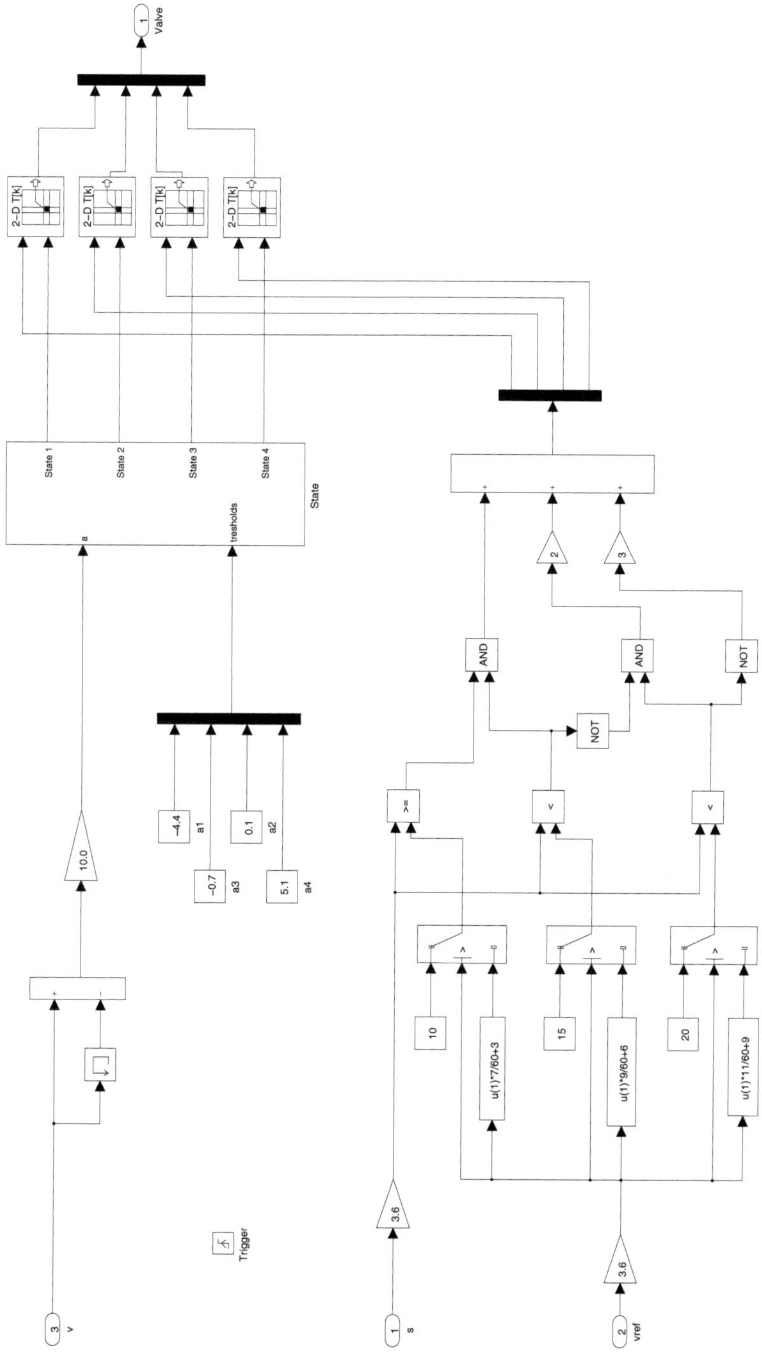

Fig. 26. Block diagram of a knowledge based WSP controller implemented in Matlab Simulink®

a → σ ↓	$a_1 \to a_3$	$a_3 \to a_4$	$a_4 \to a_4$	$a_4 \to a_2$	$a_2 \to a_1$
$\sigma < \Delta\sigma_1$	H	H	P3	H	P2
$\Delta\sigma_1 < \sigma < \Delta\sigma_2$	U1	H	P2	H	P1
$\Delta\sigma_2 < \sigma < \Delta\sigma_3$	U2	H	P1	H	H
$\Delta\sigma_3 < \sigma$	U3	U3	U3	U3	U3

Table 1. The decision table of MSG1 WSP system control algorithm (Boiteux (1999))

Simulations have been performed with a simulation model of a braked rail vehicle and controllers implemented in Matlab Simulink®. In Fig. 27 exemplary results of simulated braking from 120 km/h with a FLC reference controller at decreased adhesion have been shown.

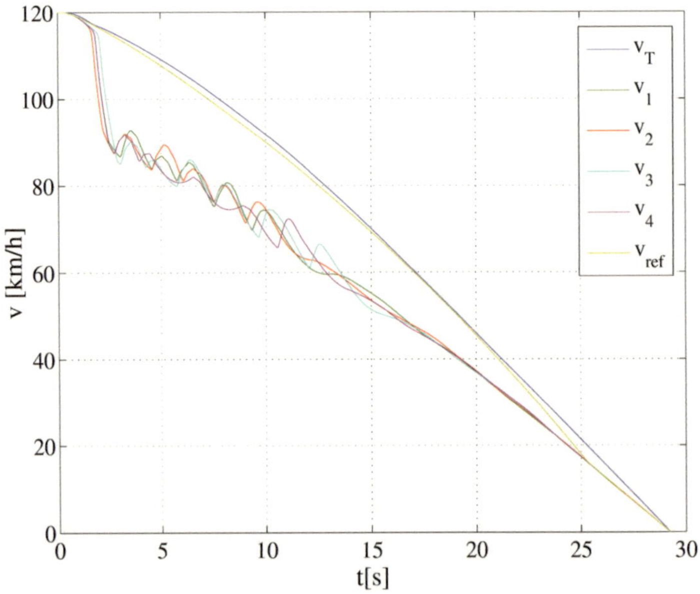

Fig. 27. Characteristics of velocities $\boldsymbol{v}$, v_T and v_{ref} for simulated braking from 120 km/h at maximum brake cylinder pressure $p_{c_{max}}$ = 385 kPa at decreased adhesion for a FLC reference controller (Barna (2009))

After running a series of tests contained to UIC 541-05 leaflet and EN 15595, simulation data have been used to develop a preliminary rule base using a dedicated C program.

The controller has been tested against the UIC 541-05 requirements with positive results. An exemplary simulated braking is shown in Fig. 28.

6.4 Testing the WSP systems

When a WSP system has been designed, simulated tests can be performed in order to check whether the WSP meets the requirements of CEN (2009) and UIC (2005). The test program consists of several tests, divided into three groups: slip tests, drag braking test and a test at low adhesion. The exact specification of tests depends on a vehicle type, which can be one of

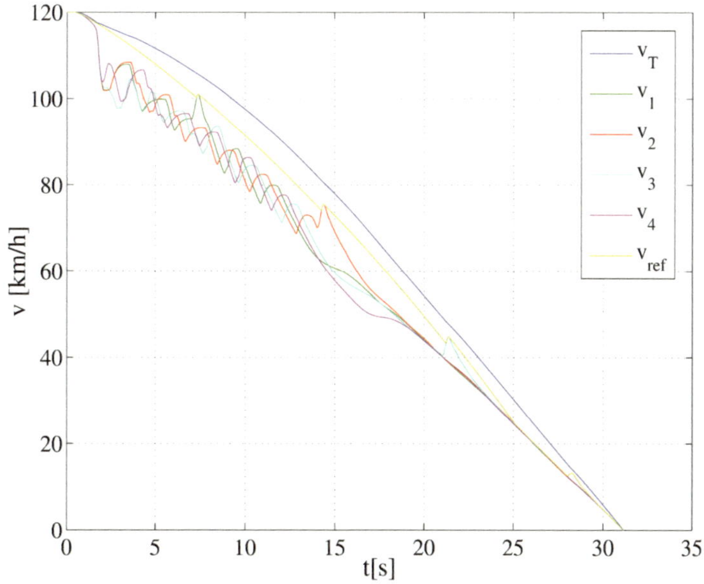

Fig. 28. Characteristics of velocities $\boldsymbol{v}$, v_T and v_{ref} for simulated braking from 120 km/h at maximum brake cylinder pressure ($p_{c_{max}}$ = 385 kPa) at decreased adhesion for a WSP controller (Barna (2009))

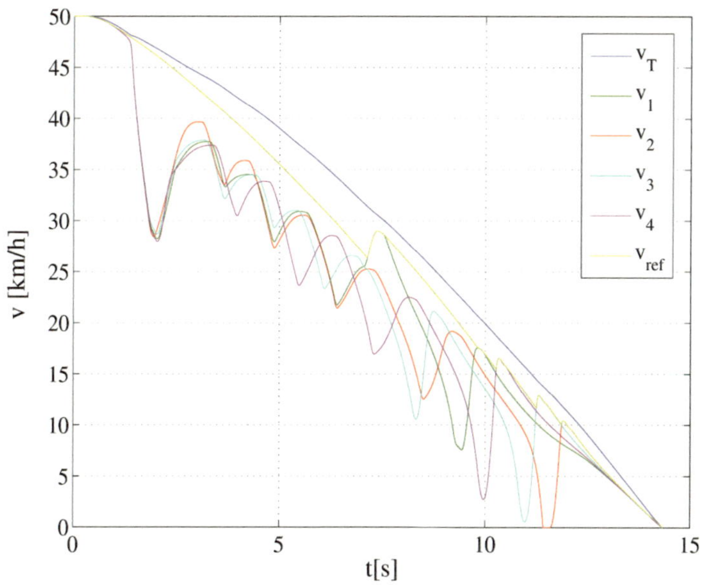

Fig. 29. Characteristics of velocities $\boldsymbol{v}$, v_T and v_{ref} for simulated braking from 50 km/h at maximum brake cylinder pressure ($p_{c_{max}}$ = 385 kPa) at decreased adhesion for a WSP controller (Barna (2009))

the following: a passenger coach, a wagon, a locomotive, a train-set or a high speed train. The initial vehicle speed and brake position, as well as additional conditions, are specified for each test. In order to check whether a WSP meets the requirements of the normative documents, appropriate simulated tests should be performed, and the results assessed.

Testing WSP systems against normative references is described in Barna (2009) and Barna (2010a). In Figures 29, 30 and 31 exemplary test results are shown: in Fig. 29 the results of tests from 50 km/h, and in Fig. 30 the results of tests for rail covered with soap. In Fig. 31 characteristic of pressure in a brake cylinder for simulated braking from 120 km/h is shown.

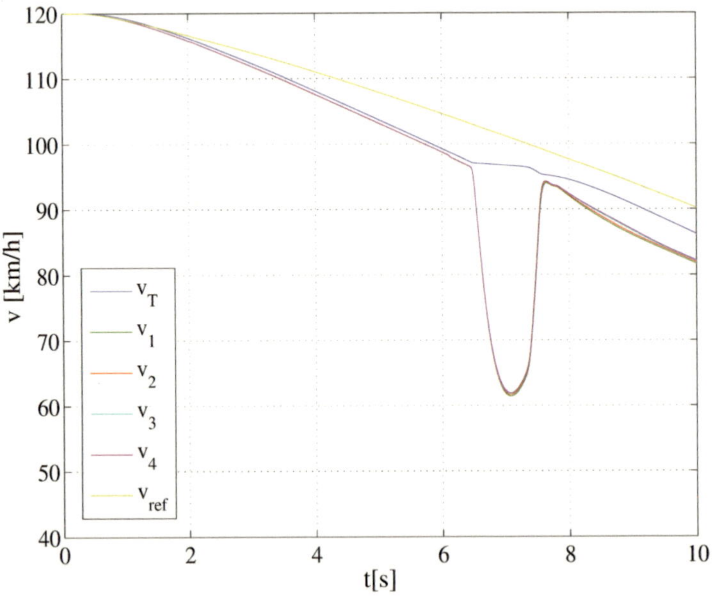

Fig. 30. Characteristics of velocities v, v_T and v_{ref} for simulated braking from 120 km/h at maximum brake cylinder pressure ($p_{c_{max}}$ = 385 kPa) for rail covered with soap for a WSP controller (Barna (2009))

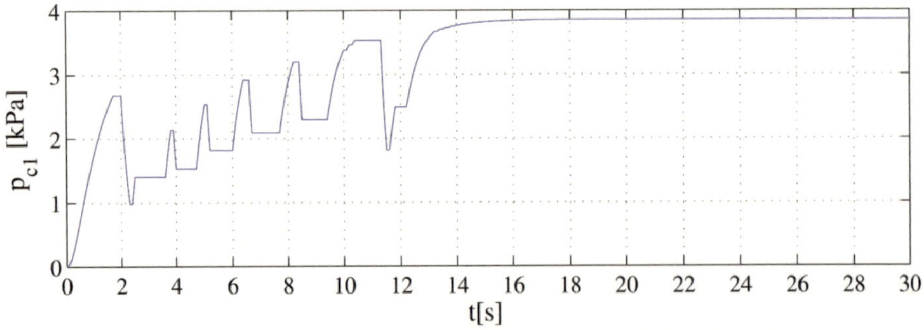

Fig. 31. Characteristics of pressure p_c for simulated braking from 120 km/h at maximum brake cylinder pressure ($p_{c_{max}}$ = 385 kPa) at decreased adhesion for a WSP controller (Barna (2009))

7. Conclusions

In order to design an efficient WSP controller, a simulator of a braked rail vehicle is indispensable. The mathematical model of the wheel-rail adhesion must comprise regeneration of adhesion by controlled slide.

The simulator can be used for manifold purposes, including developing and testing of WSP controllers.

One of possible applications is using the simulation results of the reference controllers for designing the rule bases for WSP FLC controllers. From the analysis of performance of the WSP fuzzy controller, the rule base of which has been designed in this way, it can be concluded, that this method makes possible designing efficient controllers.

The test program realized by the simulator must comply with the requirements of CEN (2009) and UIC (2005), thus making possible testing of the controllers in the whole possible range of slide and acceleration values.

The futer research concerning the simulator of the braked rail vehicle would comprise:

- further development of the mathematical model of particular sub-models, especially the model of the adhesion coefficient and model of the pneumatic system
- developing a software/hardware simulator with xPCTarget toolbox using a computer fitted with I/O boards.

8. Acknowledgements

This paper has been produced as part of the Research Projects "Microprocessor based Anti-slip System for traction rail vehicles meeting the requirements of Technical Specifications of Interoperability" N R10 0046 06/2009 with the financial support of the Ministry of Science and Higher Education.

9. List of symbols

$a\,[\mathrm{m/s^2}]$ – circumferential wheel acceleration
$a_T\,[\mathrm{m/s^2}]$ – vehicle acceleration
$A_k\,[\mathrm{m^2}]$ – area of piston of the brake cylinder
$A_x\,[\mathrm{m^2}]$ – area of friction surface of the brake disk
$d_m\,[\mathrm{m/s^2}]$ – average value of circumferential wheel deceleration from the beginning of braking and the moment when the slide value reaches 0.4
$e\,[-]$ – control error
$E\,[\mathrm{J}]$ – instantaneous value of axle set slide energy, from the start of the braking until the instant moment t
$E_o\,[\mathrm{J}]$ – value of axle set slide energy from the start of braking until reaching of the working point (s, ψ) point B
$F_f\,[\mathrm{N}]$ – force of the return spring of the brake cylinder
$F_a\,[\mathrm{N}]$ – adhesion force for an axle set
$F_{a\Sigma}\,[\mathrm{N}]$ – sum of adhesion forces for all axle sets of a vehicle
$i_p\,[-]$ – final ratio of clamp mechanisms of an axle set
$J\,[\mathrm{kg\,m^2}]$ – moment of inertia of rotating elements associated with an axle set, reduced to the axle set axis

L_h [m] – total braking distance
M_b [Nm] – braking torque of an axle set
m [kg] – vehicle mass
N [N] – vertical rail reaction force for an axle set
N_k [N] – pressure exerted by brake discs, reduced to the braking radius
n [−] – number of axle sets of a vehicle
p_c [Pa] – brake cylinder pressure
$\mathbf{p}$ [−] – vector of parameters of ψ vs. s characteristics
$p_{c_{max}}$ [Pa] – maximum pressure in a brake cylinder for a given brake position
$p_{c_{in}}$ [Pa] – instantaneous air pressure at inlet of a dump valve
p_{c_0} [Pa] – outlet dump valve air pressure value at the moment of change of the dump valve state
p_x [daN/cm^2] – unitary pressure of the friction linings of a brake block
Q [N] – instantaneous load of the axle set
r [m] – wheel radius
r_b [m] – brake radius
r_d [m] – brake disk radius
s [−] – relative slide of wheels against the rails
s_B [−] – optimum relative slide
s_α [−] – relative slide for point α
t [s] – time
T_h [s] – total time of braking until standstill
T_V [s] – time constant of dump valve venting
T_F [s] – time constant of dump valve filling
v [km/h] – circumferential velocity of axle set wheels
v_{ref} [km/h] – vehicle reference velocity
v_T [km/h] – vehicle velocity
γ [−] – coefficient of rotational mass
η_r [−] – coefficient of increasing the efficiency of the lever mechanism of the brake clamp mechanism in motion
η_s [−] – static efficiency of the lever mechanism of the brake clamp mechanism
λ [−] – braking rate
μ [−] – friction coefficient of the brake block friction lining
ψ [−] – instantaneous value of wheel-rail adhesion coefficient
ψ_B [−] – maximum exploitable wheel-rail adhesion coefficient
ψ_l [−] – adhesion coefficient for locked wheels
ψ_α [−] – available adhesion coefficient
σ [km/h] – absolute slide of wheels against the rails
$\hat{\sigma}$ [km/h] – estimated absolute slide of wheels against the rails
ω [rad/s] – angular velocity of a vehicle axle set

10. References

Barna, G. (2009). *Control Algorithms of Wheel Slide Protection Systems for Rail Vehicles (in Polish)*, PhD thesis, Poznan University of Technology.

Barna, G. (2010a). Simulation based design and tests of wheel slide protection systems for rail vehicles, *Application of System Science*, Computer Science, Academic Publishing House EXIT, Warsaw, pp. 271–280.

Barna, G. (2010b). Simulation based design of fuzzy wheel slide protection controller for rail vehicles, *Proceedings of 15th International Conference on Methods and Models in Automation and Robotics*, Miedzyzdroje.

Barna, G. & Kaluba, M. (2009). Safety and reliability of microprocessor brake control systems for multiple units, *Proceedings of XI International Conference QSEV 2009 (Quality, Safety and Ecology in Transport)*, Kraków.

Boiteux, M. (1987). Influence de l'énergie de glissment sur l'adhérence exploitable en freinage, *Revue Générale des Chemins de Fer* 106(October): 05–15.

Boiteux, M. (1990). Influence de l'énergie de glissment sur l'adhérence exploitable en freinage, *Revue Générale des Chemins de Fer* 109(Juillet - Août): 31–38.

Boiteux, M. (1998). Le problème de l'adhérence en freinage, *Chemins de Fer* 5(452): 28–39.

Boiteux, M. (1999). Auxiliaires sophistiqués du freinage d'aujourd'hui — les antienrayeurs, *Chemins de Fer* 6(459): 24–35.

Caldara, C., Rivera, M. G. & Poma, G. (1996). Software implementation of an anti-skidding control system for traction electrical drives based on fuzzy-identification techniques, *Symposium on Power Electronics, Industrial Drives, Power Quality, Traction Systems*, Capri, pp. C3–19 - C3–25.

CEN (2009). *EN 15595, Railway applications — Braking — Wheel Slide Protection.*

Cheok, A. D. & Shiomi, S. (2000). Combined heuristic knowledge and limited measurement based fuzzy logic antiskid control for railway applications, *IEEE Transactions on Systems, Man, and Cybernetics — Part C: Applications and Reviews* 30(4).

Jergéus, J. (1998). Martensite formation and residual stresses around railway wheel flats, *Proc Insts Mech Engrs*, Vol. 212, pp. 69–79.

Kaczorek, T. (1977). *Theory of Automatic Control Systems (in Polish)*, WNT, Warszawa.

Kaluba, M. (1999). *Influence of selected factors upon developing of the phenomenon of fluid friction in the disk brakes of rail vehicles (in Polish)*, PhD thesis, Poznan University of Technology.

Knorr Bremse AG. (2002). *Bremsen für Schienenfahrzeuge; Handbuch Bremstechnische Begriffe und Werte*, Knorr Bremse AG.

Kwaśnikowski, J. & Firlik, B. (2006). Excessive wear of the wheel treads of the rail bus, *Proceedings of 17th Scientific Conference "Rail Vehicles"*, Kazimierz Dolny, pp. 413–422.

Mauer, G. F. (1995). A fuzzy logic controller for an ABS braking system, *IEEE Transactions on Fuzzy Systems* 3(4): 381–388.

Ofierzyński, M. (2008). The method of automatic generation of a model for dynamic-running calculations of rail vehicles (in polish), *Proceedings of 18th Scientific Conference "Rail Vehicles"*, Vol. 2, Katowice - Ustroń, pp. 392 - 412.

ORE (1985). *Adhesion During Braking and Anti-skid Devices, ORE B 164, RP 1, Synthesis of Current Knowledge Concerning Adhesion*, Office for Research and Experiments of the International Union of Railways, Utrecht.

ORE (1990). *Adhesion During Braking and Anti-skid Devices, ORE B 164, RP 2, Fundamental Laws of Adhesion in braking*, Office for Research and Experiments of the International Union of Railways, Utrecht.

Pawełczyk, M. (2008). Mathematical model of a system: wheel with a flat spot - rail, *Proceedings of 18th Scientific Conference "Rail Vehicles"*, Vol. 2, Katowice - Ustroń, pp. 425 - 434.

Sachs, K. (1973). *Elektrische Triebfahrzeuge*, Vol. 1, 2 edn, Springer-Verlag, Wien New York.

Sanz, M. G. R. R. & Pérez-Rodríguez, J. (1997). An antislipping fuzzy logic controller for a railway traction system, *Proceedings of the sixth IEEE International Conference on Fuzzy Systems*, Barcelona.

Tao, G. & Kokotovic, P. (1996). *Adaptive control of systems with actuator and sensor nonlinearities*, John Wiley Sons, Inc., New York.

UIC (2005). *UIC 541-05, Brakes — Specifications for the Construction of Various Brake Parts — Wheel Slide Protection Device (WSP)*, 2 edn.

Will, A. B. & Żak, S. H. (2000). Antilock brake system modelling and fuzzy control, *Int. J. Vehicle Design* 24(1): 01–18.

Yager, R. R. & Filev, D. P. (1995). *Essentials of Fuzzy Modeling and Control*, Wiley-Interscience, New York.

10

Using of Hybrid Supply for Electric or Hybrid Vehicles

N. Rizoug[1], G. Feld[2], B. Barbedette[1] and R. Sadoun[1]
[1]*Ecole Supérieure des Techniques Aéronautiques et de Construction Automobile, Cedex 9,*
[2]*Ecole Normale Supérieure (ENS Cachan), Cachan Cedex, France*

1. Introduction

For automotive applications, the batteries are sized to ensure many constraints like startup, acceleration, braking and energy recovery. All these constraints give us a very heavy battery with very high energy compared to that required for these applications. To reduce the weight of the storage system, the battery can be associated with high power component like supercapacitors. This last one is used like power booster, and the battery is used just to ensure the energy needed for each application (hybrid or electric vehicles). The use of Matlab-Simulink software allows us to make a modular simulation (Fig. 1). This software resolves the differential equations using several numerical methods (Runge-kutta, Dormand-Prince, Heun, Euler,...). This paper deals with the simulation and conception of hybrid power supply composed with battery and supercapacitors for a micro-hybrid vehicles. In this case, the battery is used as energy tank and supercapacitors as power booster. This design allows to increase the lifetime of the supply and to downsize this last one.

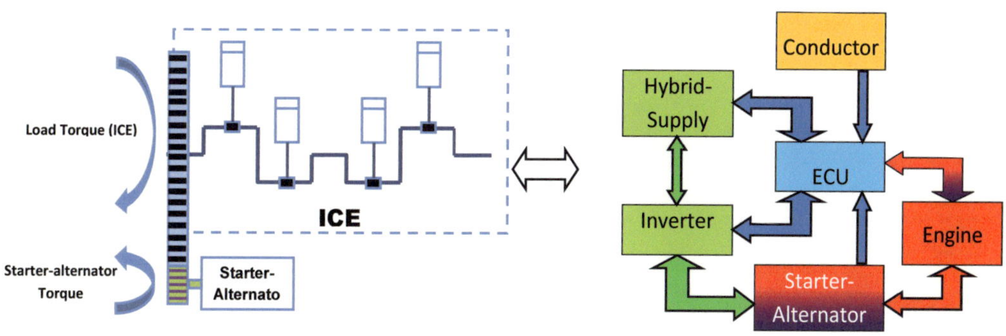

Fig. 1. Modular simulation of the system using Matlab-Simulink

2. Topology of the power system

The hybrid storage system (battery and supercapacitors) supply the starter-alternator through an inverter. Two topologies can be used to associate the battery and the supercapacitors: in series or parallel. For this last configuration, the two components are connected to the DC link through two choppers. In the series configuration (fig. 2), the supercapacitors is charged by the battery and discharged during the high power demand (startup, acceleration,...).

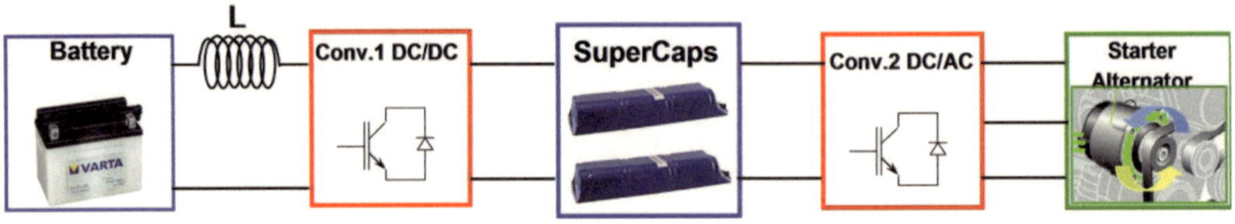

Fig. 2. Topology of the series hybrid supply for automotive application

Supercapacitors are chosen like booster because of their very high specific power, which can reach 17kw/kg. The capacitance of this component exceeds the 5000F (Maxwell technology) for a lower voltage (3V). To use this component in power applications, we must make some elements in series.

Fig. 3. Using the hybrid supply with starter or starter-alternator

3. Startup torque measurement

During the starting-up, the ICE develops a load torque applied to the starter or the starter-alternator. The computation of this torque allows us to validate the hybrid supply interest. To estimate this torque we need to know the evolution of the starter torque according to its current.

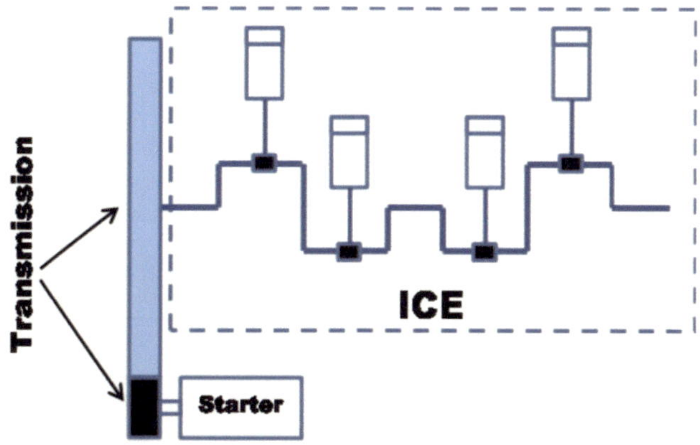

Fig. 4. The transmission between the starter and the ICE

3.1 Formula of the starter Torque

Because of their high starting torque, the series DC motors is used like a starter for the automobile applications. The torque developed by this motor can be written as follow:

$$T_{starter} = K\,\Phi\,I \tag{1}$$

The relation between the current and the flux of this type of motors complicates the identification of this torque. For that, this motor (starter) is transformed to a separate-wound DC motor.

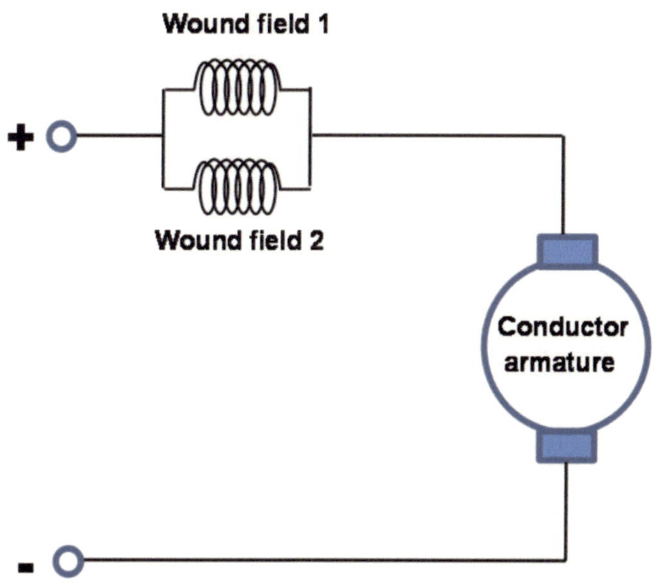

Fig. 5. Electrical diagram of starter (series motor).

Figure 6 presents the transformation of the series DC motor to a separate-wound DC motor. This transformation allows us to identify their torque.

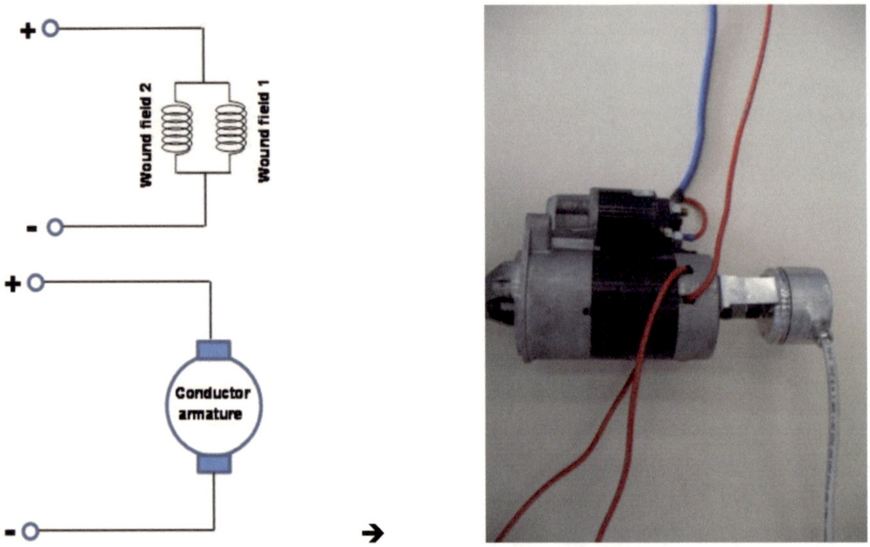

Fig. 6. Transformation of the series DC motor to separate-wound DC motor

The acquisition of the armature voltage, the armature current and the starter velocity at deferent wound current allows us to plot the evolution of the ratio K Φ according to the current (fig. 7).

$$E = V - RI = K\,\Phi\,\Omega_{starter} \tag{2}$$

According to the results plotted on the figure 7, the ratio K Φ can be written as follow:

$$K\,\Phi = -2\,E-9\,I^3 + 3\,E-7\,I^2 + 9\,E-5\,I + 0.0063 \tag{3}$$

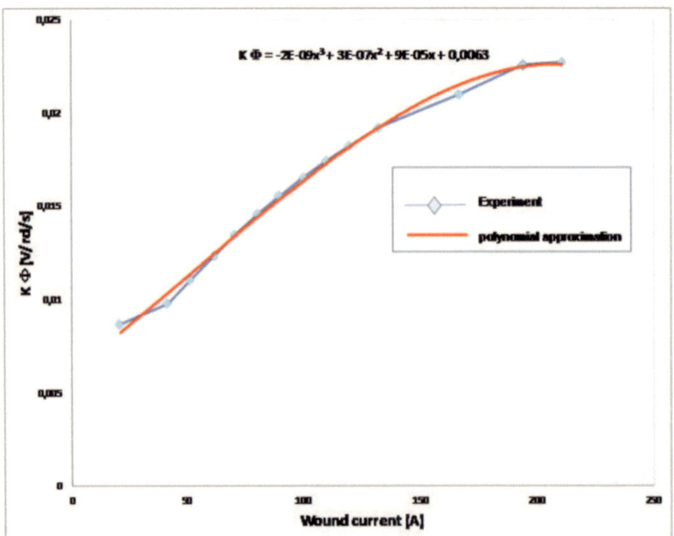

Fig. 7. Evolution of the ratio K Φ according to the wound current

3.2 Formula of the startup torque

To identify the load torque developed by the ICE during the starting-up phase, tow starting-up tests are made. The first it's without the spark plugs and the second it's with compression (with spark plug).

The first test (fig. 8) allows us to estimate the inertia and the friction torque of the ICE. Using the mechanic equation we can compute the two parameters (J and f).

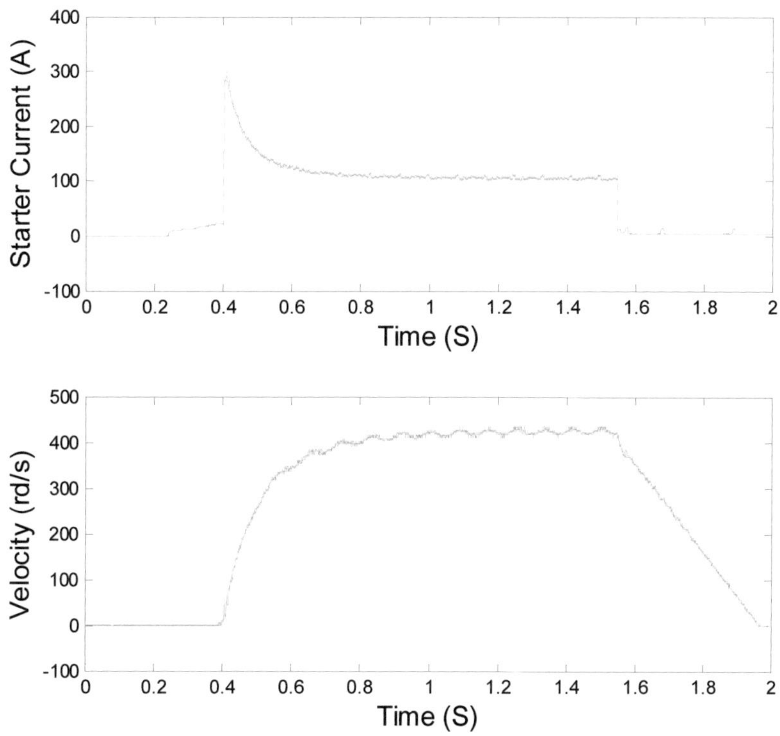

Fig. 8. Evolution of the current ant the starter velocity for the test without spark plugs

$$J\frac{d\Omega}{dt} = K\Phi I - f\,\Omega - C_0 \tag{4}$$

Using the measured current and starter velocity, we can compute the parameters J, f and C0.

$$\begin{cases} J = 1.5\,E-3\ Kg\,m^2 \\ f = 4.2E-3\ Nm/rd/s \\ C_0 = 0\,Nm \end{cases} \tag{5}$$

The second test (fig. 9) allows us to estimate the rippled torque (Tcomp) due to the compression on the ICE motor.

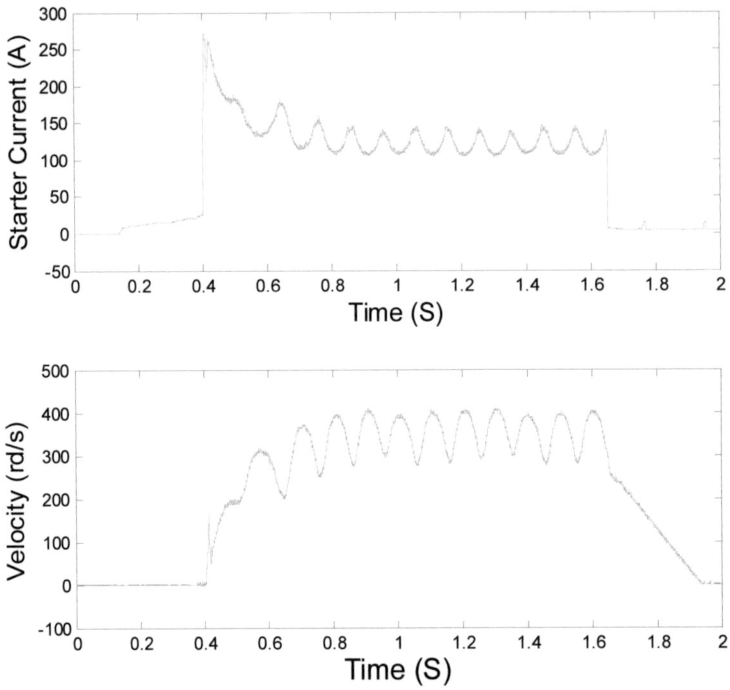

Fig. 9. Evolution of the current ant the starter velocity for the test with spark plugs

Using the parameters computed at the first test (J, f and C0), the current and the starter velocity presented in the figure 9, we can compute the torque due to the compression (Tcomp):

$$J\frac{d\Omega}{dt} = K\Phi I - f\,\Omega - C_0 - T_{comp} \tag{6}$$

Figure 10 presents the wave form of the compression torque Tcomp. This can be written as:

$$T_{com} = 1 + 5.9\sin(0.190 * \theta_{starter}) \tag{7}$$

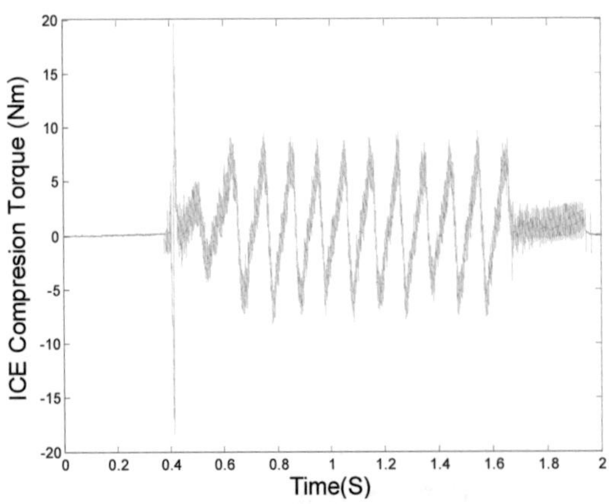

Fig. 10. Waveform of the compression torque Tcomp

4. Sizing of the supercapcitors module for the startup

The supercapacitors sizing is based on the energy and power required for the starting-up of the vehicle. Figure 11 presents the evolution of the current and the voltage of the Buggy starter at the starting-up phase. At the beginning of this phase, the battery voltage deceases to reach 9V. At the same time, the current exceeds the 250A, what gives us a maximum power of 2400W.

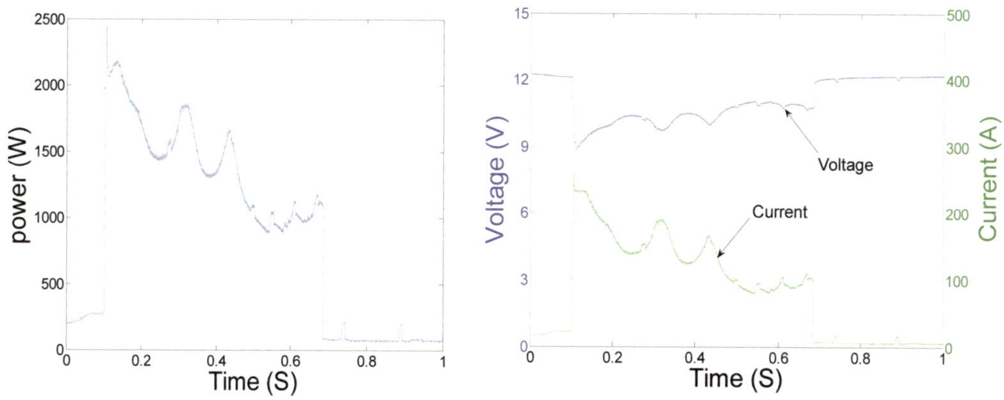

Fig. 11. Power and energy required for the starting-up of the vehicle

In order to ensure the functioning of the boost chopper, the minimum voltage of the supercondensator should not decrease lower than 12V (battery voltage). To take a safety margin, the minimum supercapacitors voltage is chosen about 15V. For this component, more than 75% of energy is stored between the maximum voltage of supercapacitors (Vmax_SupCaps) and the half of this voltage (Vmax_SupCaps/2) :

$$V_{min\_SuperCaps} = V_{max\_SuperCaps} / 2 \Rightarrow V_{max\_SuperCaps} = 2\, V_{min\_SuperCaps} = 30V \tag{8}$$

The power integral on all the starting-up duration allows us to compute the energy required for this phase.

$$E_{start} = \int P_{start} dt = 250\, mWh \tag{9}$$

The supercapcitors efficiency reaches 80% for 250A of RMS current.

By the neglecting of the Conv.2 losses, the starting-up energy can be written as follow:

$$E_{start} = \eta_{sc} \frac{1}{2} C_{sc} (V^2_{max\_SuperCaps} - V^2_{min\_SuperCaps}) = \frac{3}{10} C_{sc}\, V^2_{max\_SuperCaps} \tag{10}$$

$$C_{sc} = \frac{10}{3} \frac{E_{start}}{V^2_{max}} = \frac{10}{3} \frac{900}{30^2} \approx 3{,}34F \tag{11}$$

The best component for this application can be chosen using the characteristics of all Maxwell cells. The element 2,5V/310F gives us the best compromise between the power and the energy of the component.

	2.5V/4F		2.5V/10F		2.5V/120F	2.5V/140F	2.5V/310F	2.5V/350F	2.7V/650F	2.7V/1200	2.7V/1500	2.7V/2000	2.7V/3000
Tension (v)	2.5	2.5	2.5	2.5	2.5	2.5	2.5	2.5	2.7	2.7	2.7	2.7	2.7
Capacite d'un element (F)	4	4	10	10	120	140	310	350	650	1200	1500	2000	3000
Courant (A)	1	8	2.5	19	730	530	1500	1100	3500	3750	3900	4300	4800
Nombre d'element en série	11	11	11	11	12	12	12	12	12	12	12	12	12
Nombre de branches en parallele	240	30	96	13	1	1	1	1	1	1	1	1	1
Capacite globale (F)	87.2727273	10.9090909	87.2727273	11.8181818	10	11.6666667	25.8333333	29.1666667	54.1666667	100	125	166.66667	250
Volume unitaire (l)	0.0015	0.0015	0.003	0.003	0.027	0.027	0.053	0.053	0.211	0.294	0.325	0.373	0.475
Volume global (l)	3.96	0.495	3.168	0.429	0.324	0.324	0.636	0.636	2.532	3.528	3.9	4.476	5.7
Temps de charge à 20A	103.125	12.890625	103.125	13.96484375	14.0625	16.40625	36.328125	41.015625	88.846875	164.025	205.03125	273.375	410.0625
Resistance interne RMS (mOhm)	18.3333333	146.666667	20.625	152.307692	60	86.4	26.4	38.4	9.6	6.96	5.64	4.2	3.48

Table 1. Supercapacitors sizing

$$C_{component} = 310F\,;\; V_{component} = 2{,}5V\,;$$

$$N°_{elements-en-series} = 12\,;\; N°_{Branches} = 1 \tag{12}$$

$$Volume = 1l\,;\;\; RMS = 26m\Omega\,;$$

To reach 30V for the supercapacitors module, we must make 12 elements in series, what give a capacitance module about 26F:

$$C_{module} = \frac{310\text{F}}{12} = 26\text{F} \tag{13}$$

With this component, we can make 8 starting-up without reloading the component:

$$N_{start} = \frac{26F}{3{,}34F} \approx 8\ starting-up \tag{14}$$

5. Simulation of the system

Before the development of the test bench for this application, a simulation of the operated system is carried out using Matlab-Simulink software. In this case an inverter is used to

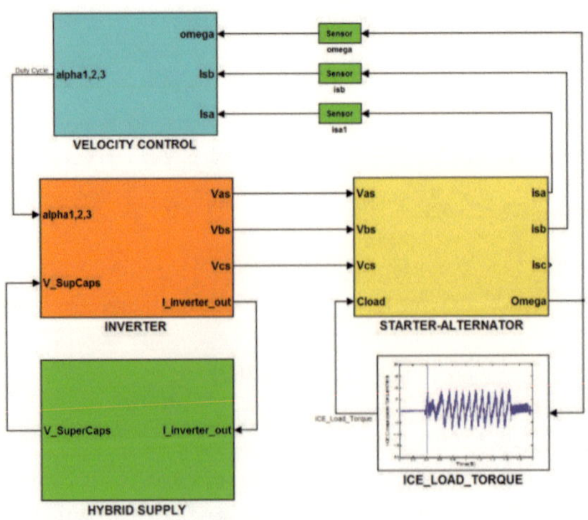

Fig. 12. Simulink model of the global system

supply the starter-alternator. In the startup phase, the velocity of the starter-alternator is controlled to reach the set point value (70 rd/S). The load torque is expressed according to the velocity using the formula 7.

Fig. 13. Test bench developed on the mechatronic laboratory

To avoid the angular representation, the starter-alternator is modeled with two phases inputs/outputs (d,q). The model is transformed into three phases inputs/outputs using the Park's transformations. The rotoric current and the load torque generates by the ICE are considered also like inputs. The starter alternator equations can write as follow:

$$\begin{aligned} V_{sd} &= R_a i_{sd} + L_{sd}\frac{di_{sd}}{dt} - pL_{sq} i_{sq}\Omega \\ V_{sq} &= R_a i_{sq} + L_{sq}\frac{di_{sq}}{dt} + pL_{sd} i_{sd}\Omega + kpM_{af} I_f \Omega \\ C_{em} &= \frac{3}{2}p\left[kM_{af} I_f I_{sq} + \left(L_{sd} - L_{sq}\right) I_{sd} I_{sq}\right] \end{aligned} \quad (15)$$

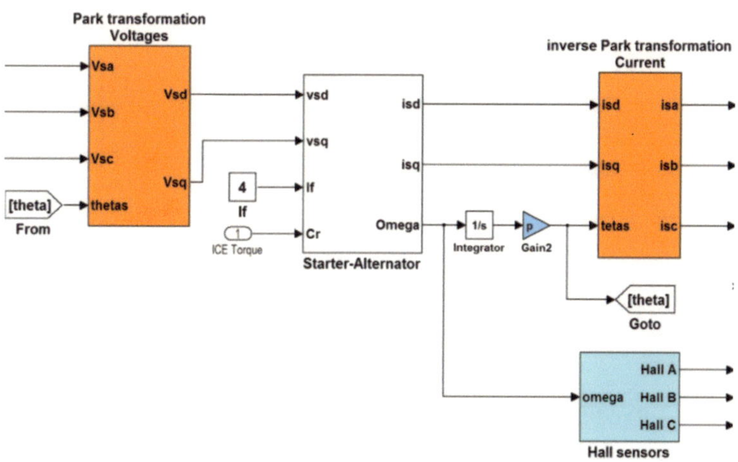

Fig. 14. Model of the starter-alternator

The starter-alternator parameters (Lsd, Lsq, Ra, Maf) are identified making some tests. The supplying of the two phases of the starter-alternator by two bridges chopper (fig. 15) at high frequency signal (20 kHz) allows to compute the values of the two inductances Lsd and Lsq. These last ones are computed for two positions of the rotor.

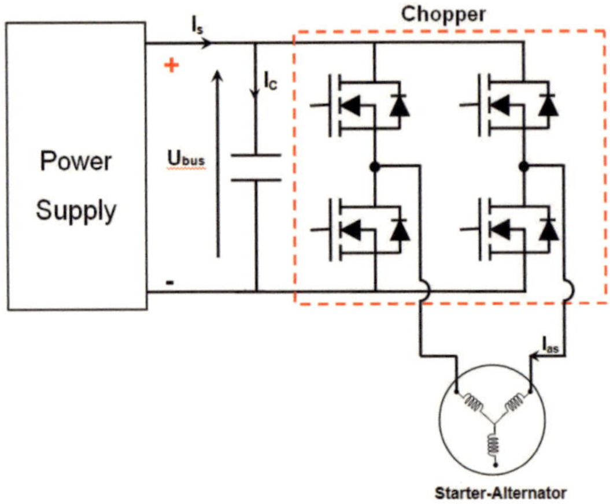

Fig. 15. Identification of the starter-alternator inductances

The first position (fig. 16.a) gives us the value of the direct inductance (Lsd), and The second position of the rotor (fig. 16.b) gives us the value of the quadratic inductance (Lsq). The same formula is used to calculate the two inductances:

$$\begin{cases} L_{sx} = U_{bus} \dfrac{\Delta t}{2\Delta i} \\ x = d \ or \ q \end{cases} \quad (16)$$

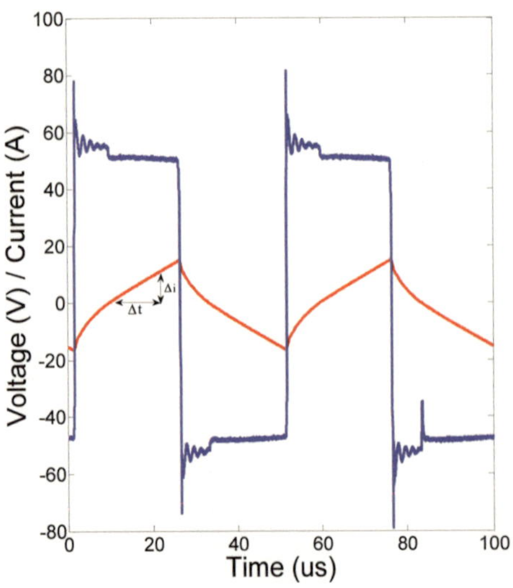

a) Test to identify the Lsd inductance

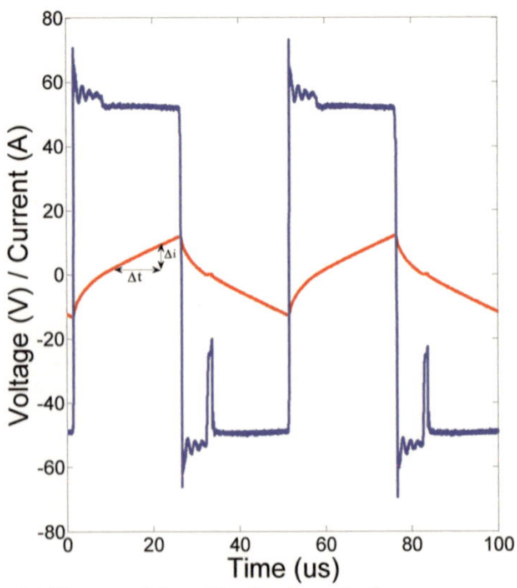

b) Test to identify the Lsq inductance

Fig. 16. Identification of the machine inductances

The applying of this formula gives us the values of Lsd and Lsq:

$$\begin{cases} L_{sd} = 40{,}7\,\mu H \\ L_{sq} = 28\,\mu H \end{cases} \tag{17}$$

To calculate the parameter Maf, the starter alternator must turn at constant velocity with the variation of the inductor current. In this case, the value of the voltage between two phases can expressed as follow:

$$\frac{U_{ab}}{\sqrt{3}} = \frac{p M_{af} I_f \Omega}{\sqrt{2}} \Rightarrow M_{af} = \frac{\sqrt{2}}{\sqrt{3}} \frac{U_{ab}}{2\pi f p I_f} \tag{18}$$

Table 2 summarizes the values of the starter-alternator parameters:

Parameter	Value	unit
Lsd	40	μH
Lsq	40	μH
Ra	13.3	mΩ
Maf	2.5	mH

Table 2. Starter alternator parameters

The inverter is modeled using the formulas between the starter-alternator voltages (Vas,Vbs and Vcs) and the control of the semiconductors (K1,K2 and K3):

$$\begin{bmatrix} V_{as} \\ V_{bs} \\ V_{cs} \end{bmatrix} = \frac{U_{bus}}{3} \cdot \begin{bmatrix} 2 & -1 & -1 \\ -1 & 2 & -1 \\ -1 & -1 & 2 \end{bmatrix} \cdot \begin{bmatrix} K_1 \\ K_2 \\ K_3 \end{bmatrix} \tag{19}$$

The voltage of the Dc link is also one of the inputs for the inverter model. On the other hand, this model imposes the current of the hybrid supply. This last one is composed with two storage systems (battery and supercapacitors) associated with a chopper (fig. 17), which is connected to the battery through an inductive filter.

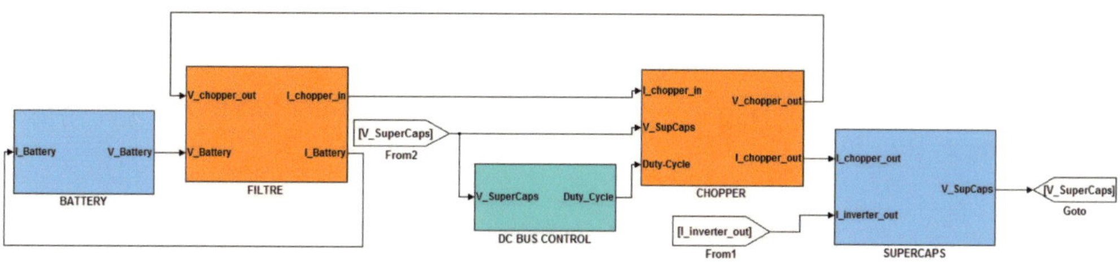

Fig. 17. Simulink model of the hybrid supply

Two models are used to represent the battery behaviour. The first one is the simplified R-C model which uses just a resistance and capacitance to modelling the battery. The second representation is based on the frequency behaviour of the battery. This method allows the representation of the component using the Shepherd model (fig. 18)

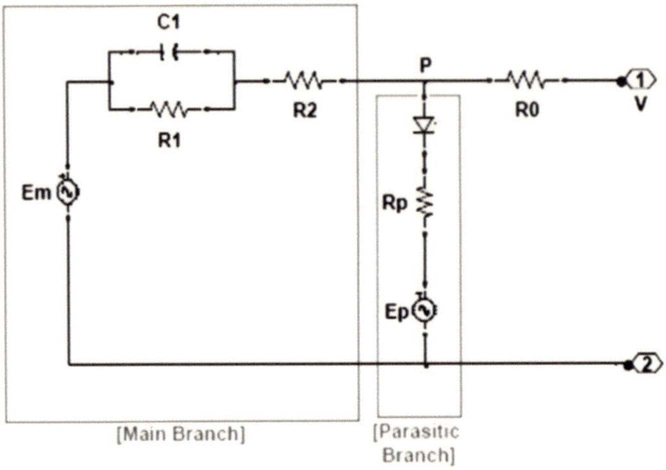

Fig. 18. Shepherd model of the battery

For the supercapacitors modeling a transmission line model is used. This approach is based on the representation of the charges propagation along the electrodes surface by RC circuits. So, the supercapacitor is considered like a capacitance distributed along the volume, with accessible areas and less accessible ones. The distribution of the capacitance depends on the electrode material and especially on the geometrical properties of the pores where ions have to access to constitute the double layer capacitance. This approach is well represented by an electrical circuit representing the transmission line and using r-c parallels branches. Then, the proposed model will only include 3 parameters (C, rs and R).

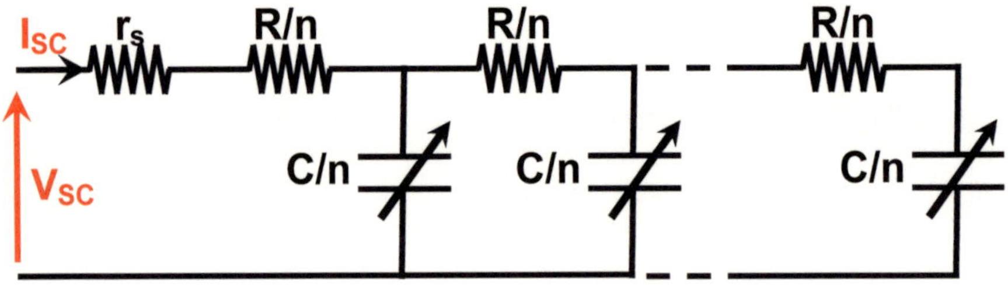

Fig. 19. Transmission line model

The modelling of the chopper is made making the formulas between the inputs and outputs of this converter (fig. 20).

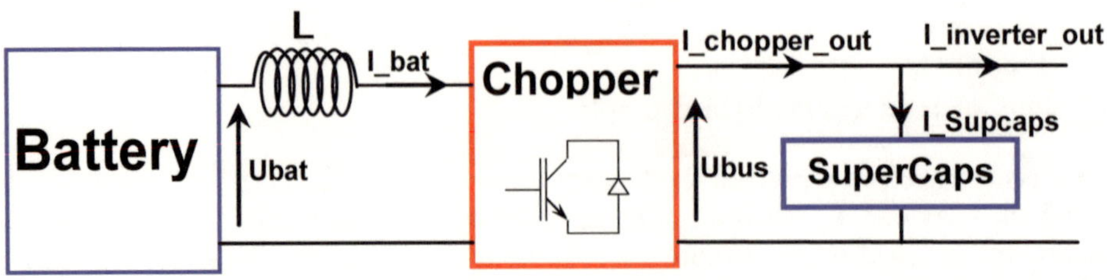

Fig. 20. Chopper inputs/outputs

The relations between the inputs and outputs of the chopper can write as follow:

$$\begin{cases} I_{bat} = \left[\left(U_{bat} - \left((1-\alpha)U_{bus}\right)\right)\right]\dfrac{1}{Ls} \\ I_{chopper\_out} = (1-\alpha)U_{bus}\, I_{bat} \\ I_{SupCaps} = I_{inverter\_out} - I_{chopper\_out} \end{cases} \qquad (20)$$

The starter-alternator velocity is estimated through Hall sensors. Using the three phases positions (fig. 21), given by these sensors we can estimate the velocity and the electric angle of the starter-alternator

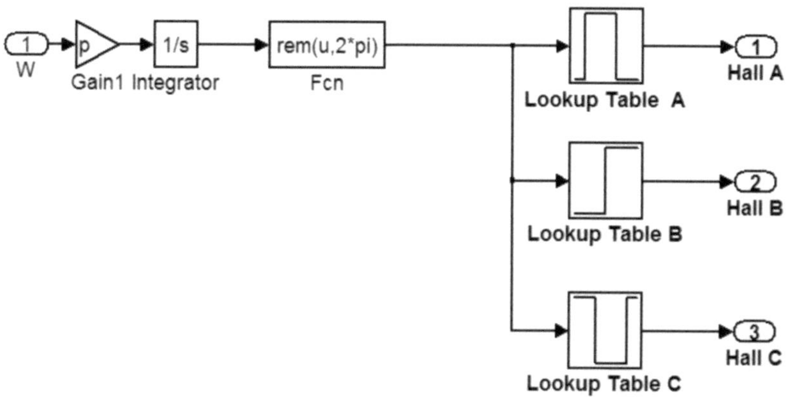

Fig. 21. Starter-alternator position using Hall sensor

6. Simulation results

Two simulations of the system functioning are made using the developed model. The first model it's to validate the startup of the vehicle using the hybrid supply. In this case, the supercapacitor discharge and the voltage of the DC link decreases. The second test is to validate the electric power generation and the charge of the battery.

6.1 Startup of the vehicle using the hybrid supply

To turn-on the vehicle, the velocity of the starter-alternator is controlled to reach the set point value (32rd/s). During this phase, the supercapacitor discharge. Figure 22 presents the waveform of the starter-alternat or velocity (real velocity) and that estimated using the hall sensors. This figure shows also that the starter-alternator velocity reaches the set-point value after 50 ms.

Figure 23 presents the waveform of the electric angle and that estimated using the hall signals. This result shows the deference between the real value of the electric angle and that estimated for the low velocity. After that the estimation gives almost the real value.

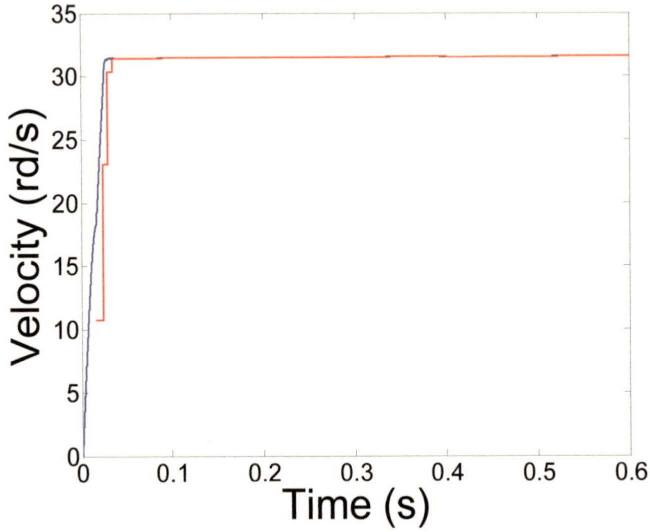

Fig. 22. Velocity of the starter-alternator during the start-up phase

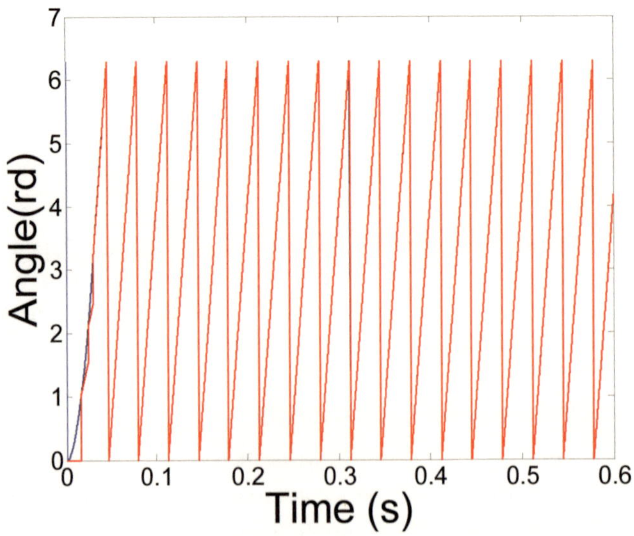

Fig. 23. Angle of the starter-alternator during the start-up phase

Figure 24 presents the evolution of starter-alternator current during the startup phase. This result shows that the current for the startup phase reach 560A at the beginning and stabilize after that at 280A.

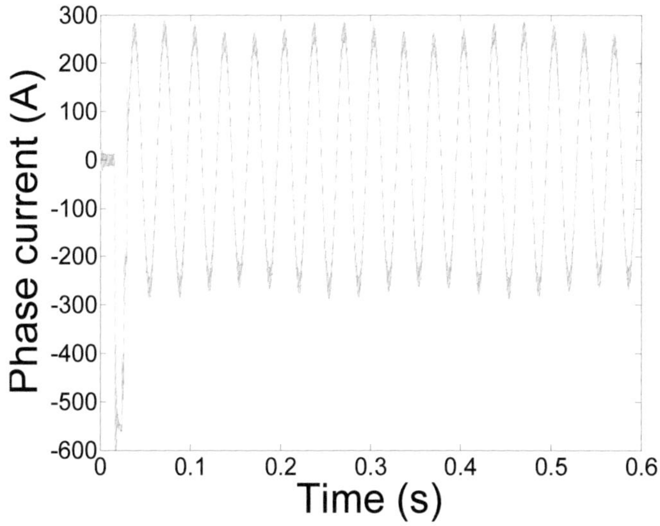

Fig. 24. Current of the starter-alternator during the start-up phase

During the startup phase, the supercapacitors current reaches -90A at the beginning and stabilizes after that at -38A. In this case, the supercapacitors discharge and the voltage of this component deceases. During this phase, the battery charges the supercapacitors at low current (20A) and the SOC of this component decreases from 100% to 99.8%.

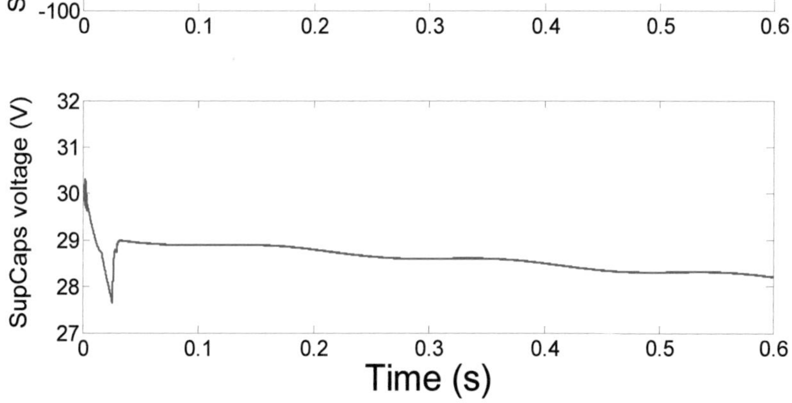

Fig. 25. Current and voltage of the supercapacitor module during the start-up phase

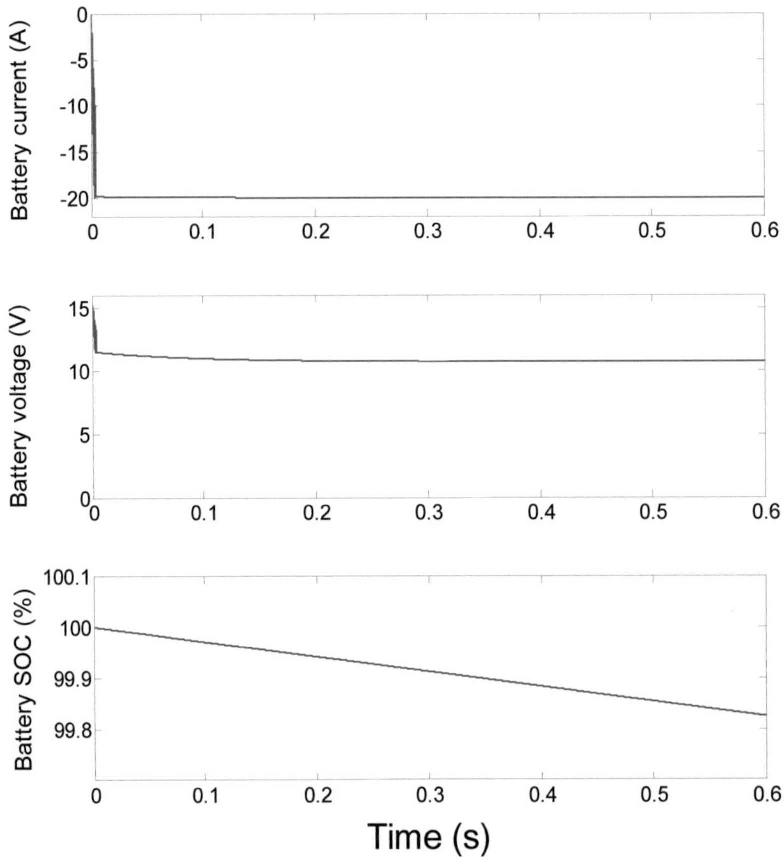

Fig. 26. Current, voltage and SOC of the battery during the start-up phase

6.2 Electric power generation

When the engine is turned-on, the starter alternator charges the battery and the supercapacitors. Firstly, the supercapacitors is charged with high current to reach 30V (fig. 27). In the same time, the chopper insures the charge of the battery. In this case, the voltage of the battery is controlled to reach the set point value (13V). During this time, the state of charge increases (fig. 28).

The battery current is limited between -20A and +20A. At the beginning, the battery participate to charge the supercapacitor module and after that the battery current reaches 20A, in the same time battery SOC increases during this phase.

The ICE drive the starter-alternator and this last one provide the power needed to charge the battery (fig. 28 and 29). The current in this case is very low compared to that of the startup phase (280A for the sturtup and 4A to charge the battery).

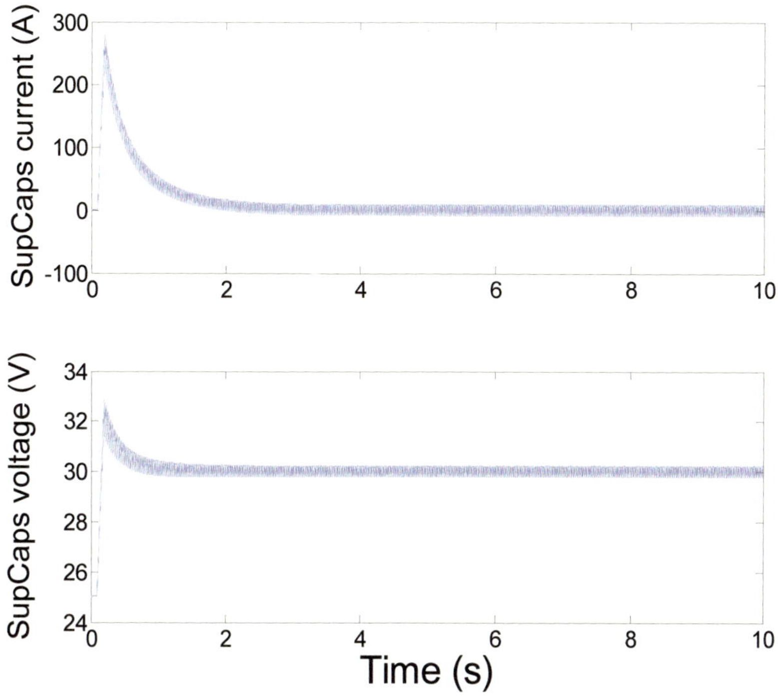

Fig. 27. Current and voltage of the supercapacitor module during the power generation phase

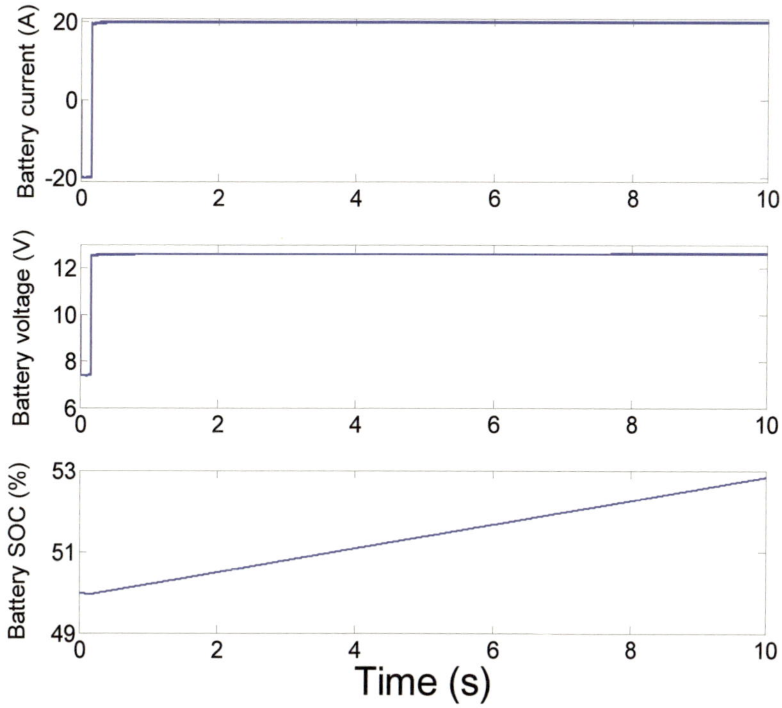

Fig. 28. Current, voltage and SOC of the battery during the power generation phase

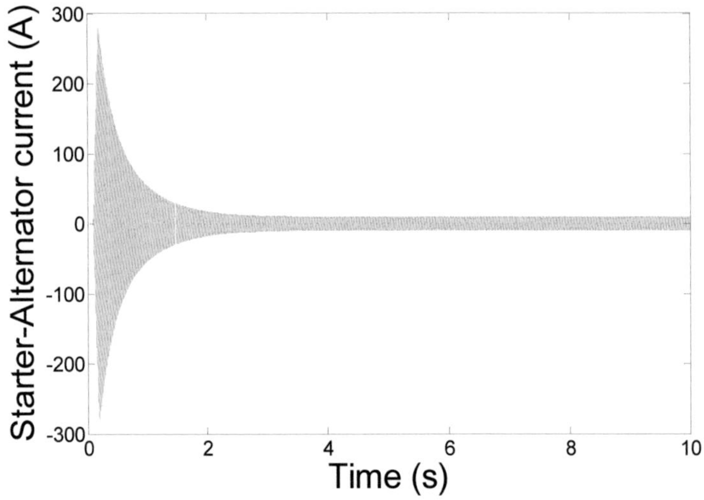

Fig. 29. Waveform of the phase current during the power generation phase (during 2 seconds)

In the power generation phase, the inverter is used like a synchronous rectifier and the signal period depends to the engine velocity.

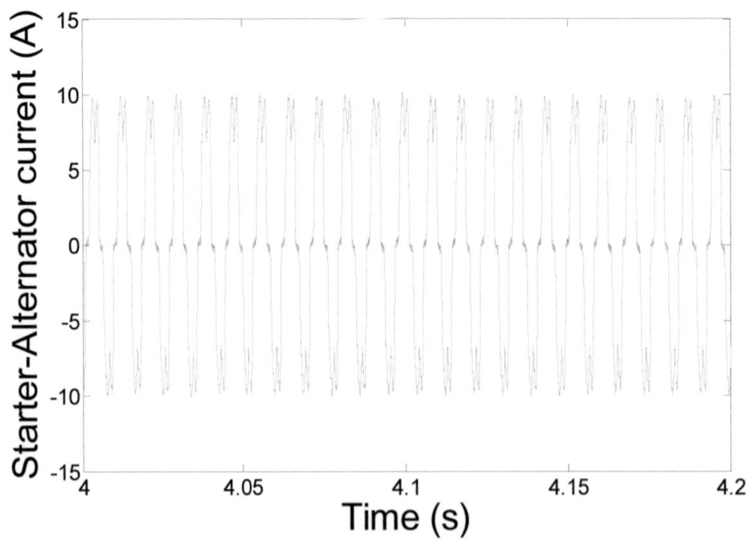

Fig. 30. Waveform of the current during the power generation phase (during 0.2 seconds)

7. Conclusion

The batteries used for the micro-hybrid vehicles have very high specific energy. Unfortunately, the power of this technology is very low compared to other technologies (Ni-Mh, Li-Ion,...). The association of battery for this application (micro-hybrid) with powerful component like supercapacitors can decrease the weight of the battery and/or ameliorate the lifetime of the supply. In this paper, hybrid supply for micro-hybrid vehicle has been presented. In this case, two storage components are used: supercapacitors like power supply and battery like energy supply. The power density of supercapacitors makes them very interesting for the applications which need high power during short time.

Two architectures are possible to implement the association of supercapacitors and battery: a parallel architecture by connecting the two sources to DC bus through two choppers. The drawback of this architecture is the very large size of the induction coil in series with the supercapacitor module. In the case of series architecture, the size of the induction coil used to smooth the battery current is less important because of the weakness of the current charge/discharge.

After the choose of the architecture of the power supply and the identification of the load torque, the parameters of the starter-alternator are identified. In the next part, the sizing of the two storage system (battery and supercapacitors) is presented.

Matlab-simulink software is used to simulate the supplying of the starter-alternator by the hybrid supply through an inverter. The association of battery and supercapacitors is made using a boost chopper. For the startup phase, the velocity of the starter-alternator is controlled to follow the set point value (32rd/s).

8. References

N. Rizoug (2006), *Modélisation électrique et énergétique des supercondensateurs et méthodes de caractérisation : Application au cyclage d'un module de supercondensateurs basse tension en grande puissance* , Thesis, feb 2006, Ecole centrale de Lille.

P. Bartholomeüs, B. Vulturescu, X. Pierre, N. Rizoug, P. Le Moigne (2001), *A 60V-400A test bench for supercapacitor modules*, EPE'2003, Toulouse, Septembre 2003.

S. Buller, E. Karden, D. Kok, R.W. De Doncker (2001), *Simulation Of Supercapacitors In Highly Dynamic Applications*, ESV, 2001, Berlin, Germany.

N. Rizoug, P. Bartholomeüs, P. Le Moigne and B. Vulturescu (2004), *Electrical and thermal behaviour of a supercapacitor module: on-line characterization*, ESSCAP'2004, Belfort, France.

Y. Hyunjae, S. Seung-Ki, P. Yongho and J. Jongchan (2007), *System Integration and Power-Flow Management for a Series Hybrid Electric Vehicle Using Supercapacitors and Batteries*, IEEE Trans. Ind. Applic, Vol. 44, N° 1, pp. 108–114, Jan.-feb. 2007.

C. Plasse, A. Akémakou, P. Armiroli and D. Sebille (2003), *Lalterno-Demarreur, Du Stop And Go Au Groupe Motopropulsseur Mild Hybride*, Prop'Elec 2003, France 2003.

J.M. Dubus, P. Masson and C. Plasse (2003), *The Starter Alternator Reversible Systems Of Valeo*, Valeo Systèmes Electriques.

S. B. Ozzturk, B, Akin, H. A. Toliyat and F. Ashrafzadeh (2006), *Low-Cost Direct Torque control of Permanent Magnet Synchronous motor using Hall-effect sensors*, IEEE APEC 2006.

D. Feroldi, M. Serra and J. Riera (2009), *Design and Analysis of Fuel-Cell Hybrid Systems Oriented to Automotive Applications*, IEEE Trans. Veh. Technol., vol. 58, no. 9, Nov. 2009.

W. Gao (2005), *Performance Comparison of a Fuel Cell-Battery Hybrid Powertrain and a Fuel Cell-Ultracapacitor Hybrid Powertrain*, IEEE Trans. Veh. Technol., vol. 54, no. 3, May 2005.

J. Bauman and M. Kazerani (2008), *A Comparative Study of Fuel-Cell–Battery, Fuel-Cell–Ultracapacitor, and Fuel-Cell–Battery–Ultracapacitor Vehicles,* IEEE Trans. Veh. Technol., vol. 57, no. 2, Mar. 2008.

S. Lu, Keith A. Corzine and M. Ferdowsi (2007), *A Unique Ultracapacitor Direct Integration Scheme in Multilevel Motor Drives for Large Vehicle Propulsion,* IEEE Trans. Veh. Technol., vol. 56, no. 4, JULY 2007.

Y. Yang, J. Liu, T. Wang, K. Kuo and P. Hsu (2007), *An Electric Gearshift With Ultracapacitors for the Power Train of an Electric Vehicle With a Directly Driven Wheel Motor,* IEEE Trans. Veh. Technol., vol. 56, no. 5, Sep. 2007.

11

The Uses of Artificial Intelligence for Electric Vehicle Control Applications

Brahim Gasbaoui and Abdelfatah Nasri
Bechar University, Faculty of Sciences and Technology,
Department of Electrical Engineering,
Algeria

1. Introduction

This chapter presents a novel speed control design of electric vehicle (EV) to improve the comportment and stability under different road constraints condition. The control circuit using intelligent fuzzy PI controller is proposed. Parameters which guide the functioning of PI controller are dynamically adjusted with the assistance of fuzzy intelligent control. Actually, electric vehicle (EV) including, full cell and hybrid vehicle have been developed very rapidly as a solution to energy and environmental problem. Driven EVs are powered by electric motors through transmission and differential gears, while directly driven vehicles are propelled by in-wheel or, simply, wheel motors [1, 2]. The basic vehicle configurations of this research has two directly driven wheel motors installed and operated inside the driving wheels on a pure EV. These wheel motors can be controlled independently and have so quick and accurate response to the command that the vehicle chassis control or motion control becomes more stable and robust, compared to indirectly driven EVs. Like most research on the torque distribution control of wheel motor, wheel motors [3, 15] proposed a dynamic optimal tractive force distribution control for an EV driven by four wheel motors, thereby improving vehicle handling and stability [4, 5].

Research has shown that EV control methods such as, PI control are able to perform optimally over the full range of operation conditions and disturbances and it is very effective with constant vehicle torque, Moreover these non-linear vehicle torque are not fixed and change randomly. However EV with conventional PI control may not have satisfactory performance in such fast varying conditions, the system performance deteriorates. In addition to this, it is difficult to select suitable control parameters K_p and Ki in order to achieve satisfactory compensation results while maintaining the stability of EV traction, due to the highly complex, non-linear nature of controlled systems. These are two of the major drawbacks of the PI control. In order to overcome these difficulties, adaptive PI controller by fuzzy control has been applied both in stationary and under roads constraints, and is shown to improve the overall performance of EV.The Direct Torque Control strategy (DTC) is one kind of high performance driving technologies for AC motors, due to its simple structure and ability to achieve fast response of flux and torque has attracted growing interest in the recent years. DTC-SVM with PI controller direct torque control without hysteresis band can effectively reduce the torque ripple, but its system's robustness will be fur there enhanced. DTC-SVM method can improve the system robustness, evidently reduce the torque and flux ripple, and effectively improve the dynamical performance. The DC-DC converter is use with a control strategy to assure the energy require for the EV and the propulsion system. The aim of this chapter is to contribute to understanding the intelligent fuzzy PI controller for utility EV tow rear deriving wheel applied direct torque control based space vector modulation under several scenarios.

2. Electric vehicle description

According to Fig. 1 the opposition forces acting to the vehicle motion are: the rolling resistance force F_{tire} due to the friction of the vehicle tires on the road; the aerodynamic drag force F_{aero} caused by the friction on the body moving through the air ; and the climbing force F_{slope} that depends on the road slope [1,2 3].

The total resistive force is equal to F_r and is the sum of the resistance forces, as in (1).

$$F_r=F_{tire}+F_{aero}+F_{slope} \tag{1}$$

The rolling resistance force is defined by:

$$F_{tire}=mgf_r \tag{2}$$

The aerodynamic resistance torque is defined as follows:

$$F_{aero}=1/2\ \rho_{air}A_fC_dv^2 \tag{3}$$

The rolling resistance force is usually modeled as:

$$F_{slope}=mg\sin(\alpha) \tag{4}$$

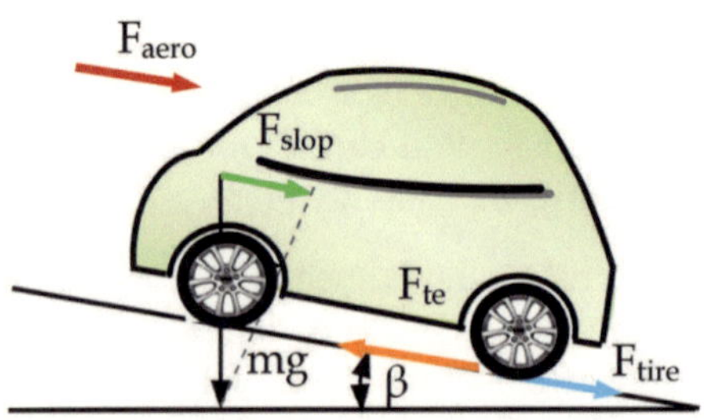

Fig. 1. The forces acting on a vehicle moving along a slope.

Where M_v is the total masse of vehicle r is the tire radius, f_r is the rolling resistance force constant, g the gravity acceleration, ρ_{AIR} is Air density , C_d is the aerodynamic drag coefficient,A_f is the frontal surface area of the vehicle, v is the vehicle speed, is the road slope angle. Values for these parameters are shown in Table1.

r	0.32 m	A_f	2.60 m^2
m	1300 Kg	C_d	0.32
f_r	0.01	ρ_{air}	1.2 Kg/m^3

Table 1. Parameters of the electric vehicle model

3. Direct torque control strategy based space vector modulation (SVM-DTC)

With the development of microprocessors and DSP techniques, the SVM technique has become one of the most important PWM methods for Voltage Source Inverter (VSI) since it gives a large linear control range, less harmonic distortion, fast transient response, and simple digital implementation. The induction motor stator flux can be estimated by:

$$\varphi_{qs} = \int_0^t (V_{qs} - R_s i_{qs}) dt \tag{5}$$

$$|\varphi_s| = \sqrt{\varphi_{ds}^2 + \varphi_{qs}^2} \tag{6}$$

$$\varphi_s = \tan^{-1}\left(\frac{\varphi_{qs}}{\varphi_{ds}}\right) \tag{7}$$

And electromagnetic torque T_{em} can be calculated by:

$$T_{em} = \frac{3}{2} p(\varphi_{ds} i_{qs} - \varphi_{qs} i_{ds}) \tag{8}$$

The SVM principle is based on the switching between two adjacent active vectors and two zero vectors during one switching period. It uses the space vector concept to compute the duty cycle of the switches.

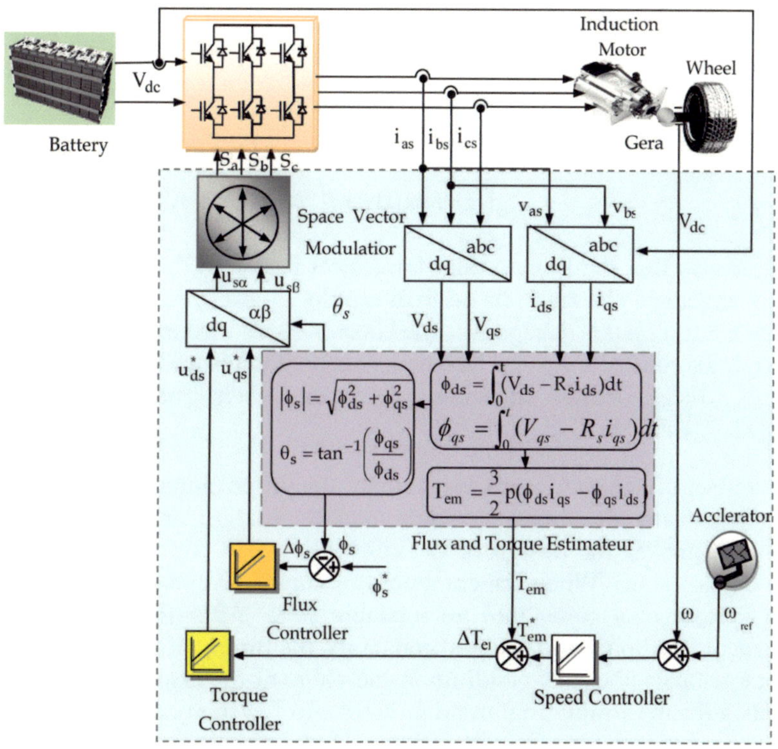

Fig. 2. Bloc diagram for DTC strategy based space vector modulation

4. Conventional PI controller

The reason behind the extensive use of proportional integral (PI) ..controller is its effectiveness in the control of steady-state error of a control system and also its easy implementation. However, one disadvantage of this conventional compensator is its inability to improve the transient response of the system. The conventional PI controller figure 3 has the form of Eq. (9), where T_{em}^{*} is the control output. Kp and Ki are the proportional and integral gains respectively, these gains depend on the system parameters. ε is the error signal, which is the difference of the injected voltage to the reference voltage.

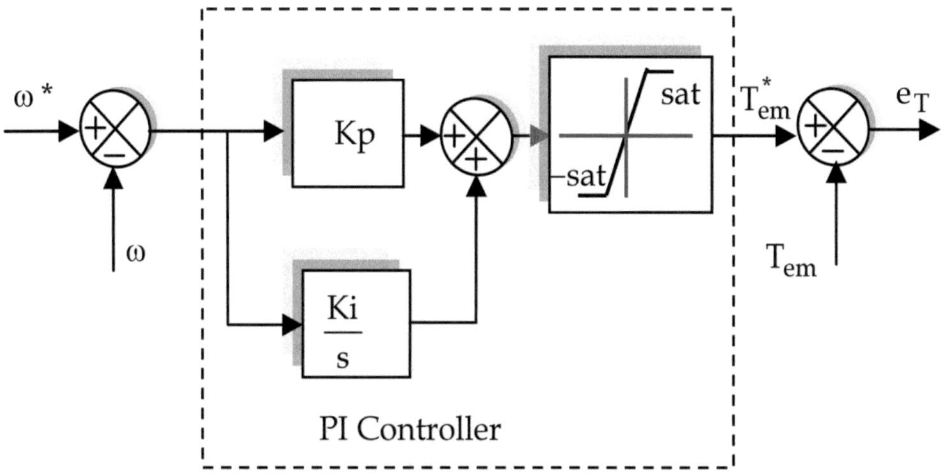

Fig. 3. Control of the injected speed using conventional PI controller

$$T_{em}(t) = Kp\varepsilon(t) + Ki\int_T \varepsilon(t)dt \tag{9}$$

Equation (9) shows that the PI controller introduces a pole in the entire feedback system, consequently, making a change in its original root locus. Analytically the pole introduces a change in the control system's response. The effect is the reduction of steady-state error. On the other hand, the constants Kp and Ki determine the stability and transient response of the system, in which, these constants rely on their universe of discourses: $Kp \in [Kp_{\min}, Kp_{\max}]\,and\quad Ki \in [Ki_{\min}, Ki_{\max}]$

Where the values of the minimum and maximum proportional and integral constants (gains) are practically evaluated through experimentation and using some iterative techniques. This makes the design of the conventional PI controller dependent on the knowledge of the expert. When the compensator constants exceed the allowable values, the control system may come into an unstable state. After the determination of the domain of the proportional and integral constants, the tuning of the instantaneous values of the constants takes place. Depending on the value of the error signal, ε, the values of the constants adjusts formulating an adaptive control system. The constants Kp and Ki changes to ensure that the steady-state error of the system is reduced to minimum if not zero.

5. Adaptive fuzzy PI controller

Fuzzy controllers have been widely applied to industrial process. Especially, fuzzy controllers are effective techniques when either the mathematical model of the system is nonlinear or not the mathematical model exists. In this paper, the fuzzy control system adjusts the parameter of the PI control by the fuzzy rule. Dependent on the state of the system . The adaptive PI realized is no more a linear regulator according to this principle. In most of these studies, the Fuzzy controller used to drive the PI is defined by the authors from a series of experiments [21, 22, 23, 24].

The expression of the PI is given in the equation (10).

$$y(t) = Kp * [e(t) + \frac{1}{T_i}\int_0^t e(t)dt] \tag{10}$$

Where:

$y(t)$: Output of the control.

$e(t)$: Input of the control. The error of the reference current $w^*(t)$ and the injected speed $w(t)$

kp: Parameter of the scale

Ti: Parameter of the integrator.

The discrete equation:

$$y(k) = Kp * [e(k) + \frac{1}{T_i}\sum_{j=1}^{k} e(j)T] \tag{11}$$

Where:

$y(k)$: Output on the time of k th sampling.

$e(k)$: Error on the time of k sampling

T: Cycle of the sampling

$$\Delta e(k) = e(k) - e(k-1)$$

$$y(k) = Kp * [e(t) + \frac{1}{T_i}\sum_{j=1}^{k} e(j)T]$$

$$y(k) = Kp * e(t) + K_i \sum_{j=1}^{k} e(j)$$

On-line Tuning:

The on-line tuning equation for kp and ki are show above:

$$kp = 20 + 0.8(Kp - 2.5) \tag{12}$$

$$ki = 0.0125 + 0.003(Ki - 2.5) \tag{13}$$

The frame of the fuzzy adaptive PI controller is illustrated in figure 4.

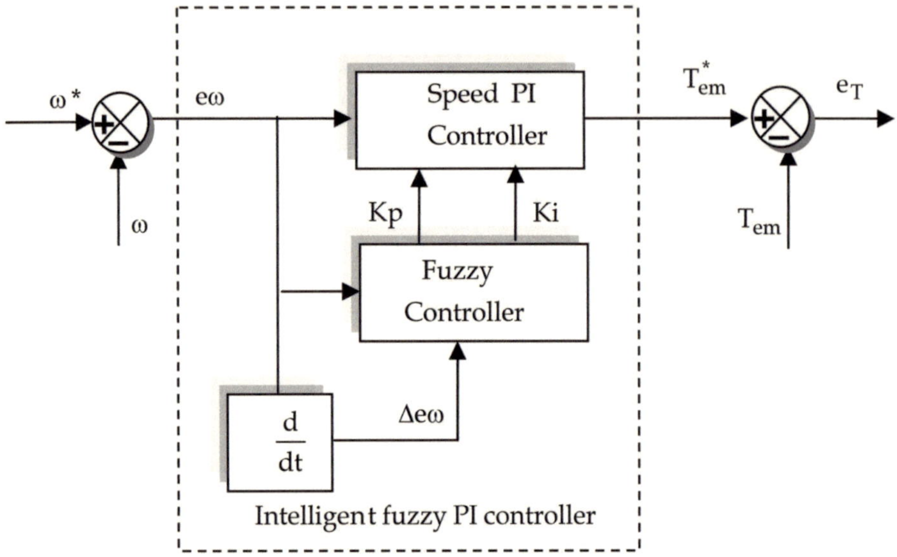

Fig. 4. PI gains online tuning by fuzzy logic controller

The linguistic variables are defines as {NL,NM,NS,Z,PS,PM,PB}meaning negative large, negative medium ,negative small, zero, positive small, positive medium, positive big.

The Membership function is illustrated in the figures 7, 8, 9 and 10.Figures 9 and 10 shows the view plot of fuzzy controller for kp and ki respectively.

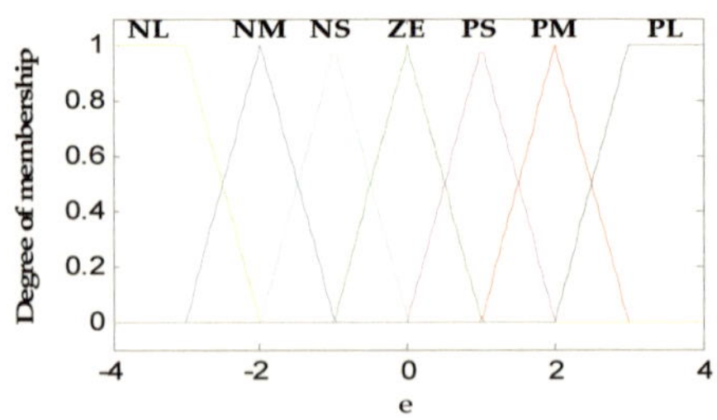

Fig. 5. The Membership function of input e(k).

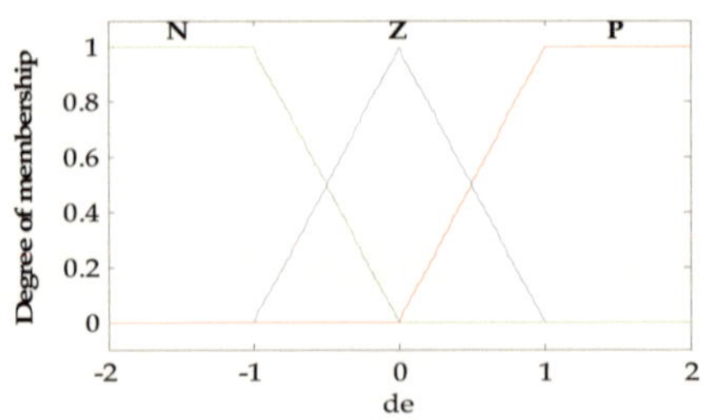

Fig. 6. The Membership function of input $\Delta e(k)$.

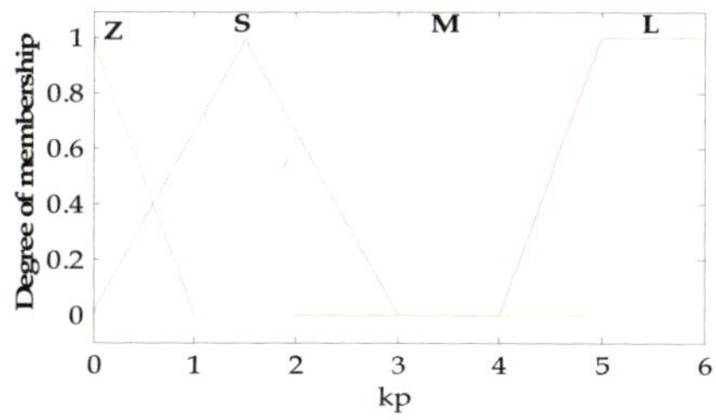

Fig. 7. The Membership functions of output kp.

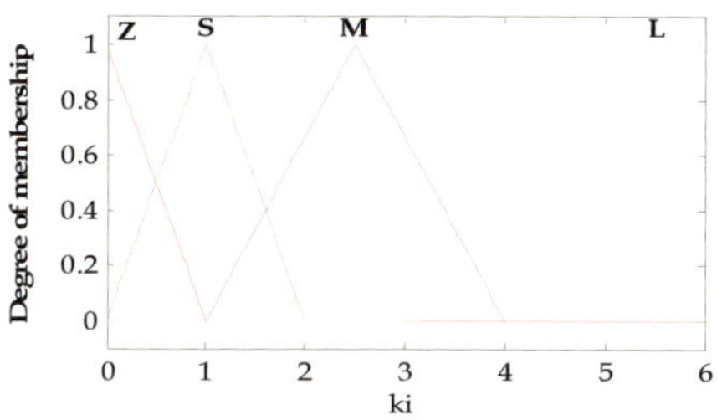

Fig. 8. The Membership function of output ki.

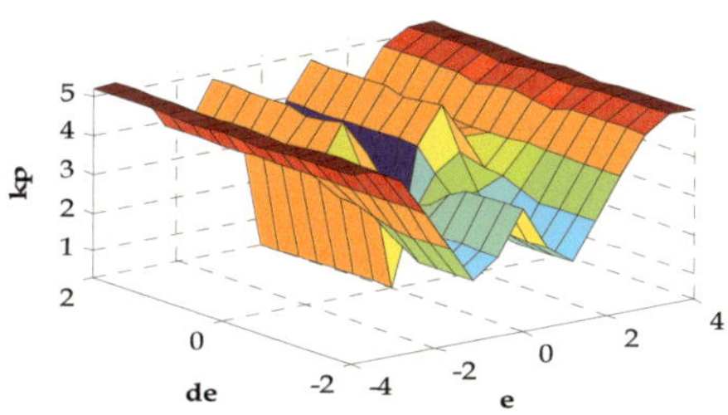

Fig. 9. View plot surface of fuzzy controller for kp

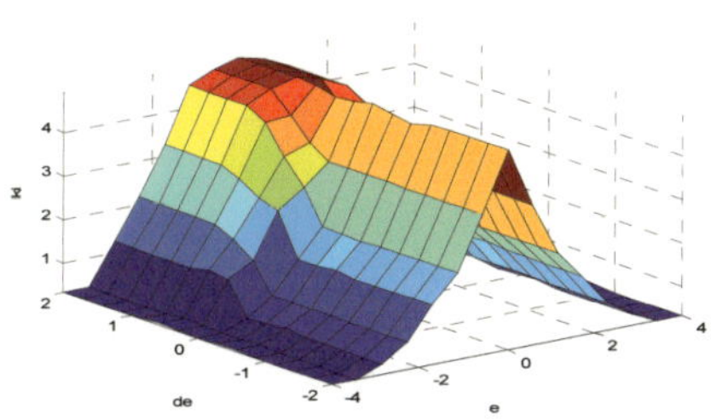

Fig. 10. View plot surface of fuzzy controller for ki

kp and ki	$\Delta e(\omega)$ \ $e(\omega)$	NL	NM	NS	ZE	PS	PM	PB
kp	N	L	M	S	M	S	M	L
	Z	L	M	L	Z	L	M	L
	P	L	M	L	Z	L	M	L
ki	N	Z	S	M	L	M	S	Z
	Z	Z	S	M	L	M	S	Z
	P	Z	M	L	L	L	M	Z

Table 2. Fuzzy tuning rules

6. Implementation of electronic differential

The proposed control system principle could be summarized as follows:

A speed control is used to control each motor torque. The speed of each rear wheel is controlled using speed difference feedback. Since the two rear wheels are directly driven by two separate motors, the speed of the outer wheel will need to be higher than the speed of the inner wheel during steering maneuvers (and vice-versa). This condition can be easily met if the speed estimator is used to sense the angular speed of the steering wheel. The common reference speed ω_{ref} is then set by the accelerator pedal command. The actual reference speed for the left drive ω^*_{left} and the right drive ω^*_{right} are then obtained by adjusting the common reference speed ω^* using the output signal from the DTC speed estimator. If the vehicle is turning right, the left wheel speed is increased and the right wheel speed remains equal to the common reference speed ω^*. If the vehicle is turning left, the right wheel speed is increased and the left wheel speed remains equal to the common reference speed ω^* [7, 9, and 11]. Usually, a driving trajectory is adequate for an analysis of the vehicle system model. From the mode show in Fig. 6, the following characteristic can be calculated:

$$R_\omega = \frac{L_\omega}{tg(\delta)} \tag{14}$$

Where δ is the steering angle. Therefore, the linear speed of each wheel drive is given by:

$$\begin{cases} V_1 = \omega_v(R - d_\omega/2 \\ V_2 = \omega_v(R - d_\omega/2 \end{cases} \tag{15}$$

And their angular speed by:

$$\begin{cases} V_1 = \omega_v(R - d_\omega/2 \\ V_2 = \omega_v(R - d_\omega/2 \end{cases} \tag{16}$$

$$\begin{aligned} \omega_{mr}^* &= \frac{L_\omega - (d_\omega/2)\tan(\delta)}{L_\omega}\omega_{mr} \\ \omega_{ml}^* &= \frac{L_\omega - (d_\omega/2)\tan(\delta)}{L_\omega}\omega_{ml} \end{aligned} \tag{17}$$

Where ω_v is the vehicle angular speed according to the center of turn.

The difference between wheel drive angular speeds is then:

$$\Delta\omega = \omega_{mr}^* - \omega_{ml}^* = -\frac{d_\omega \tan(\delta)}{L_\omega}\omega_v \tag{18}$$

And the steering angle indicates the trajectory direction:

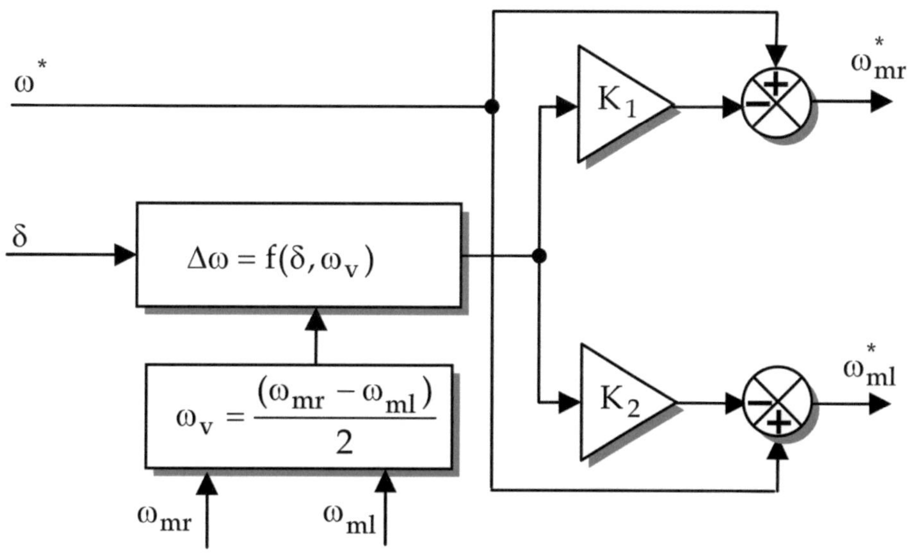

Fig. 11. Differential electronic.

$$\begin{aligned} &\delta > 0 \Rightarrow Turn\,left \\ &\delta = 0 \Rightarrow Straight\,ahead \\ &\delta < 0 \Rightarrow Turn\,raight \end{aligned} \tag{19}$$

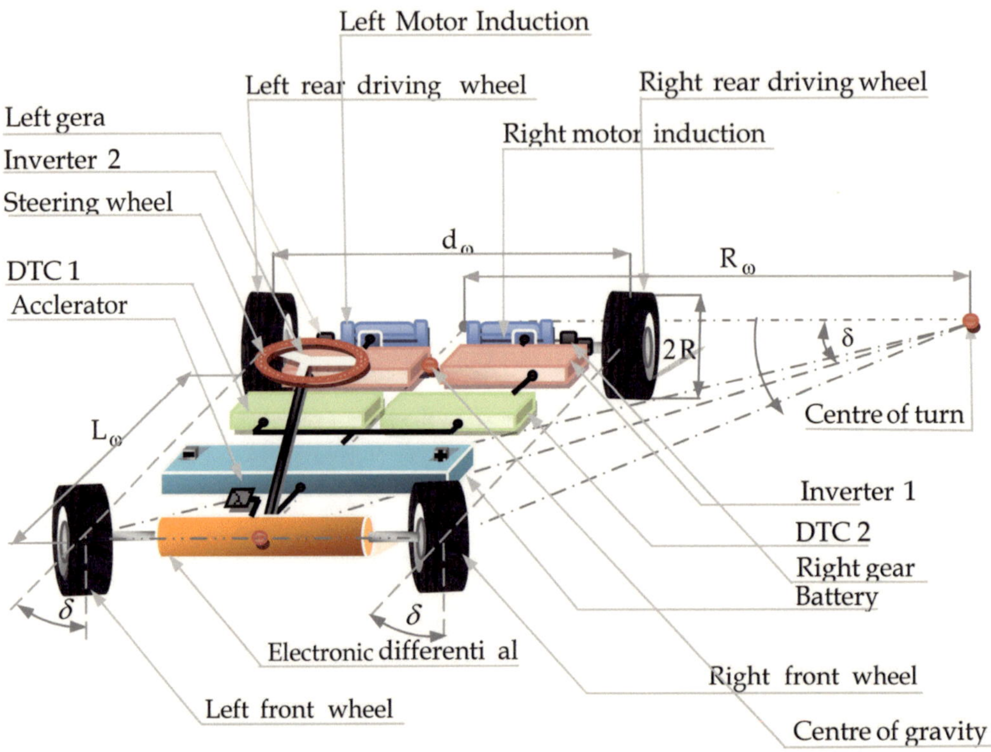

Fig. 12. Structure of vehicle in curve

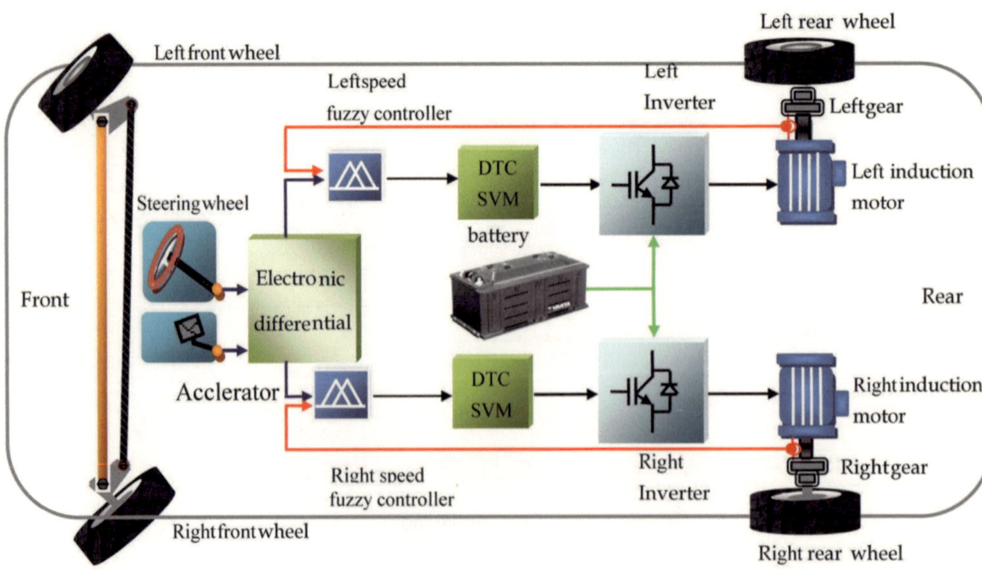

Fig. 13. The riving wheels control system

7. Simulation results

In order to characterize the driving wheel system behavior, Simulations were carried using the model of Fig 13.The following results was simulated in MATLAB .The test demonstrate the EV performances using an intelligence fuzzy PI controlled with DTC-SVM strategy under several speed variation.

A: Intelligent fuzzy PI controller with space vector modulation

The topology studied in this present work consists of three phases: the first one represent the acceleration phase's beginning with 60 Km/h in straight road, the second phase represent the deceleration one when the speed became 30 Km/h, and finally the EV is moving up the slopped road of 10% under 80 Km/h, the specified road topology is shown in Fig. 14, when the speed road constraints are described in the Table 2.

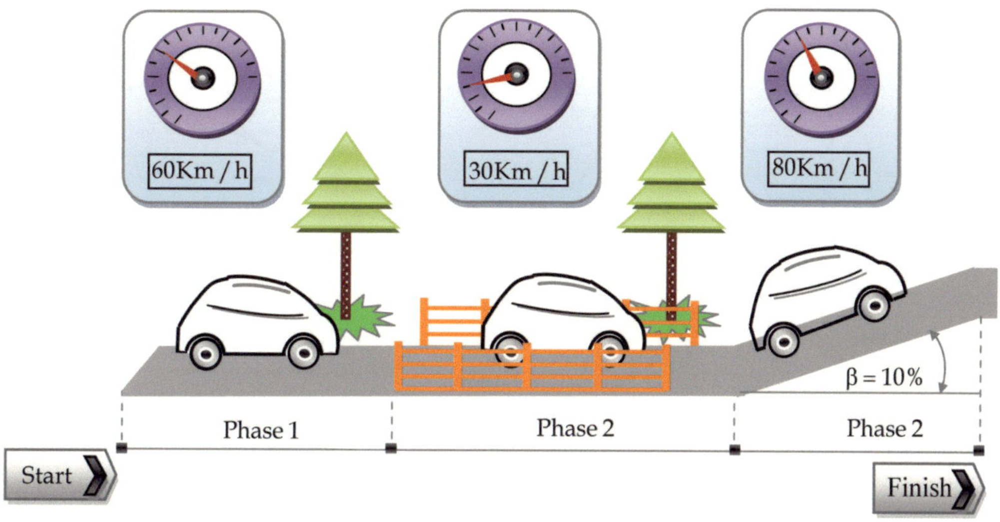

Fig. 14. Specify driving route topology

Phases	Event information	Vehicle Speed [km/h]
Phase 1	Acceleration	60
Phase 2	Bridge, Break	30
Phase 3	Acceleration and climbing a slope 10%	80

Table 3. Specified driving route topology

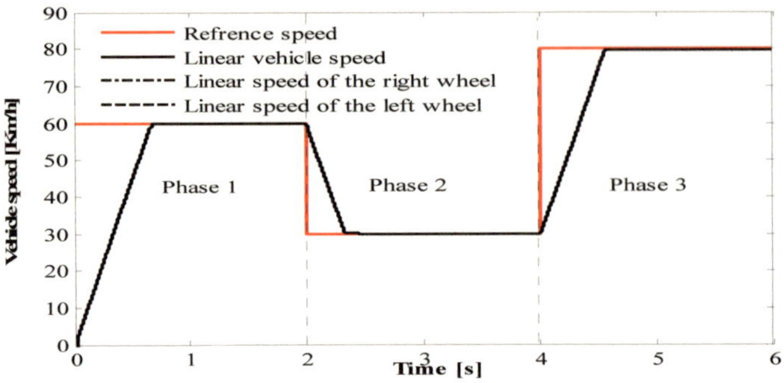

Fig. 15. Variation of vehicle speeds in different phases.

Refereed to Fig. 15 at time of 2 s the vehicle driver move on straight road with linear speed of 60 km/h, the assumption's that the two motors are not disturbed. In this case the driving wheels follow the same path with no overshoot and without error which can be justified with the good electronic differential act coupled with DTC-SVM performances.

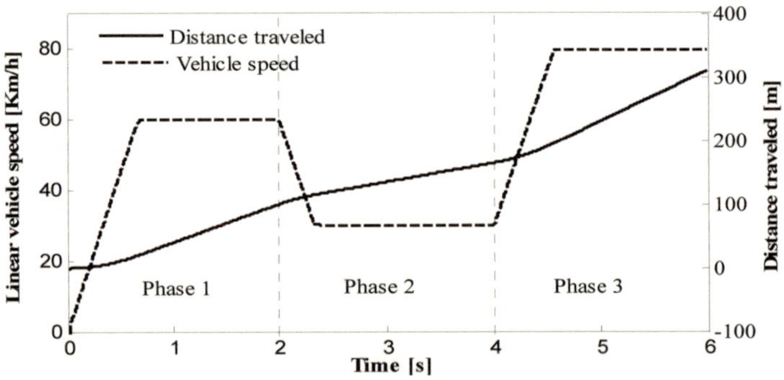

Fig. 16. Evaluation of vehicle and distance travelled in different phases.

Fig. 16, reflect the relationship between vehicle speed's variation and distance traveled in different phases. The distance travelled of 310 m in three electronic differential references acts 60 then break of 30 and acceleration until 80 km/h.

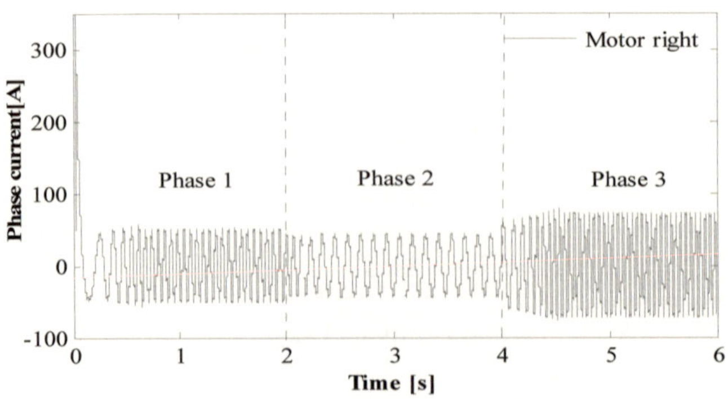

Fig. 17. Variation of phase current of the right motor in different phases.

Figs 17 and 18 explains the variation of phase current and driving force respectively. In the first step and to reach 60 km/h The EV demand a current of 50.70 A for each motor which explained with driving force of 329.30N. In second phase the current and driving forces demand decrees by means that the vehicle is in recharging phase's which explained with the decreasing of current demand and developed driving forces shown in Figs 14 and 15 respectively . The last phases explain the effect of acceleration under the slope on the straight road EV moving. The driving wheels forces increase and the current demand undergo double of the current braking phases the battery use the maximum of his power to satisfy the motorization demand under the slopped road condition which can interpreted physically the augmentation of the globally vehicle resistive torque illustrate in Table 4. In the other hand the linear speeds of the two induction motors stay the same and the road drop does not influence the torque control of each wheels. The results are listed in Table 3.

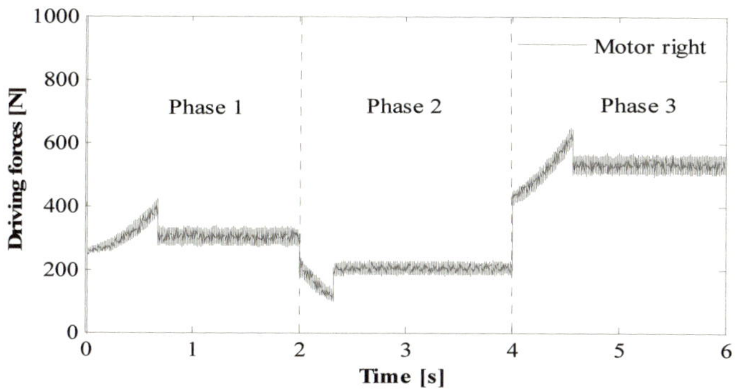

Fig. 18. Variation of driving force of the right motor in different phases.

Phases	1	2	3
the Vehicle resistive torque [N.m]	95.31	68.53	168.00
the globally vehicle resistive torque Percent compared with nominal motor torque of 476 Nm	20.02 %	14.39 %	35.29 %

Table 4. Variation of vehicle torque in different Phases.

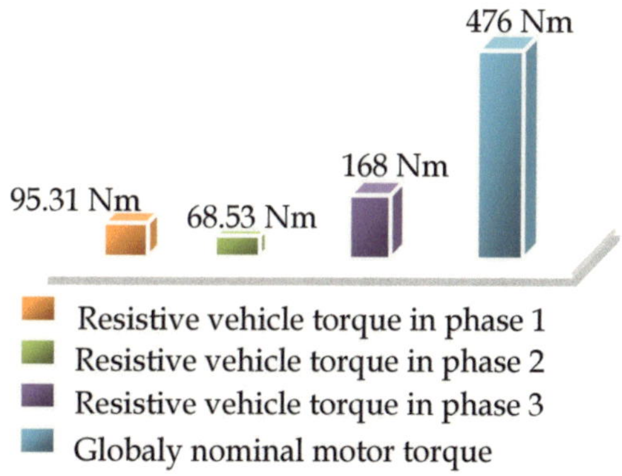

Fig. 19. Evaluation of the globally vehicle resistive torque compared to nominal motor torque in different phases.

According to the formulas (2),(3),(4) and Table. 3, the variation of resistive vehicle torques in different cases as depicted in Table 4. , the vehicle resistive torque was 95.31 N.m in the first case (acceleration phase) when the power propulsion system resistive one is only 68.53 Nm in the breaking phases (phases 2) , the back driving wheels develop more and more efforts to satisfy the traction chain demand which impose an resistive torque equal to 168.00 N.m .The result prove that the traction chain under acceleration demand develop the double effort comparing with the breaking phase case's by means that the vehicle needs the half of its energy in the deceleration phase's compared with the acceleration one's as it specified in table 2.

B. Comparative study of two method of controlling

In simulations the two different methods to control the EV were used .Because of the sweeping of the kp on the interval [15 43] and the ki on the interval [228 243] as shown in the figure 20 and 21.The DTC with Fuzzy Adaptive PI Control method improves EV performance. The intelligent fuzzy PI controller was proved in efficiency adaptation for stability of the vehicle. The results obtained by simulation show that this structure permits the realization of the robust control based on intelligent fuzzy inference system, with good dynamic and static performances for the multi-converters/multi-machines propelled system.

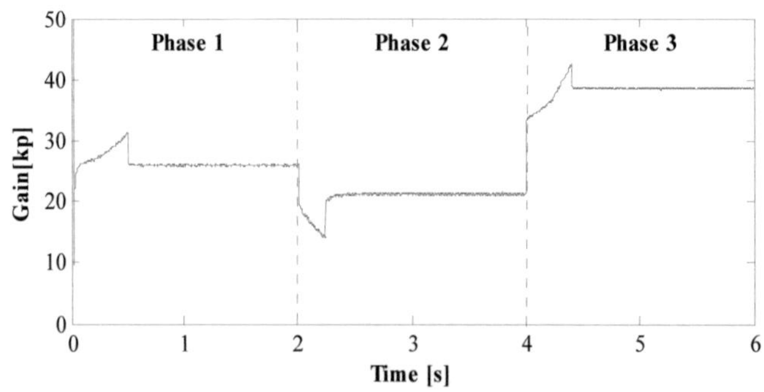

Fig. 20. Variation gain kp of intelligent fuzzy PI controller

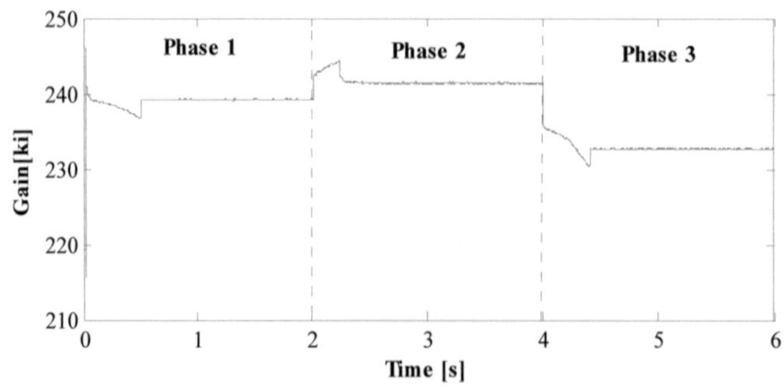

Fig. 21. Varaition gain ki of adaptive fuzzy PI controller

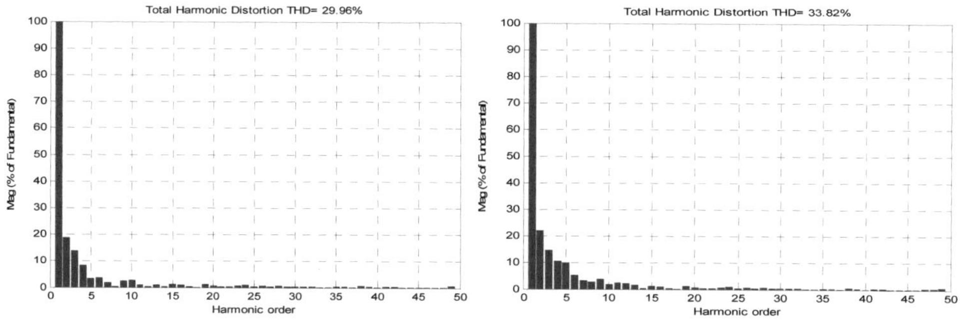

(a) (b)

Fig. 22. (a) Total harmonic distortion using DTC with intelligent fuzzy PI controller, (b) Total harmonic distortion using DTC-SVM with classical PI.

Referring to figures 20 (a) and (b) we show harmonic analyses of stator current. DTC-SVM with intelligent fuzzy PI controller present 29.96%, DTC-SVM with classical PI controller give 33.82 %. The first controller offer an reduction of 13.84% .This remarkable change obtained enables us to say that the current inject by voltage source inverter in DTC-SVM classical PI controller is harmonics current polluting what to justify the great oscillations of the torque and the attraction force .as a consequence this ripple present negative effects on the autonomy of the battery and heating of the both motors and increase power losses.

Designation	PI controller	intelligent fuzzy PI controller
THD [%]	33.82	29.96
Comportment of electric vehicle in sloped road	Less adaptive	More adaptive
Driving forces and electromagnetic torque	More oscillation	Less oscillation

Table 5. Comparative between PI and intelligent fuzzy PI controller

8. Conclusions

The research outlined in this paper has demonstrated the feasibility of an improved vehicle stability which utilizes two independent back drive wheels for motion by using DTC-SVM controls. DTC-SVM with intelligent Fuzzy control is able to adapt itself the suitable control parameters which are the proportional and integral gains kp and ki to the variations of vehicle torque. This method was Improved EV steering and stability during different trajectory. The advantage DTC-SVM controller is robustness and performance, there capacity to maintain ideal trajectories for two wheels control independently and ensure good disturbances rejections with no overshoot and stability of vehicle perfected ensured with the speed variation and less error speed. The DTC-SVM with intelligent fuzzy PI controller is more adaptive for propelled systems. The electric vehicle was proved best comportment and stability during different road path by maintaining the motorization error speed equal zeros and gives a good distribution for deriving forces. The electric vehicle was proved efficiency comportment in the different road constraints.

Te	Motor traction torque	238 Nm
Je	Moment on inertia of the drive train	7.07Kgm2
Rw	Wheel radius	0.32m
M	Vehicle mass	1300Kg
fe	Bearing friction coefficient	0.32
Kd	Aerodynamic coefficient	0.32
A	Vehicle frontal area	2.60 m2
fv	Vehicle friction coefficient	0.01
Lw	Distance between two wheels and axes	2.5m
dw	Distance between the back and the front wheel	1.5m

Table 6. Vehicle Parameters.

9. References

[1] Yee-Pien Yang., Chun-Pin Lo. Current Distribution Control of Dual Directly Driven Wheel Motors for Electric Vehicles, *Control Engineering Practice, vol.* 16, no. 11, pp. 1285-1292, 2008.

[2] P. He., Y. Hori., M. Kamachi ., K. Walters., H. Yoshida. Future Motion Control to be Realized by In-wheel Motored Electric Vehicle, *In Proceedings of the 31st Annual Confer- ence of the IEE Industrial Electronics Society, IEEE Press, Raliegh South Carolina,* USA, pp. 2632-2637, 2005.

[3] Jun-Koo Kang ., Seung-Ki Sul. New Direct Torque Control of Induction Motor for Minimum Torque Ripple and Constant Switching Frequency, *IEEE Trans. Ind. Applicat., vol.* 35, no. 5, p. 1076-1082, 1999.

[4] C. C. Chan . Electric vehicles charge forward, *IEEE Power Energy Mag, vol.* 2, no. 6, pp. 24–33, 2004.

[5] Z. Q. Zhu ., David HoweZ. Zhu . Electrical machines and drives for electric, hybrid, and fuel cell vehicles, *Proc. IEEE, vol. 95, no. 4,* pp. 764–765, 2007.

[6] P. Vas. Sensorless Vector and Direct Torque Control, *Oxford University Press*, 1998.

[7] K. Itoh ., H. Kubota. Thrust ripple reduction of linear induction motor with direct torque control, *Proceedings of the Eighth International Conference on Electrical Machines and Systems, ICEMS 2005, vol.* 1, pp. 655-658, 2005.

[8] Lin Chen j, Kang-Ling Fang chen . A Novel Direct Torque Control for Dual-Three-Phase Induction Motor, *Conf. Rec. IEEE International Conference on Machine Learning and Cybernetics,* pp. 876-88, 2003.

[9] P. Vas. Sensorless Vector and Direct Torque Control, Oxford University Press, 1998.

[10] [10] A. Schell., H. Peng., D. Tran., E.Stamos. Modeling and Control Strategy development for Fuel Cell Electric Vehicle, *Annual Review in control Elseiver, vol.* 29, pp. 159-168, 2005.

[11] A. Haddoun., M. Benbouzid., D. Diallo., R. Abdesseme.,, J. Ghouili., K. Srairi. Modeling ,Analysis and neural network control of an EV Electrical Differentiel, *Transaction on industriel electronic vol.* 55,N 6 June 2008.

[12] A. Nasri., A .Hazzab .,I.K. Bousserhane., S. Hadjeri., P. Sicard., Two Wheel Speed Robust Sliding Mode Control For Electric Vehicle Drive, Serbian Journal of Electrical Engineering , vol. 5, no.2, pp. 199-216, 2008.

[13] K. Hartani., M.bourahla,. Y.miloud, M.sekour., Electronic Differential with Direct Torque Fuzzy Control for Vehicle Propulsion System, Turk J Elec Eng & Comp Sci, vol.17, no.1, 2009, TUBITAK.

[14] L.T. Lam., R. louey. Developpement of ultra-battery for hybrid-electric vehicle applications, *Elservier, power sources, vol.* 158, pp. 1140-1148, 2006.

[15] Larminie. Electric Vehicle Technology Explained, *Edited by John Wiley and John Lowry, England,* 2003.

[16] A. Haddoun et al. Analysis, modeling and neural network traction control of an electric vehicle without differential gears, *in Proc. IEEE IEMDC, Antalya, Turkey, May* 2007, pp. 854–859.

[17] M. Vasudevan., R. Arumugam ., New direct torque control scheme of induction motor for electric vehicles, 5th Asian Control Conference, vol. 2, pp. 1377 - 1383, 2004.

[18] M. E. H. Benbouzid et al. Advanced fault-tolerant control of inductionmotor drives for EV/HEV traction applications, *From conventional to modern and intelligent control techniques, IEEE Trans. Veh. Technol., vol.* 56, no. 2, pp. 519–528, Mar. 2007.

[19] A. Gupta., A. M. Khambadkone. A space vector pwm scheme for multilevel inverters based on two-level space vector pwm, *IEEE Transaction on Industrial Electronics, vol.* 53, October 2006.

[20] T. G. Habetler., F. Profumo., M.Pastorelli., L. Tolbert. Direct torque control of induction machines using space vector modulation, *IEEE Transaction on Industry Applications, vol.* 28, no. 5, pp. 1045-1053, septembre/October 1992.

[21] Mingqian Gao., Shanghong He. Self-adapting Fuzzy-PID Control of Variable Universe in the Non-linear System, *2008 International Conference on Intelligent Computation Technology and Automation.*

[22] J.-Y. Chen, P.-S. Tsai and C.-C. Wong .Adaptive design of a fuzzy cerebellar model arithmetic controller neural network, *IEE Proc.-Control Theory and pplications, vol.* 152, no.2, pp. 133-137, 2005.

[23] Chih-Min Lin., Ya-Fu Peng., Adaptive CMAC-Based Supervisory Control for Uncertain Nonlinear Systems, IEEE Transactions on systems, man, and cybernetics-part b: cybernetics, vol. 34, no. 2, april 2004.

[24] Hugang Han., Chun-Yi Su., Yury Stepanenko. Adaptive control of a class of nonlinear systems with nonlinearly parameterized fuzzy approximators, *IEEE transactions on fuzzy systems, vol.* 9, no. 2, april 2001.